REOPENING

THE FRONTIER

Reopening the Frontier

HOMESTEADING IN THE MODERN WEST

Brian Q. Cannon

UNIVERSITY PRESS OF KANSAS

Published by the University Press of Kansas (Lawrence, Kansas 66045), which was organized by the Kansas Board of Regents and is operated and funded by Emporia State University, Fort Hays State University, Kansas State University, Pittsburg State University, the University of Kansas, and Wichita State University

Library of Congress Cataloging-in-Publication Data
Cannon, Brian Q.
Reopening the frontier : homesteading in the modern West / Brian Q. Cannon.
p. cm.
Includes bibliographical references and index.
ISBN 978-0-7006-1657-2 (cloth : alk. paper)
1. Frontier and pioneer life—West (U.S.) 2. Reclamation of land—West (U.S.)—History—20th century. 3. West (U.S.)—History—1945– 4. West (U.S.)—Social life and customs—20th century. 5. Community life—West (U.S.)—History—20th century. 6. Farmers—West (U.S.)—History—20th century. 7. Veterans—West (U.S.)—History—20th century. 8. World War, 1939–1945—Veterans—United States. 9. Environmental policy—West (U.S.)—History—20th century. 10. West (U.S.)—Environmental conditions. I. Title.
F596.C2395 2009
306.3′4909780904—dc22 2008052227

British Library Cataloguing-in-Publication Data is available.

Printed in the United States of America

10 9 8 7 6 5 4 3 2 1

The paper used in this publication is recycled and contains 30 percent postconsumer waste. It is acid free and meets the minimum requirements of the American National Standard for Permanence of Paper for Printed Library Materials Z39.48-1992.

CONTENTS

PREFACE AND ACKNOWLEDGMENTS

Twelve years ago as I was beginning what I thought would be a book on reclamation homesteading in the Progressive Era, I stumbled upon a brief description in a county history of homesteading after World War II. Until that time I had no idea that it was possible to homestead outside of Alaska after 1934. That brief description sparked my curiosity, and after I completed two articles on reclamation in the Progressive Era I turned my attention to the years after World War II. One question led to another, one interview led to another, and this book is the end result.

I owe a debt of gratitude to many who have assisted me over the course of this project. I thrived professionally and intellectually through my conversations with graduate students concerning their work and my own. My colleagues in the history department and the Charles Redd Center for Western Studies at Brigham Young University encouraged me as they effectively balanced research, writing, teaching, and administration. I particularly thank members of the History Department Writing Group, who read and critiqued drafts of several chapters. I appreciate the gentle prodding, generous advice, and friendship of Jay Buckley, Jessie Embry, Ignacio Garcia, Mark Grandstaff, and Susan Rugh. I benefited greatly from the diligent and careful research as well as the friendship of Amy Reynolds Billings, Clint Christensen, Teri Mayfield, Samuel Peterson, and Dale Topham, student research assistants who labored on this project. The College of Family, Home and Social Sciences and the Charles Redd Center provided indispensable funding. Deans Clayne Pope and David Magleby supported and encouraged my endeavor. In the Redd Center, Kris Nelson transcribed most of my interviews and Jason Thompson assisted me in preparing the photographs. Pam Smith, a reporter with the *Yuma Sun*, and Anders Tomlinson, a photographer in San Diego, generously permitted me to use their photographs.

Early in the writing process, Nancy Jackson of the University Press of Kansas expressed interest in my work. As acquisitions editor for the press, Kalyani Fernando encouraged me to complete the manuscript, acquired it, and shepherded it through the review and publication process.

Scores of people who homesteaded invited me into their homes and generously permitted me to interview them about their experiences. My work was greatly enriched by their stories. Many who shared their experiences with me have since passed away. I am grateful to have made their acquaintance and captured their words on tape. I appreciate administrators of irrigation district offices and regional and local offices of the Bureau of Reclamation, who permitted me to examine documents in their historical files. Historians Brit Storey and Toni Linenberger at the Bureau of Reclamation in Denver shared their knowledge and provided opportunities for me to share my work at reclamation conferences and seminars. I thank Don Pisani, who critiqued an early version of one of my chapters, and Doug Hurt and Walter Nugent, who reviewed the entire manuscript for the University Press of Kansas.

My children, Michael, Jared, Seth, Miriam, and Joseph, accompanied me on numerous research trips. While some of my colleagues' families accompanied them in their research travels to foreign capitals like London, Paris, and Vienna, my family good-naturedly motored with me to less exotic locales. My father, Don Cannon, also a professional historian, nurtured my interest in history long before this project commenced. I cherish our mutual interest. My mother, JoAnn, inspires me by her expectations to be the best I can be. My parents-in-law, Pete and Suzanne Black, have successfully pursued a simple lifestyle similar to that of the modern homesteaders described in the epilogue of this book. Finally, I thank my wife, AnnaLea, for believing in me.

REOPENING THE FRONTIER

INTRODUCTION

In 1893, a young historian at the University of Wisconsin, Frederick Jackson Turner, boldly positioned westward migration and settlement at the center of American history. "The existence of an area of free land, its continuous recession, and the advance of American settlement westward, explain American development," he proclaimed. Quoting the Superintendent of the Census to show that a frontier line no longer stretched across the nation, Turner concluded, "The frontier has gone, and with its going has closed the first period of American history." Turner's nostalgic observations rang true to a generation of Americans experiencing the effects of rapid urban growth, industrialization, and immigration. Many had grown up in rural regions where land ownership enhanced economic security. They shared Turner's anxieties about the prosperity and political stability of a nation without an agricultural frontier.[1]

Turner's announcement that the frontier had closed turned out to be premature. By 1900, not counting Alaska and Hawaii, 560 million acres of the public domain remained open to settlement. In 1902, when Congress passed the Newlands Reclamation Act, some reclamation enthusiasts optimistically predicted that government reclamation would transform 100,000 arid and semiarid acres into fertile farmland. A phenomenal surge in homesteading ensued during the Progressive Era, climaxing in 1913 but continuing at nearly record rates through 1917. Not until the passage of the Taylor Grazing Act in 1934 did Congress close most remaining public lands to settlement, and even after that the Homestead Act continued to operate on a limited basis.[2]

Although Turner's timetable for the closing of the settlement frontier was inaccurate, the general trend he envisioned ultimately unfolded: after World War I progressively fewer Americans claimed farms on the public domain, partly because promising opportunities to homestead diminished and the prices of farm products plummeted. Youth who had grown up on the farm now turned their attention to other endeavors. "The answer was not to try another homestead farther west, as so many generations had done, but to find a wage-paying job," writes Walter Nugent. The number of Americans residing on farms dropped, too, as the capital requirements for farming rose and economic opportunities in urban areas multiplied. The Great Depression temporarily reversed the farm-to-city migration; during the 1930s people returned to their rural roots seeking a bare subsistence, but thereafter the number of people living on farms fell drastically from 30 million in 1940 to 9 million in 1970. Those who left were dispensable; machinery, new pesticides and chemical fertilizers made it possible to grow more food with fewer laborers.[3]

Seeing that capitalism and democracy survived the frontier's closing and that rural migrants prospered in urban areas, Americans set aside their concerns about the closing of the frontier. As David Wrobel has indicated, anxiety about the frontier's closing, which "helped shape the period from the late nineteenth century through the New Deal," ceased to be "an important strain in intellectual thought in America" after the 1930s. Scholars increasingly regarded Turner's frontier thesis as a relic that revealed more about the anxieties of Americans during Turner's lifetime than about the shaping of American institutions. One influential critic, Henry Nash Smith, observed in 1950 that Turner's "archaic assumptions" about agriculture and the frontier "hampered his approach to twentieth-century social problems."[4]

Others questioned whether the abundance of cheap land and the process of settling it had ever been as integral to America's national character or institutions as Turner had claimed. They criticized Turner's triumphal depiction of western settlement as unduly celebratory, ethnocentric, sexist, and environmentally insensitive. Regionalists claimed that the continuities between the pre- and postfrontier eras in the West were more striking and important than the differences.[5]

Patricia Limerick memorably synthesized and elaborated much of the criticism in her 1987 classic *The Legacy of Conquest.* She argued that frontier "is an unsubtle concept in a subtle world." The closing of the frontier was an artificial divide that diverted attention from underlying continuities in "the continuous sweep of Western American history." The myth of the frontier's closure was a noteworthy "historical artifact," but Turner's thesis was "entirely irrelevant to the [lived] history of the Trans-Mississippi West," Limerick contended. Committed to excising Turner from western history, Richard White avoided the word *frontier* and Turner's ideas entirely in his prizewinning 1991 western history survey, *"It's Your Misfortune and None of My Own."* For many western historians of the 1990s *frontier* became the "F" word.[6]

But as Limerick observed eight years after *The Legacy of Conquest* was published, despite the whipping, Turner's ideas persisted. In fact the debate that Limerick, White, and other New Western historians provoked had "revitalized Turner's reputation" rather than burying it. Far from being confined to professional conferences and journals, the debate played out, too, in the national media. It turned out that the frontier myth articulated by Turner "remained an integral part of the national culture," David Wrobel observed, and was "vital to the question of American self-esteem." When historians criticized Turner's ideas, they undermined fundamental national myths. Reflecting renewed interest in Turner, Yale University Press in 1999 issued a new collection of ten of Turner's essays edited by John Faragher. In prizewinning books, historians near the turn of the twentieth century focused upon frontier processes and themes although they did not necessarily echo Turner's conclusions. Elliott West and James Brooks probed the collision of competing worldviews and cultures on western frontiers. Walter Nugent built much of his acclaimed 1999 narrative of western history around a solidly Turnerian insight: "the rise and collapse of homesteading underpinned the entire history of the United States for over 200 years from the Atlantic to the Sierras and beyond." Homesteading, he wrote, "engaged the spirits and dominated the lives of tens of millions of Americans" from colonial times to the end of World War I.[7]

Although Nugent masterfully chronicled the experiences of settlers and homesteaders over the long sweep of western history through the early twentieth century, his survey turned to metropolitan and industrial themes after 1920. "Homesteading withered away, already over with when the Taylor Grazing Act closed the public lands to new entries in 1934," he wrote, reinforcing a common misperception.[8]

This book takes up the subject of western agricultural settlement and homesteading in the 1940s, more than a decade after the passage of the Taylor Grazing Act, and follows it through the end of the twentieth century, focusing upon homesteading on federal reclamation projects. Near the end of World War II, officials in the Bureau of Reclamation and Secretary of the Interior Harold Ickes proposed creating new farms for up to 400,000 veterans on 415 irrigation projects at a cost of $5 billion. The logistics and costs of establishing so many Americans on the land overwhelmed the Bureau, and Congress prioritized other water storage objectives in its appropriations. Nevertheless, the Bureau's homesteading program proceeded slowly, and between 1946 and 1966 the Bureau opened over 3,000 farms on public lands in the West. The Bureau received over 150,000 applications for those farms, an indicator of a widespread, continued interest in homesteading in the middle decades of the twentieth century. Reporters and journalists chronicled the experiences of these modern homesteaders in popular magazines for large reading audiences. Historians have paid scant attention to this last wave of homesteading in the lower forty-eight states, partly because it involved few people. As Paul Gates observed, the number of homesteaders after World War II was "slight compared with the great floods of people migrating to the West [in the same era], not for land to farm but for jobs and urban residences."[9]

At first glance, these episodic outbursts of homesteading appear to be anachronistic throwbacks to an earlier era, romantic and entertaining sideshows that curiously brought new lands into production at the same time that the government was paying other farmers to withhold land on existing farms from cultivation. It might even be argued that the entertaining story of this last wave of homesteaders diverts attention from more consequential forces shaping the modern West such as urban growth, environmentalism, and the evolution of industrial tourism. Nothing could be further from the truth. The unfolding of a quintessential element of the Old West—homesteading—within an urbanizing, modern West created exceptionally vivid contrasts. The juxtaposition of elements of the Old and New Wests facilitates a critical examination of Limerick's central argument that the continuities in western history override the temporal differences. We can better understand change and continuity in western history by examining the West after World War II through the lens of postwar homesteading.

The history of postwar homesteading illustrates a significant ideological continuity: the myths of the frontier and Jeffersonian yeomanry with their linkage of virtue, independence, and life on the land flourished after "free land" was no longer widely available. As Catherine Stock and Robert Johnston have observed, stories of rural Americans in the twentieth century "have the power to move us" because they illuminate "values, dreams and ideals at the core of the . . . American experience." None of those dreams is more venerable than the age-old, "well-nigh universal" desire for land with its promise of economic security, independence, virtue, industry, and familial stability. Most homesteaders embraced that dream, as did thousands of others who unsuccessfully applied for a homestead. So did politicians and journalists who recounted the postwar homesteaders' stories for large audiences. The homesteaders' experiences engaged many who had grown up on farms earlier in the century or had been taught by their parents and others from rural backgrounds to regard land as security. The new metropolitan West that emerged after World War II was populated by people who traced their roots to the countryside. Rural "worldviews" therefore persisted as parents and grandparents

Hundreds thronged the armory in Klamath Falls, Oregon, on 18 December 1946 for the Bureau of Reclamation's first postwar land lottery. Reporters from across the nation relayed the news to a public who associated free land with economic security, independence, virtue, industry, and family solidarity. (Photograph by Ben L. Glaha, Reclamation Photographs, National Archives and Records Administration [NARA], Rocky Mountain Region)

passed them on to succeeding generations. These ways of viewing America, economic opportunity, and the common good contributed to the conservative ascendancy of the 1970s and the Reagan Revolution. As Douglas Hurt has observed, "late in the twentieth century, most Americans considered farm life preferable to urban living. A poll indicated that 58 percent of the people questioned believed that farm life was more honest and moral than city life, while 64 percent of the interviewees contended that farm men and women worked harder than urbanites, and 67 percent thought that farmers had closer ties to their families than other people." Indeed, at the end of the twentieth century "the Jeffersonian ideal died hard, if it died at all."[10]

Despite this significant intellectual and cultural continuity, the experiences of modern homesteaders also reflect sharp differences between the Old and Modern Wests. While the yeoman myth and the connection between private land acquisition and public virtue retained much of their luster, competing visions of the land countered and increasingly overwhelmed those Jeffersonian ideals as the twentieth century progressed. In the decades following World War II increasing numbers of Americans viewed the rural West as what William Cronon has called a "non-working" landscape. As the number of Americans who depended directly upon farming, mining, and ranching plummeted and the population of metropolitan regions skyrocketed, Americans increasingly viewed the rural West through the lens of "non-rural values." This value system privileged recreation, aesthetics, and environmental protection over economic growth and efficiency. This new value system scored significant victories in the passage of the Wilderness Act of 1964, the National Environmental Policy Act of 1969, and the Endangered Species Act of 1973. The Bureau of Reclamation's agenda for constructing new dams and developing irrigated homesteads collided with these developments beginning in the 1950s. For a time the Bureau maintained the upper hand, but in the 1960s the agency was forced to abandon its plans for additional homestead openings. In 1976 the Homestead Act itself was repealed.[11]

Historians have described how recreational, aesthetic, and environmental values shaped national policy and affected the resource base of timber- and mining-dependent communities in the modern West. They have paid less attention to the impact of those values upon agricultural communities. As Douglas Hurt observed in 1998 historians "have given little attention to the . . . rural West," defined as "the agricultural, small-town, and reservation West," in the post-1945 era. To redress that neglect, Hurt commissioned essays on the topic. The authors of three of the essays, James Sherow, Donald Pisani, and Mark Friedberger, outlined some of the key federal policies that have affected western farmers and ranchers. The authors lacked the space in their brief essays, though, to develop detailed case studies. By following the farming careers of the postwar homesteaders and their descendants over six decades, this book illuminates pivotal effects of changing national values and policies upon the fortunes of western farmers. In the process, it illustrates significant discontinuities between the 1940s and the turn of the twentieth century, particularly with regard to national water policy. Although the general public remained generally sympathetic to small farmers, the postwar homesteaders and their successors lost ground in their fight to maintain water rights in the face of competing claims from environmentalists, wildlife advocates, and urban water users.[12]

Another disjuncture between the old and modern Wests illustrated by the history of homesteading involves the homesteaders' relationship to the state. Homesteaders had always looked to the federal government for land, but not for money. The legendary homesteader was a gambler who bet his brawn and brains against economic and environmental obstacles. Homesteaders who succeeded in that gamble, living on the land and improving it for five years, became landowners. Recognizing that the odds were stacked against them, especially in semiarid regions, homesteaders between the 1860s and the 1920s clamored for government assistance. Aside from the right to claim larger parcels of land in semiarid regions, they received little direct aid until the 1910s and 20s when Congress granted homesteaders on federal reclamation projects more time to repay the government for their irrigation systems. During the 1920s, bills in Congress that would have provided federal price supports for farm products failed to become law, and Congress refused to furnish low-interest loans to reclamation homesteaders for livestock and equipment.[13]

Homesteading after World War II unfolded in a climate of expectations shaped by the New Deal and the generosity of the GI Bill. In 1944 Congress considered but rejected a bill that would have involved the government more directly in the fortunes of homesteaders. The abortive bill would have authorized technical assistance and credit for reclamation homesteaders. But lawmakers soon changed their minds; as Commissioner of Reclamation Floyd Dominy indicated, Congress "encouraged" the Bureau to "assume greater responsibility for the settlers' success" on its projects during the 1950s. Dominy believed this mandate amounted to a "change in [the Bureau's] entire philosophy" of its relationship to its clientele. In 1953–1954, Congress guaranteed every postwar homesteader on a federal reclamation project a sufficient quantity and quality of land to support a family. Homesteaders who could prove that their lands were inadequate were entitled to receive additional lands or be resettled. Ten years later, Congress handsomely rescued beleaguered homesteaders on the Bureau's Riverton Project, paying them far more than the market value of their lands. Thereby lawmakers shifted the financial risk of homesteading from the settler to the taxpayer. The history of postwar homesteading reveals the reasons for this revolutionary redefinition of homesteading. Dominy attributed the redefinition to Congress, but the process originated at the grass roots with discontented farmers, opportunistic attorneys, and muckraking journalists. The story of that process supports Robert Johnston and Catherine Stock's observation that rural Americans in the twentieth century played "active roles both in resisting and in constructing the state and the role of its agencies in their lives."[14]

The history of homesteading following World War II also furnishes an opportunity to reexamine Donald Worster's influential characterization of the modern West as a "hydraulic society," an "increasingly coercive, monolithic, and hierarchical system, ruled by a power elite based on the ownership of capital and expertise." At the center of this "concentrated power and hierarchy based on the command of scarce water" is the Bureau of Reclamation and its "water lords." Worster acknowledges that the Bureau's projects were environmentally "vulnerab[le]" in the postwar era and that "a scrutinizing, distrusting people" halted the expansion of the hydraulic society late in the 1970s after the collapse of the Teton Dam. The history of the Bureau of Reclamation's postwar land development illustrates that the Bureau's power was sharply limited and contingent from 1944 onward, though. As political scientists Robert Dahl, Nelson Polsby, and Raymond Wolfinger have argued, the decisive power of large bureaucracies is often overestimated. The story of postwar homesteading illustrates many ways in which the judiciary, Congress, other federal agencies, secretaries of the interior, and presidents repeatedly curtailed the Bureau's activities and clipped its wings. The Bureau was less an empire than a vassal of Congress, the president, and secretary of the interior. Worster is correct that the control of water in the modern West has coercive overtones; witness the experiences of homesteaders and their neighbors whose water rights were contested and limited. But as often as not the Bureau of Reclamation acted in these contests as the agent of the courts and Congress and in response to pressure from interest groups.[15]

In addition to enabling us to reassess important interpretive arguments about the West, the history of the postwar homesteaders illuminates the lifeways, values, and attitudes of family farmers at a pivotal era in the history of American farming. As Allan Kulikoff has indicated, American agriculture from colonial times to the 1930s was characterized by a dialectical tension between "dependence on markets" and "subsistence activities." He argues, though, that between the Great Depression and the mid-1960s, market agriculture superseded household activities as farm women stopped gardening and left the home for wage work and as farmers replaced family members with hired labor. Commodification was complete. Despite the climactic significance of these decades, few historians of agriculture have closely studied them. The homesteaders' experiences enrich our understanding of the economic and technical challenges farm families encountered in this era. They reveal the complex array of impulses including desires for personal fulfillment, material wealth, and family stability that made farming meaningful. They illustrate how and why farm families, and especially farm women, assumed new roles and abandoned others in the middle decades of the century. They also demonstrate that many farm women resisted these changes and continued to engage in subsistence activities even when experts advised that they no longer made economic sense.[16]

This book begins by examining the Bureau of Reclamation's experiments with homesteads for veterans after World War I, the lessons the Bureau learned thereby, and the campaign in Congress during the 1940s to offer similar but improved opportunities to World War II veterans. Champions of western reclamation on Capitol Hill argued that greater technical and financial assistance would enhance the veterans' chances of success in homesteading. But narrow bureaucratic interests and jealousies, sectional loyalties, and valid questions about agricultural surpluses roiled the waters and often diverted lawmakers' attention from the veterans themselves.

The lands opened for reclamation homesteading after the war were vacant but had been previously occupied by others including Native Americans, dryland homesteaders, and Japanese American internees. As it prepared to open these lands to homesteaders, the Bureau worked with local examining boards to establish minimum criteria for applicants. The criteria privileged singles and husbands over married women and excluded the poorest applicants and those who lacked agricultural experience. The names of winning applicants were drawn in gala ceremonies, and the winners were then invited to visit the projects to select their farms.

This book traces the homesteaders' experiences in establishing a farm, proving up, and gaining title to the land. The realities of modern homesteading often clashed with iconic views of the frontier as a contest between individual men and nature, but most homesteaders still perceived homesteading as a means of proving themselves. After they had gained title to their land, the homesteaders were free to leverage it to pursue their dreams. The courses men and women followed and their retrospective assessments reveal the complex relationship between homesteading, material wealth, family relationships, and personal satisfaction in a transitional era in agricultural history.

Disappointment particularly stalked settlers on the Bureau's Riverton Project in central Wyoming. Having lived on their homesteads rent-free for as long as fifteen years, a cadre of settlers convinced Congress that the government owed them more than the combined value of their land and improvements. Homesteading had become as soft as possible, and too expensive for the government to underwrite.

Not only finances but Americans' shifting understanding of the optimal usage of natural resources foreclosed further homestead openings. The impact of changing values was particularly striking on the Bureau's Klamath Project in northern California where attempts to open new homesteads aroused nationwide opposition from wildlife and sportsmen's organizations. At last Congress and the secretary of the interior intervened to prevent further homesteading in the Klamath Basin. A decade later, Congress repealed the Homestead Act itself, following a tedious round of investigations, deliberations, debates, and negotiations.

Many homesteaders or their children remained on their farms into the twenty-first century. They struggled to retain their water rights as municipalities and wildlife advocates, among others, demanded a larger share of the West's scarce water. A dramatic standoff in 2001 pitted farmers in the Tulelake Irrigation District against the courts and federal agencies including the Fish and Wildlife Service and the Bureau of Reclamation.

This book concludes with a brief examination of the continued appeal and adaptive nature of the homesteading ideal in the late twentieth and early twenty-first centuries. Free irrigated land is no longer available, but individuals seeking to reorient or reinvigorate their lives, as well as local governments eager to repopulate their towns and counties, have reinvented homesteading to achieve their objectives.

CREATING A "NEW FRONTIER OF OPPORTUNITY" WORLD WAR II VETERANS AND THE CAMPAIGN FOR WESTERN HOMESTEADS

1

Americans who served in the military during World War II returned to a hero's welcome. Convinced that veterans were entitled to educational and economic benefits because of their military service, Congress conferred a wide array of privileges upon them in 1944 when it passed the Servicemen's Readjustment Act, popularly known as the GI Bill of Rights. Earlier in the nation's history veterans had received grants from the public domain as a reward for their military service, but this benefit was impractical by the 1940s: when it had enacted the Taylor Grazing Act in 1934, Congress had foreclosed settlement on most of the remaining public lands outside of Alaska. It was still possible in the 1940s, though, to homestead on federal reclamation projects because the Taylor Grazing Act permitted homesteading on lands that had previously been reserved and withdrawn for reclamation. Moreover, the act also allowed the secretary of the interior to reopen any lands for entry deemed to be "more valuable or suitable for the production of agricultural crops than for the production of native grasses and forage plants."[1] Acreage being developed by the Bureau of Reclamation could not accommodate every veteran, but at least some Americans' land hunger could be satisfied thereby. Congress had already established a precedent in 1920 after World War I for offering veterans priority rights in land openings on reclamation projects. As World War II wound down, Congress considered whether to continue that policy, revise it, or scrap it entirely.

Although Congress overwhelmingly supported the idea of

granting veterans preferential rights in applying for reclamation homesteads, a constellation of regional, bureaucratic, and philosophical issues and interests roiled the political waters. Complicating the picture was the fact that the nation's agricultural economy was rapidly changing. The percentage of American farms with tractors had nearly doubled between 1939 and 1945, rising from 22 to 40 percent. During the war harvests increased as farmers used more chemical fertilizer such as anhydrous ammonia and insecticides such as the newly introduced DDT.[2] Was it economically feasible or desirable to develop new farms when existing farms were already satisfying domestic demand? The debates and hearings on Capitol Hill in 1944–1945 regarding homesteads for veterans illuminated significant disagreements and tensions regarding reclamation and development of western lands, the Bureau of Reclamation's role within the government, the fit between homesteading and a modern economy, and the degree to which government should minimize the risks inherent in homesteading. At this early date, though, no one who weighed in on the debate questioned the propriety of subdividing the public domain to reward and enrich individual citizens.

In the legislative debates and hearings of the 1940s proponents of homesteads for veterans looked to the post–World War I era for both precedents and lessons. Following that war the Department of the Interior had received close to 196,000 inquiries regarding settlement opportunities on western reclamation projects. In February 1920, responding belatedly to these inquiries over a year after the fighting had ended, Congress through Public Resolution 29 granted a sixty-day preference right to veterans in applying for homesteads on public lands, including federal reclamation projects. Later the preference period was lengthened to ninety days. Only if an insufficient number of qualified veterans applied for those lands during that time period would others' applications be considered. Although most veterans who had written to the Department of the Interior had already chosen other opportunities, 10,875 would-be homesteaders applied for 1,311 farms that were opened to settlement on federal reclamation projects. Particularly from 1920 to 1922 lands opened to entry were awarded almost exclusively to veterans. Most of these new farms were located on the Klamath Project along the border between California and Oregon and on the Shoshone and North Platte Projects in Wyoming. The farms were awarded by lottery.[3]

The post–World War I homesteading frontier had its share of impressive success stories. Take the case of Frank Vancluira, one of eighty veterans who took up a homestead on the North Platte Project's Fort Laramie Division early in 1920. A Bohemian immigrant who had moved to the United States in 1911, Vancluira had farmed in New York and Nevada and worked in a sausage factory before joining the army in 1917. During the war Vancluira suffered a severe leg injury. With $2,000 and a dependable monthly pension from the Veterans Bureau as a result of his wartime injury, he managed to develop his farm and construct a home without having to borrow money. His knowledge of irrigation, stemming from previous farming in Nevada, combined with his industriousness and good fortune in receiving an exceptionally fertile homestead, allowed him to prosper. Within four years his farm was valued at $10,000—far beyond the amount of money he had invested in the place.[4]

Despite the success stories, barely 60 percent of the 1,311 homesteaders on reclamation projects during the interwar years "proved up" by complying with the requirements of federal homestead law and thereby obtained title to their farms. Of those who did prove up, 75 percent (or about 45 percent of all 1,311 original claimants) retained their farms until 1944—an impressive rate considering the economic volatility of the 1920s and 1930s. However, nearly half (46 percent) of those who had gained title to their homestead no longer farmed the land themselves by 1944. The homesteaders were more likely to continue farming on projects that were more fertile: on the highly productive Klamath Project, 65 percent of the homesteaders who had proved up continued to farm their land in 1944, whereas on the North Platte Project, only 19 percent still did so.[5]

The high percentage of homesteaders who departed without proving up, coupled with the failure of many veterans to continue farming the land personally after they gained title to it, concerned the Bureau of Reclamation. Commissioner Elwood Mead assigned Andrew Weiss, superintendent of the North Platte Project, to probe into the matter, focusing upon the Shoshone and North Platte Projects. Weiss found that most veterans had arrived on the projects with insufficient funds. For instance, Sam Monaco, an industrious immigrant and World War I veteran, had come to the North Platte Project in 1920 with practically no capital. Monaco "made a very courageous trial for three years, being obliged to undergo every privation to get along." Unable to afford lumber for a pigpen or a henhouse, he had sheltered the hens in his own shack and had dug a clay pit for the hogs. Despite his pluck, Monaco was eventually forced to quit. No amount of ingenuity or hard work could compensate for his penury. Many other homesteaders had rented out their farms after proving up, Weiss reported, because they needed more money than their farms could provide. For instance, E. G. Phelps, a homesteader in southeastern Wyoming described by the project manager as "a very fine type farmer" and a "splendid type of man," was "intelligent and anxious to learn" but found he "could not make it" financially. Finally he opted to rent his farm and work full time as a powerhouse operator in order to support his family. Weiss estimated that over half (53 percent) of the veterans, like Monaco and Phelps, who homesteaded on the Fort Laramie Division in 1920 were poorly prepared financially for homesteading. Only about one in four had arrived with sufficient money for "the necessary fixed improvements" and the "necessary farm equipment and livestock."[6]

On the Frannie Division of the Shoshone Project in northern Wyoming, Weiss discovered that only five of the fifty-seven veterans who had settled there in 1920 remained four years later. Even on better farms that had been opened to settlement the following year, only one-fifth of the settlers remained. Weiss identified their principal impediment as the lack of capital.[7]

In addition to insufficient capital, defects in the land itself such as poor soil, waterlogged land, and small farm size handicapped some veterans. Hundreds took up lands in the Goshen Irrigation District in southern Wyoming between 1921 and 1927, and roughly one-fifth "had very little chance of success" because of "poor or submarginal" farms, project superintendent Fred Roush estimated in hindsight. In 1924, the president of the water users' association on the Frannie Division reported that nearly two-thirds of the farmland there was "practically valueless" because of seepage, alkali, and other problems. It would cost an estimated $30 per acre to drain lands that were worth no more than $25 an acre. A commission appointed by the secretary of the interior to study reclamation concluded in 1924 that "the lands on the Frannie Division are of such low agricultural value as to make it impossible for them to pay the cost of operation and maintenance of the irrigation works much less to return the construction costs."[8]

Weiss reported that inexperience, coupled with underestimation of the rigors of farm life, had driven others from their farms. Roughly one in three veterans who homesteaded on the North Platte Project in 1920 had never lived or worked on a farm. "Too few of us knew much about irrigated farming when we started here," observed homesteader George "Doc" Haas, who had come to the Goshen Irrigation District in 1921. "We had every kind of ex-soldier, from piano tuners to paper hangers. . . . We did not realize that there was no let-up in work, season after season."[9]

Other veterans quickly sold or rented out their farms after proving up because they had always regarded their homesteads as speculative property. Weiss's report showed that 35 percent of those who homesteaded on the Fort Laramie Division of the North Platte Project in 1920 had no interest in farming, preferred some other occupation, or disliked the country and therefore had never intended to remain there. For instance, Paul J. Hall, a thirty-year-old veteran, was characterized by the project superintendent as "not hav[ing] much energy." He lacked capital, farming experience, and had "no desire to farm." Moreover his wife disliked farm life. Willard Wertman, a thirty-five-year-old homesteader who had grown up on a farm in Milford, Nebraska, only cultivated his tract for one season. He "always seemed to dislike the country and was dissatisfied with nearly every thing in connection with his farm, the community and the government." Some had homesteaded largely for speculative reasons. A. R. Baker, who had constructed a 10 x 12–foot shack on his homestead, had come from a wealthy family but invested little capital in the place and engaged only in "poor and nondescript farming." A graduate of the Washington School of Finance, he worked as a financial expert and had remained on the farm only long enough to prove up. He retained title to the land, though, "with hopes of higher values and oil boom."[10]

Poor health dogged other homesteaders like L. C. Anstine, a veteran with a fair education, farming experience, and a "good personality," who suffered from a wartime injury. The project manager gauged his prospects for success in 1924 as "poor" because of his "physical handicap," although he noted that Anstine had "made a creditable effort." Likewise, Bruce Morton, a forty-year-old veteran with farming experience, had made only "fair" progress as a farmer although he knew how to farm, was "industrious," and possessed a "good personality." Having been "gassed" while fighting in the trenches, he suffered from a "severe physical handicap." The project manager believed Morton would "no doubt make a success if he were able-bodied and had sufficient capital."[11]

In Weiss's view, then, insufficient capital, liabilities of the land itself, inexperience, lack of commitment, and poor health largely explained the lackluster performance of most veterans who homesteaded following World War I. Twenty years after Weiss filed his report, his successor as project manager,

Fred Roush, revisited the issue of homestead abandonment. With the benefit of two additional decades of hindsight, Roush identified many of the same impediments to successful homesteading that Weiss had cited. Reversing the order Weiss had assigned to the foremost factors in homestead abandonment, Roush deemed the most significant factor to be "poor and submarginal units," followed by "lack of financial aid" to the homesteaders during the farm development phase. Other causes of farm abandonment were the agricultural depression of the 1920s and 1930s (an issue that Roush had not identified), lack of managerial ability or ambition on the part of the veterans, and insufficient knowledge of or instruction in irrigation and farming techniques.[12]

Shortly before Weiss completed his investigation of veteran homesteading and two decades before Roush offered his evaluation, the Fact Finders, a blue ribbon commission appointed by the secretary of the interior to study the reclamation program, had cited similar problems on reclamation projects generally and had advocated reforms to correct these problems. They recommended against approving any project until studies of "water supply, engineering features, soil, climate, transportation, markets, land prices, probable cost of development and other factors upon which the success of the project must depend" showed that the project could succeed. Retreating from the laissez-faire approach to homesteading that had allowed virtually any head of household to try their luck at homesteading, the Fact Finders had also advocated screening applicants for reclamation homesteads on the basis of their "industry, experience, character, and possession of a part of the capital needed in improving their farms." Additionally, to soften the edges of pioneering, they had recommended that the government provide agricultural and economic advisors and short-term, low-interest loans to settlers for livestock, equipment, and farm development.[13]

A conservative Congress in 1925 not surprisingly rejected the Fact Finders' calls for loans and agricultural advisors for settlers. In what became known as the Fact Finders' Act, Congress did stipulate that no project should be approved until scientific studies had been conducted showing that the project was "adaptable for actual settlement and farm homes." Congress also authorized the secretary of the interior to appoint examining boards to review the qualifications of prospective homesteaders and to establish minimum qualifications for homesteaders on reclamation projects in terms of "industry, experience, character, and capital."[14]

By 1940, the Bureau of Reclamation was relying upon scientific studies to ensure that proposed projects were feasible and had established minimum standards of industry, farming experience, character, and capital for prospective homesteaders. Homesteaders still were receiving no training or farm development loans from the Bureau, and this became a major issue in congressional debates over postwar homesteading.[15]

In 1940, the twenty-year veterans preference legislation Congress had passed after World War I lapsed. Soon thereafter Congressmen James Scrugham of Nevada and John R. Murdock of Arizona discussed the possibility of extending homesteading benefits to veterans for two more decades. Murdock proceeded to introduce a bill to that effect in the Seventy-Seventh Congress, but it was never considered.[16]

Murdock was not about to abandon the matter, though. Sincerely interested in rewarding veterans, he viewed reclamation partly as a means to that end. Murdock was convinced that "of all the programs being pushed because of the capacity to aid the veterans, Reclamation offers most—at least in the long run." But he also recognized that a fashionable cause like honoring veterans might win support among skeptical easterners for an enhanced reclamation budget, leading to new agricultural communities, wealth, and population in the arid West. Murdock was a tireless booster of the West. One of his favorite sayings was "An underdeveloped West and a fully prosperous Nation do not—and never can—go hand in hand." As he stated on another occasion, "My heart is in the cause of reclamation. It means very much not only to my State, but to the entire West."[17]

In 1944, with national interest in the returning veterans crescendoing rapidly, Murdock believed the time had come to publicize the desirability of reclamation for veterans. As the House Committee on World War Veterans' Legislation held hearings in the spring of 1944 on Senate bill 1767, the GI Bill of Rights, Murdock capitalized upon Congress's interest in the future of America's soldiers and scheduled a meeting with the committee. Addressing the committee on March 28, he reminded them that "after every war our veterans have been taken care of in the public domain, lying in the West." By the end of the First World War, though, "all the good land had [already] been taken." After the Great War many who attempted to "make a living out on the desert with the jack rabbits" had failed. The answer to the problem of insufficient homesteading opportunities on the public domain for veterans in the twentieth century was not to point veterans toward the cities. Instead it was to develop irrigable tracts through the Bureau of Reclamation and open them to settlement. More than 100,000 veterans might be accommodated in this fashion within a handful of years. "I feel that we ought to turn our attention to that land of sunshine and health and husband our water resources that our land-hungry veterans may have the help of the Government in making good land available as homes, on which they can make a living," he told the committee.[18]

Murdock proposed an amendment to the GI Bill that would entitle veterans to preference over all other applicants for homesteads on reclamation projects. Such an entitlement would naturally increase the stake of millions of soldiers in the Bureau's construction program. Murdock's amendment sought to make reclamation homesteads even more inviting for veterans and enhance their chances for success by waiving over half of each veteran homesteader's share of the Bureau's cost of constructing the irrigation system. Thereby the congressman sought to shift the costs of reclamation from the direct beneficiaries to all taxpayers. After discussing Murdock's amendment to the GI Bill, the committee rejected it. Some felt that Murdock's amendment had merit but should be considered as a separate bill because it dealt only with the West; others believed the proposal was "too generous." Murdock later claimed that he had only been testing the waters to determine how favorably disposed others were to the idea. "I offered the . . . proposal to that committee, not that I expected them to include it, although I think it would have been appropriate in an omnibus bill of that nature. But I got the reaction of the members of that committee."[19]

Having failed to persuade the committee to incorporate homesteading benefits within the GI Bill, Murdock addressed the entire House as the bill was being discussed on the floor. Rather than offering the amendment anew, Murdock said he "merely wanted to call the attention of Congress to it" and to inform them that he had drafted a new bill along the lines of his amendment, H.R. 3179; the Committee on Irrigation and Reclamation would soon conduct hearings on the bill, he announced, and he hoped his colleagues would support it.[20]

H.R. 3179 stipulated that any qualified veteran "shall have preference as an applicant for entry on any public lands irrigated or reclaimed by the Bureau of Reclamation." Moreover, in an effort to reduce the financial burdens that had plagued earlier generations of reclamation homesteaders, the bill waived over half of each veteran's repayment obligations to the reclamation fund for project construction. Murdock's bill was referred to a subcommittee of the House Committee on Irrigation and Reclamation chaired by Murdock and comprised of five westerners. In May of 1944 the subcommittee devoted a day to the bill, focusing upon the ways that reclamation could be justified as a means of serving the needs of veterans and boosting the economy.[21]

Everyone in the room assumed veterans wanted to homestead although no one presented hard evidence in support of the assumption. It would be several months before the army would test that assertion in surveys of its personnel. As historians John M. Blum and Mark Grandstaff have observed, though, the typical soldier portrayed in the media hailed from a farm or small town in the American heartland. It seemed natural in light of this stereotype to assume that soldiers wanted to return to live in the country. Murdock noted that veterans after every previous war had been "land hungry." Why should veterans of the present conflict be any different? Assistant Commissioner of Reclamation William Warne quoted Secretary of Agriculture Claude Wickard's statement that "our best information indicates there are about 1,500,000 farm boys now in the armed services." These young men had "every right to expect" the opportunity to farm, Warne maintained. Warne indicated that the Bureau's proposed program of postwar land development could bring an astounding 6,500,000 acres under cultivation on 190 irrigation projects within three to five years, as well as delivering supplemental water to 9,500,000 acres—if Congress appropriated enough money. Taken together, these projects would open anywhere from 125,000 to 150,000 new farms for veterans. Warne added that he hoped Congress would also make "adequate provision" to assist those who settled on these farms through loans and technical training.[22]

It seemed clear that existing farms could not accommodate the hundreds of thousands of veterans who intended to become farmers. A report by H. H. Wooten of the Bureau of Agricultural Economics estimated that the number of veterans who might be accommodated on existing farms was slim: about 22,000 elderly farm operators might be expected to sell their farms to returning veterans, but only about half of these farms would be economically viable enterprises. Other underutilized land on existing farms might be cleared, drained, or irrigated to create 100,000 more farms. Still, only a small percentage of veterans could be accommodated on existing farms.[23]

In light of the presumed demand among veterans for farms and the stunning outline Warne presented to the Committee on Irrigation and Reclamation of how the Bureau could help to meet that demand, Murdock urged the committee to strike while the iron was hot. William Lemke of North Dakota worried, though, that the veteran was "entitled to a great deal more than Congress will ever give him." The committee concluded that it needed to redraft Murdock's bill to come up with "something we can get through Congress." They must be prepared, Walt Horan of Washington observed, to dismantle the "old argument, Why develop the West when we are paying men all over the United States to take land out of cultivation?" The proposal would appear economically irrational to many of their eastern colleagues.[24]

Despite plans to call other witnesses and to determine ways to build a convincing case for subsidizing the move of veterans to the West, the committee chaired by Murdock was forced by the press of business to defer those matters. Meanwhile, another veterans preference bill that was likely to raise little criticism was making its way through the Committee on Public Lands, to which Murdock also belonged.

Florida Representative J. Hardin Peterson, who chaired the House Committee on Public Lands, introduced H.R. 5025, a bill granting preference to veterans in applying for public lands "under the homestead or desert land laws," in June of 1944. Partly because it appropriated no money, developed no new programs, and mentioned neither the Bureau of Reclamation nor the West but theoretically applied to the entire nation, the measure inspired little opposition. One day after the bill had been referred to the Committee on Public Lands, Murdock as a member of that committee referred the bill without amendment to the House, recommending its passage and noting that the Interior Department had endorsed it. Four days later the House approved the bill and submitted it to the Senate. Later that summer the Senate Committee on Public Lands reported the bill favorably and on 13 August the Senate approved it. On 27 September, President Franklin D. Roosevelt signed the bill into law. Although the law was far less specific than the one Murdock had drafted, it did ensure veterans would receive preferential treatment in applying for any land on federal irrigation projects.[25]

At the same time that many policy makers were forecasting that hundreds of thousands of veterans would return to the farm after the war and that the Bureau of Reclamation could accommodate many of them on new projects, the House Committee on Post-war Economic Policy and Planning began to question the economic feasibility of thousands of new farms. In August 1944, Secretary of Agriculture Claude R. Wickard warned the committee that although "a great many" soldiers might want to farm, agriculture would "offer no large-scale possibilities" for them. In fact, because of mechanization, it was likely that "a somewhat smaller, rather than larger, farm labor force will be needed to turn out full farm production." The nation's farms could not even reabsorb those soldiers who had farmed before the war. Wickard hastened to add that he "didn't mean to say that there will be no opportunity," but he insisted that "there is no possibility . . . for us to put a large additional number of workers on the lands as compared with what we have now." Several months later, the committee heard Karl Brandt of the Food Research Institute at Stanford University, who was even more skeptical of the economic prospects for veterans who desired to farm. Although new lands might be brought under cultivation, particularly in the West, and although "nothing is more popular in the country than the idea of paying our tribute to the veterans by giving them a chance to found a home on a farm," Brandt questioned the wisdom of placing hundreds of thousands of veterans on farms "because they will have to meet the hard competition in a market that will be glutted in many ways." Murdock responded to these pessimistic forecasts with an optimistic faith in America's ingenuity and capacity to consume. He maintained that Congress had no choice but to accommodate "a lot of veterans [who] will want to go on the land." Americans would simply have to "find other uses for farm products" to overcome the problems of supply and demand.[26]

With veterans preference for homesteading on public lands in place, the Bureau of Reclamation and its friends in Congress ignored concerns about agricultural surpluses and pushed for more irrigated farms for veterans. From their perspective, the veterans preference law Congress had just enacted was insufficient in three respects. First, the law said nothing about the Bureau of Reclamation's role in developing the West for veterans; second, it provided no financial or technical assistance to the veterans for developing their farms. During the Gilded Age, such assistance would have been viewed as an unconscionable interference with natural processes that insured that only the fittest farmers would survive. But the liberal reforms of the Progressives and the New Dealers had thrust a greater responsibility for social welfare and support upon the federal government. One representative from the Bureau explained, "We feel that a man should be assisted sufficiently to increase to the optimum point his chances of success on the land. . . . I think we have had some failures on our projects that could have been avoided if we had given a little additional attention to getting the farm into production quickly and seeing that the farmer was properly coached in the methods of using his water." The Bureau was reacting, another employee later recalled, to the widespread perception that on the Bureau's projects "it took three generations of farmers to make an irrigation farm. The first one who came in and subjugated the land usually wore out and went broke. Another man would buy it. By the time he got it pretty well along he was also gone. It took the third investment before a fully successful family farm, economically sufficient, was available." To counteract this perception, the Bureau was eager to "improve our ways of doing business." A third deficiency arose because of some of the lands the Bureau was developing in the Columbia Basin and Arizona's Wellton Mohawk Valley. There the bureau planned to buy, subdivide, and resell privately owned tracts that were too large to be irrigated under the 160-acre limitation imposed by reclamation law. Veterans should have preference in obtaining these tracts, the Bureau's representatives believed, but inasmuch as these lands could not technically be offered as homesteads, the veterans preference law did not apply. If these deficiencies were remedied, the interests of veterans and those of the Bureau of Reclamation might be made to serve one another.[27]

In tandem with John Murdock, officials in the Bureau worked to draft a new bill, H.R. 520, which they hoped would be more acceptable to the House than the "generous" provisions of H.R. 3179. Murdock introduced the new bill in the spring of 1945. It provided "a ninety-day preferred right of purchase" for veterans on lands being made available for sale on reclamation projects. The bill also permitted the Bureau to purchase and resell any land "within or adjacent to" any project, authorized the Bureau to extend technical assistance to farmers on reclamation projects, permitted the Bureau to contract with settlers or with water users' associations for clearing and leveling land to prepare it for irrigation, and authorized "necessary" appropriations for these activities. Having decided in their deliberations the previous summer that Congress would insist that the homesteaders shoulder their full share of the government's investment in each reclamation project, the bill proposed other alternatives for assisting the veterans financially: it permitted governmental agencies "authorized to make provision for the reestablishment of veterans in civil life" to become involved "to the fullest extent" that was legally and administratively feasible in extending "financial assistance" to the veterans "for the acquisition or erection of housing, farm buildings and adjuncts, improvements, equipment, chattels, and operating capital, and for transportation to the project."[28]

Referred to the House Committee on Irrigation and Reclamation, with Murdock as the chair, the bill became the committee's first item of business. Through the committee's hearings, stretching from 12 April to 22 May, Congress probed the relationship of veterans to irrigation and federal reclamation more closely than at any other time during the war.

Much was said in the hearings of the veterans and their desires. Murdock admitted that some might say that "all you want to do is further the cause of reclamation and ride the wave of patriotic feeling which is running high now, to do the right thing by returning veterans," but he insisted that "it is the interest of the veterans primarily that I have in mind." Murdock opened the hearings by reading a letter from President Roosevelt. Although Roosevelt had not reviewed H.R. 520, he did "commend and urge [the committee's] favorable consideration of Federal Reclamation projects as an important opportunity for returning veterans" and urged Congress to furnish "such forms of assistance" to veterans "as will be needed to make their pioneering efforts fruitful to the country and truly beneficial to themselves and their families." The committee's first witness, Secretary of the Interior Harold Ickes, spoke in favor of the bill, saying that it would bestow "one of the most valuable privileges ever conferred upon veterans by the Government," affording them "the opportunity through hard work to build a place where they can spend their lives in comfort, good living, and happiness." Modest assistance to the settlers in the short run would result in their long-term financial independence.[29]

William Warne, assistant commissioner of the Bureau of Reclamation, told the committee that demand among veterans for irrigated farms would be heavy. In recent months, the Bureau had received close to 100 letters per month from soldiers who wanted to know about "job and settlement opportunities" on western reclamation projects—especially in the Southwest and in the Columbia Basin. For instance, Will Menaker, a merchant seaman, had written the previous November that "many" soldiers and seamen aboard his cargo vessel "desire[d] to return to agricultural pursuits." Byron Lowry, a discharged veteran, had written that same month because he hoped to "locate on some irrigated project that is being constructed." Early in 1945, Private Jesse Jensen wrote that he, "among many other boys . . . [was] wondering what's to become of us after this war." Jensen had heard rumors that lands were to be opened by the government in the Columbia Basin. Since he was "very much interested in farming," he wanted "to learn more about this opportunity." Technical sergeant Robert E. Nixon, stationed at an army air base in Yuma, wrote that he hoped to "get some of this land" slated for homesteading near Yuma. He had "talked to at least 20 servicemen [at the air base] about such a project to find what they thought about an opportunity of this kind" and "almost everyone was very much interested and anxious to find out more about it." Although the Bureau had received only a few hundred such inquiries in recent months, at least 400,000 farm boys from irrigated regions were serving in the military, noted Bureau administrator Goodrich Lineweaver. He estimated that "at least" 300,000–400,000 soldiers like the letter writers "would like to settle on an irrigated farm" and could meet the Bureau's qualifications for homesteading in terms of startup capital and agricultural experience.[30]

Representatives from the Regular Veterans' Association and the American Legion also appeared before the committee to testify in favor of the bill, and the legislative representative for the Veterans of Foreign Wars sent a letter expressing his organization's support for veterans preference. John Taylor of the American Legion stated that he had "been in contact with literally hundreds of thousands of soldiers overseas" and therefore knew the "mental attitude of the veterans." Contrary to popular opinion, many veterans had no former job to which they could return. "I think what they really want is . . . real property." After living on "boxed up rations," "literally hundreds of thousands" of soldiers were eager "to be somewhere actually producing the things [they] required and living from that and off that, and having a surplus so that [they] could get ahead and make [their] own way in life."[31]

Although veterans and their interests received considerable attention in the hearings, those who spoke also offered additional arguments in favor of the legislation. Secretary of Agriculture Claude Wickard endorsed the idea of opening new lands for veterans in the West. He had seemingly overcome the scruples about overproduction he had expressed a few months earlier because he now testified, "It is always desirable to open up new lands that can be operated economically," adding, "as time goes on we will need all the good agricultural lands we have in this country to take care of the demand." The secretary urged, "We should go ahead with all the irrigation projects that are economically feasible that offer an opportunity of producing good crops and a good living for the farmers that live on them."[32]

Harry S. Bashore, Commissioner of Reclamation, likewise emphasized the economic benefits of reclamation for the entire nation. Citing bleak forecasts of a recession that would follow demobilization and the cancellation of defense contracts, Bashore testified that the Bureau's construction program would directly employ over 400,000 workers as well as indirectly furnishing work for 640,000 people in factories where goods requisitioned by the Bureau would be produced. Thus, he concluded, "H.R. 520 is an important step in the direction of full post-war employment and a high level of income." Postwar economic needs and particularly the postwar agenda of the Bureau of Reclamation received so much enthusiastic attention that the committee chair felt obliged, at the end of the fourth day of the hearings, to remind the committee that "the main purpose of this legislation is to provide as many homes for veterans on good agricultural lands as it is possible for us to provide." The committee had become so enthralled with the developmental possibilities of reclamation that the ostensible justification for that development—the interests of veterans—had received relatively little attention.[33]

Several days into the hearings, substantial opposition to the bill finally surfaced. The sole committee member from east of the Mississippi River, Chester Gross of Pennsylvania, argued that he disliked H.R. 520 because it ran counter to the interests of the veterans, and, incidentally, the economic interest of his own region. "You can take a run-down, cheap farm [in the East] and you would be further in 10 years than in 30 years on a farm in your sagebrush country," he alleged. A veteran settling on an inexpensive eastern farm would be "more likely to stick" because he "would have opportunities available where he could go and work in a nearby community or town and earn some money very often." Although Frank Barrett of Wyoming retorted that the West offered veterans who desired a family farm superior opportunities because "the air is clear and pure and the sun shines most of the time," permitting people to "raise a family under healthful and decent living conditions," Gross would not concede; sunshine would not pay a mortgage. He charged his western colleagues with "hav[ing] in mind the development of the West rather than the welfare of the soldiers," a charge that seemed meritorious in light of the keen interest they had manifested in the Bureau's postwar plans for their own states.[34]

Roland Curran, a westerner representing the Central Valley Project Association, likewise opposed the bill. Curran's association opposed the bill primarily because it threatened to extend the Bureau's power to enforce the acreage limitations of reclamation law through authorizing purchase of excess lands, something that would adversely affect many growers in the Central Valley. But Curran was shrewd enough to attack other vulnerable features of the bill in the name of veterans' interest: he charged that the bill had "been conceived in a department bureau that seems more concerned with enlarging its powers and sphere of activity than it is with either the veteran or the people already operating farms in the various project areas." If Congress really wanted to assist veterans, they would leave the Bureau out of the picture entirely and loan funds to veterans who desired to buy a developed farm anywhere in the nation, rather than "mak[ing] them pioneers" on raw lands. Although Curran attended the hearings because of his interests in the Central Valley Project, he had identified a fundamental assumption underlying the Murdock bill: the idea that veterans would be better served by an elaborate support system of governmental employees than by their own judgment and resourcefulness.[35]

Ultimately representatives of the Department of Agriculture expressed the most influential opposition to the bill. Praising the idea of veterans preference, Secretary of Agriculture Claude Wickard sharply criticized the bill's second section, which authorized the secretary of the interior to purchase and sell lands within or near irrigation projects, to predevelop project lands for settlers by clearing and leveling them, and to provide technical and agricultural guidance and advice to settlers. Such provisions, warned Wickard, would "duplicate machinery already set up for the whole of agriculture in the Department of Agriculture" and would therefore be a "wasteful" use of governmental resources. As Representative J. Will Robinson put it, section 2 appeared to be "setting up some super-agency to take care of the veterans" alone.[36]

As a result of these objections, the committee, in concert with representatives from the Bureau, modified the bill. The new version specified the Veterans Administration rather than the Bureau as the government agency authorized to loan funds to the homesteaders and it permitted the secretary of the interior to purchase, subdivide, and resell only irrigated tracts that were too large to be legally irrigated by their former owners. In response to Secretary Wickard's concerns, the modified bill authorized the secretary of the interior to "obtain through or in cooperation with the State colleges and appropriate agencies of the Government guidance and advice for settlers on lands within the projects in matters of irrigation farming; and to disseminate information by appropriate means and methods," whereas the original bill had authorized the Interior Department "to extend guidance and advice to settlers . . . and to disseminate information," without any reference to cooperation with other government agencies. Still, the initiative for consultation under the new bill remained vested in the Interior Department.[37]

The committee reported the revised bill to the House on 5 June 1945. In their report to the House, the majority of the committee justified their support for the proposed law by observing that "several hundred thousand veterans of World War II have indicated that upon their release from the service they wish to have an opportunity to take up farming as a career." Although farms on reclamation projects could not accommodate all who desired to farm, "veterans, having earned the Nation's gratitude, [deserved] a preferred position with respect to obtaining such farms."[38]

Over three months after receiving the committee's report, the House turned its attention to the bill. President Truman had urged Congress to approve it in order to give "outstanding opportunities for returning veterans." As had been the case in the committee hearings, no one vocally opposed the concept of veterans preference. John Flannagan of Virginia, the influential chair of the House Committee on Agriculture, claimed, "We are all in accord that the veterans should be given preference in the purchase of this reclaimed land." Adolph Sabath of Illinois attested that he knew it was "the aim of the Members of this House that everything possible shall be done to aid returning veterans." Similarly, Leo Allen of Illinois said that "every Member of Congress irrespective of party, wants the returning soldier to be benefitted in every way" and August Andresen of Minnesota maintained, "There is no disagreement in giving the veterans preference."[39]

Although rewarding veterans seemed desirable to all, representatives objected to several other features of the bill. At this stage, no one mentioned possible overproduction of farm products as an objection to the bill, despite the phenomenal pace of mechanization, which had caused production to skyrocket during the war years. Although some easterners questioned the quality of life on a western homestead, none questioned the quality of life including standards of living or educational and cultural opportunities in rural America generally, even though these factors had induced many rural residents to relocate in urban areas. Environmental objections to reclamation, which would become dominant by the 1960s, were not mentioned either.

The foremost argument was that the bill authorized the secretary of the interior to become involved in agricultural training and technical assistance although the Department of Agriculture already had similar programs in place. The House Committee on Agriculture, which had met to review the bill that morning, had drafted an amendment eliminating all key provisions of the bill aside from granting of preferential rights to veterans and the provision of information and financial assistance by the Veterans Administration. Irrigation and Reclamation Committee member Robert Rockwell noted that the committee had not even consulted with the new secretary of agriculture, Clinton Anderson, who had opposed the bill in writing. Everett M. Dirksen of Illinois charged that the bill unduly broadened the activities of the Bureau of Reclamation and the Department of the Interior, duplicating services that were already being furnished by the Department of Agriculture. Similarly, Clarence Cannon of Missouri, who said he believed "the veterans are entitled to anything the Nation can offer," opposed the duplication of services by two bureaus.[40]

Others objected to the bill's focus upon western lands, arguing that few genuine opportunities awaited the veterans in the rural West. The bill would play "a dirty trick on the veterans," claimed Jessie Sumner of Illinois, forcing them into unwinnable pioneering situations rather than loaning them funds so that they could buy improved farms. Chester Gross questioned the wisdom of veterans' homesteading in the West, even more colorfully than he had done in the committee hearings on the bill. "It induces them now to go out into the West on new lands, where rattlesnakes might bite their children and coyotes and wolves endanger the lives of their wives, and where their greatest asset is sunshine, which never pays mortgages or educates their children and where foxes will kill their chickens and crows pick the eyes out of any livestock that is born outside," he claimed, concluding, "It is just not right." Rising to the challenge, William Lemke of North Dakota retorted that "in many places east of the Mississippi River nothing worthwhile grows even if they have water."[41]

Committee members who favored the bill attempted to refute the criticism of their colleagues. The new secretary of agriculture must have not compared the former bill with the newly revised version, some insisted; he had merely repeated the objections of the former secretary, which had been addressed and resolved by the committee in redrafting the bill. Strenuously opposing the amendment proposed by the Committee on Agriculture, which would excise most of the bill, committee members argued that it would reduce veterans preference to a meaningless gesture. Antonio Fernandez of New Mexico maintained that a veterans preference law that contained no provisions for financial or educational assistance to homesteaders would be "nothing but an empty shell," similar to the preference right that veterans received after World War I. John Murdock called the amended bill "a mockery" and Will Robinson of Utah accused those who wanted to strike most of the bill and claimed to be "so strong for the veterans" with "leav[ing] a hollow shell for the veterans, helping them with one hand but . . . taking everything away [with the other] that was given them by a committee that studied this bill for 3 or 4 weeks." Murdock agreed that "the powers of the Bureau of Reclamation are somewhat extended by the terms of this bill" but maintained that this was necessary because the projects to be developed were "more difficult" ones with more "difficult engineering problems" than the first projects that had been developed.[42]

At length, opponents of the bill carried the day, although the vote was close: the House voted 76 to 68 to approve the first section of the bill, with its provision for veterans preference, but to jettison most of the other provisions, including any expansion of the Interior Department's jurisdiction over assistance to homesteaders. The amended bill was sent to the Senate where it was referred to the Senate Committee on Irrigation and Reclamation, but the bill as amended had no strong supporters in the House who would pressure the Senate to act; after all the lip service that had been paid to the veterans, no one seemed to be very interested in this watered-down bill. Certainly Murdock and his associates on the Irrigation Committee, along with the Bureau of Reclamation, saw no charm in it. Perhaps their lack of interest stemmed from their belief that the amended bill offered nothing substantial to veterans, although it did instruct the Veterans Administration to assist the homesteaders financially. Certainly the bill clipped the Bureau of Reclamation's aspirations for assisting homesteaders technically or monetarily. Preoccupied with other matters, the Senate committee never held hearings on the bill or referred it back to the full Senate, and so the bill died in the Senate.[43]

Congress had rejected the alternative vision of homesteading proposed by the Bureau and the House Committee on Irrigation, with its attempts to overcome some of the handicaps homesteaders had encountered after World War I. Waivers of construction payments, assured loans, guaranteed predevelopment of farms, and a wealth of technical assistance were intended to reduce the risks of homesteading and the historically high attrition rate among homesteaders. Such measures could have enhanced future homesteaders' prospects of financial success. For reasons that had less to do with the perceived needs of veterans than with bureaucratic turf wars between the Departments of Agriculture and Interior, the Murdock bill had been allowed to die. Nevertheless, in an almost perfunctory manner Congress had assured veterans of preferential treatment in any land openings that did occur. Officials in the Bureau hoped there would be hundreds of such openings on reclamation projects in the coming years.

2 "AH, FOR THE LIFE OF A FARMER" THE CHIMERA OF FREE LAND

On 12 April 1945, Secretary of the Interior Harold Ickes met with the House Committee on Irrigation and Reclamation to outline the Bureau of Reclamation's plans for developing the West. Across the Atlantic Ocean in Europe, Allied forces were surging toward Berlin, the German army in shambles. Within four weeks Adolf Hitler would be dead and Germany would surrender. Ickes and those with whom he met anticipated the Third Reich's imminent collapse, foresaw Japan's eventual defeat, and expected increased funding would become available following the war for domestic programs like reclamation. To that end, Ickes roughly sketched the outlines of Reclamation's proposal to develop 415 projects in fifteen western river basins at a cost of $5 billion. As had been the case in previous hearings, the numbers were rough estimates intended to dazzle and impress lawmakers. The nation's postwar "prosperity" and its "future strength and greatness" would be magnified by these projects: as many as 400,000 returning veterans could obtain farms on these postwar projects, but the benefits of reclamation would extend far beyond them. New farms on reclamation projects would "provide a market for all manner of goods produced in other sections." These projects would enhance river transportation, prevent flooding, and generate hydroelectric power for cities and industry. Thanks to reclamation, a prosperous nation where "good food, good schooling, and opportunity for leisure and travel" were available would permit "our men and women to perform their necessary economic tasks with less effort and greater profit, and to devote more time to citizenship and cultural growth." This dazzling vision of federal investment in western development, "offer[ing] servicemen an important stake in . . . a tremendous expansion of agriculture, industry, and trade in the West" electrified the western members of the committee.[1]

Although reclamation had its skeptics on Capitol Hill in 1945, particularly when the Bureau pushed for funds to develop training programs for homesteaders, Congress in the immediate postwar years allocated unprecedented sums to support dam building and irrigation. Appropriations for the Bureau of Reclamation soared to over $36.6 million in 1946, an increase of 378 percent over the previous year, and well beyond any previous annual allocation. In the two decades following the end of the war, the Bureau's annual appropriations aggregated over $1.6 billion. During these decades, the Bureau constructed over 110 storage dams and dikes including the 710-foot high Glen Canyon Dam, dozens of diversion dams, and over 140 major canals, along with tunnels, pipelines, and pumping plants.[2]

Despite substantial appropriations, the Bureau of Reclamation received far less than the $5 billion Ickes had envisioned and it developed far fewer than 400,000 new farms for returning veterans. Instead, in large measure the Bureau's postwar projects furnished supplemental water for existing farms or facilitated reclamation of privately owned land: between 1946 and 1966 the Bureau advertised the opening of only 3,041 new farms on government land. Additionally, in the Columbia Basin, other new irrigated farms were established on the Bureau's Columbia Basin Project as private owners reduced their holdings to 160 irrigable acres in order to obtain irrigation water from the government. By 1967, there were 5,463 farms under irrigation on that project—a substantial number albeit much smaller than the 10,000–15,000 that planners in 1946 had envisioned for the Basin.[3]

Aside from four farms in Oregon, one in Montana, and six in Wyoming, all of the farms offered by the Bureau of Reclamation to veterans between 1946 and 1966 were concentrated on ten reclamation projects in Arizona, California, Washington, Idaho, and Wyoming. As had been the case on earlier frontiers, much of the land made available to homesteaders in the postwar era seemed pristine—one homesteader described it as being "just the way that God made it." But even seemingly pristine lands had previously been claimed, traversed, occupied, and utilized by others. The story of homesteading began decades prior to World War II with the dispossession of previous claimants, long before plans for federal reclamation projects were contemplated.[4]

Post-1945 reclamation homesteading sites

In Arizona, the Bureau of Reclamation opened lands to farming after the war on its Yuma and Gila Projects. One of Reclamation's earliest ventures, the Yuma Project stretched across 67,000 acres of the Colorado River flood plain in both Arizona and California. Congress had deprived the Quechan Indians of all but 15,000 acres of this riverine region when it established the Fort Yuma Reservation in 1884. In 1912 under the terms of the Dawes General Allotment Act federal authorities parceled out roughly half of the reservation to individual households within the tribe and then opened the remaining 7,000 acres west of the river for general settlement. Some of this acreage was still owned by the government and available for settlement after World War II. East of the river in Arizona much of the land that awaited settlement had once been embroiled in litigation surrounding a grant Mexican officials in Sonora had allegedly made in 1838. In 1893, the U.S. Court of Private Land Claims had upheld claims stemming from the grant. Five years later the Supreme Court reversed the claims court decision, ruling that Sonoran officials had lacked authority under Mexican law in 1838 to award the land. Shortly after this court ruling, which restored lands on the eastern side of the river to the public domain, the land was opened in 1901 to homesteading. Reclamation's Yuma Project was authorized in 1904 on some of this land. Although Reclamation Service canals conveyed water to portions of the Yuma Project as early as 1910, a handful of tracts were still available for homesteading by the 1940s, either because they had reverted to the government in the intervening years or because they had only recently become cultivable with the construction of levees. These scattered tracts, comprising 1,297 acres and divided into twenty-six farms, were advertised for settlement by veterans after the war.[5]

As part of the Gila Project the Bureau of Reclamation opened several dozen additional homesteads on thousands of acres of sandy tableland directly east of Yuma that were watered by the Gila Canal. Between 1936 and 1942 canals and pumping plants had been built to convey, lift, and distribute Colorado River water on Yuma Mesa. During the war, the army established an airfield on the mesa and the Bureau began developing adjacent terrain, partly in order to reduce the severity of dust storms at the airbase but also with an eye toward eventually opening the land for settlement. After the war, the Bureau accelerated its development work, and by 1947 the Bureau was ready to open fifty-four farms; five years later it opened twenty-seven more.[6]

East of Yuma Mesa and across the Gila Mountains along the Gila River drainage, the Bureau began developing a second division of the Gila project known as Wellton-Mohawk in 1949. Until early in the eighteenth century Maricopa Indians farmed and lived along the river as far west as the Mohawk Mountains; thereafter they retreated eastward under pressure from whites and other Indian groups, settling with Pima bands near Gila Crossing. In the nineteenth and early twentieth centuries, white settlers moved into the former homelands of the Maricopa and attempted to irrigate the lands with river water and groundwater. Stymied by drought, floods, saline groundwater, and dropping water tables many of these early settlers abandoned their farms. In 1949 in order to boost water supplies for the region's remaining farmers, the Bureau began constructing two branch canals and three large pumping plants to furnish supplemental water from the Colorado River. In the process, water became available not only for existing farms along the Gila but for over 4,000 acres of government land, which the Bureau subdivided into fifty-two new farms. Because the Bureau had acquired these lands through purchase from former settlers and other landholders, the government sold it at nominal prices ranging from $496 to $787 per farm rather than opening it to homesteading. But buyers were required to comply with the legal requirements of reclamation homesteading.[7]

Northwest of the Yuma Project in the stark Salton Basin lay the Coachella Valley. Spanish explorers traversing the area in the 1770s had visited several Cahuilla villages there. A smallpox epidemic in 1863 wiped out nearly two-thirds of the Cahuilla population. Between 1875 and 1876 the federal government set aside five small reservations for the remaining Cahuilla. In 1891 Congress clarified and reduced the reservation boundaries but also established three more reservations. Three years later in 1894 non-Indian farmers who had moved onto the Cahuillas' former lands began irrigating with groundwater. Crops could be grown year-round in the hot, desert climate, but the groundwater supply was uncertain. The farmers agitated for a long-term, dependable supply of water from the Colorado River. In 1949 their dreams materialized with the completion of the Coachella Main Canal and a labyrinth of underground pipes for delivering Colorado River water to their lands. Although the 77,000-acre project primarily benefited existing landowners, 1,369 acres of irrigable public land were subdivided into twenty sandy farms with phenomenal economic potential and opened for homesteading in 1954.[8]

Hundreds of miles north of the Coachella Valley near California's northern border lay the Tule Lake Division of the Klamath Project. Some of the

Tule Lake Basin's Modoc inhabitants had signed a treaty with California officials in the 1850s guaranteeing their rights to the region, but the United States had never ratified it; in 1864 at Klamath Lake some of the Modoc signed a second treaty less favorable to their interests. Thereunder they renounced their claims to lands in California. Shortly thereafter they moved to a reservation in southern Oregon, but a disillusioned band led by Captain Jack soon returned to Tule Lake. White settlers in the area attempted to evict them and the Modoc War of 1872–1873 ensued, culminating in the execution of Captain Jack and the exile of over 150 Modocs to Indian Territory. Over thirty years later the secretary of the interior in 1905 authorized the Reclamation Service to develop the Modocs' former lands for irrigated farming. By 1912, a dam near the headwaters of the Lost River, a diversion dam, and an 8-mile channel further downstream had been completed, diverting much of the Lost River for irrigation and consequently reducing the size of Tule Lake. Within five years, the lake level fell by 11 feet, and the fertile alluvial soil that was exposed was offered to homesteaders in 1917. In 1921–1923, Reclamation completed a second diversion dam on the Lost River and another canal, opening additional lands in the basin for agriculture. Between 1917 and 1937, the Bureau sponsored six land openings for homesteaders. Plans were under way to open additional lands in 1942, but they were derailed by World War II. After the war, reclamation of lands in the basin resumed, and 216 homesteads were awarded between 1946 and 1949.[9]

Nearly 400 miles northeast of Tule Lake the Bureau created more homesteading opportunities on its Yakima Project. This project straddled the Yakima River and its tributaries in south-central Washington, a region that had been used by the Yakima Indians prior to a land cession in 1855. Subsequently Congress awarded title to much of the region to the Northern Pacific Railroad, which in turn sold the land to farmers. Reclamation's original Yakima project, approved in 1905, primarily furnished supplemental water to privately owned farms in the area. Local boosters then petitioned the Bureau to expand the project. One extension, the Roza Division, was authorized by Congress in 1935 but not completed until after the war. On that division thirty-nine new farms were opened for homesteading after the war. An additional seventeen farms were created in the 1950s after Congress approved new construction on another division, the Kennewick, in 1952.[10]

The Bureau of Reclamation's grandest postwar venture in creating farms took place east of the Yakima Project in the Columbia Basin. The mammoth

Columbia Basin Project included former homelands of the Sinkayuse, or Moses-Columbia, Indians. The United States had pressured Chief Moses to exchange those lands for a reservation north of the Columbia River in 1879. During the 1910s, homesteaders unsuccessfully attempted to farm much of the region without irrigation and then pled with the government to furnish irrigation water. In 1932 the Bureau of Reclamation released a 1,845-page report recommending construction of a huge dam on the Columbia River at Grand Coulee, and New Deal funds were allocated by executive decision early in 1933. Although the dam was essentially completed before the Japanese attacked Pearl Harbor, work on a distribution system including pumping plants was delayed during the war, and the first irrigation water was not delivered until 1948. As was the case on the Gila Project, federally owned lands in the Columbia Basin were offered primarily for sale rather than as homesteads, the federal government having purchased them from individuals who owned more land than they could legally irrigate. Between 1948 and 1966, the Bureau advertised the sale of 1,229 full-time farms in the basin, as well as 190 small part-time farms, and required buyers to comply with the reclamation homesteading regulations. Hundreds of other new farms were created as private landowners sold their excess lands to would-be farmers. By 1967, the Bureau reported that there were 5,463 irrigated farms on the project.[11]

Southeast of the Columbia Basin on the Payette Division of the Boise Project in Idaho the Bureau also developed lands for irrigation and homesteading. This region, along with much of southern Idaho, had been utilized by bands of Northern Shoshone before their claims were reduced in 1867 to a reservation in the eastern part of the state at Fort Hall. Although Reclamation studied the feasibility of irrigating lands east of the Snake River between Payette and Caldwell as early as 1905, over three decades passed before the construction of two dams and a 29-mile canal at last assured water for 24,000 acres within the area. In 1946, the Bureau built Cascade Dam on the north fork of the Payette River along with a pumping plant and canal to convey water to 26,000 more acres of rough and rolling volcanic soil on the project. Most of this land was already privately owned, but the Bureau carved out fifty farms from the remaining public domain and opened them to settlers in 1950.[12]

East of the Payette Division along the semiarid, sagebrush-covered Snake River Plain in south-central Idaho lay the Minidoka Project. The construction of an 8-mile canal north of the Snake River and a 13-mile canal south of the river prior to World War I brought irrigation water to hundreds of farms on the project. In 1908 the secretary of the interior withdrew lands north of those irrigated farms from entry, anticipating that the area, known as the North Side, might be irrigated as an extension of the original project. When Reclamation began constructing the American Falls Reservoir in 1925, it tentatively reserved 500,000 acre feet of water in the reservoir for the North Side. Two years later, the Bureau scrapped plans for the North Side and instead developed the Milner-Gooding Division, a less expensive extension northwest of the original project. Construction of a 70-mile canal for conveying water to the Milner-Gooding Division commenced in 1928 and ended in 1932. Over the next decade as connecting laterals were completed the Bureau opened various tracts on the division for homesteading. As a continuation of that development, between 1946 and 1949, eighty-nine more farms were opened for settlement by veterans.[13]

East of Milner-Gooding on the North Side over 600 homesteads were finally developed beginning in the 1950s. In 1947, representatives from Reclamation and water users in southeastern Idaho tentatively allocated 47,593 acre-feet of water for developing approximately 13,650 acres on the North Side. The Bureau subsequently subdivided these lands into 107 farms and opened them for settlement in 1957. In order to develop an additional 64,000 acres, the Bureau drilled wells and pumped groundwater from the Lost River aquifer 150–200 feet below the surface. Between 1953 and 1961, nearly 200 wells were drilled to furnish water for 532 new homesteads.[14]

After World War II the Bureau of Reclamation also developed lands for homesteading in Wyoming on terrain that had been reserved for the Mountain and Kicked in the Bellies clans of Crow Indians under the Fort Laramie Treaty of 1851. In 1868 under the terms of a second treaty some of the Crow had been pressured to cede their lands in Wyoming in return for a reservation in southern Montana. The removal of the Crow paved the way in that same year for the Eastern Shoshone, who had hunted and camped on lands west of the Bighorn River since the sixteenth century, to obtain a reservation in the Wind River valley. Part of the Wind River Reservation was opened to white settlement under the terms of the Dawes Allotment Act following a 1904 purchase agreement. Eventually Reclamation developed three divisions of its Riverton Project, comprising 57,184 acres. Prior to World War II, Reclamation advertised 260 homesteading opportunities on the first two divisions. In 1944 Congress authorized an irrigation system for a third division of the project, consisting of 11,831 acres. Between 1947 and 1950, Reclamation opened 159 more homesteads to settlement.[15]

Under the same land cession that paved the way for creation of the Wind River Reservation representatives of the Crow signed over lands in the Shoshone River Valley in northern Wyoming that eventually became part of Reclamation's Shoshone Project. Between 1907 and 1938 the Reclamation Service opened 72,000 acres for irrigated farming on three divisions of its Shoshone Project: Garland, Frannie, and Willwood. In 1936 construction of a tunnel and canal to convey water to a fourth division, Heart Mountain, commenced. World War II delayed the opening of that division, but in the postwar era 216 Heart Mountain homesteads were opened to settlement.[16]

The succession of previous claimants, treaties, court decisions, and armed conflicts on lands that were opened for homesteading following World War II belied glib assertions about pristine western lands being naturally "available" for settlement. A combination of armed force, negotiations, treaties, annuities, and allotments along with devastating epidemics had wiped the lands clean of Indian inhabitants prior to the public notices that offered the lands to homesteaders. Here and there on some homesteads, pottery shards, arrowheads, or other artifacts bore silent witness that others had occupied these "unclaimed" lands. In other places weather-beaten remains of fences, houses, or wells served as reminders that earlier generations had tried their hand at dryland homesteading on the same tracts and failed.

Far more apparent on three projects was evidence of another much more recent occupation: some of the choicest homesteads on the Minidoka, Klamath, and Shoshone Projects had been developed and cultivated by poorly paid Japanese and Japanese American internees at the Tule Lake, Heart Mountain, and Minidoka Relocation Centers.

The War Relocation Authority (WRA) decided to situate three of the nation's ten wartime relocation centers on undeveloped reclamation projects in the spring of 1942. After government agencies had identified 300 possible sites for relocation centers, representatives from the WRA visited the most promising ones. Thereafter WRA administrators in cooperation with the Bureau of Reclamation, the Farm Security Administration, and other agencies provisionally selected ten sites for internment camps. Through the Engineer Corps, the War Department negotiated the terms of land transfers and leases. Although historian Roger Daniels has written that the centers were situated "in places where nobody had lived before and no one has lived since," the Bureau of Reclamation had long planned on opening many of the lands that were developed by the internees on the Minidoka, Heart Mountain, and Tule Lake Projects for irrigated farming. In fact, Reclamation believed the relocation centers would actually advance the agency's own agenda because WRA director Milton Eisenhower had pledged to engage residents in developing infrastructure and the land itself for irrigation. For its part, the WRA found the sites attractive because they were federally owned and remote from major population centers or sensitive governmental installations but reasonably close to highways and railroads.[17]

Internees in the camps did much to improve the lands and irrigation systems that others would one day use. At Heart Mountain in the spring of 1943 nearly 200 camp residents per day labored for a pittance—$16 to $19 per month—to line the most porous portions of the recently constructed 26-mile main canal leading from Shoshone Dam to the division. The laborers lugged 100-pound bags of bentonite and wheelbarrow loads of native clay to cement mixers, blended the compound, and then pressed it against the bottom and sides of the 32-foot-wide and 9-foot-deep canal. A Japanese American writer for the *Heart Mountain Sentinel* optimistically speculated that "the evacuees who put in thousands of man-hours through the heat and cold will have the satisfaction of knowing they helped put the final touches on a valuable, permanent project." Perhaps some of the laborers were that altruistic. What is certain is that without their efforts the canal would have been useless; when water had been experimentally turned into the unlined canal in 1941, the seepage had been so heavy that the canal banks nearly gave way in several vulnerable spots.[18]

In addition to their vital labor on the main canal, internees cleared debris from distributing laterals—the arteries stretching from the main canal to the farm plots—and they dug field ditches. They also developed close to 1,700 acres of farmland; with tractors and heavy equipment they broke off the sagebrush and other shrubs, piled them in windrows, and burned them. They then chiseled, disked, and leveled the raw land, going over some plots with tractor-driven implements a dozen times. Subsequently field laborers from the internment camp planted, tended, and harvested crops including cucumbers, tomatoes, melons, corn, potatoes, celery, and daikon for consumption at Heart Mountain and for export to other relocation camps. Much of the back-breaking field work with shovels and hoes was performed by women, many of them first-generation immigrants from Japan who spoke little English.[19]

Internees at the Minidoka Relocation Center performed a similar array of tasks, constructing irrigation systems and improving and cultivating lands that would one day be turned over to homesteaders. Although tractors were used, as they had been at Heart Mountain, to clear most of the land, in the fall of 1942, shortly after their arrival from the west coast, some of the first residents laboriously grubbed sagebrush from nearly 80 acres using hoes. All told, the evacuees prepared close to 1,200 acres for farming, roughly the same amount that was farmed at Heart Mountain. Over two dozen camp residents built irrigation structures including checks, headgates, and drops in order to make a 6.5-mile lateral functional, and others excavated over 30 miles of field and drainage ditches and drainage.[20]

Most internees at the Minidoka Center hailed from cities and towns in the Northwest and were "inexperienced and disinterested in agricultural production." One city slicker expressed most residents' lack of interest in fieldwork when he quipped that "he would like to work in the farming department if he could get an indoor job." Even most of the farmers had never irrigated. To make matters worse for these neophytes, the powdery volcanic soil on the project "seemed to flow like liquid as the water reached it," repeatedly washing out farm ditches and furrows. Despite these obstacles, in 1943 camp residents under the supervision of evacuee Shintaro Kamaya grew over twenty varieties of vegetables. At the peak of the harvest season, over 400 internees labored in the fields, harvesting 2.2 million pounds of vegetables.[21]

Internees at the Tule Lake Relocation Center developed nearly three times as much land for farming as did workers at Heart Mountain or Minidoka. WRA administrators hoped that the fertile soil there would produce enough food for several relocation centers where farming was not feasible. By 1943, laborers were farming over 3,100 acres at Tule Lake. Each workday a caravan of army trucks transported hundreds of workers 7 miles from the relocation town site to the fields where they labored on irrigation, cultivation, and weeding crews for forty-four hours per week, earning $3 per week in 1942 and $4 beginning in 1943. Prevailing wages in the area were 4–5 times as high. At the peak of the harvest season over 600 residents toiled in the fields. As had been the case on the other two projects, evacuees also developed and

Japanese American internees irrigating head lettuce on the Tule Lake Relocation Center farm, 29 August 1942. Following the war this prime, fully developed farmland was awarded to fortunate homesteaders. (Reclamation Photographs, NARA, Rocky Mountain Region)

improved the irrigation system; at Tule Lake they excavated an 18-mile, 8-foot-deep drainage ditch and lined portions of an irrigation canal with reinforced concrete.[22]

Did the laborers see their voluntary work as unfair exploitation? Some journalists and administrators claimed the answer was no. A Japanese American writer for the Tule Lake center newspaper rhapsodized, "Ah, for the life of a farmer," and went on to depict the "beautiful ride" that workers took each day to and from the farm with "such a marvelous, scenic view." After describing the hearty lunches the workers consumed and their "boat riding in the levies" during their lunch break the writer concluded that the farmer's life in the "peaceful" countryside was "really swell." Stressing that all labor on the farm was voluntary, an Anglo administrator called the farm "the pride of the Newell [Tule Lake] project." Journalist Bill Hosokawa acknowledged that few internees at Heart Mountain volunteered for farmwork, a sign that not all regarded it positively. Still, on pleasant days, he wrote, people would walk out to the fields, "picking up shovels and hoes to help" because they "just wanted to get in and help" with the work.[23]

Perhaps working for low wages was preferable to sitting by idly, but the laborers were not as contented with their situation as the foregoing reports would imply, partly because the government paid them poorly. William Jarrett, who supervised agricultural operations at Tule Lake, criticized the WRA for being insensitive to labor requirements. He did "not believe any consideration was given to labor" in planning the camps; instead it was simply "taken for granted." Similar attitudes prevailed at Heart Mountain where the chief of the agricultural section, former University of Wyoming professor Glen Hartman, assumed erroneously that "all able-bodied people would be eager to work hard" on the farm simply because many had formerly worked as farmers even though no one was required to do so and the pay was abysmal. To his dismay he discovered that few were interested in working in the fields for $16 a month. The work was arduous, the weather severe, and the pay low. Those who did volunteer for farmwork faced caustic criticism from their neighbors, who branded them "suckers" for working for so little money. At every camp, worker morale plummeted. At Tule Lake laborers bristled with resentment at working "for such small pay when the rest of the world was getting good [wartime] wages"; when supervisors reprimanded them for working slowly or quitting early they retorted, "What in hell do you expect for fifty cents a day?"[24]

At each camp, agricultural workers went on strike to protest their treatment. The most protracted and subversive strike occurred at Tule Lake in the Fall of 1943. On 15 October, a farm truck carrying twenty-nine Japanese American harvest workers rolled over, seriously injuring four passengers who were pinned under the truck and killing another. The accident brought simmering tension regarding the WRA's treatment of farmworkers to the boiling point. The next day, with hundreds of acres of crops still unharvested, elected representatives from each work crew on the farm met and resolved "to stay away from our places of employment until our demands are met." They insisted upon compensation for those who had been injured and prosecution of those who were responsible for the accident. Moreover, they desired a public funeral for the man who had been killed in the accident and stipulated that the camp administrator, Raymond Best, speak at the funeral and send a letter expressing his condolences to the family of Kashima, the deceased worker. Later that day resident managers of each residential block in the internment camp voted to "support unconditionally" the farmworkers by calling a camp-wide election of a committee to present the farmworkers' demands to the administration. On 21 October, Best refused to permit a public funeral or to apologize to Kashima's family. "I do not recognize demands," he insisted. Best's rigidity infuriated the farmworkers, as did the news that the WRA would compensate Kashima's family at the rate of only two-thirds of his monthly wage. The niggardly compensation policy refocused attention on the workers' oldest grievance: what one sarcastically called their "kingly wage of sixteen big dollars."[25]

Eleven days after the accident ten elected representatives finally met with Best. He rejected most of their demands but when they complained that much of the food that was raised on the project was being shipped to other internment camps while their own tables at Tule Lake were poorly provisioned, Best did agree that all of the food raised on the project would stay there, beginning in 1944. For the time being, though, the crops in the ground must be harvested and made available to other relocation centers. Nearly a week earlier Best had threatened to "request harvesting by the Army and consequent loss of the crops to the evacuees" if the strike did not end. Referring obliquely to the work stoppage during his meeting on 26 October, Best threatened to make arrangements to harvest the crop one way or another. Because of their "attitude," he later explained, he did not tell them that he had already arranged to circumvent the strike by bringing in strikebreakers from other internment camps. After all, many of the crops would be "going to the other centers." Two days after his meeting with the committee, Best dropped a firebomb, shocking the committee by announcing that he had decided to fire every farmworker at Tule Lake because of the strike. On 30 October the first recruits from other centers arrived and bivouacked in a tent city; Best raised the ire of residents all the more by withdrawing foodstuffs from camp warehouses to feed the strikebreakers and by paying them as much for a single day's work as camp residents had earned in a full week.[26]

Early in November rumors that more food was being removed from the community storehouse to feed the strikebreakers ignited a riot. A handful of young thugs assaulted the camp Chief of Security, gathered angrily around Best's home and reportedly threatened to "get" him, and taunted camp workers. In the ensuing melee "a score or more of evacuees were very badly beaten." Fearing for his life, Best requested military support and within a few hours army tanks, armored trucks, and jeeps were rumbling through the compound. For the next two months the camp operated under martial law. "No one can go out from 7 P.M. to 6 A.M.," wrote one resident. "Right now there's no movies or Engei Kai [Japanese entertainment] or anything." Another internee remembered, "After the Army came in I really felt like a prisoner. . . . All during the time when the Army was controlling the camp, naturally, we were sad. There were no activities. Everything stopped. We had a curfew. Oh, it was a miserable life. . . . We got baloney for Thanksgiving." As a result of the work stoppage, some of the crop could not be salvaged. Still, nearly 200 railroad cars of potatoes and other vegetables were shipped out to other relocation centers at the end of the year.[27]

The strike at Tule Lake manifested agricultural workers' discontent with being unjustly compensated while working for the benefit of others. Ill fed and paid substandard wages without assurance of governmental accountability for injury or death on the job, they resented the fact that many of the crops they planted, tended, and harvested were not reserved for their own families or community. At Tule Lake, Minidoka, and Heart Mountain thousands of acres were irrigable after the war because of the internees' development and improvement of irrigation and drainage systems. Moreover, while a relatively small portion of the lands homesteaded by veterans after World War II had been meticulously developed and farmed by Japanese American internees, the contributions of those internees to the prosperity of that fortunate subset of veterans were substantial. As a reporter for *Newsweek* observed in 1946, veterans who were awarded homesteads on lands farmed by the Japanese at Tule Lake received "$2,000,000 worth of the finest bottom land in Tule Lake, Calif., all fenced and cleared, on what had been the wartime Japanese relocation settlement." Each of these farms developed by the ethnic Japanese was valued at $20,000. In 1942 some WRA administrators, hoping to compensate the internees more fairly for the developmental work they had performed, investigated the possibility of permitting internees to lease some of the lands that they had developed for agriculture after the war but the plan went nowhere. In June of 1942 an agency spokesman announced that "evacuees will not be eligible for any rights or interest in the land they work."[28]

Following the war, the WRA's camps closed; control of lands at Tule Lake, Heart Mountain, and Minidoka reverted to the Bureau of Reclamation;

and the Bureau, flush with fresh peacetime appropriations, accelerated its construction program. As irrigation systems on a reclamation project neared completion, the Department of the Interior prepared public notices inviting Americans to apply for a homestead on the project. The notices invited all to apply but explained that veterans' applications would be considered first. Each notice set forth information regarding soils on the project, climate, major crops, water requirements, markets, and public schools.[29]

Each public notice also set forth the minimum qualifications applicants must meet in order to be eligible for a homestead. Congress in 1924 had authorized such eligibility requirements in order to enhance the likelihood that settlers on each irrigation project would succeed. Recognizing that conditions "var[ied] from project to project," Reclamation left the particulars of those qualifications on each project to local examining boards. The Bureau's regional director typically appointed prominent local farmers and entrepreneurs to the board, along with a representative from Bureau's local office. Board members sought to promote opportunities for those who needed them while at the same time working to ensure that those who received a homestead would succeed.[30]

On the Klamath Project, where the first postwar land opening occurred, the five-member examining board, wanting to be fair, agonized over establishing minimum qualifications, which betrayed the illusion of equal opportunity that had been so central to the western mystique. As Horace Greeley had boasted, "The one great point of superiority enjoyed by our countrymen over their cousins in western Europe is the facility with which every American who is honest, industrious and sober may acquire, if he does not already possess, a homestead of his own." The board members were loathe to abandon this cherished notion, although they did not question the propriety of dispensing lands that had been taken from the Modoc and developed by the ethnic Japanese. During the 1930s the project office had employed a flexible rating system with 100 points possible; the system awarded 20 points to applicants with \$2,000–\$2,999 in capital but permitted those with larger amounts to accumulate as many as 30 points. In 1937 with nearly 1,300 applicants vying for sixty-nine farms, the system had automatically excluded from consideration all who possessed only the \$2,000 minimum. Most local residents strongly opposed continuing the prewar policy. For instance, F. D. Rockbice, a World War I veteran and longtime farmer in the Tule Lake Basin, reasoned with the examining board, "Because a man has 10 or 50 thousand dollars does not make him a better farmer, a better man, or a better citizen than the little fellow who wants a home for himself and family and a chance to better himself." Rockbice conceded that wealthy applicants would be more likely to succeed because of their capital reserves, but he believed that rewarding them for their wealth betrayed "the homestead laws [which] was [sic] made to give the man that did not have a home a chance to make one."[31]

In light of arguments such as these, the Klamath Project examining board scrapped the flexible rating system. After the first land drawing a regional official observed that if they had retained the system, "no veteran with less than $10,000 could possibly have gotten a farm." This he surmised, "would have given rise to a damaging national scandal." Perhaps he was correct, but examining boards appointed for some drawings such as one in 1947 on the Shoshone Project employed flexible rating systems and encountered little opposition.[32]

Alongside questions of applicants' wealth, examining boards debated how much farming experience they should require of applicants. Dale Johnson, a veteran who spoke at a hearing on the Klamath Project, condemned standards that shut out those who possessed the "willingness and ability to learn" but happened to have "little or no farming experience." Such standards smacked of elitism and offended the populist sensibilities of many veterans. When the Bureau's regional settlement officer retorted that "farming background should be necessary" because otherwise "a lot of fellows [lacking farm experience] would get tired of it [homesteading] in a hurry," the district commander of a local veterans group accused him of discrimination. Ultimately the examining board voted to require two years of farming experience, although the requirement was not always strictly enforced.[33]

Once qualifications had been established and printed in a public notice, the Bureau sought to publicize the land openings, circulating the notice along with press releases to newspapers, veterans' organizations, and magazines aimed at farmers or veterans. The agency especially advertised its early postwar land openings. For instance, employees in the Bureau's Boulder City, Nevada, regional office sent press releases to 400 newspapers in connection with a land opening on the Yuma Project in 1946. The Bureau maintained a file of inquiries it received regarding homesteading opportunities and also mailed public notices to thousands of inquirers whose names were in its files; Reclamation mailed over 12,000 notifications of the first postwar land opening.[34]

Due to the Bureau's multifaceted advertising campaign, veterans heard about land openings through correspondence, newspaper and magazine articles, and radio announcements. The news traveled quickly, as friends, relatives, and coworkers shared their knowledge with others. Arland Van Zant of Oklahoma decided to apply for a farm after he learned about a land opening on the Boise Project from his instructor in a vocational class for veterans. A friend in Phoenix told Jake Colvin that he could apply for a homestead on the Yuma project. Beldon Reynolds first heard about homesteading opportunities on the Shoshone Project through a conversation with a coworker in a Vernal, Utah, furniture store. Don and Violet Hurlburt of Oregon first learned about a land opening near Tule Lake from Violet's mother.[35]

Most applicants were married men, but their wives' involvement in applying for a homestead varied considerably. In some cases, wives seized the initiative; when Vernie Morrison returned home from work one evening, his wife excitedly relayed the details from a radio announcement of a homestead opening in Wyoming and urged him to apply. After reading an article about farms for veterans in the *Denver Post* Lola Frank shared the news with her husband, seized the initiative, requested an application form, completed it for him, and mailed it. In other instances, homesteading was purely the husband's idea; Frosty Poore was working for the Veterans Administration in Oakland, California, when he heard about homesteading in southern California's Coachella Valley. When he came home, he asked his wife, Verna, a city girl who said she had never even heard of homesteading let alone considered doing it, if she "would be willing" to move to the Mojave Desert.[36]

Regardless of who first heard about homesteading, most couples, like Mary and Chester Blackburn of Chase County, Kansas, consulted and negotiated before applying for a farm. From the perspective of some women, though, their husbands more or less unilaterally decided to apply. Evaleen Hulet George recalled how her husband, Wally, seized the initiative when her brother told him about homesteads for veterans. "Sure we ought to look into it," he decreed, and so he applied. When Evaleen learned that Wally's application had been selected in a drawing, she tried to reassure herself; "We're not going to do anything about it, are we?" she suggested, but Wally responded, "We['d] better look into it."[37]

Applicants for a homestead were required to submit three letters of recommendation, testimonials of their farm experience, proof of military service, the results of a medical examination, and an itemized list of their assets.

Thousands of veterans were sufficiently interested in homesteading to solicit and prepare these supporting documents. From 1946 to 1966 the Interior Department received over 150,000 applications—some veterans applied for farms on several projects—for 3,041 farms. Bureau officials who had predicted that thousands of veterans were interested in obtaining a homestead had been right.[38]

Applicants hailed from every state in the Union, but a high percentage lived in the same state as the homesteads for which they were applying. Forty percent of the applicants for farmland in northern Wyoming in 1946 were Wyoming residents, and an additional 19 percent lived in neighboring Montana. Nearly nine in ten applicants for farms being opened that same year on the Klamath Project near the California-Oregon border lived in those two states. Sixty-seven percent of those who applied for a farm in the following year on the Yuma Project lived in either Arizona or California. A disproportionate number of applicants came from existing reclamation projects, not only because the Bureau's land openings were well publicized there, but because the children of those who had homesteaded in the area were familiar with irrigation and with the Bureau of Reclamation's policies. For all of the Bureau's efforts in advertising, those living on a reclamation project were most likely to be aware of the land openings.[39]

After the application period had closed, Bureau employees in the project office laboriously sifted through the applications, weeding out any from applicants who did not meet minimum qualifications. The applications exuded the hopes of America's veterans on matters ranging from equality of opportunity to the agrarian dream, hopes that were central to the homesteading ideal. The yeoman tradition suffused many letters: "I believe this will be the chance of a lifetime to become independent and to develop a farm which will compare in productiveness to any other in that region," wrote one veteran. "It's a thing a fellow dreams about." A Japanese American veteran of the Italian campaign who had sustained over 100 shrapnel wounds encouraged the examining board to overlook his ancestry. He hoped that the examining board would agree that "the fact that I am of Japanese descent should not be of issue," but he chose to address the matter because he knew that "in the past other agencies have passed up qualified people of my race simply because of the difference in skin color." He pled with the examining board to "show no discrimination due to race." While he did not win a farm, other Japanese Americans did.[40]

On the Shoshone Project a full-time settlement specialist, John K. ("Jack") Black, and two clerks examined the applications. Black explained, "I had to determine if they had an honorable discharge from the U.S. Armed Services. Did they have two years of farming experience in their background? Did they have $2,500 in assets in a truck or in farm machinery or in money? Did they have all those qualifications? . . . I checked those all out and made a notation, a footnote with their application whether they actually met these three basic requirements. . . . All I did was do mechanical work to check those features. [Then] I would take it to my board."[41]

Rejecting applications was a thankless task. One veteran who desperately wanted a farm but did not possess the requisite capital applied anyway. Anticipating that he would be denied, he chastened the examiner on his application for a Bureau policy that deprived the least fortunate of assistance: "You know very well that a veteran out of the army does not have $2,000. Nor can I raise it. Now if you do not want me to have one of the little farms just stick them all where the sun doesn't shine." Occasionally, a bit of humor or a quaint expression in an application enlivened the reviewers' work. One writer recommended a young man whom he had known "since he was a gleam in his father's eye and a blush on his mother's cheek." Another claimed to have known the applicant since he was "large enough to get his hand around a cow's teat."[42]

Humor or no, once the preliminary review of applications had been completed, the project office prepared for a land lottery, the gala event where the winning applicants were selected and announced. As an agency dependent upon taxpayer support, the Bureau of Reclamation campaigned vigorously to secure and maintain popular support for its programs. Tapping into the nation's patriotic fervor and desire to reward veterans for their wartime valor, the Bureau's public relations team, known as information specialists, fulsomely publicized the first postwar land opening, which occurred in 1946 on the Klamath Project. Months before the opening, Max Stern, an administrator in the Bureau's Sacramento regional office, seized upon the lottery as a public relations tool. The unassuming local examining board preferred a low-key event with minimal publicity, but they were overruled by Stern and other regional officers who hoped that the land drawing would "dramatize the terrific land hunger" of young veterans and show how the Bureau was satisfying that craving. To attract nationwide attention, Stern envisioned "a humdinger of a celebration" in conjunction with the lottery, one that would be publicized nationwide by "news reel men, radio coverage and newspaper correspondents in numbers." To that end, the Bureau sent announcements to roughly 450 newspapers and magazines and "thoroughly briefed" radio and newsreel producers regarding the drawing. Stern's hopes for national and regional media coverage of the drawing materialized: major Oregon and California dailies, the *New York Times*, the *Christian Science Monitor*, *Life*, and newsreel producer RKO-Pathe News dispatched reporters to cover the land lottery. The cover of *Life* sported a photograph of veteran Dale Sprout, his wife, and their two children gazing with rapt enchantment over the land they had won. The accompanying story claimed inaccurately that the land opening was "one of the biggest legal lotteries the nation has ever seen" and concluded that the "lucky" winners were "now established for life."[43]

National media coverage declined after the first postwar opening, partly because the Bureau was embarrassed after some of the winners who were announced and featured in news coverage of that first drawing were later disqualified in interviews with the examining boards. However, on the local level the festivities associated with land lotteries remained elaborate and the proceedings were broadcast live by area radio stations. Often a high school band kicked off the occasion with a half-hour concert, as dignitaries including business leaders, representatives of veterans organizations, politicians, and Reclamation administrators took their seats on the stand. Generally the mayor of the town where the drawing was taking place welcomed the crowd, followed by speeches from three to five dignitaries.[44]

Speakers at the drawings compared the modern homesteaders to their venerable and mythicized historical counterparts. For instance, Arizona governor Sidney Osborn reminded applicants attending a drawing in Yuma that "like those early day Arizonans, you are the type of progressive, industrious citizens which every great state needs." Wyoming's deputy secretary of state T. C. Thompson called homesteaders "the pioneers of civilization." Speakers liked to chart the transformation of the landscape and the escalating values of land produced by reclamation as an indicator of what the veterans could expect on their own farms in the future. Wyoming governor Lester Hunt told an audience at a land drawing in 1947 that he had "crossed and recrossed many times every portion" of the Riverton Project and had "seen this land, valued in the early days at $1 and $2 per acre, which has now reached the value of $100 and in many cases in excess of $100 per acre." Speakers reiterated the Jeffersonian view of prosperous, independent yeomen; Lawrence

Carr, representing California governor Earl Warren, told veterans at a land opening in 1945, "You are being given an opportunity to become self-reliant, independent, American farmers." The mayor of Riverton, Wyoming, W. B. Glass, assured veterans that "this virgin soil will be your land of opportunity." Idaho Land Commissioner Edward Woozley, representing the governor, averred that homesteading "builds good citizenship and resourcefulness."[45]

Following the speeches, politicos, Bureau officials, beauty queens, and small children took turns drawing names sealed in gelatin capsules from a receptacle such as a wire basket called a squirrel cage, a tumbler, or a three-gallon glass jar turned by a crank. Each name drawn was announced by the master of ceremonies, recorded by a stenographer, and written on a chalk board. After the drawing was finished, the crowd was often treated by local merchants to a luncheon or barbecue.

A drawing for farms on the Minidoka Project in August 1953 was typical. Over 4,000 people thronged the Rupert town square. Harold Nelson from the Bureau's regional office told the crowd that the lands being awarded as homesteads were part of "the last frontier," while Idaho lieutenant governor Edson Deal rejoiced in this evidence that the frontier had not really closed and that "new horizons have not vanished." Local merchants awarded prizes to the first veteran present whose name had been drawn, the oldest and youngest winners, the winning veteran with the most children, the first Idahoan present whose name had been drawn, and the successful applicant who had traveled the greatest distance for the drawing. Then the entire crowd was treated to barbecued beef sandwiches and coffee, compliments of the Rupert Chamber of Commerce, followed by a horse show.[46]

Few out-of-state applicants who applied for a farm traveled to the drawings; the chances of receiving a farm were simply too slim to justify the expense. At the first postwar drawing in Arizona only four of the twenty-six winners were present. Not one of the twelve winners in a lottery with over 2,900 applicants in Indio, California, was present to hear his name called. Despite the claim of a Klamath Falls reporter that "electricity . . . charged the air" at a drawing as the "applicants, their families and friends waited" for their names to be called, even some of the applicants in attendance lost interest or dozed off as the announcer droned on. Elizabeth Fowers had to shake her husband, Leslie, awake when his name was called at a drawing in Idaho. Others apparently listened with rapt attention. Velma Robison re-

Intently focused on her task, six-year-old Patty Worrell draws capsules containing the names of lucky applicants for twenty-eight homesteads on the Roza Division of the Yakima Project. Assisting her is William Farmer, land use specialist for the Bureau. Project Superintendent O. W. Lindgren looks over Patty's shoulder while regional official Hu Blonk addresses the audience, 25 April 1947. (Photograph by Stan Rasmussen, Reclamation Photographs, NARA, Rocky Mountain Region)

called, "You just sat there with your heart in your mouth wondering if you were going to be a lucky one." Mabel Rogers likened the land lottery to the draft, "only this time I was praying that [her husband] Paul's number would be called." When Martin Ross's name was called at a drawing in Arizona he responded with a "rafter-shaking whoop" that "no one who heard [it] is likely to forget," a Bureau official reported.[47]

In some places, other extravaganzas staged by local boosters coincided with the land openings. In the Columbia Basin in 1952 following a media blitz, local merchants spearheaded a "Farm-in-a-Day" celebration in which volunteer laborers developed a lucky veteran's land and built him a home within twenty-four hours. The fortunate veteran was Donald Dunn, a

Elated by their good fortune, Fred and Velma Robison posed for this photograph after Fred's number was drawn for the sixty-first homestead to be awarded 18 December 1946 on the Klamath Project. "You just sat there with your heart in your mouth wondering if you were going to be a lucky one, and our number was finally called," recalled Velma. (Photograph by Ben L. Glaha, Reclamation Photographs, NARA, Rocky Mountain Region)

Kansan whose farm in the Sunflower State had been ruined in a flood the previous year. Hundreds of volunteers began work at 12:01 A.M. on 29 May 1952, with fireworks blazing overhead and spotlights illuminating the ground. Twenty-four hours later eighty acres had been leveled, a seven-room house had been constructed, and Dunn was ready to move in.[48]

Although some celebrants believed that the veterans whose names were drawn with such pomp were sure to receive a farm, such was not the case. Before awarding any farms the examining committee further scrutinized the qualifications of each winner and interviewed each one, and in the process some were disqualified. In the first postwar land opening, one of the two veterans who had been featured in the article covering the opening in *Life*,

Elmer Metz, was disqualified because he lacked the requisite farm experience—a great embarrassment not only to Metz but to the Bureau. In that same drawing it appeared for a time that Eleanor Bolesta, the only woman whose name had been drawn for a farm—ten had applied—would also be disqualified. Married women were legally ineligible to apply for a homestead on a reclamation project unless they could demonstrate that they were "the head of the family." Originally this policy had been intended to prevent married couples from double dipping under the Homestead Act. Although this was no longer a possibility in an era when homesteads were so scarce, the policy remained in force. The Bureau's published policy stipulated that "the head of a family is ordinarily the husband, but a wife or a minor child who is obliged to assume major responsibility for the support of a family may be the head of the family." In her interview with the examining board a member asked Bolesta if "I could prove I was head of the household," a question that "stumped" her. After some thought she replied that she was the primary breadwinner for the time being because her husband was convalescing from wartime injuries and "they accepted that." Years later, Bolesta reasoned that "they shouldn't have asked only me that question"; each husband should have had to prove that he was the head of his household, too. An examining board on the Boise Project did not let Lucy Evers, the thirteenth person whose name was drawn for a farm, off the hook as readily. Evers had claimed on her application form to be head of the household because her husband had been employed for only three of the preceding fourteen months. The examiners refused to accept this rationale, arguing that if her husband's health was "good" there was no reason he should not be classified as the household head. Somehow, Evers managed to convince the committee that she deserved a homestead, demonstrating other "circumstances [that] prevent your husband from supporting your family."[49]

Winning veterans who met all of the minimum requirements received letters requiring them to report at the project office and select their farms; Jack Black, settlement specialist on the Shoshone Project, described the farm selection process, which he supervised. At an orientation meeting each applicant received a packet with maps, legal descriptions of each unit, and information regarding topography, soils, and other features of the units. Then the applicants in company with Black drove out over dusty trails to examine the farm units, with Black never selecting the farms for the veterans but willingly answering their questions about the advantages and disadvan-

Settlement specialist John Black shows rough, brush-covered land on homestead number sixty-two to Mr. and Mrs. Rex Stanton and their son on the Shoshone Project, 15 November 1946. (Photograph by Arthur Fawcett, Reclamation Photographs, NARA, Rocky Mountain Region)

tages of different farm units. "Number one [the first person whose name had been drawn] didn't have to worry," Black recalled. "He just picked his first choice. . . . As the time went by, the [remaining] units became less and less and less desirable. There wasn't as much irrigable land in the perimeters of the homestead. They'd say, 'It's a damn, dumb homestead. I don't want that; I'm going to go home.'"[50]

Veterans chose their farms based on a variety of criteria. Bill Gunlock chose his farm unit because it was larger than many others. Fred and Velma Robison chose theirs because it had been previously farmed by residents of the Tule Lake Internment Camp and was therefore ready for farming. Eliot Waits selected his land because it ran parallel to a section line; Waits knew that county roads were constructed along section lines and he wanted a farm along a good road. Wilbur Andrew's father advised him to choose a farm that was "near a town, near a main road and one that did not require a big expense to get into production," and he used those standards in selecting his unit.[51]

Within six months of making their selection, the veterans were required to relocate on their new farms. As they prepared for the move, the first group of postwar homesteaders received sage, even prophetic advice from the chair of the examining board: "Even though these lands of yours are some of the best in this country of ours, life will not be all smooth sailing. All of you at the start will be cursed with shortages of machinery and materials. Many of you and your wives will have to get used to living in a strange land. You will experience the usual troubles with climate, bugs and blights. . . . On behalf of this Board and the representatives of the Bureau of Reclamation, I am very pleased to welcome you to this country. After all, you are probably the only friends we made out of over 2,000 original starters!"[52]

PROVING UP AND PROVING THEMSELVES

3

At its core, homesteading entailed transforming raw land into productive farms. This enterprise was a "meaningful," deeply appealing one to veterans like Ted Aston, who had dreamed since childhood of "do[ing] as the pioneers did . . . making wilderness ground productive as farmland." As Laura McCall has observed, many Americans attributed the "loss of opportunity for the self-made man" to the closing of the frontier, which deprived would-be pioneers of the opportunity to prove their manhood by "transform[ing]" a frontier landscape and "tam[ing] a wilderness." In the mid-twentieth century, reclamation promised to recreate such opportunities for self-definition. Tapping into the homesteading myth, one reporter writing for the Bureau of Reclamation went so far as to claim that these modern pioneers faced a battery of challenges to be overcome and opportunities to be seized "entirely through man's own endeavor." As inheritors of these iconic notions, many postwar homesteaders viewed pioneering as a test of their worth and capacity.[1]

The task of reordering the landscape was breathtaking and exhilarating—but also overwhelming. Gazing out over the brush-covered expanse that he intended to reclaim, Leslie Fowers confided that he was "scared" by the magnitude of the task ahead. Van Sorensen remembered being frightened of failure, too. "You just worried, worked, worked, worked and drove all day and all night," he recalled. "You would work all the hours you could possibly stand it and still there was more to do than you could get done." Knowing he had to start somewhere, Bill

Leslie and Elizabeth Fowers inspect available lands after his name was drawn for a farm on the Minidoka Project, 5 July 1954. "Just looking at it scared me," Leslie told a reporter. (Reclamation Photographs, NARA, Rocky Mountain Region)

Nolan, a settler in the Columbia Basin, commenced by swinging a grubbing hoe, hacking away at the brush that covered his land, one plant at a time.[2]

While the image of Nolan driving a grubbing hoe into the scrubby bark of the sage or Sorensen straining under exhaustion resonates nicely with the bootstrap tradition of homesteading evoked by the Bureau's claim that the land would be reclaimed "entirely through man's own endeavor," it is somewhat misleading. In an era of powerful tractors and mechanization, few farmers cleared their lands manually as Nolan did. Moreover, postwar homesteaders enjoyed unprecedented access to training, mechanized equipment, and funding. A Wyoming journalist was correct when he claimed in 1948 that homesteading still "require[d] determination, hard work, courage and grit" and that developing a farm was a "herculean task—especially the first few years." It was simply that these virtues were only part of the equation; homesteaders would draw upon far more resources than self-discipline and brawn to sustain themselves.[3]

The mystique of man against the land died hard, though. Homesteads in the mechanized postwar era may not have been "a grand proving ground for white male individualism" in the Turnerian tradition, but they were promoted as such. In American folklore the westering drama was masculine to its core. Ignoring the fact that some single women were being awarded homesteads and that most of to veterans were married and would work with their spouse on the farm in order to gain title to it, a 1947 promotional brochure for the Columbia Basin project expressed the dominant perception: the Grand Coulee Dam and, by extension, the lands being opened thereby to irrigation in the basin were "a man's world," part of the "last frontier where men vie with the forces of nature, that in the years to come and for untold generations she will do their bidding."[4]

Not only homesteading, but its occupational corollary, farming, was broadly viewed as manly work, directed and largely performed by the yeoman. As historian Mary Neth has observed, "the 'manly' virtues of physical labor, independence, and self-sufficiency" are "embodied in the image of the farmer," a central motif in American culture. In the nineteenth century the middle class had idealized self-mastery and restraint as manly qualities, but middle-class Americans in the twentieth century associated masculinity primarily with aggressiveness and physical force. According to this physically grounded definition of masculinity, nowhere was a man's mettle better tested than on a homestead where masculine strength and stamina were pitted against raw land and the forces of Nature. Thus, publicists covering the postwar homesteaders resorted to gendered terms, employing images of "men vying with female nature," as Richard White has observed. For instance, Bill Hosokawa, a staff writer for the *Denver Post*, described the Shoshone Project in northern Wyoming as "an environment to test a man" and illustrated his point by highlighting the experiences of Glen Mangus, a homesteader who had served as a hand-to-hand combat instructor and was certainly "no softie." Mangus "could throw half a dozen of the navy's huskiest recruits and hardly work up a sweat," the writer maintained, but in his first summer of homesteading Mangus "peeled off thirty pounds of weight, none of it excess . . . in a weary series of sixteen-hour days."[5]

Hosokawa's depiction of homesteading and farm making as an unmediated contest between male breadwinners and the natural world is too simple for historians to accept, but it is related to the disposition of some scholars to portray agricultural settlement and conquest as "metaphorical rape" in which men and their technology overwhelm nature "by force." This creative construction of technological mastery is also flawed: even in an irrigated environment where human engineering can cushion the impact of drought, farming is still a gamble; what Mark Fiege has aptly labeled a "resilient and protean" nature often frustrates human designs.[6]

The men who homesteaded knew that it would be reckless and foolish to rely upon brute force and sheer will alone when they could lessen the strain through wise use of credit, machinery, the federal government's resources, and hired or family labor. Still, nearly all of them assumed primary responsibility for farm making on their homesteads. Even in the households of married female veterans who drew a homestead, the husband ultimately directed the farming. In most cases, proving up, or fulfilling all of the legal prerequisites for gaining legal title to one's lands, thus became a means for men to prove themselves to society in the "manly" roles of farmer and provider.[7]

Whether they intended to remain on their farms for the rest of their lives or to sell out quickly, every serious settler's goals hinged upon proving up. While the process had been simplified by Congress and the Bureau of Reclamation in the years since passage of the original Homestead Act, homesteaders were still required to inhabit and improve the land. Within six months of the award date, the winner was required to settle on the land. Homesteaders with no military service had to live on the land for three years, but veterans could apply two years in the military toward the requirement, thereby reducing the residency requirement to twelve months. On projects in the southwestern deserts where temperatures soared to over 120 degrees in the summer, homesteaders were permitted to substitute seven months' residence for a year. No one who really wanted free land could reasonably feel this requirement was excessive. But there was more to the process. Each homesteader was required to create a substantial, permanent dwelling on the farm and to develop and cultivate at least half of the land successfully for the two years immediately preceding their application for a deed to the land. Veterans who purchased their land from the Bureau of Reclamation for nominal prices in places such as the Columbia Basin were likewise bound by the Bureau's reclamation, cultivation, and residency requirements, with title to the land being contingent upon fulfilling those requirements. Once the homesteader had complied with all requirements, affidavits and other docu-

A solitary man in a vast landscape, homesteader Art Willis, a bachelor, hauls culinary water to his tent, with his tractor, farm machinery, and newly cleared land on the Yakima Project in the background, 22 August 1947. When his photograph was taken, Willis had been camping for months, too busy with farm work to worry about housing. (Reclamation Photographs, NARA, Rocky Mountain Region)

ments were submitted as evidence, and after they had been reviewed and accepted, a final certificate was issued, followed by a patent. These were the stipulations that caused so many homesteaders to fret and to lose sleep. Barbara Adams, the daughter of a homesteading couple on the Minidoka Project, vividly remembers her parents' concerns about proving up: "They talked about it constantly, and I worried that we would never get that done." As Van Sorensen recalled, the big uncertainty gnawing at the homesteaders was "if we could handle that first two or three years." Many labored 17–18 hours per day in the growing season to fulfill the requirements. Bill Casper's normal work day began at 3:00 A.M. and ended at 9:00 P.M. The regimen left everyone "pretty exhausted," Stan Buckingham told a reporter.[8]

In practice, the magnitude of these homesteading requirements caused over 90 percent of the homesteaders to take at least three years to meet the requirements; for instance, of the 86 homesteaders who settled on the Klamath Project in 1947, only 7 percent completed all of the requirements for proving up within two years. An additional 31 percent finished by the end of their third year, 21 percent did so during the fourth year, and 35 percent did so during the fifth year. Six percent did not submit final proof until sometime during their sixth year.[9]

One of the first tasks to be performed in improving most homesteads entailed removing brush and other vegetation. Stands of brush varied in size and thickness, depending in part upon the richness of the soil, level of precipitation, and previous usage of the land by humans and livestock. In some areas vegetation was so small and sparse that it could be cleared manually with a grubbing hoe. More commonly, homesteaders chained heavy articles such as railroad irons to their tractors, dragging them across the fields so that the brush snapped off near the ground and "cut a swath . . . just like it was grass." Others snapped the brush loose with a blade cultivator or dislodged it by plowing shallowly. Working on their own in this fashion, homesteaders labored for up to three months clearing brush, rocks, and other debris from a quarter section (160 acres) of land. Some homesteaders conscientiously removed all traces of the brush, not realizing that the plants could be their allies: root materials mixed in with the soil provided a valuable safeguard against erosion, particularly for finely textured soils. Defying the myth of the solitary male homesteader subduing the land, a few married women did as much if not more than their husbands in clearing their farms. Barbara Patterson's husband held a full-time job off the farm. At home with a four-year-old child, she "did a lot of outside work" while her husband was at work in town, including pulling sagebrush. Other settlers felt they could not spare the time and instead hired a contractor to perform the work. Nearly half of the first group of postwar homesteaders on the Shoshone Project made such arrangements with contractors.[10]

After the brush had been cut it was collected and piled, frequently using a dump rake. Others improvised with whatever machinery they could find; one settler on the Shoshone project pulled a harrow behind a jeep to rake the brush. In the evening the homesteaders burned the brush in huge bonfires that lit the sky. While men were generally in charge of land-clearing operations many wives worked with their husbands, particularly in raking the

Bill and Claire White prepare to burn brush on their homestead on the Shoshone Project, April 1950. Claire recalled, "We disked [the sagebrush] and then we picked it up by hand 'cause we didn't have the rake then. [We'd] pitch it up and have all these piles and start them on fire." (Reclamation Photographs, NARA, Rocky Mountain Region)

brush, with one person driving the tractor and the other operating the dump rake, periodically raising the rake teeth and releasing the brush into piles. Nora Bovee's secondary but significant contribution in land clearing was typical of married women: "We did it ourselves," she explained. "When Les [her husband] wasn't working by himself, I was helping him."[11]

As they cleared the land, homesteaders disturbed the habitat of rodents, rabbits, and snakes, forcing them out into open fields. Rattlers were especially plentiful on lands being developed at Riverton. One homesteader, Ted Gies, carried a large wrench on his tractor and dismounted whenever he saw a rattlesnake to hit it over the head. Crossing fields on foot, farmers were more vulnerable than they were on tractors. Another homesteader at Riverton, Van Sorensen, "kept [his dog] out in front . . . no matter where [he] went" in order to be aware of snakes.[12]

Lands also had to be leveled before they could be irrigated efficiently. On relatively flat land some homesteaders chose to water "in whatever direction we could" until they had the time and money to adjust the contour properly, but on farms like Leon Machen's homestead, where the elevation fell over 50 feet in a quarter mile, leveling was imperative. Earlier generations of homesteaders on reclamation projects had scraped off the high spots and filled in the low ones with horse-drawn scrapers or fresnoes. But in the postwar decades, those who chose to do the work themselves, like Glen Olsen on the Boise Project, used tractors to move the earth. With a borrowed quarter-yard scraper and his 1941 John Deere tractor Olsen "moved thousands and thousands of yards" of powdery volcanic soil. Some farmers spent three months trying to level rough terrain properly with a tractor and small scraper. Others borrowed funds and hired either a private contractor or the Bureau of Reclamation to do the work, justifying the added expense and reliance on others with the rationale that it would enable them to farm the land during their first season. Practicality trumped myth.[13]

In addition to clearing and leveling their fields, homesteaders on raw land needed to create ditches and other irrigation structures such as dikes or ridges around the perimeter of their fields. In southern California's Coachella Valley where the intense heat made above-ground ditches impractical because of evaporation, a network of underground irrigation pipes had to be installed on each farm. Elsewhere the Bureau had excavated supply ditches to convey the water to each farm, but each settler was responsible for constructing the ditches that would bear water to their fields. In earlier eras farmers had excavated ditches using picks and shovels. Now most could do so more swiftly by pulling a digging implement called a ditcher behind their tractors. Still, the operation consumed enough time that a few homesteaders chose to hire someone else to excavate the field ditches. On farms where the natural slope was steep enough that water coursing through the ditches at high speeds would cause the ditches to erode, the ditches had to be excavated in levels or steps, with concrete check drops or bulkheads installed at critical junctures over which water would spill as it moved from one level to the next. Some, like Phil Bare, poured their own concrete drops in the fields, often working late into the night. Others purchased prefabricated drops, hauled them out into the fields with a tractor, and then positioned them in the ditches. Here was a test of physical strength: Ed Hoff recalled that it was "generally all one man could do to wrestle them around or . . . stand on one end and walk them to where we were going to put them." In lieu of concrete checks others improvised by taking empty fertilizer or concrete bags, filling them with dirt and packing them into the sides of the ditch, changing the bags every two to three irrigations.[14]

Preparing land required so much time or money that few farmers were able to cultivate all of their land in their first year of homesteading. On the Shoshone Project, for instance, only 44 percent of the lands that were opened to homesteading in 1947 were actually farmed that year. The percentage would have been even lower were it not for the fact that some of the lands had previously been developed by Japanese American internees.[15]

Those who were fortunate enough to acquire land that had been tilled previously under leasing arrangements with the Bureau of Reclamation found themselves well ahead of their counterparts on undeveloped lands.[16] Settlers on these "predeveloped" lands had the option of either farming the land personally in anticipation of a respectable harvest or of leasing their land to farmers in surrounding areas for the first year, leaving themselves free to work on their homes, barns, and other buildings. About 12 percent of the 1947 homesteaders at Tule Lake leased all their lands to local farmers during their first year.[17]

After the land had been cleared and leveled and supply ditches had been excavated the fields were ready for the plow. The challenges of plowing varied depending upon the nature of the soil. Some tracts were so sun-baked that they could not be plowed until the soil had been softened by flooding. On the other hand, much of the dirt on homesteads in southern Idaho had a fine, volcanic texture; a person stepping onto it could easily sink seven or eight inches, and heavy implements and tractors sank much further. In some places the topsoil was thick whereas elsewhere it was only two or three inches deep. Barring unusual soil features, the farmer plowed the land and then dragged a spike-tooth or disk harrow over the fields to break up any clods. Then using a tractor-drawn cultivator the farmer would corrugate the fields, creating furrows to convey the water to the crops. Some farmers inexperienced in irrigation, including Clinton Rogers, excavated such deep furrows that they were unable to drive their machinery across the fields to harvest the crops. The mistake was "a costly one," he admitted.[18]

High winds that whipped dust and dirt into the air complicated farmers' efforts to plow and furrow the land. As Bill Casper quipped, during a windstorm in the Columbia Basin "everything moved." A "powdery dust" filled the air, clogging tractor air filters and the farmer's nostrils and lungs. In Casper's first year of farming, after he had invested "a lot of work" in furrowing his fields, high winds whipped volcanic soil into the furrows, leveling the field "just like a table again."[19]

Even if plowing was supposedly a man's job, women commonly plowed farmland, especially during the first years of farming. For instance, Frances and Jerry Johnson assisted each other, with Jerry plowing and Frances disking the fields. Likewise, Joan Casper "was out there with us" in the fields, her husband Bill recalled. He thought she was "the best four-bottom plow operator on a 135 horsepower tractor there was in the country."[20]

After plowing and furrowing their fields the homesteaders were ready to plant and water their crops. Most of the settlers had planted crops previously—all were supposed to have done so in order to qualify for a farm—but most were accustomed to planting and then depending upon the rain and sun to coax and nurture the plants. On a reclamation project, the farmer's work had just begun when the planting was completed. Most homesteaders' ignorance of irrigation techniques was profound. When Carroll Riggs heard his neighbor say he was going to town to purchase some "dam canvas" he thought the man was cussing. Vernon Egbert saw one homesteader trying to suction irrigation water from the ditch into siphon tubes using his mouth—"quite a sight." Although sprinkler systems had been developed by the 1950s, they were inflexible, cumbersome, and extremely expensive so nearly every homesteader learned to irrigate from ditches.[21]

Irrigation methods varied across the West and in learning to irrigate, the homesteaders benefited from visiting with experienced farmers in their area and watching them; a seasoned farmer showed Vernon Egbert on the Minidoka Project how to use siphon tubes to divert water from ditches into furrows on the Minidoka Project, and a nearby farmer's experienced hired hand showed Eldon Paulsen some of the tricks of irrigation on Yuma Mesa. Bureau of Reclamation personnel and county extension agents also demonstrated irrigation techniques in workshops. Some settlers were loathe to ask questions, though, not wanting to appear stupid. Minidoka homesteaders George Falkner and Milt Reese debated whether wheat should be planted

Lawrence W. Hartley irrigates potatoes with siphon tubes on his Klamath Project homestead, 31 July 1950. (Photograph by A. M. Bergloff, Reclamation Photographs, NARA, Rocky Mountain Region)

before or after they furrowed their fields for irrigation. It embarrassed their pride when they had to ask the wife of an established farmer, but they thought it was better to lose face with a woman than with a man.[22]

Even if a homesteader received excellent advice regarding irrigation, implementing that advice was difficult. Initially the water seemed to have a mind of its own. Eldon Paulsen's first head of irrigation water—flowing about 20 cubic feet per second—"looked as big as the Missouri River" to him. Phil Bare was working in his fields one morning when he heard his neighbor yelling. The man had turned so much water into the ditch that it had washed away each of the dams he had set. He was furious, "wet from his neck down and muddy." Bare helped the man divert some of the water into a drainage ditch and then showed him how to set the dams properly. Bob Fagerberg, a settlement specialist for the Bureau of Reclamation, reported that most homesteaders needed two years of trial and error before becoming proficient at irrigating.[23]

Recently formed ditches in light soil were unstable, which compounded the challenge of irrigating. The Bureau of Reclamation recommended that farmers turn a small amount of water into new ditches, allowing them to soak gradually and to stabilize for several days before the first full-scale watering turn. Even so, ditch banks in finely textured volcanic soils often eroded. On his first day of irrigating, Rolly Powers experienced seven washouts in nineteen hours. Lyle Esser likened irrigating from new ditches in the Columbia Basin's powdery soil to "putting water on sugar." On soils of similar consistency in southern Idaho, Vernon Egbert carefully monitored the water in his fields until midnight during his first watering turn. The ditches had held so well to that point that Egbert had no compunction about going home to bed and leaving the water running. By the time he returned to his fields the next morning, "the ditches had all dissolved and run away" and water was everywhere. As the years passed, organic material accumulated in the soil and ditch banks became firmer, permitting many farmers to set their water and leave for several hours, especially if they were watering resilient crops like alfalfa that could tolerate a ditch break.[24]

In the first months of homesteading, though, homesteaders devised ingenious means of stabilizing soft ditch banks. Sometimes husbands and wives worked together to solve the problem. Doris Esser "would sit in the ditch" while her husband, Lyle, "shovel[ed] the dirt around her" to plug a leak. Old feed or fertilizer bags filled with dirt also served to reinforce ditch banks. In order to prevent furrows in his fields from washing away when water was turned into them, Mark Sweet "carried five-gallon buckets, one in each hand, full of pea gravel . . . and graveled the mouth of every corrugate by hand." After working the pea gravel into the soil with his hands and a shovel, his "hands looked like claws and [his] fingers were all split wide open and bleeding." Sometimes while Sweet was irrigating, shovel in hand, "it'd get so slick from all the blood that I couldn't hang on to the shovel handle. It didn't do any good to wear a pair of gloves," he remembered, "because . . . they'd just get soaked and it'd be worse." By releasing small amounts of water into the ditches, monitoring the situation around the clock, and using siphon tubes to divert water from field ditches, others managed to minimize ditch breaks.[25]

Irrigation was exhausting as well as challenging. Everett Miller dislocated his back during his first watering turn. "He came to the house—barely moving and with glazed eyes," recalled his wife, Marty. Eldon Paulsen and his neighbors generally spent "36–48 hours straight by ourselves" when they were irrigating. The time and effort entailed in irrigation varied depending upon the mode of irrigation and the crop. Flood irrigation, or releasing water into fields surrounded by dikes, was possible in places where the Colorado River furnished an abundant water supply. Generally this method required less attention than the more common method of watering in furrows. Walter White, a veteran who exchanged his marginal homestead on the Riverton Project for a farm on the Gila, was surprised by the "ease" of flood irrigation in Arizona where an acre of alfalfa could be watered in under half an hour. On the Minidoka Project where the furrow method was used, the Bureau of Reclamation advised farmers to plan on devoting four hours each year to watering an acre of small grains, seven hours a year per acre of alfalfa, twelve hours for potatoes, and thirteen for sugar beets. The frequency of irrigation also varied with the climate and soil. In the Tule Lake Basin, where temperatures were relatively cool, farmers growing grain needed to irrigate only once during the season, compared to four to five irrigations in the sandy soils of the Snake River Plain.[26]

A few who managed to irrigate their crops successfully in their first years of farming reaped remarkable harvests. Previously untilled soil in some regions was wonderfully fertile. In sections of the recently drained Tule Lake Basin, lake bottom sediment rich in organic material yielded bumper crops. In Wyoming, some homesteaders harvested prodigious amounts of seed peas and alfalfa seed on previously untilled, nitrogen-rich soil. One farmer harvested an average of 2,000 pounds of seed peas per acre; another raised enough alfalfa seed to buy an airplane at the end of the first season. Some made comebacks that became the stuff of legends: in his first year of homesteading in the Big Horn Basin, Forrest Allen's seed peas turned sickly yellow after a week of heavy rain. When two executives from Associated Seed Growers visited the farm in mid-July they wrote off the crop as a "total loss." The fields dried out, though, and the plants not only recovered but thrived. Allen's crop was so large that he was the "top grower" the seed company had that year.[27]

But these were the exceptions, and aside from the Tule Lake Basin, nitrogen and other nutrients stored in the soil were quickly depleted. Generally raw desert lands lacked organic material and proper nutrients, leading to inferior crops. On the Minidoka Project, the soil lacked sufficient nitrogen. In some areas, sand and soil covered volcanic rock to a depth of 40 feet, but in other places only a few inches of topsoil overlaid the rocks. Similarly, "natural organic matter" constituted less than 2 percent of the soil on some homesteads on the Boise Project. Farmers on such lands could expect disappointing harvests and little if any income for at least one year and relatively low yields for the second, third, and fourth years. After building up the nutrients and organic matter in their soil for several years by planting and plowing under alfalfa, farmers in the Southwest who planned to grow specialty crops such as grapes would have to wait an additional 3–4 years for the grapevines to mature fully.[28]

Homesteaders did apply fertilizer to boost their harvests but few felt they could afford the optimal amount, along with all of the other expenses associated with developing a farm. Consequently, many applied as little as 10 percent of the recommended treatment. Where they could, homesteaders supplemented chemical fertilizers with manure. Most had no choice but to develop most of their soil over 3–5 years with soil-building, nitrogen-fixing crops such as alfalfa or sweet clover that would eventually be plowed under. In the process of building up the soil in this fashion, a few managed to harvest and sell large amounts of alfalfa or alfalfa seed at a premium price. More commonly, the nitrogen-fixing, soil-building crops themselves fared poorly for several years. Even after the soil had been coaxed in this fashion, commercial fertilizer was still needed. After growing alfalfa for three years on the Riverton Project, Harold Holmes plowed under the crop and planted wheat. He was disappointed with the results. "I've tried to keep it all green, but once you break up the alfalfa [and plant grain] it doesn't do very well," he told a visitor.[29]

Individual projects presented homesteaders with added, unique challenges related to soils. On some farms on the Boise Project patches of sterile hard pan or adobe ground made up as much as a tenth of the irrigable acreage. Hard pan could be reclaimed by plowing with a subsoiler, a 36- to 40-inch prong that would hook into the hard pan and lift it to the surface in slabs as large as a kitchen table. Once the slabs had been brought to the surface they could be pulverized with a diesel-powered crawler. At a cost of $60 an acre, though, few homesteaders could afford to deep plow with the requisite heavy equipment at the outset. Some opted for a less expensive but more painstaking approach to rehabilitating adobe ground: periodically raking straw and manure into the soil and then turning it over with a disk. After several years of this treatment, some former adobe land produced decent crops.[30]

In the Coachella Valley, most of the land that was opened to homesteading following the war was so alkaline that it had originally been blacklisted by the Bureau of Reclamation. Responding to pressure for new land openings in a region where specialty crops like premium table grapes could be grown, the Bureau had reclassified the land and opened it to settlement. The Bureau advised farmers to apply four feet of water to each acre before planting in order to force the salt deep into the ground beyond the root zone of the plants. Then, with each subsequent irrigation, they were told to apply an extra 15 percent of irrigation water to maintain the leached conditions. The soil itself was woefully deficient in organic material and this, in tandem with heavy irrigation that leached nutrients as well as salts from the soil, necessitated heavy applications of expensive fertilizer.[31]

The challenges associated with soils and irrigation were enough to discourage even an inveterate optimist, but in their first year of farming the homesteaders could also lose their crops to livestock that "aided the homesteader in harvesting," as one farmer euphemistically phrased the problem. The Big Horn Basin in Wyoming had been open range land since the nineteenth century, and cattle continued to graze on the homesteaders' unfenced land after they plowed and planted it. The Cowboy State had long been partial toward stockmen, and county officials advised homesteaders there to fence their land or put up with the animals. Time and money were in short supply that first year of farming, though, so more than one farmer "took the thirty-ought six out" to ward off the animals.[32]

On newly developed farms, wild animals that ranged freely over the land also devoured crops. Allen Talbott planted nine acres of wheat next to a hill on his homestead in Riverton but "the antelope and the jack rabbits kept it pretty well mowed down." Rolly Powers only harvested eleven sacks of wheat from seventeen acres his first year on the Gooding Division. "Jack rabbits and mismanagement of the water took care of the rest," he quipped. Homesteaders trapped, shot, and poisoned the rabbits—Powers and his neighbors killed 900 in four hours—but a common joke on western rangelands was that if you killed 1,000 rabbits, 10,000 would show up for the funeral.[33]

In common with all farmers, homesteaders also gambled against the weather, but those on new farms whose projected harvests were already low were especially vulnerable. High winds frequently blew seeds out of the freshly plowed soil, especially if it contained little organic matter. One Yuma

Mesa homesteader had to replant his cotton crop four times because the wind carried the seeds away. If the plants managed to germinate, blowing sand could also bury them or sever them from their roots. Another cotton grower on Yuma Mesa recalled that "about every two weeks it would blow and the sand would come and race around the cotton stalks and then they'd fall over." Similarly, Lyle Esser lost an entire crop of tender sweet peas in the Columbia Basin when blowing sand "just cut them all up."[34]

Windstorms wreaked havoc at harvest time, too. One year Asil Dobson swathed twenty-five acres of alfalfa on the Gila project, cutting the seed pods loose and raking them into "nice big fluffy windrows" where he left them to cure. High winds destroyed his hard work, leaving the cuttings jumbled and rolled into huge mounds. Although he tried to process the cuttings after the wind abated, they were so tangled and choked with sand that they "plugged up" the combine. Ultimately Dobson "didn't get enough out of that to be worth fiddling with."[35]

Exceptional heat and cold could also spell disaster. Homesteaders near Yuma gained little from their first few cuttings of alfalfa because they mowed and raked the hay in the heat of the day, causing the cuttings to wilt. Cold weather could be even more devastating, wiping out a crop overnight. "When the cold night came you were just at the mercy of the frost and everything . . . was gone," recalled Lowell Kenyon, a homesteader in the Tule Lake Basin. Cold temperatures and heavy snow in August decimated the bean crop one year on homesteads in the Big Horn Basin. In 1955, about 500 acres of potatoes froze in the ground and were written off as a "complete loss" on homesteads under development in the Snake River Valley. Carl Skinner, a homesteader on the Yakima project, described his first harvest for a reporter in 1949: "It was late before I got anything planted last year, but it came up good. I had eight acres in beans. I took 20 rows out and the next morning the rest were buried under a foot of snow." Hard freezes were especially frightening to citrus growers on homesteads in the Southwest because they jeopardized not only a single crop but the trees themselves. To save a citrus grove during a hard freeze when the mercury fell into the mid-20s for several hours, farmers would flood the groves with 6 inches of water. As the water froze it would release heat that would be picked up and circulated by wind machines to preserve the trees. If temperatures plunged into the lower 20s or teens, farmers would "burn everything we could burn, rubber tires, and baled hay, anything that would burn and create heat."[36]

A single hailstorm could also wipe out a year's effort. When a freak storm crossed Van Sorensen's homestead on the Minidoka Project the "elongated, jagged pieces of ice" beat down the alfalfa "like a ragged mat," stripped the sugar beets of foliage, and decimated the grain to the point that Sorensen "didn't harvest one kernel of grain that year." Individual homesteaders attempting to develop farms in sections of the Riverton Project lost between 40 and 100 percent of their crops in an August 1950 hail storm. The next year on the same project, three farmers in their first year of homesteading lost their entire harvest in a hailstorm.[37]

Heavy rains at the wrong time of year could be equally ruinous. Varian Wells planted beans on his entire farm in 1959 in the Columbia Basin and had a "real good" crop. In the fall he cut the bean stalks and was ready to thresh them when "it started to rain and ruined every bean I had." September thunderstorms also ravaged Bill and Myrtle Gunlock's alfalfa seed. "If it rains on a seed crop we can just as well forget it because it gets wet and after it dries all the seed just pops out of the alfalfa pods," Myrtle explained.[38]

The homesteaders would always be vulnerable to hailstorms and extreme heat or cold, but in their first years of farming as they were proving up on their lands, they did learn through trial and error, observation and conversation, how to respond effectively to some of the weather-related challenges distinctive to their particular locations. Even though it seemed counterintuitive to water heavily after a rainstorm, on the Coachella Project farmers discovered that by so doing they could counteract spring rains that pushed alkali from the surface into the root zones of plants. On the Minidoka Project, where winds generally subside at dusk in the spring, homesteaders learned that they could plant more easily with less loss of seed if they worked at night and tried to sleep during the day. In southern Arizona, where temperatures soar to 120 degrees in the summertime, farmers learned to bale their hay at night when the temperatures were cooler and the "dew was up" so that the alfalfa leaves would not become brittle and fall from the stems. Homesteaders in areas with finely textured soil learned that they could reduce wind erosion by leaving clods of dirt on the surface after plowing.[39]

The veterans faced some of their greatest obstacles to proving up in the economic arena as they struggled to break into farming in an era of capital-intensive agriculture. The need for credit dogged homesteaders since the 1860s, but no generation faced greater capital requirements than farmers in the second half of the twentieth century. Farming was a business, and many found themselves wishing they had taken classes in economics, marketing, and finance. Fortunately for the homesteaders, payments toward their prorated share of the cost of the irrigation system that delivered water to their farms did not begin for ten years. However, beginning with the first year of farming they received a bill annually for the expenses of operating and maintaining that system. On the Minidoka Project's North Side Extension, operation and maintenance charges averaged $10.50 per acre, although they were levied on a graduated basis over the first decade, beginning with a payment of $4.20 in the first year.[40]

Those like Carlyle Butler, a homesteader on the Hunt Division of the Minidoka Project, who believed that they must "make our farms produce the maximum in the least amount of time," assumed additional obligations by hiring others to clear, level, and develop their lands. On the Minidoka Project in the 1950s the cost of clearing and leveling land, constructing farm ditches, drops, and other irrigation works, and applying fertilizer averaged $57 per acre. Homesteaders could easily spend an additional $17,500 for a home, farm buildings, machinery, and a well. Nearly every homesteader who did not already own equipment purchased a tractor, plow, and harrows, and many invested in grain drills, combines, power mowers, rakes, pick up balers, and machinery for specialty crops such as potatoes or sugar beets, sometimes purchasing equipment jointly with their neighbors or relatives. On average between 1949 and 1954 homesteaders on the Klamath Project spent over $5,000 for farm equipment. A reporter who interviewed homesteaders in the Big Horn Basin found that many had spent between $10,000 and $15,000 on equipment.[41]

The costs of developing and equipping their farms quickly depleted whatever cash reserves the homesteaders brought to the projects. By his third year of farming, A. L. Wursten admitted, "It has taken a lot of money to make this a productive farm and our savings are about gone." Under the GI Bill, veterans who attended vocational training courses received up to $65 monthly from the Veterans Administration—$90 if they were married. Every veteran qualified automatically for twelve months of training, with an additional month of training allotted for each month they had served in the military. These stipends kept food on the table and gasoline in the car but left little money for defraying farm expenses.[42]

Aside from settlers in the Tule Lake Basin where the soil was so fertile that bankers willingly extended credit to first-year farmers on the basis of a crop lien, the homesteaders found that options for credit were sharply limited. Generally bankers were "very reluctant" to loan money until the settlers had proved up and could offer their land as collateral. A banker in Moses Lake, Washington, told David Hunt that he expected "the first three farmers on these farm units were going to go broke before one made it" just as had happened on earlier reclamation projects. Unless they had grown up in the area, the farmers themselves were also an unknown commodity whom the bankers eyed warily. Their policy was no collateral, no loan. Even for a loan of $100, a banker on the Minidoka Project insisted that George Falkner mortgage his truck. Merchants were likewise suspicious. A settler on Yuma Mesa who tried to buy a refrigerator was denied in-store credit after the sales clerk checked his application and saw that he lived along Rural Route B—the homesteading district.[43]

For most homesteaders who had not yet proved up and gained title to their land the Farmers Home Administration (FHA) was their only recourse. As Laverda Allen of the Minidoka Project observed in 1959, "If it weren't for the FHA most of us wouldn't be here." Farmers could apply for production and subsistence loans to purchase farming supplies such as seed, livestock, and equipment and to meet household expenses. In 1947, the total amount that any farmer could borrow in a single year was $3,500, and maximum indebtedness could not exceed $5,000. Additionally, farmers could borrow from the agency for land development and construction. The amount of money they could borrow varied depending upon the philosophy of local loan officers and the potential productivity of the farms. On the Minidoka Project, FHA farm development loans of $15,000 were common, and by 1957 the average homesteader there owed $20,000. On the Boise Project the FHA typically loaned homesteaders smaller amounts; standard loans for farm development and home construction ranged between $7,500 and $8,500. Farmers there and elsewhere complained that the funds were insufficient and that they came with too many strings attached. Glen Olsen found the agency's approach to expenditures on the Boise Project "authoritative," meaning that the FHA loan officers generally insisted that borrowers invest in a few dairy cows and a milking shed or dairy barn so that they would have a consistent source of cash. Consequently, "many of us . . . milked cows for our tenure as homesteaders."[44]

Homesteaders could and did appeal to officials in Washington, DC, in an effort to extract additional money and greater freedom in spending it. A loan agent for FHA told Phil Bare that he would not approve a loan unless Bare agreed to invest in dairy cattle. Bare had milked cows when he was younger and wanted nothing to do with dairying, so he contacted Wyoming Senator Joseph O'Mahoney and asked him to intercede. The ploy worked; Bare received the money without having to develop a dairy. A fellow-homesteader at Riverton, Ted Gies, applied for money to buy a milking machine for eight cows and was told that he should buy a portable machine that could handle one cow at a time instead. Gies appealed to officials in Washington and secured a large enough loan for a grade-A milking barn.[45]

On the other hand, some homesteaders believed they were encouraged to borrow more than they needed. Carroll Riggs walked into the FHA office in Riverton intending to borrow $1,100 to finish building a house. Instead, he walked out with a standard $7,000 loan for not only a home but a barn, fencing, and other supplies. He was "sorry a lot of times after that I did that" because he had to devote so much of his income to loan repayments. Farmers on the Minidoka Project expressed their frustrations with indebtedness to the FHA by adapting the popular song "Sixteen Tons" to their own situation: "I thin my beets / And I haul my hay / And the money all goes / To the FHA. I change my siphons / Six times a day / All for the LOVE / Of the FHA. Forty-five cows / You milk twice a day / At the insistence / of the FHA. Forty five cows / Now ain't that grand! The power's off again / So you milk 'em by hand."[46]

Financing farming operations was only one of the economic challenges homesteaders faced. They also struggled to market crops successfully. The influx of new farmers on reclamation projects growing the same crops as more established farmers often created an oversupply in the region, driving down the prices of farm products. On the Minidoka Project, for instance, the balance between local alfalfa supplies and demand for livestock feed in the area collapsed as hundreds of new homesteaders began planting alfalfa, with hay prices falling to $8 a ton. Wary of high transportation costs, many farmers hoped to sell vegetables, fruit, and dairy products locally, but local demand was limited. In the thinly populated county where his ranch was located in Wyoming, Wally George felt fortunate to be able to sell a sack or two of potatoes per day to a restaurateur; that was the extent of his local market. Bob and Deloris Fram, who tried to establish a dairy on the outskirts of Yuma, could not sell their milk locally at all; the closest good market was 5–6 hours away in Tucson.[47]

If they turned to national networks and markets homesteaders likewise encountered difficulties. Aside from the Columbia Basin, the lands onto which postwar settlers moved were extensions of reclamation projects that had been established previously, and so markets for some irrigated crops were already well established; hay buyers customarily visited Yuma, for instance, while potato buyers regularly came to Tulelake. Agricultural economists had warned that America would produce more food than it could consume in the postwar era, though, and their forecasts were accurate. "We could raise most anything but there wasn't a market for a lot of the stuff," explained Lyle Esser, a settler in the Columbia Basin. For two years in a row another Basin farmer, Anthon Price, raised potatoes and "never made a dime." Established farmers west of the Basin in the Yakima Valley jealously guarded their markets. Farmers like Price had to undersell the Yakima Valley growers to attract buyers: "We had to develop all those markets . . . the hard way: you sold cheap." It took about five years before potato warehouses and grain elevators were built in the basin. The problem of attracting buyers was especially daunting in the Columbia Basin because irrigated crops had not been grown there previously, but it plagued farmers elsewhere, too, who wanted to try different crops than those that were routinely grown in the area. Swede Olson, a homesteader in northern Wyoming, was sure he could grow "beautiful head lettuce and carrots" but despaired that he could find no market for them. "If we could find a market, I'd like to try truck crops," he admitted wistfully in 1954.[48]

In addition to marketing challenges that were endemic to new agricultural regions, the homesteaders also faced economic challenges shared by all farmers such as erratic prices and unscrupulous buyers. When a journalist visited Allan Talbot, a homesteader on the Riverton Project, in his third year of farming, Talbot rejoiced in the prospect of a bountiful alfalfa seed harvest. In earlier years he had fretted about "how good the crop is going to be" but now he was worried about "how low the price of seed will drop." Talbot and his associates on the project had good reason to worry given what they had seen in the previous two years: in 1951 one Riverton homesteader, James Van Trump, had earned nearly $10,000 from alfalfa seed. The following year the price was so low that Van Trump cleared only $1,500. Similarly, on the Klamath project homesteaders watched helplessly as the average price of barley fell by 43 percent in one year.[49]

Unscrupulous buyers from out of state got the best of some farmers who were eager to sell at the highest rate possible. Bill Nolan's neighbor contracted early in the summer to sell his potatoes at a good price. Then the market value of potatoes dropped and "for some reason his potatoes could never meet the contract criteria." During his first three years of farming at Riverton, Art Over and his neighbors raised alfalfa seed and "made some hellacious production on that." A buyer from Colorado contracted to purchase most of the seed, loaded it into a truck, and "went on out of state" and the farmers "never got a penny." The corruption of hay buyers, who seldom paid up front for the crop, was legendary.[50]

Despite the obstacles they faced some homesteaders sold crops at enviable prices in the early years while they were proving up. As a new homesteader Ted Gies of the Riverton Project made enough money on alfalfa seed to repay his loans and pay for a new automobile. One homesteader's gross income in his first year on the Klamath Project exceeded $16,000. After three years on his ninety-six-acre homestead on the Minidoka project, Dale Stoller was "practically debt free" and was honored by the local Jaycees as "Young Farmer of the Year."[51]

Aside from those who were fortunate enough to acquire rich lake bottom soil at Tule Lake, though, penury and disappointment were the more common outcomes of farming on each reclamation project in the first 1–3 years. Rolly Powers's gross income in his first year of farming in southern Idaho was under $500. Riverton homesteader Stanford Clark's gross income in his first year amounted to only $700. No one starved, but many homesteaders were in dire financial straits. Reflecting upon the meager returns from farming on a homestead, Windy Dobson mused, "I'm not sure that they told us, 'Hey, be prepared. It's going to be five years before you get a paycheck out of this.'" Glen Olsen felt he had to forego "needed medication" for his family because "we just didn't feel that we could afford it." At times Anthon Price had no discretionary money at all because "we just didn't have a way to make a living." One Christmas the Prices "didn't have a dime."[52]

In order to make ends meet and furnish a consistent income while they were developing their soils and "there was hardly anything coming in off the farm," many homesteaders held down part- or full-time jobs. Some worked off the farm only during the slack season, others worked as teachers during the school year and many others labored year round on construction sites or in mills, factories, and offices. For those who spent 40 hours a week off the farm, the work day never seemed to end. Thomas Pierce, a school teacher, worked from four o'clock in the morning until eleven o'clock at night in the fall and spring "in order to do justice to both jobs." Similarly, Anthon Price spent nine hours each day at a construction job and then attempted to farm in the evenings and on weekends. Physically and mentally, such a rigorous schedule taxed the homesteaders almost to the breaking point. "We were trying to farm and work out almost full time as well. We were burning the candle at both ends," recalled Asil Dobson.[53]

The prospects became so dismal for some homesteaders owing to bad luck and miscalculation that they walked away from their farms without having acquired a clear title to them. Such was the case with one homesteader on the Klamath Project. Emboldened by a strong showing in his first year of farming, he planted sugar beets on his entire farm the following year and borrowed heavily to install an expensive sprinkler system. Results from the initial planting were mixed, so he reseeded his field, complicating his task later in the season when he had beets at two stages of maturity in the same fields. A late summer frost hit the plants hard, leaving him with "practically no crop" that year. Discouraged and heavily in debt, he decided to abandon the homestead.[54]

Despite the privations and obstacles they encountered, most of the homesteaders proved up on their lands, with the exception of portions of the Riverton Project, a special case that is treated in Chapter Six. On the Boise Project, for instance, 92 percent of the original entrymen obtained title to their homesteads. On the first unit of the Yuma Mesa Project, where fifty-four entrymen took up homesteads, all but one proved up. By contrast, under 48 percent of those who filed homestead claims in Kansas between 1873 and 1890 proved up. With concessions such as reduced residency requirements; low-interest, federally financed loans; guidance from government employees; and a ten-year exemption from construction payments for the irrigation systems they used, the bar had been lowered to the point where proving up was within the reach of most homesteaders who were willing to apply themselves.[55]

Old-timers shook their heads in disbelief when they heard the veterans complaining about the rigors and uncertainty of homesteading or boasting about their achievements as pioneers. In their minds, the homesteaders had not proved themselves sufficiently to be honored as manly pioneers. Some of the homesteaders themselves acknowledged that they had not proved their mettle as fully as earlier generations of pioneers. Lyle Esser adamantly stated that he and his neighbors in the Columbia Basin "did not consider ourselves pioneers." Anthon Price admitted, "We talk about the old pioneers coming west. Well, we had some of that. Not as much as they did, but some of that." Ted Aston's childhood dream of "do[ing] as the pioneers did . . . making wilderness ground productive as farmland" had been fulfilled—with qualifications.[56]

For the time being, notwithstanding the programs and policies that smoothed the veterans' path, their dependence upon technology and family labor, and the disjuncture between "notions of iconic western masculinity" and their lived experience, the knowledge that they had proved up was still exhilarating confirmation to the homesteaders of their yeoman status. Van Sorensen recalled that when he and his neighbors proved up, "you felt like you were no longer just a tenant on the land." As another homesteader stated, "It meant a lot because if you're raised on a farm or if you're born in the generation I was, having land is a kind of security that nothing else quite meets." Ownership meant independence and the chance to "build something for myself," as Francis Martin expressed it, rather than "working for the other fellow." Martin spoke in the singular, but many men spoke of an identity and objectives they shared with others. Soon after proving up on the Shoshone Project, Alex Brug told a reporter, "Both our families worked all their lives and they never had a place to call their own. Well, this land is ours. It isn't much, but it's the first land we've ever owned."[57]

For those who intended to make a living on the land, though, the challenge had just begun when they finished proving up. Most owed substantial sums for their homes and the development of their land and they had not even started paying for the cost of the irrigation system itself. When those debts could no longer be deferred, the homesteaders would be called upon to prove themselves a second time.

4

"GOLD MINE IN THE SKY" THE FARMERS' DREAMS FOR THEMSELVES AND THEIR LAND

The veterans relished their newfound albeit incomplete independence as landowners. As Assistant Commissioner of Reclamation William Warne observed, "When title passes to [the homesteader] there is no [legal] limitation upon him." As heirs to the agrarian dream and the pastoral promise of American land, these owners were free to sell, mortgage, or rent out their land if they chose. Their choices would unmask their dreams for themselves and for their land.[1] Each farm remained heavily encumbered with prorated charges for improvements made by the government, including the irrigation system itself, but those who chose to sell their farms shortly after proving up could still expect to make some money from the improvements they had made. From the outset some settlers had expected to sell as quickly as possible. Van and Bell Sorensen, for instance, planned to sell their homestead in Wyoming and use the income as a down payment on a ranch in a less remote location. Butch Woodman, a homesick bachelor from northern California, likewise intended to leave the Sonoran Desert as soon as he could unload his homestead on Yuma Mesa. Leon Machen did not expect to till his land west of Boise for long, either; with luck, he hoped, he would be able to make enough money in the first few years of farming to get out of the business and bankroll a college degree in veterinary medicine. All of these homesteaders changed their plans; like Woodman, by the time they proved up they owed so much that they reckoned they were "too broke" to leave.[2]

While some like Woodman who had originally planned on

moving changed their minds, between 10 and 15 percent of the homesteaders on most projects sold their farms soon after proving up. On the Shoshone Project one in ten homesteaders departed within the first seven years, selling their farms for as much as $27,000. North of the Snake River, 11 percent of the 623 homesteads that were established between 1954 and 1958 changed hands by the end of 1960. Similarly, 12 percent of those who filed on lands at Tule Lake between 1947 and 1949 sold by the end of 1953, receiving up to $35,000 for their farms. The intense heat drove even more from Yuma Mesa; by 1951, only four years after the first homesteaders had arrived, 15 percent had sold out, for an average price of $200 an acre. The fact that settlers managed to sell at a profit after such a brief stint on their homesteads frustrated some lawmakers who believed that the government had been hoodwinked into underwriting and abetting "speculation."[3]

Others who retained title to their lands could also be characterized as speculators; rather than selling, they rented their farms to someone else, using part of the income to pay property taxes and other obligations. In the most productive districts of the Tule Lake Division, homesteaders in 1952 could earn as much as $100 per acre by leasing their farmland to potato growers. Thirteen percent of the postwar homesteads at Tule Lake were farmed by lessees that year. Even on less productive lands, leasing was common: on the Riverton Project, renters farmed 9 percent of the postwar homesteads by 1952.[4]

Dissatisfaction induced others to rent out their farms. In places where the climate was especially harsh, leasing was most common: by 1951, roughly four in ten homesteads on Yuma Mesa were cultivated under leases. Others who discovered they disliked farming likewise became landlords. Mark Sweet, a Marine Corps veteran who had grown up on his father's homestead in Oklahoma, "raised some beautiful crops" and "wound up with a pretty good herd of Holstein cows" on his Idaho homestead. But "after I spent five years proving up, I knew that I didn't want to farm," he reflected. Farming was "tough" and exhausting. Sweet moved to town, began working for the railroad, rented the farm and used the rental income to repay his $12,000 farm development loan. He retained the land, hoping that it would appreciate in value. He finally cashed in on his investment in the 1980s.[5]

Rather than leasing their land to someone else, a few absentee owners like Roy Rucker hired a manager to farm for them. Rucker owned a construction company in Tucson, so he and his family stayed on their homestead in the Coachella Valley only long enough to prove up. Rucker had "always wanted to farm," but largely from a business perspective. He periodically visited his new farm in his Tri-pacer plane to supervise matters but he paid a manager to water and fertilize his citrus groves. For the first three years while the trees were maturing Rucker invested "$10,000 or $20,000 a year to hang onto" the land as an absentee owner. The capital requirements "pretty well drained" his construction company, creating a "nip and tuck" existence. But then the trees began to produce and he recouped his investment, clearing $50,000 in good years. By 1974 the farm itself was worth $400,000.[6]

While many homesteaders became absentee owners shortly after proving up, providing some justification for allegations that the Bureau's postwar homesteading program benefited shrewd investors and speculators as much as would-be yeoman farmers, the majority—at least two-thirds on most projects—retained their lands and farmed them personally in the years immediately after proving up. In an era of America's international economic dominance when opportunities in education and industry proliferated and millions of Americans were leaving the countryside, a blend of economic and nonpecuniary motives caused these homesteaders to buck the rural-to-urban population trend and continue farming.

All expected that the enterprise would make them financially stable. With luck, some hoped, they might even become wealthy, viewing farming as a means to increased wealth rather than a sacrifice of it. W. A. Galbraith, chair of the Columbia Basin Commission, expressed the dominant perception among farmers on reclamation projects when he stated that each settler should be assured "that by hard work, ingenuity and husbanding his resources, he can expand his operations, provide things a little better for his family, boost his standard of living and contribute more to the community in which he lives."[7]

The Bureau of Reclamation encouraged aspirations toward upward mobility; farmers who subscribed to the Bureau's monthly magazine, *Reclamation Era*, were frequently treated to rags-to-riches tales of homesteading. Shortly before the first postwar homestead drawing on the Yakima Project, the magazine's lead article, "I Finally Struck It Rich," recounted the adventures of C' deVere Fairchild, a man who had spent five years prospecting for gold on the Klondike. Fairchild had found a small amount of gold but after moving to a farm on the Yakima Project in 1912 he had achieved such "great" wealth that the Klondike's riches seemed "insignificant by comparison." Farmers in the Yakima valley had harvested crops valued at nearly $321 million over a three-year period—allegedly more than the value of all the gold mined during the Klondike rush—and Fairchild's share of the agricultural wealth had made him "rich," allowing him to live in "social and economic comfort." Readers of *Reclamation Era* were encouraged to believe that the economic possibilities for postwar homesteaders were just as great; an article covering a postwar land opening in a high mountain valley on the Klamath Project was entitled "Gold Mine in the Sky."[8]

Some postwar homesteaders lived a storied rags-to-riches existence, proving that Fairchild's story was more than a quaint artifact from a bygone era. Jerry Lindsey acquired forty acres that no one else wanted in the Gila River valley in 1962, willing to take the chance that the land would grow crops once the Bureau of Reclamation installed an elaborate system of drains. Locals derided the place as the farm where it "snow[ed] all the time" because white alkali dust blanketed the ground. After the drainage system was completed Lindsey set out to prove them wrong. He leveled his land, excavated irrigation ditches, and turned prodigious amounts of water onto the soil hoping to leach out the salt. Then he planted Bermuda grass, a seed crop well suited to salty ground. Even so, after the first irrigation water had soaked into the newly planted soil, the surface "was just white all over. It wouldn't grow a weed." Lindsey tried every chemical remedy he could think of over the next four years to no avail. Finally at his "wit's end" he plowed down five feet, turned over the soil and flooded the field for over a month to leach out the salt before leveling the land for a second time and replanting. His efforts were at last rewarded: Bermuda grass finally germinated on some of the land, and over the next few years grass spread slowly over the rest of the land. In Lindsey's seventh year of farming the price of grass seed soared; Lindsey had an excellent crop, and he netted $120,000. Eventually the land where it "snowed all the time" became prime farmland; when Lindsey sold it he made a small fortune.[9]

Although Lindsey's saga proves that homesteaders could make substantial money, wealth was not many homesteaders' paramount reason for living on the land. As Lyle Esser explained, he and many of his peers possessed "college educations . . . or were trained in other things. . . . So they all could have made money in some other place." Some bypassed more lucrative careers because they "wanted to farm"—for reasons that had little to do with

Photographs such as this one distributed by the Bureau of Reclamation's Public Relations staff emphasized the economic success and prosperity of homesteaders. The caption written by the staff for this photograph is: "Mr. and Mrs. W. O. White seem well pleased with their wheat harvest, and rightfully so, for successful crops such as this have provided them with this beautiful farmstead and a well-developed farm." (Reclamation Photographs, NARA, Rocky Mountain Region)

money and much to do with the rural ideal that scholars have termed *pastoralism*, or the "affinity for land and farming as a way of life." For instance, Eliot Waits could not imagine a more fulfilling occupation than working on the land. Waits reflected, "I grew up on a farm and I followed my dad around every place he went on the farm. I guess I just loved it as a kid. . . . That's what I want[ed] to do. I'm happy doing that." Waits felt spiritually invigorated when he was in the fields. It gave him "a lot of time to think and talk." Once he commented to his minister, "I go out driving the tractor at night and I bet I'm closer to God than you are." Others coveted the independence that came with being their own boss; Bill Nolan, a settler in eastern Washington, explained that for many in his generation the chance to labor "on their own" without taking orders from anyone else or conforming as an organization man was "the biggest thing," a far more important objective than having "a nice house and a new car."[10]

Some preferred farm life because of its putative benefits for their families. When Elmer Metz's name was drawn for a homestead at Tule Lake, a journalist asked him if he "plan[ned] to make a lot of money." Metz reportedly told him that he wasn't "worried or even particularly interested about that." Instead he was "just interested in making a good home." The values of home also animated Jake Colvin, who regarded farming as "a means to a way of life" rather than "my total way of life." Colvin expected the farm would provide stability for his children and nurture positive character traits as they matured and learned to work. Some parents whose children struggled with physical or mental disabilities hoped that farm life would enable their children to thrive; Ralph Issler relocated on a farm in Arizona's Wellton Mohawk Valley largely because doctors advised that the dry climate would help his son's frail health. Similarly, Glen and Evelyn Olsen hoped that farm life would give their youngest son, who was struggling academically, "an opportunity to do something" well. In contrast to his marginal performance in school, his effort on the farm would be "something [they] could praise." For some homesteaders, the vision of providing for one's children on the farm extended into their adult years. Dale Lorensen located on a homestead in western Idaho with "dreams . . . looking ahead" to "what we were going to have some day": a farm that would remain in the family for multiple generations.[11]

The varied motives of these modern homesteaders counter traditional and surprisingly resilient characterizations of American farmers as crass materialists. As historian Elliott West has observed, "The traditional view of the frontier . . . portrays pioneers as moving with a single-minded motivation to profit by making over the land." For generations, historians of American agriculture, for whom the "metaphor of the frontier" was also central, likewise believed in the centrality of markets. Allan Kulikoff characterized the traditional assumptions about economic motivation: "'The market' has been a powerful metaphor in the history of American farming. . . . The metaphor presumes that commercial (even capitalist) agriculture arrived with the first European immigrants and that farmers still outside the market were merely waiting for the building of canals or railroads to open their way to the world market." As Catherine McNicol Stock and Robert D. Johnston have observed, journalists and scholars have perpetuated the myth in recent decades that "all contemporary farmers care about is their own crude material self-interest."[12]

In 1978, James Henretta drew upon evidence from other studies to challenge this monochrome portrait of early American farmers. He argued instead that "economic gain was important to these men and women, yet it was not their dominant value. It was subordinate to (or encompassed by) two other goals: the yearly subsistence and the long-run financial security of the family unit." In the intervening years the challengers in agricultural, western, and colonial history mounted an impressive array of evidence to support their revisionist argument. Summarizing the point of view of the challengers in 1989, Elliott West wrote, "A typical adult pioneer, to be sure, was an optimist inspired by dreams of gain. Yet pioneers did more than transform the country, and certainly they worried about more than making profits. They went west also determined to build what they considered a proper social order. The focus of that was not the field and the mine, but the family, the home, and the children."[13]

As scholars examined the motives of farmers, they recognized the flaws of an either-or dichotomization of farmers' value systems. Allan Kulikoff has argued instead for viewing the history of agriculture from colonial times to the mid-twentieth century "dialectically, as farm families balanced dependence on markets with independent subsistence." Sometime in the second third of the twentieth century, Kulikoff posits, "the market engulfed the nation," but up until then "household activities mediated market forces" as farmers "look[ed] backward to subsistence and the perpetuation of their farms and forward to the market exchange that made agriculture possible." The point at which the transition to the market was complete, Kulikoff posits, was when farmers no longer grew food to feed themselves, women left the home to work for wages, and farmers relied primarily upon wage laborers rather than the labor of family members. These factors, along with immersion in markets and the purchase of agricultural machinery, meant that everything had been commodified.[14]

Kulikoff points to 1933–1966 as the era when market dominance became total. Because few of the revisionists have focused their research upon this era, though, we know less about the attitudes of farm families in this era than in earlier ones. The veterans' accounts of their experiences enrich our understanding of farmers' negotiation of the dialectic between household and market in this critical era of transformation. Their stories suggest that even in this watershed era when the market supposedly triumphed, some small farmers continued to view money as a means rather than an end to their labors, even if they worked off the farm for wages and no longer planted vegetable gardens or milked cows to feed themselves.

Whether or not money was the veterans' paramount objective in farming, most expected to achieve what Andrew Biorn, a settler in the Columbia Basin, called "a decent standard of living" in contrast to what he called "subsistence level living." To that end they worked to obtain additional land, purchased new machinery, borrowed money, and played the market. While they also "oppose[d] wholeheartedly large scale undesirable corporate farming" they believed farming should sustain their families comfortably rather than at a bare subsistence level. W. A. Galbraith described for the Bureau of Reclamation the middle road between subsistence farming and commercial agriculture that they sought: farmers should

> have the right to earn for themselves a living equal to those in any other pursuit, to build up an estate for retirement, to earn sufficient for their comfort, to pay for their medical and dental needs the same as anyone else, to feed, clothe and shelter their families the same as those in all other walks of life and to provide for educations of their children the same as anyone else.[15]

The small size of farms on reclamation projects held the veterans back in their quest for economic stability. As a legacy of both the Homestead Act of 1862 and the Reclamation Act of 1902, the Bureau of Reclamation had inherited a nineteenth-century definition of family farm size: 160 acres in individual ownership. Michael Straus, Commissioner of Reclamation from 1945 to 1953, believed the 160-acre limit was consonant with the Bureau's mission to furnish "opportunity for the maximum number of actual settlers or farmers on the land." Many farmers contested these regulations, though, recognizing that the Bureau had made exceptions elsewhere. For instance, between 1938 and 1957 lawmakers authorized the Bureau to deliver water to farms larger than 160 acres on five projects: Colorado–Big Thompson, Truckee River, the Owl Creek and East Bench Units of Pick-Sloan, and Santa Maria. In 1947, Straus informed a congressional committee that a landowner with 1,600 acres could continue to farm the land, "bring himself into technical compliance with the law," and "never hear from the Bureau of Reclamation on the subject" by deeding 160-acre tracts to nine friends, relatives, or business associates and reserving 160 acres for himself.[16]

Despite these exceptions, on each of the Bureau's postwar projects where new farm units were platted and offered to veterans, the lines were drawn in compliance with the Bureau's acreage limitations. Every farm contained fewer than 160 irrigable acres. Straus claimed to have been influenced in this matter by the parting advice of his predecessor in the Bureau, Harry Bashore, who urged him, "'No matter what the future brings to reclamation, stand firm on the family-sized reclamation farm. Follow the wisdom of the reclamation law, and don't start turning over reclamation to corporate farming.'" Farms in the Columbia Basin, which politicians in the 1930s had intended as a solution to the woes of dust bowl refugees and the unemployed, were especially small; the project's authorizing legislation prohibited settlers there from acquiring water for more than a single unit, and the average unit contained barely 75 acres.[17]

Many homesteaders complained that antiquated laws dictated farms that were too small to provide an adequate return in an era when the costs of farming were rising more rapidly than farm income. A key cause of the rising costs was replacement of draft animals with tractors and other new machinery. It made sense to nearly everyone to invest in the machinery because it reduced manual labor and enabled people to accomplish more in a limited amount of time. But it was also expensive. As Eleanor Bolesta explained, "You couldn't afford [to farm only] 110 acres when you had to start buying expensive equipment." Using his own experiences to illustrate the financial crunch veterans faced, Harold Eidemiller tried to convince a congressional committee in 1957 that the average farm in the Columbia Basin was too small to support a family. During the Depression, Eidemiller explained, he and his brother had farmed 80 acres in Idaho using horses. The farm had supplied both of them "with a more or less satisfactory income" and had occupied them full time. The value of their equipment approximated $5,000; their home, built in 1925, cost $3,500. By 1957, that same farm was being leased to a man who farmed a total of 200 acres with modern equipment valued at $25,000. A home similar in size to the one Eidemiller had formerly inhabited would now cost at least $12,000. Having carefully laid out the facts and figures, Eidemiller cogently summarized their meaning: "we on the Columbia Basin Project are expected to make an investment of from $25,000 to

$35,000 and repay the investment on 60 to 70 acres of comparable land. It just cannot be done." In the same hearings another farmer argued, "A farmer using modern methods can farm 160 to 320 acres with no more capital investment than he has in the equipment necessary to farm an 80 acre unit but the difference in income from the added acres is the difference between subsistence level living and a decent standard of living. In many cases it means the difference between success and failure."[18]

Persuaded that the costs of modern machinery justified slightly larger farms, Congress and the Bureau increased the size of some of the smallest farms that were "too small to support a family" to bring them closer to 160 *irrigable* acres, but always stopped short of that limit in the 1950s. An act passed 13 August 1953 permitted the secretary of the interior to enlarge homesteads in individual ownership on reclamation projects up to 320 acres (including dryland pasture) in order to support a family, but stipulated that no more than 160 acres could be irrigable. Four years later, Congress permitted individual land owners on the Columbia Basin Project to receive water for more than one farm unit, provided that the total acreage watered did not exceed 160 acres. Thus Jim Foster, whose original farm unit in the Columbia Basin was only 65 acres, was permitted to reconfigure his tract, adding part of an adjacent plot, to bring the entire farm to 119 acres. Federal land exchange programs also helped. In 1956, one of Forrest Allen's neighbors traded a homestead back to the government, and Allen was allotted 45 acres from that farm, bringing his total irrigable acreage to 143. The demand for more arable land exceeded the supply, though, so few obtained a full quarter section of irrigable land. On Yuma Mesa, for instance, only homesteaders having fewer than 80 irrigable acres were allowed to augment their farm units with additional government land.[19]

Although Congress and the Bureau increased the size of some of the smallest homesteads, the 160-acre limit remained in force until 1982. Those who required more land than the government could supply often rented additional ground. Wilbur Andrew, who moved to his 80-acre Idaho homestead in 1950, was farming an additional half section under lease by 1960. Claude Briddle augmented his original 160-acre homestead on the Riverton Project by purchasing a neighbor's farm and leasing more land, bringing the total that he farmed to roughly 700 acres. Both relied largely upon household labor and continued to see their operations as family farms.[20]

Eventually some farmers became sufficiently prosperous to mimic the techniques adopted by large landholders on reclamation projects in California, purchasing land in the name of relatives or friends: Bill Casper bought out his neighbors as they left the region and eventually farmed 1,000 acres in the Columbia Basin. "I had to put these farms all in my kids' names or someone else's names because the limit that you could own at that time was 160 acres per person or your husband or wife could own 320 acres," he explained. "So I had put in my father-in-law's name on these contracts and my brother-in-law's name." This strategy enabled farmers such as Casper to develop significant commercial farms. Finally in 1982, this legal fiction became unnecessary after Congress in the Reclamation Reform Act raised the legal limit of irrigated land in individual ownership to 960 acres. In Casper's case, his objective in acquiring land was not only to increase profits but also to provide farming opportunities for the next generation. By 1996 three of his sons and a son-in-law operated portions of the farm they had purchased from him.[21]

In their quest for a comfortable living standard, the veterans were hampered by indebtedness as well as small farm size. As we have seen, few were able to secure significant loans from private lenders until they held title to their lands, but once they proved up credit became fairly easy to obtain. Credit enabled many families to develop their farms rapidly in anticipation of the greater profits a fully developed farm would generate. By 1957, the average postwar homesteader on the Minidoka Project owed $20,000 to the government and other lenders, an amount five times greater than their annual cash income. Those who purchased large, new equipment rather than used or smaller implements doubled their debt load in the process. When their income fell short of their optimistic expectations, many felt hopelessly trapped. Asil Dobson, who owed $20,000 to the FHA, described a typical scenario: "Well in our case this is what's happening, we're not gaining enough, we're not getting ahead enough to pay a whole lot of our debt with this Farmers Home Administration. So they're breathing down our neck all the time, plus we got the fertilizer people breathing down our neck and we . . . have to expend the money to get the [irrigation] water." Ted Aston, a homesteader on the Minidoka Project who took out a loan for a barn, milk cows, and dairy equipment "felt [himself] continuing to slip financially." In reality he was making nominal financial progress, but it was so slow and his debts were so heavy that the situation was "discouraging." Looking back on the situation he reflected, "Debt in itself isn't bad. However, when you're connected with the type of economy and the type of industry that requires you to operate on such a small margin of profit, such as farming required in those days, you can't help but feel the pressure."[22]

Alongside their indebtedness for machinery, livestock, homes, and farm buildings, the farmers also owed thousands of dollars to the Bureau of Reclamation for construction of their projects' irrigation systems. Despite the fact that the payments were spread out over decades, the cumulative obligation deeply discouraged some settlers because of its implications not only for themselves but for their children's financial prospects. "The charge is so great my kids will be fifty years old by the time the debt is paid off. I don't think that's right," complained Swede Olson of the Shoshone Project.[23]

Volatile markets complicated the challenge of repaying debts and achieving an acceptable standard of living on the farm. Farming was a gamble against the vagaries of national and international markets; as Ralph Wright, a homesteader on the Boise Project, observed, "Farming is luck. You can't control it. You have no control [over] what farming is going to do for you. You just have to ride along with the waves and do the best you can." Prices fluctuated erratically for many crops. Homesteaders on Yuma Mesa sold their hay for as little as $12 per ton in some years and as much as $140 a ton in others. Likewise, the price of lemons grown on the project ranged from $1 per box in some years to $20 in other years. Within a single growing season, prices could rise or fall meteorically; Bill Casper contracted to sell his wheat one year in the 1970s for $1.25 a bushel. By harvest time, Soviet demand for the grain had driven the price up to $5.[24]

In years when the market was unkind, some farmers specializing in a single crop earned little if any profit. Eldon Paulsen "had one grove of grapefruit and at the end of the year I got a bill for about $2,000 an acre. The fruit lacked that much of paying the picking and the packing." Bill Casper had nearly $50,000 invested in an apple crop one year including expenses for thinning, pruning, harvesting, watering, and spraying. The price plummeted and he "got a check for $125" after paying all his expenses.[25]

Discouraging financial challenges including small farms, heavy indebtedness, volatile markets, and insufficient income induced many homesteaders who had hoped to remain permanently on their farms to get out after only a few years. Saron Minden was one who threw in the towel. Minden and his wife and three children had settled on a farm north of Moses Lake in the Columbia Basin in 1951. The Mindens were featured in a 1952 article in the

Seattle Post Intelligencer describing their rosy dreams for the future. Minden had recently planted thirty-five acres of wheat and expected a gross income of $3,500 from the crop. He planned to use the rest of his land for pasture and cash crops like potatoes or seed peas. In a move that many of his fellow-farmers would have considered extravagant, Minden invested $100 per acre in a sprinkling system, borrowing the money from the FHA; he also owed money for his new home; an electric stove; 500 young chickens; and equipment including a tractor, fertilizer spreader, and disk harrow. During his first two years of farming Minden made so much money on a small acreage of seed peas that he was able to begin repaying the FHA, and the newspaper again featured him in an article updating readers on his success. But the glory days were nearly over; the price of seed peas plummeted at about the same time that Minden's entitlement to an educational stipend under the GI Bill lapsed. Along with hundreds of other new settlers in the Columbia Basin Minden tried his hand at dairying, borrowing funds for livestock and a milking parlor. Soon more milk was being produced than could be marketed; Minden had specialized to the point that he lacked money for basic necessities yet still owed thousands of dollars. The dire economic straits strained his marriage to the breaking point. Minden's dream of a comfortable lifestyle had degenerated into a nightmare, a living "hell." To pay the bills he began working as a boiler operator at Larson Air Base and eventually sold the farm. Minden's experiences with fluctuating markets and indebtedness, leading to departure from the family farm, were repeated by hundreds of settlers on reclamation projects in the 1950s and 1960s. Whether or not money was their primary objective, as it likely was in Minden's case, their homesteading dreams could not be sustained without it.[26]

Despite the obstacles to profitably operating a small farm with limited capital and uncertain markets, a substantial minority of the homesteaders retained their land and continued to farm it for decades. At Tule Lake, where the soil was especially rich, 43.5 percent of the homesteaders remained on their land in 1968, 20–22 years after their arrival. On the Minidoka Project 31 percent of a cluster sample of 83 veterans retained their land 20–22 years after their arrival. Similarly, at Yuma Mesa, after 20 years one-third of them remained.[27]

Some remained on the farm at great personal sacrifice, revealing the depth of their commitment to farm life. For instance, Eliot Waits defied disheartening financial reverses in order to continue farming. Waits had borrowed heavily in 1953 after he proved up in order to plant citrus groves on his homestead. The trees would not produce for several years, and in order to provide for his family that year, Waits leased nearly 1,000 acres and planted cotton. The cotton crop failed because of severe sand storms. "We'd borrowed from everyone we could borrow from and when we finished up the season, I was in the hole $30,000," he recalled. Waits tenaciously held onto the farm and gradually repaid his creditors over the next decade. In order to be able to meet his obligations he worked in town as a mechanic while his wife drove the tractor and did much of the farmwork during the day. In the evenings and on weekends Waits did what he could on the farm.[28]

While the Waits family retained their farm through strenuous financial sacrifice, others with an equally heartfelt commitment to farming failed to do so. The unhappy experiences of one veteran, David Hunt, reveal the profound psychological and emotional depth of some settlers' desire to farm—and the despair that haunted some whose dreams never materialized. After serving overseas in the navy during World War II, Hunt returned home, married, and searched for an affordable farm. Unable to find one with a decent water right Hunt enrolled instead in college and studied refrigeration. But he continued to dream of working independently on his own farm. When a friend told Hunt that irrigated farmland was being opened in eastern Washington, the news elated him. When the snow melted the following spring, Hunt and his brother-in-law set out for the Columbia Basin. Arriving on a Sunday afternoon, they toured the area. "You never saw such beautiful land in your life," Hunt recalled. There was one hitch: almost all of the land being developed by the Bureau of Reclamation for small farms in the Columbia Basin was already privately owned. Supposedly the Bureau was regulating land sales and prices, but Hunt discovered to his chagrin that a "black market" operated in which "you would buy the ground and then perjure yourself, say that you only paid so much for the ground and [then] you'd pay so much money under the table to get the ground." His only chances with his limited finances were the land lotteries being conducted by the Bureau of Reclamation and the Northern Pacific Railroad. Hunt applied and was surprised but overjoyed to be awarded farm unit 89, a tract with sixty irrigable acres, in block 40. The tract would cost him little more than a homestead—only $566—but he must comply with the same stipulations regarding land improvement and residency that applied to homesteaders.

Hunt bought a shack, loaded it onto a truck, and hauled it through the sagebrush to his new farm, and he and his family moved in. They had no electricity, telephone, or running water. He secured a loan of $25,000 from the Farmers Home Administration and the family went to work full time preparing the land for farming; after his first crop failed, Hunt determined that his land was better suited for pasture and forage crops so he invested in dairy cattle and a milking parlor. Unfortunately, as Saron Minden also learned, so many new settlers in the basin had similar ideas that a milk surplus soon developed. Hunt reacted to the situation by selling his dairy cattle and buying steers. The following summer six of them died. By this time, Hunt was "in pretty deep trouble" financially; he was mired in poverty and unable to persuade anyone to lend him more money. His creditors advised him to walk away from the farm. Trapped in the wreckage of his dreams, Hunt's stress rose to a fevered pitch, he was "run raw with so much tension," and one morning he "just went all to pieces, started bawling and couldn't quit." He was hospitalized after the breakdown and then taken to his parents' home near Las Vegas to convalesce.

Even after his breakdown, when his better judgment told him he should walk away from the farm, on the subconscious level the dream of farming persisted. After he returned to his farm in Washington, one night as he slept Hunt dreamed of a productive family farm with hogs, Holsteins, corn, and hay fields. As he awoke a "most peaceful feeling" engulfed him. Waking his wife, he told her, "We're not going back. We're going to stay." Hunt's creditors took no stock in the dreams of a broken man, though, and "everything [he] tried to do to make that dream come true, it just seemed like it turned to dust." Eventually he fell so far behind in his payments that his creditors repossessed the farm.

Hunt moved to Utah where he found stable work as a refrigeration mechanic at a military base and eventually was able to build "a beautiful home." Still, the dream of a family farm haunted his sleep, eventually pulling him back to the Columbia Basin because, as he explained to his wife, it was something "I've got to do." Back in the basin, Hunt applied for land in another government drawing but did not win. Determined to acquire a farm, he worked there as a refrigeration mechanic in packing plants, setting aside money to buy land. With some of his savings he purchased some Holstein calves on the coast, brought them back to the basin, fattened them on surplus french fries from the plant where he worked, and sold them at decent profit. With the proceeds he made a down payment on some land and hired someone to drill a well, hoping against odds to tap into a large aquifer that would facilitate irrigation. After drilling down 400 feet, he still was unable to pump enough water for his family's domestic needs. Again admitting defeat Hunt sold the place in the 1970s.

But the dream persisted. Hunt bought a rundown irrigated farm, moved a mobile home onto the land and began to fulfill his dreams. He "lived that dream, the very particular thing," except that doing so necessitated off-farm work. Hunt found a job to support his farming but lost it after attending a union meeting. Next he worked part time at a beet dump, and next on the graveyard shift at a potato factory, leaving little time for farming. One day he was loading a cow into a trailer, using the tail gate as a ramp. As Hunt was trying to lift the tail gate, the cow stepped back onto it, pinning Hunt underneath and crushing some of his vertebrae. He was placed in a cast for a year and told he would "never be able to lift more than five pounds." Unable to work, he lost his farm to creditors. He would never farm again although he did manage to salvage a small piece of ground for his home on a hilltop overlooking the fields he had once owned.[29]

Hunt's dogged devotion to his dream and the physical, emotional, and financial costs of it illustrate how deeply some veterans desired to farm and how devastating the failure of that dream could be. Wealth mattered little to Hunt; indeed he frittered away money in pursuit of a farm of his own in the hope that it would satisfy his dreams. Yet Hunt like every veteran who tried to farm in the postwar era needed some money to support his dream, and he never had enough of it. Money would have translated his dream into reality, even though the object of the dream itself was not wealth.

While financial crises and failures were common among settlers who deeply desired to farm, some veterans managed to broker their small farms into significant businesses. To the extent that money could buy their dreams they experienced enviable success. One of these successful homesteaders was Lowell Kenyon, a veteran who had flown thirty-eight combat missions for the air force during World War II. Kenyon was working as a commercial pilot when his name was drawn for a seventy-two-acre farm at Tule Lake. A native of the area, Kenyon was eager to return although he would be giving up a secure, stable job and income to do so. Kenyon seized the opportunity and worked in the off season in potato sheds in the area in order to supplement his meager farm income. He managed to set aside some money and borrowed more to buy out neighbors as they left; he limited his risk by leasing other ground. By 1962 he was farming over 150 acres of potatoes along with other crops, as well as working part time in the sheds. Through his continued work in the potato sheds Kenyon became familiar with the packing business. In 1962 after dabbling in the futures market, Kenyon's employer at the packing shed filed for bankruptcy and the shed closed. With Kenyon's contacts and experience and with the encouragement and backing of brokers he knew from Los Angeles, Kenyon mortgaged his farm and built his own shed in 1962, fifteen years after he had filed on his homestead. Potato prices were high that year, and Kenyon made good money, which he invested in new machinery. With his earnings in subsequent years he purchased and leased others' homesteads until he was farming close to 2,000 acres. In the early 1970s, profits were high enough that Kenyon was able to build a cold storage facility, offering him additional leverage with buyers. By the late 1970s he was operating entirely on a cash basis, carrying no debt. Kenyon purchased a twin engine Cessna and used it to fly to southern California, meet buyers there, bring them to his packing shed near the Oregon border for tours and negotiations, and then return them in a matter of hours to Los Angeles or San Diego. In 1983 he was elected president of the National Potato Board.[30] Rising land values added to the wealth and success of persistent farmers like Kenyon. In the Southwest, where crops could be grown year round, land values rose to dizzying heights. Land on the Gila Project that had sold in the 1950s for $200 per acre was worth as much as $6,000 an acre by the 1990s, and settlers like Jack Grout who had invested wisely, were worth millions.[31]

Some veterans embraced the market to the point that they measured their success or failure as farmers in dollars and acres. Money validated their efforts, provided fulfillment, and enhanced the comfort and security of life for themselves and their loved ones. Some maintained this economically oriented outlook throughout their careers. Others who initially had other priorities came to believe through the school of hard knocks that money mattered most. Yet financial success rang hollow for others like Dale Lorensen, who learned that money alone could not fulfill their deepest yearnings.

Lorensen moved to Idaho from California to homestead with "dreams . . . looking ahead" to "what we were going to have some day": a multigenerational family farm. At age forty-eight, he shared his hopes for the future with his seventeen-year-old son, inviting him to jointly operate the farm until Lorensen's seventieth birthday, when the son would become the sole proprietor. Lorensen expected the farm would not only support two households but also forge an enduring bond between father and son. Shortly after he struck this bargain with his son, Lorensen's health failed and he was hospitalized. When he was sufficiently well to come home he could neither bend over nor mount a tractor. All he could do was "crawl around [the farm] on [his] hands and knees," pointing out what had to be done. Lorensen's son was unable to farm the place alone, so Lorensen auctioned the machinery and livestock and sold the land. In a classic understatement he recalled, "That hurt."[32]

Lorensen did not blame his poor health on farming, but others did. As their health failed, some decided that success in farming as they had once defined it had come at too high a price. Lyle Esser mourned the loss of friends and neighbors in the Columbia Basin who had "worked themselves to death; a lot of them died in their 50s because they just worked . . . from before sunup in the morning 'til way after sundown at night" hardly ever eating "a regular meal" with their families. Ralph Wright, a dairyman who raised grain and hay for two decades on his homestead west of Boise, routinely worked eighteen or nineteen hour days during the growing season. In old age when his physical strength was fading he lamented, "I worked too blame hard and worked myself down."[33]

Farming and family were so closely linked in the minds of some homesteaders that a large, productive farm lost much of its significance when the family collapsed. Ed Hoff's primary objective was to build a lasting *family* farm. By business standards Hoff more than fulfilled his dreams. During Hoff's first year of homesteading, a researcher from the Department of Agriculture visited him and inquired about his aspirations. "You homesteaded this; what [are your] goals?" he asked. Hoff remembered replying, "If we had a 200 cow outfit, if I ever achieve that, it's all that I would want to achieve." Using his 120-acre homestead as a nucleus, he developed an 800-acre ranch with 460 mother cows. He pastured the cattle every summer on 400 acres adjoining the Payette River while he raised feed for the upcoming winter on 227 acres of irrigated land including the original homestead. Every autumn, Hoff and his son drove the cattle 18 miles from the river to the homestead. For Hoff's impressive achievements as a rancher he was named Canyon County Grassman of the Year by the Idaho Extension Service and Idaho Power Company. Hoff viewed the farm as a means of uniting his household in a common cause; in fact, he dreamed of one day passing the ranch on to his only son—his right-hand man on the farm. He and his three children worked together "very diligently on the farm" and together were "all very capable." They called their ranch the Spurline. Together they made, painted, and installed a large sign emblazoned with the ranch's name at the entrance to their property. Hoff's pride in his children was boundless. The death of Hoff's son at age twenty-one in an automobile crash in 1971, shortly before the boy was to be married, devastated the family and blasted their sense of common purpose and hope. After that "things went to hell," and ranching lost much of its meaning for Hoff. Without his son to help him "in the saddle" Hoff sold his cattle, leased out his land, and bought a home in town. The family "went further apart," and he and his wife, Agnes, eventually divorced. In 1998, Hoff felt "fortunate" to have saved the original homestead and he was still "proud" of his achievements as a rancher, but the ranch reminded him of many lost possibilities, too, and those losses made him "sad."[34]

Reviewing their farming careers in hindsight, others felt cheated by what they considered to be their shortsighted perspectives of yesteryear. Successful farming, the perceived vehicle to fulfillment of their dreams, had diverted their attention from the people they loved. Throughout his working life, Leon Machen was "totally devoted" to his work. His wife, Ruth, observed, "He has no hobbies, nothing at all except just work." Machen bred high-producing milk cows using artificial insemination and developed one of the most productive small dairies in the Boise region; his achievements buoyed him, but he developed ulcers from the stress and work of farming and was hospitalized three times in 1962. "It was just more than he could do to do all the field work and the dairy and everything," Ruth explained. Ironically, the family farm interfered with Machen's responsiveness to his family. "I didn't treat my family as good as I should have done," he believed. Although his wife had disliked farm life and feared animals he had doggedly persisted on the land until his health failed.[35]

If farm life could compete with personal and familial needs, it could also meet personal needs for peace, solitude, or development while yielding at least a modest income—at least some homesteaders perceived this to be the case in retrospect. The pleasures of life on his homestead included the chance to be surrounded by deer, pheasants, and other wildlife and to live in privacy and quiet, free from "boom boxes or a neighbor leaning over the back fence criticizing," remarked Glen Olsen. Most importantly, Olsen believed, home-

Bureau photographer Stan Rasmussen captured the centrality of home and hearth in this image of the Otto Jorstad family in their new living room on the Hunt Unit of the Minidoka Project, 19 April 1950. (Reclamation Photographs, NARA, Rocky Mountain Region)

steading had made him a better person. "I don't know if perhaps there were any [thing] that would have pushed me to the extent that homesteading did, as far as determining what kind of mettle I had. It is physically exhausting, and it's mentally draining because you always have more problems than you could really contend with. . . . [But] you can, over a long period of time . . . mold yourself into a position where some beneficial things can result." For Olsen, that was "the major benefit of homesteading."[36]

The land has always pandered to Americans' dreams; the second half of the twentieth century was no exception even though the amount of government land available for the taking was relatively small. Proving up and gaining title to land freed the homesteaders to pursue their dreams, using the land as leverage. Many behaved as speculators, quickly selling the land and moving on. Yet others expected more of their farms, dreaming of a comfortable standard of living, familial security and unity, personal fulfillment, character development, or an independent lifestyle. The costs associated with developing a farm and farming, along with the prospect of making money, made market obligations and opportunities central to the homesteaders' outlook and experiences. Yet in the pivotal era when market dominance supposedly became complete, many chose farming over other occupations because of what they hoped it would do for their family unity, familial security, character development, or personal satisfaction and fulfillment. Those intangibles required income, too, as Saron Minden and David Hunt learned, but they also depended upon the human element—a web of values and interpersonal relationships associated with the household and the family farm.

5 THE BEST YEARS OF THEIR LIVES? WOMEN ON WESTERN HOMESTEADS

While he was stationed in Iceland during World War II, Wally George often dreamed of life after the war. In a letter to his wife, Evaleen, he shared some of his dreams. Evaleen recalled, "He said he'd like to start out small, he'd like to be close to the mountains . . . and we could get a few cattle and . . . gradually build up. He would like us to get a home soon so that we wouldn't be living in an apartment." In 1998, ten years after Wally's death, Evaleen still liked to read that letter because it reminded her of her family's good fortune in acquiring their own dairy farm in the shadows of Heart Mountain in northern Wyoming. "You know, not a lot of people get to see their dreams fulfilled," she reflected; her husband had been one of the lucky ones. Shortly before Wally died, Evaleen took him for a drive so that he could gaze at the homestead once again. She would never forget the look of dreamy satisfaction that crossed his face as they inspected the fruits of their labor. At one point, Wally turned to her and said, "You know, Mama, this place has got[ten] to be just like I always dreamed."[1]

Wally's dreams of farm ownership, like those of thousands of veterans, nearly all of them male, were at least partly fulfilled in homesteading, as we have seen. Wally's choice of the singular pronoun "I" was telling, though. "This place has got[ten] to be just like I always dreamed," he exulted. But what of the dreams of women like Evaleen George whose husbands acquired a postwar homestead?

In planning postwar homesteading neither Congress nor the Bureau of Reclamation paid much attention to the attitudes, needs, or dreams of spouses who would homestead alongside the winning veterans. Examining boards scrutinized the fitness of male farm applicants, poring over their assets, employment history, farming experience, character, and industriousness, but they never formally considered the suitability of applicants' marital partners for homesteading. As we have seen, even in the case of married female veterans who applied in their own right, boards were as interested in documenting the inability of these women's husbands to support the family as in scrutinizing the women's qualifications. Thus the Bureau of Reclamation and its local examining boards reflected the broader biases of American society which, in the words of historian Sandra Schackel, "views farming as a male occupation" and has therefore often "ignored" farm women. As Katherine Jellison has observed, those biases grew in the years following World War II, an era when women's control over and involvement in traditional subsistence activities from gardening to poultry raising dwindled, giving men "even greater control" on the farm. Academic research at the time reflected these biases. As late as 1958, social scientist Murray A. Straus could identify "no empirical studies of the wife's role in successful [agricultural] settlement." That bias persisted in historical studies of irrigation. As Susan Armitage observed, historians portrayed the irrigated landscape almost exclusively as "Hisland."[2]

Even if government planners and academics did not bother to investigate the attitudes of prospective homesteaders' wives, folk wisdom acknowledged that those attitudes mattered. S. E. Hutton, one of the builders of Grand Coulee Dam on the Columbia Basin project, articulated this folk wisdom when he observed that a wife and children who harbored the same "hopes and ambitions" as the husband were one of the greatest assets a homesteader could exploit. Phyllis Gies, who homesteaded with her husband in Wyoming, recalled a common witticism that expressed the same concept: "Whether you end up with a nest egg or a goose egg depends upon the chick you're married to." In a study of postwar settlers in the Columbia Basin Murray Straus found that women on the most prosperous farms possessed significantly more "pioneering spirit," long-range perspective, willingness to endure inadequate equipment and facilities, and stoicism in the face of opposition than their counterparts on the least successful farms. Whether it reflected their husbands' actual abilities or their own docility, wives of successful farmers also expressed greater confidence in and trust of their husbands' managerial abilities than did the spouses of less prosperous farmers.[3]

Not only their attitudes but their work shaped the outcomes of homesteading. As Joan Jensen has observed, American farm women have been "active participants . . . in every period of agricultural history." Despite their active participation, most women as well as men on postwar homesteads perceived farming and homesteading as ideal measures of men but not of women. This was the case because, as Sandra Schackel has observed, rural women's "primary postwar role remained that of homemaker . . . according to prevailing cultural values." As was the case in rural America at large, women on homesteads usually tended the yards, gardens, and chicken coops, taking pride in those endeavors, but few women with children identified those activities as either their primary roles or as full-fledged farming. When women worked in the barns or the fields—real farming enterprises from their perspective—they generally did so under their husbands' direction and referred to that work as "helping" their husbands who were "farming." Even those like Norma Eppich Price who spoke of their work in the fields as "farming" did so in a patriarchal context wherein the crop redounded to their husbands' success: the wives who "were home farming with the men . . . their husbands were the successes," explained Price. "It took the wife and the kids to help." As Katherine Jellison has written, generally "the postwar farm woman's work in the field . . . was viewed merely as an extension of her role as dutiful wife."[4]

Women's attitudes and their work may have been consequential for the farm's success, but anthropologist Deborah Fink has argued that historically farm life has "offered little to most mothers" and that agrarianism in America has always been "a white male vision that failed to consider the full human integrity of other persons." By contrast, historian Barbara Handy-Marchello has argued that North Dakota farm women "did not view their roles as drudgery" or "express the desire for a very different life than they had lived." What did homesteading and agrarianism offer to women in the short term, and more fundamentally, in the long run?[5]

Views of hardships can change as time passes. Thus, reminiscences and life stories convey different perspectives than do contemporary documents like letters and diaries. Unquestionably, women on homesteads worked hard and did without modern conveniences. Bertie Snider, a Wyoming homesteader, attested, "We worked our butts off . . . and there were a lot of things we didn't do, or we did without." Yet the passage of time confers added perspective. Looking back upon her privation long after it had passed,

Snider reflected that it "d[id]n't seem so darn important" any more. Given the high premium most women on homesteads placed upon motherhood, Anna Kamm's analogy between homesteading and mothering is apt. When asked if she would do it again she reflected: "Well, you always say, 'Well I wouldn't go through that again,' like 'I wouldn't have five kids again for nothing.' Well, I wouldn't give any of them back. No, I think it [homesteading] was worth it."[6]

Whether or not with the benefit of hindsight they would homestead again if they could turn back the clock, some women, Evaleen George included, do not remember feeling their husbands' enthusiasm at the outset, notwithstanding Seena Kohl's contention that in the history of women in the West "there is no evidence that men and women did not share similar views regarding homestead settlement as a way to ensure a future for themselves and their children." "I wasn't sure that we had made a very good move," Evaleen George confessed. Likewise, Mary Rucker, who could see that her husband "just wanted to farm so bad" could not bring herself to embrace his ambition. "I couldn't believe that we would actually move over there. I couldn't believe he'd do that. . . . We had a nice home. . . . We bought it as a new home and fixed it just like we wanted it and then he tells me he's going to move me over there." Rucker "cried privately through one solid month" before the move. Facing stiff opposition from their wives, some veterans backed down. Over 40 percent of the 47 veterans whose names were initially drawn for farms on the Boise project turned down the offer, some of them renouncing their dreams of farming in order to preserve their marriages. Clyde Brummell, who was awarded a homestead in Jerome, Idaho, turned down the opportunity after his wife "decided we did not need to live in a tent until the first harvest."[7]

Conversely, some women maintain they embraced agrarianism and fully shared their companions' dreams from the outset. Mary Blackburn was "all excited" by the news that her husband's name had been drawn because she had always "wanted to get on a farm." Likewise, Phyllis Gies remembered feeling "elated" when her husband won a farm. Bertie Snider shared her husband's ambition: "We wanted to get out on our own." Alberta Jackson regarded homesteading "as an opportunity" because she wanted to live on a farm and knew that in eastern Colorado where she and her husband were living "young people who don't have any money and don't inherit any money have no opportunity to buy that land." Seven years into the homesteading

Alexander Brug drives away on his tractor to begin drilling operations on his Heart Mountain Division homestead while his wife, Betty, waves goodbye from their tent home, 29 April 1947. (Photograph by Charles Knell, Reclamation Photographs, NARA, Rocky Mountain Region)

venture, Betty Brug told a reporter that she had never been happier than in her first year of farming with her husband. "We were at it seven days a week, building the house, getting the crops in. We were never happier . . . because we were working together to make our dreams come true."[8]

In retrospect, others who would not have chosen a homesteader's life remembered feeling pleased *for their husbands* because their husbands' happiness mattered to them. Dorothy Hedrick, who had grown up in a small town in Illinois but had never lived on a farm, reasoned, "If that is what my husband wanted, fine . . . we'd try it." Pearl Mayfield could see how "very happy" her husband was with the prospect of homesteading in the Mojave Desert. She feared that it would be "hot and horrible" there but she acquiesced, believing that "the husband is the important one in the family, just like he's the one that's got to make a living. He should do what he has to do." Similarly, although the idea of homesteading near Powell, Wyoming, "didn't sound so big" to her, Pat Jones "went along" with the idea because she could see that her husband was "real happy" with the opportunity.[9]

Whether or not they were eager to homestead, most women remember being discouraged or intimidated by their first views of the land. This was especially the case in the deserts of Arizona and southern California. Mary Rucker was "totally unimpressed" with the Coachella Valley and its sandy soil, commenting that they had "better dirt than that" in their sand lot in Tucson. Even on projects where large sagebrush and native grasses dotted the landscape, the prospects seemed daunting. Virginia Reynolds took heart as she passed through Cody, Wyoming, with its green trees and lawns, but as she and her husband motored out of town into "nothing but dry sagebrush flats" she felt "devastated." Driving out onto a new division of Idaho's Minidoka Project in a convoy of other prospective homesteaders, Mildred Egbert thought that the dusty, windswept sagebrush plain "looked like the ends of the earth or worse." The powdery dirt "just sift[ed] up" around the cars. Wondering if she would always look "like a powder puff" if she moved there, she "want[ed] to go home and forget the whole thing." Recalling her first impressions of the brush-covered land that would become her home, Dora Adams confessed, "I hated it. I hated it. . . . I didn't like it. I never did for years and years."[10]

Some recall being as disappointed in the cultural environment as in the physical landscape. Shortly after she arrived in the Wellton Mohawk Valley, Windy Dobson drove to the nearest telephone, located 7 miles away in a ditch rider's shack. The home was "just a little makeshift thing that they'd put together themselves." As she crossed the threshold she saw a pet pig sprawled on a chaise lounge in the living room and thought, "Oh, dear! If this is what living in the Mohawk Valley is going to be, why, forget me." Nelda Haney was equally disturbed by the backwardness of old-timers in the vicinity of her homestead in the Columbia Basin who "hadn't been very far away from home" and "didn't know what was hardly going on." Soon after she moved to the basin, two old-timers came to call. "They set a sack of candy bars on the table and they said, 'This is for the kids.' And we looked at it and the candy bars had all gone white. They [were] probably twenty years old." The message of these retrospective accounts is clear: the physical and cultural landscapes on the homesteading frontier seemed inauspicious and alien, and the women felt out of place.[11]

Memories are selective, though, and it appears from documents produced

Barracks similar to these buildings from the Yuma Army Air Base were cut in half, placed on flatbed trailers, and hauled to many homesteads on the Gila Project for use as homes and outbuildings. The surrounding sandy terrain of Yuma Mesa, pictured here, appeared bleak and uninviting to many settlers. 22 September 1950. (Photograph by S. B. Watkins, Reclamation Photographs, NARA, Rocky Mountain Region)

at the time that practical rather than aesthetic concerns were uppermost in most women's minds when they first viewed the land they would homestead. "It certainly looks like a lot of work to me," Mrs. Walter Klosterman, of Iowa, told a reporter following a tour of the Minidoka Project. Jane Grosch told the same reporter that she was "thrilled" but also "scared." On the other hand a woman from Illinois whose uncle had moved to nearby Twin Falls and liked it there offered nothing but praise for the land: "It's wonderful country. And it looks like a healthier country, too [than Illinois]."[12]

Within six months of selecting their homesteads, the veterans were required by law to relocate on them. Some wives moved at the same time as their partners, but many remained behind for several months while their husbands arranged housing for the family. By doing so they enabled their children to finish the school year before moving or helped to bankroll the new homestead by working for wages or selling property. At least one couple reversed the usual pattern of husbands moving before their wives: Roy Rucker continued working in Tucson to finance his homestead, commuting 600 miles on weekends, while his wife, Mary, and their five children complied with the homesteading residency requirements by moving into a crowded two-room house on their "farm." For seven months, Roy was seldom there except on weekends.[13]

Wives who accompanied their husbands rather than waiting behind until semipermanent housing was available occupied trailers, tents, the closest motels, apartments in town, barracks left over from Japanese internment, or shacks that had been hastily moved to the homestead. Ted and Phyllis Gies rented a fifty-year-old log cabin near Riverton, Wyoming. The rustic home excited their six-year-old son—it looked like something out of the Wild West—but didn't seem "that nice to me," Phyllis recalled. Skunks lived beneath the cabin floor, and after the neighbor's dogs "got in there and riled up all the skunks," the odor was too strong for the Gieses to remain. Hastily gathering food, clothing, and "whatever we had to have," they moved into a house that was still under construction. That night the temperature outside plunged below zero. The unfinished house still had cracks in the roof, but Phyllis and Ted built a fire in the stove, wrapped their children in blankets, and "spent the night putting up sheet rock to close it in so it would be a little bit warmer."[14]

Some homesteaders in the Columbia Basin initially occupied 16 x 16–foot military surplus Quonset "hutments" with toilet paper stuffed into cracks in the walls for insulation. "If the wind blew the streamers came out," remembered Norma Eppich Price. With all of their belongings crammed into such a tiny space, the makeshift homes were crowded. Price had boxes of bottled fruit and vegetables stacked in one corner of her "hutment," boxes of clothes in another, and three open shelves where she stored her dishes. A cook stove provided heat. In short, "everything was pretty quaint."[15]

Such primitive living conditions offered women a strong incentive for building more substantial homes. Although husbands were generally responsible for housing, either arranging for contractors to do the work or doing it themselves, many women participated. They would, after all, be spending more of their time at home than their husbands and, like most

Mr. and Mrs. John Burns lay brick for their new home on the Yakima Project while their daughter Patricia holds the trowel. The photographer noted, "Since moving to their unit, the Burns have centered most of their attention upon improving living conditions." (Reclamation Photographs, NARA, Rocky Mountain Region)

American farm women in the 1950s, they identified homemaking as a primary role. After logs for their new home in Wyoming arrived, for instance, Nora Bovee stripped or "peeled" their outer bark. On the same project, Ruth Otto salvaged brick for their home's foundation from chimneys at the Heart Mountain Japanese relocation camp and then mixed mortar while her father and husband laid the brick. Alberta and Bill Jackson worked together in building their home, too. "Everything we did, we did together. I learned how to drive nails and saw boards and everything else," she recalled.[16]

Women also generally took charge of beautifying the yard surrounding their new homes—sometimes by default. Ted Gies "didn't think a yard was necessary," but Phyllis Gies wanted one so she hauled a load of sheep manure home, dumped it in the yard, spread it, mixed it into the soil, and "put in a yard and a garden" complete with rosebushes. On the Minidoka Project in southern Idaho, Laverda Allen planted 400 seedling fruit trees and evergreens "all by myself" because her husband was occupied with work in the fields. Beautifying a yard was not a priority for all women, though. Mary Blackburn "never planted a lot of flowers [and] never had much of a garden."[17]

Women almost always took the lead in decorating their homes, too. Verna Poore painted the interior of her home—a discouraging task in a desert valley where the wind blasted the walls with sand before the paint could dry—Lola Frank made curtains for her windows, Virginia Reynolds "put down a few rugs and put some pictures up," and Barbara Patterson papered the walls of her home. At Yuma Mesa, where women organized a club shortly after their arrival, they used club meetings as a forum for sharing their experiences and accomplishments in finishing and beautifying their homes with one another. "We'd come to a meeting and somebody'd say, 'Oh, we got such-and-such a room painted this week and we were able to put up some drapes.' Any time anyone got some kind of an improvement you were just thrilled with each other," recalled one participant. The emphasis her American female neighbors placed upon decorating the interior of their homes surprised Mrs. Bill Ross, who had grown up on the Australian frontier in Queensland before marrying a GI and moving to a Wyoming homestead. Unlike homesteaders' quarters in the United States, most houses where she came from were "not decorate[d]" and the walls were "mostly bare," she told a reporter. It seemed strange to her that so many of her female neighbors devoted so much time that might have been used more productively to beautification.[18]

Even after layers of wallpaper or coats of paint had been applied, many of the more permanent homes built by homesteaders were still fairly primitive, initially lacking electricity, indoor plumbing, or furnaces. Most women found this aspect of the great American homesteading dream repulsive. Virginia Reynolds described her first home in the Big Horn Basin as "liveable" but explained "that there are two different [definitions] of liveable. There is liveable what you have, and liveable what you would like and what you are used [to]." Those who were "used to the modern conveniences" had the greatest difficulty. Claire White had grown up in a comfortable farm home in the Midwest and had spent her early married life in a high-rise apartment in Chicago. "I wasn't quite ready for it when we came out here," she explained. "I wanted to be a city gal." Some like Mary Blackburn who had already lived in homes without conveniences claimed that it was fairly easy to adjust to the lack of plumbing and electricity. Most women disagreed. The adjustment was "rough" for anyone, believed Nora Bovee, who had grown up in a primitive sod house in South Dakota. While their friends and acquaintances who lived elsewhere enjoyed electricity, running water, nice yards, and modern homes, "we didn't have all the things that we thought we should have," and that made it "pretty hard emotionally," explained Barbara Patterson.[19]

Wives tended to miss electricity more than their husbands did because many of their routine household tasks were harder without it. Ruth Otto believed the absence of electrical appliances was the greatest challenge women faced on a modern homestead. In the California desert, not having a refrigerator "was kind of bad," explained Pearl Mayfield because she could not store perishable items. Even in colder climes Dorothy Hedrick found it hard to prepare meals for special occasions without a refrigerator. When she received a card in the mail announcing that a friend intended to visit that evening, Dorothy decided to prepare a nice dinner for her. Her husband had their only vehicle, though, and she had no meat on hand because she had no way of keeping it cold. Having seen her husband catch a chicken and pop off its head, she decided to do that. Having failed in the attempt, she then tried to chop off the head but "didn't chop [it] all the way through" before "the chicken jumped up and ran" with blood "just squirting" everywhere. With the help of a dog she apprehended the chicken, finished the job, cleaned the chicken, baked it, and had dinner waiting when her friend arrived.[20]

Lacking electricity, most women cooked on wood and coal stoves. "You started out like your grandma did" with "an old cook stove," Ruth Otto explained. When the supply of coal ran low, Norma Eppich began burning sagebrush in her stove because she and her husband were too poor to buy fuel. The brush burned too hot and fast for baking, though. Others cooked on coal oil camp stoves, particularly in places like Yuma Mesa where the heat of a wood stove would have been unbearable for much of the year. Yuma Mesa homesteader Myrtle Paulsen was accustomed to cooking on electric stoves and was "scared to death" to light her coal oil camp stove, fearing that it would explode. Unless her husband was home to light the stove for her, she refused to cook. Anxiety about kerosene lamps, camp stoves, and wood stoves was warranted; after visiting homesteads at Heart Mountain in 1954 a reporter noted that "house fires are an ever-present hazard." At least four veterans' homes had already caught fire on the project.[21]

With no electricity, water also had to be hauled, complicating tasks such as laundering clothes. Water for bathing and washing clothes was taken from the irrigation ditch during the summer and heated on the stove. Drinking water had to be hauled longer distances year round. In the winter water for all purposes had to be brought in. Anna and Earl Nelson filled a large metal garbage can with water whenever they went to town and wedged it between the front and back seats of their car to transport it. "If you filled it too full you had water all over the car," recalled Anna. Husbands were often responsible for trucking water over long distances, but many women routinely hauled water from nearby irrigation ditches for laundry, walking dozens of miles yearly in all kinds of health. "We carried our water from the pump into the house, every drop that we used, and it was pretty hard to do when you are sick and couldn't walk. You had two kids to keep clean and get to school and everything and a baby. Why it was pretty tough," explained Dora Adams.[22]

Whether or not they had hauled the water the women were responsible for heating it—no small task. Ruth Otto and her husband purchased a gasoline-powered washing machine. Before he left in the morning Ruth's husband would start the motor so that she could begin washing as soon as she had heated enough water on her cook stove. Unfortunately, the motor often stopped before the job was finished, and try as she might, Ruth could never restart it. "I had to take all the water out of the machine and put it back on the stove and heat it. Then when he'd come home, he'd start it." Women were also responsible for washing the clothing once the water had been heated—including diapers. Joan Casper had three children in diapers and no bathroom or running water in her first house in the Columbia Basin. "That was kind of a struggle," she said with characteristic understatement.[23]

After months or even years without electrical service, the arrival of electricity was a red-letter event and marked a significant turning point for many women on their homesteads. As Pearl Mayfield, who spent eleven months in the California desert without electric power for lights, an air conditioner, or water pump, stated, "life was much easier" with electricity. She had vowed that if she "ever had electricity and water I'd never complain about another thing in my life," and she never forgot the vow, even if she didn't honor it fully. One woman recalled cooking "a whole meal of just toast" after waiting for five months for electricity because "it was so nice to have a toaster." After living five years without electricity, with no electric vacuum, refrigerator, radio, or washing machine, Edna McClaflin celebrated the arrival of electricity on Christmas Eve by stringing electric lights on the Christmas tree. "We were so anxious to get the electricity," she recalled.[24]

The lack of electricity on homesteads was not the only factor complicating women's efforts to keep themselves, their families, their laundry, their dishes, and their homes clean and proper. Not all women placed a premium upon cleanliness, but many measured their success as homemakers partly by the appearance of themselves and their surroundings. Unfortunately for them, dirt and dust were omnipresent on the homesteads as new lands were being cleared of native vegetation and placed under the plow. Keeping a clean house in the Tule Lake area was "next to impossible," explained Barbara Krizo. In the Columbia Basin, "the air was just full of dirt. It was hard to get along," recalled Norma Eppich Price. Sandstorms in the desert east of Yuma arose always, it seemed, "right after you did a really good job of cleaning," Myrtle Paulsen recalled. West of Yuma in the California desert, Verna Poore "had a few tearful times" after the pockets in freshly laundered clothing filled with blowing sand while hanging on a clothesline.[25]

The inability to stay clean was "one of the hardest things" about homesteading, believed Eileen Buckingham of Tule Lake. "You'd get yourself fixed up as well as you could and then wade out through the barley stubble to the car. By the time you got there, you weren't fixed up any more." Frances Johnson, who lived on the same project, had grown up in the area, and knew from the outset that dust was a fact of life there, but "a lot" of women, including one of her close friends, pressed their husbands to sell out and leave their homesteads, partly because of "the mud and the crud"—they "could not tolerate not being real, real clean."[26]

In addition to dirt, the abundance of insects, snakes, rodents, and other animals in or under their homes annoyed and sometimes frightened homemakers. One woman living on a Yuma Mesa homestead found "black widows all over the house." Another feared putting her baby on the floor because black widows were so common. One evening Norma Eppich was heating water in her small "hutment" in Pasco, Washington, and preparing to wash the dishes. Reaching for the dish drainer, which was suspended from a nail on the wall, she nearly grabbed a snake that was "sticking out" through it. She had seen the snake before in the yard and knew it was not poisonous—her husband had refused to kill it because it was a good mouser—but Eppich was nevertheless "scared to death." Racing outside, she grabbed her son, who was playing under a tree, jumped into the car, and

A newly developed farm in the Columbia Basin. Primitive living quarters made housekeeping difficult on a homestead. Dust blowing off the land seeped into bedding and laundry. (Reclamation Photographs, NARA, Rocky Mountain Region)

drove toward her husband who was working in a distant field. When the road ended and she could drive no further, she left her son in the car and waded out into the fields, the sandy soil "just powder dry clear to [her] knees," screaming for her husband to kill the snake.[27]

Homesteading complicated not only women's housework but also their maternal responsibilities. Given the centrality they and their families attached to their role as mothers, it was only natural that women would weigh the challenges and opportunities of homesteading in light of its implications for their children. Limited access to medical care, especially when unimproved roads were blocked by snow or rendered impassable by rain, frightened many mothers. During the winter of 1950, when Edith Powers's son lapsed into convulsions, she had no way to transport him from their snowbound homestead in southern Idaho to the doctor in Twin Falls and no means even of telephoning for help. Mothers in such circumstances simply had to improvise as best they could. When Edna McClaflin's son Wayne suffered a severe asthma attack at home during a Wyoming blizzard the only thing she felt she could do for him was "kneel down beside the kid's bed and pray for him." Many expectant mothers took precautions to avoid being stranded when their time came, temporarily moving to town or even returning to their parents' homes shortly before their babies were due. Some who failed to take precautions were marooned when they went into labor. When Bill Nolan's wife began experiencing hard labor pains on their farm in eastern Washington one night in mid-January, drifting snow had blocked the road to town. Bill got his wife into the car and managed to maneuver it through a 20-foot drift, but then the engine died and refused to turn over again. Leaving his wife in the car—it was 15 degrees below zero outside—he raced on foot to the nearest farm home and knocked and yelled frantically until the occupants awakened and agreed to try to drive the Nolans to the hospital. After plowing through several drifts they reached Mrs. Nolan, who "was nearly froze[n]" and doubled over with pain after having been stranded in the snowbound car for nearly two hours.[28]

Mothers worried that not only the isolation but also the poorly insulated buildings on their homesteads threatened their children's health, particularly in the case of infants. Lola Frank, whose baby was born during their first winter in northern Wyoming, became concerned when bottles of milk left overnight in her baby's bassinet froze solid. To keep the baby warm while she bathed him, she opened the oven door of her wood-burning stove and placed the bathtub on a card table nearby. Ruth Otto of the same project spent the winter in Nebraska visiting relatives after her baby was born, fearing that "it was too cold" in their cabin for the infant.[29]

Nearly every homesteader had at least one encounter with a rattlesnake, and many mothers especially worried that their children might be harmed by a rattler. One morning Mary Rucker glanced outside and saw a coiled diamondback rattler 10 feet from her two youngest children. Alone with the children, she "had no way to do anything except to chop his head off with a hoe," and, steeled by adrenalin, she quickly did so. Virginia Reynolds was so frightened of snakes that she only got close enough to kill one in over fifty years on her Wyoming farm. Normally, she would have avoided the snake entirely, but because her children would soon be arriving home from school and walking down the lane where the snake was sunning itself, she felt she had to act. Her fear for her children's safety was "the only reason I had the courage to kill that snake."[30]

While the practical hardships of being a homemaker and mother on a homestead were substantial, they were compounded by the isolation and loneliness that many women felt, particularly those with small children, in their first few months on the farm. In their histories of rural America scholars have disagreed regarding the extent to which women on homesteads felt isolated. The debate is possible in part because women's experiences with loneliness varied depending upon their stage in the life cycle; those with infants and small children were more confined to the home than were childless women or mothers with older children.[31]

The fact that women struggled with loneliness even in an era when motor vehicles and radio reduced the isolation of their farms suggests that feelings of isolation on earlier frontiers in the first phases of settlement were acute. One woman who homesteaded with her husband east of Yuma likened her loneliness to hunger pangs: "we were so hungry for people, friends," she recalled. Men felt lonely, too, but wives were more isolated than their husbands. Establishing a home and farm left them with little time for visiting, and in some cases their husband had the only car or truck, leaving them with no way to get out for a short visit. In her first months on the Minidoka Project, Mildred Egbert recalled, her husband always "seemed to be so busy and tired." For her, physical exhaustion was secondary to being "homesick" and depressed because she had no visitors to relieve her from the monotony of her routine for weeks on end. As another homesteader on the same project, George Falkner, explained, "The men actually got acquainted borrowing each others' tools and helping each other and just visiting on the ditch," but the women were occupied with matters at home and therefore "did not at first get out and mix as much." Visiting a household on the Hunt Division in 1950, a journalist found a similar situation. The husband, Rolly Powers, was well known to his neighbors, having traded equipment with them and having met them at Farm Bureau meetings and agricultural training courses sponsored by the Veterans' Administration. But his wife, Edith, "pregnant annually the first years on the project" and very busy at home, "was not too well known." Her busy schedule at home had made her a "virtual shut-in."[32]

Women's social isolation was compounded by the lack of telephones, the absence of electricity (those who lacked a battery-powered radio could tune in to the airwaves only when they were in the car), and the distance separating them from parents and members of their extended families. For instance, the first years of homesteading in Idaho were "hard" for Ercell Flood partly because "she was very close to her mother" in Nebraska. Myrtle Paulsen, a new bride from Iowa who moved to Yuma Mesa, "bawled all the time" because she missed her parents' home so much. Although Paulsen, a young wife with no children to care for, was able to return to Iowa for a few weeks while her husband held down the farm, other women were not so fortunate. Evaleen George remained on the Shoshone Project for five years without visiting her relatives—an era she downplayed as merely a "disappointing time" in her life. The work rhythms of farming kept many homesteading families—particularly those who established dairy farms—close to the farm. As Ruth Machen explained, "With a dairy farm you are tied; it's seven days a week. You could never get away."[33]

Rudimentary housing, the necessity of performing housework without running water or electricity, scant protection from extreme temperatures, the omnipresence of dirt and dust, pests such as snakes and insects, hazardous conditions, isolation from medical care, and loneliness weighed heavily upon many women on homesteads. Although they recognized that earlier generations of homesteaders had faced even greater privation and isolation, their own struggles were particularly jarring in the postwar era because the general standard of living in America was rising so rapidly, creating a vast contrast between their circumstances and those of their relatives and friends who lived elsewhere. Barbara Patterson admitted, "At times it got pretty hard. When you'd come to Powell [a nearby town] everybody had electricity, water and everything, and we didn't have much out there . . . We didn't have all the things that we thought we should have 'cause our friends had it all." When combined with the precarious financial standing of many homesteaders, these pressures exacted a heavy price psychologically and "probably helped some marriages break up" although they "ma[d]e others stronger," believed Joan Casper, who homesteaded with her husband near Basin City, Washington.[34]

The pressures of life on a homestead physically and emotionally overwhelmed some women. Reared on farms in western Wyoming and eastern Idaho, Ruth Machen disliked farm animals and had decided after observing her parents that farming was "too much work, too much worry. . . . It just takes so much out of you." Her husband, Leon, became convinced that a homestead in western Idaho was his ticket to prosperity, though, and she reluctantly acquiesced. Living conditions were primitive. When Ruth's mother visited she "just kind of shook her head. . . . Everybody thought this was just about the end." Unable to stand being on the farm day in and day out, Ruth quickly took a full-time job in town "to keep [her] sanity." At age twenty-eight, the disappointments and privations of farming, coupled with other stresses, pushed her to the brink emotionally and she suffered a nervous breakdown. Ruth made a comeback, but it was not easy. Candidly and courageously summing up her experiences, Ruth reflected, "I am not a pioneer. I will never pioneer again. . . . I keep thinking there are easier ways to make a living and enjoy life along the way somewhere."[35]

Few women suffered emotionally to the extent that Ruth Machen did, but many who left their homesteads after a few years share her assessment that it was not worth the effort. That conviction on the part of wives, some believed, undergirded many couples' decisions to give up on homesteading: although factors including economic reverses, illness, and attractive opportunities elsewhere impelled some families to leave their homesteads, Bill Hosokawa, a journalist who visited the Bureau's Shoshone Project in 1954, found that "it is generally agreed that among couples who have left the project, dissatisfaction on the wife's part was usually the underlying reason." If folk wisdom was correct, women wielded decisive power over their families' decision to remain on the homestead or to depart.[36]

While women allegedly cast the deciding vote in many households in the matter of farm abandonment, over one-third of the families who homesteaded in the postwar era remained on their homesteads for at least two decades, with women playing pivotal roles in that outcome, too. In 1950 Rolly Powers attributed his persistence on his homestead in southern Idaho to his wife, Edith. He recalled that after his first night and day of irrigating in southern Idaho he had seriously considered giving up. Edith had taken his cracked hands, "tenderly coated on Vaseline," wrapped his swollen fingers in torn sheets, and "insist[ed] that he not blame himself for inexperience, that everyone had a lot to learn." Her encouragement offered him the "fresh resolve" to return to the fields each day. By her own account, Ruth Otto practically insisted that her husband, Loran, remain on their homestead in Wyoming when he suggested that they should give up and move back to Nebraska. Ruth "really held out," remonstrating that Loran was "crazy" to want to go back to Nebraska where they had no irrigation water. She won. They remained on the farm until they retired. Similarly, when Anna Nelson's father-in-law encouraged her husband to sell his homestead and invest the money in the bank she "listened to [it] about as long as I could" and then retorted, "Well, that's fine [i]f he wants to put it up for sale, but I bet he's going to have to find some old bachelor that wants a wife and four kids." That was the end of the discussion.[37]

The persistence of large numbers of families was attributable not only to attitudes and advice but also to the economic contributions of wives, including their involvement in agricultural production. As we have seen, women cleared, fenced, plowed, and planted land, particularly in the early years as the farm was being developed. After the farm was established, some women continued to work regularly with their husbands in the fields or in the barn—a trend that increased nationwide during the 1950s as the number of hired hands on family farms dropped. A survey of groups of settlers on the Columbia Basin Project published in 1958 showed that 33–44 percent of the wives in various groups "helped with farm work." The homesteaders were typical farm women in this respect; a survey of Iowa farm women conducted in 1958 for *Wallace's Farmer* showed that 38 percent of the respondents worked on the farm. The amount of farmwork women on homesteads did depended partly upon the number and ages of their children, becoming more frequent as children "got a little older and went to school," recalled Claire White of Heart Mountain. Still, "there weren't very many of the women who didn't work some, work as far as the farming was concerned." White, who had no children, worked "full time" as a "farmhand" on their land. On the same project, Ruth and Loran Otto "worked together just an awful lot," taking their children out into the fields with them. Likewise, Joan Casper "was out there with us" in the fields, her husband, Bill, recalled. He thought she was "the best four-bottom plow operator on a 135 horsepower tractor there was in the country." Although her husband spent more time in the fields than she did because of her responsibilities in the house, Norma Eppich toiled regularly in the fields, planting, hoeing, cultivating, and driving a tractor—whatever her husband assigned her to do. Evaleen George, who operated a dairy with her husband, milked twice a day for over thirty-eight years and estimated that she routinely spent 8–10 hours per day in the barn.[38]

Even many women who did not normally work in the fields assisted at harvest time or in tasks where two people were needed. On Yuma Mesa, Eliot Waits enlisted his wife's help in loading and hauling hay: Mrs. Waits would

Homesteader Eleanor Bolesta posed on a tractor for this photograph in March 1947. She applied for a homestead because "if you're raised on a farm or if you're born in the generation I was, having land is a kind of security nothing else quite meets." Bureau regulations stipulated that only heads of households could qualify for a homestead, so Bolesta, a married woman, encountered tough scrutiny from the examining board. The photographer noted, "Mrs. Bolesta, despite the fact that she does not look the part, can handle a tractor efficiently." (Photograph by J. E. Fluharty, Reclamation Photographs, NARA, Rocky Mountain Region)

drive their tractor and trailer through the fields, Eliot would hoist hay bales onto the trailer, and then she would haul the hay to the roadside where "she would get up on the trailer and roll the bales off" to him. During the potato harvest at Tule Lake, Joe Victorine drove a tractor with a potato sacker, which dug potatoes and lifted them up to a conveyor belt where his wife, Mary, removed the dirt clods from them before the potatoes fell into the sack. While the sugar beet harvest was underway in the Big Horn Basin everyone helped, and there were "more women driving [sugar beet trucks] than men," Claire White recalled.[39]

Although working in the fields was more common, a small group of women supplied much of the operating income for the farm by working in town—largely a "new phenomenon" in American farm families in the 1950s. One study completed early in the 1950s reported that 10 percent of Illinois farm women worked for wages. Pearl Mayfield, who had no children to care for, always worked as a bookkeeper and accountant, providing what she called "a stable source of income" that was particularly important before their vineyards and orchards began producing fruit. Claire White, who had worked with her husband on the farm for several years, went to work in town as a clerk when they had several bad years on the farm. As Dorothy Hedrick, a young mother who worked off the farm, recalled, though, "not too many women . . . worked outside the home" if they had young children. In a random sample of farm families in the Columbia Basin in 1958, under one-fifth of the wives worked for wages. Young mothers who did work, like Hedrick, justified their labor as an extension of their parental role, because their salary "helped to buy the groceries" for the family.[40]

Women usually took charge of planting and caring for the vegetable garden if the family had one. As an extension of their household responsibilities, women had traditionally been responsible for growing and preserving food. These duties were all part of being "a good farm wife," many believed. As Edna McClaflin explained, "The yard and garden were my department." Due to specialization on farms, increased commercial canning, and commercially produced frozen food, the proportion of farm wives who gardened or canned food decreased in the postwar era; still most of the women on western homesteads grew and bottled food: in 1957, Murray Straus divided a random sample of 210 settlers on irrigated farms in the Columbia Basin into six groups based upon their economic success. He found that 56 percent of the least successful group had a vegetable garden, compared to 83 percent of the most successful subset. Wives of the most successful farmers canned an average of 350 quarts each year, compared to an average of 67 quarts for the least successful group.[41]

In addition to gardening and canning, many women raised chickens and marketed fryers and eggs. For instance, Barbara Patterson of Heart Mountain ordered 300 baby chicks each spring and kept them in a brooder house until they were ready to lay eggs. Then she moved them into the hen house; moved the old hens out; and slaughtered, dressed, and marketed them. "That was my project," she explained. Such work had traditionally belonged to women, although the proportion of American farm women who raised chickens plummeted during the postwar era.[42]

Ironically, women's involvement in food production on homesteads and on farms generally, which was valued by their families, was often ignored or discounted by off-farm observers. Social scientist Murray Straus in 1958 documented farm wives' persistent yet economically "irrational" involvement in gardening, reasoning that if women spent more time working under their husbands' direction in the fields or took a job in town, the economic returns would be greater. Some averred that food could be purchased more cheaply than it could be grown in home gardens or that frozen foods were preferable to bottled fruit and vegetables. Under these circumstances, gardening and preserving food was seen as no longer "practical" by some experts like Straus. The fact that Straus himself found that prosperous farm families were more likely than unprosperous ones to have a vegetable garden and to bottle large quantities of fruit and vegetables suggests that he and others may have been too quick to discount the economic value of these activities. As Deborah Fink has observed, the "basis" for the capitalist family farm has lain to a far greater degree than most agricultural pundits have admitted in "subsistence production and women's labor"—factors that have economically enabled families to live on commercial farms. In most cases women working in town could have earned more money than the value of food they produced in their gardens, but gardening and canning were nevertheless practical household activities that allowed them to harmonize their traditional roles and expectations; they could produce nutritious food for their families, reduce expenditures for food, and promote their family's health without separating themselves from their children. Such activities permitted them to defy urban middle-class norms that were increasingly segregating economic activity and productive labor from motherhood and homemaking.[43]

Wives on western homesteads also often ran farm errands for their husbands, picking up parts or recruiting help in town. As Laverda Allen of the Minidoka Project explained, such responsibilities took precedence even over a woman's central homemaking roles; she often had to leave her housework "half done" to "drive ten miles, or even twenty in search of a replacement for a broken loader chain or a do-dad for the whatchamacallit." Likewise, when her husband "got stumped with some project," Ruth Otto of Heart Mountain was in charge of "find[ing] somebody who knew how to do whatever the project was, any machine or whatever."[44]

When their husbands were ill or out of town, wives and their children managed the entire farm. Virginia Reynolds's husband periodically worked on construction projects in Wyoming and Montana to supplement the farm income. When he was home, her "responsibility was the home," but when he was out of town, "of course I had to oversee the farm."[45]

Although most women occasionally filled in for their husbands, they insist in interviews that they regulated their own contributions, limiting their involvement as they saw fit by rarely if ever engaging in "men's work" if their husbands were there. John Mack Faragher has argued that farmers on earlier frontiers engaged in "the exploitation of women as wives," using their labor to reduce their own work regimen and free them for recreational pursuits and politics. In light of these modern farm women's agency, their influence, and the pride they expressed in their work, Faragher's generalization poorly describes men's and women's interdependence on homesteads in the mid-twentieth century. Certainly husbands benefited from their wives' work, sometimes disproportionately, but wives also benefited from their husbands' labor, sometimes disproportionately. Although power dynamics varied among households, women by virtue of their husbands' dependence upon them exerted influence over the division of labor. The work women performed on the farm—including clearing and fencing land, plowing and disking fields, harvesting crops, operating farm machinery, running errands, growing gardens, raising chickens, marketing eggs, and managing the entire farm when their husbands were unable to do so—was vital. Confident that their contributions mattered, many women used normative gender roles to their advantage, refusing to engage in certain onerous tasks. Most, although not all, women on postwar homesteads viewed irrigation as men's work and let their husbands know that they generally would not irrigate, just as most also refused to milk cows. Virginia Reynolds "occasionally" helped her husband by driving a tractor or doing other farmwork, but "that wasn't a standard thing." Once when her husband asked her to milk so that he could go to town she "looked him straight in the eye and said, 'Beldon, I don't go out and milk.'" Dorothy Hedrick "never did milk very much," either. She also rarely drove a tractor because doing so was very difficult for her. Lola Frank occasionally drove a tractor but "didn't do the hard physical labor." Pressured by creditors who wanted him to have a consistent income, Ruby Van Zant's husband purchased a dozen milk cows. Although her husband "hated" to milk she insisted that he as the farmer do the work. "I just said, 'I'm not going to milk them,'" she recalled.[46]

If we can believe their husbands, at least some women chafed at being unable to do more on the farm. Wilbur Andrew's wife taught school during the first six years they lived on their homestead in Idaho. Although she thought he was "being mean" by not taking advantage of her assistance on the farm, Andrew "thought it completely stupid that she put her labor in to keep the farm going when she could earn twice what [he] was paying a man to do the work that she was doing." She had "a hard time understanding that."[47]

In a patriarchal culture in which men were the farmers and women helped on the farm women occupied a subordinate position in farm management as well as farm ownership. Bob Fagerberg, a settlement specialist for the Bureau of Reclamation who worked closely with homesteaders in northern Wyoming, likened the wives to hired hands: "many of the wives were the hired men of the farmer because they just weren't able to hire. Maybe the exceptions to that would be the women who were city born and so forth that were not acquainted with farm machinery." As Deborah Fink has observed, the meaning scholars attach to "the entailed differences between husband and wife" gives rise to their "disagreement between a rosy assessment and a negative assessment" of the interdependence of men and women on farms. At least in the case of women who settled on homesteads after World War II, the negative assessment is largely a scholarly imposition. Few women on modern homesteads viewed these realities as exploitative ones that robbed them of their volition or denied them satisfaction. Assertions of agency and expressions of pride in their achievements punctuate their reminiscences. "You just learned to work together. I know when we were working in the beet field, I put in just as long of hours as he did because he dug the beets and I hauled them and most of the time he got inside the house

Holding hands, Lola and Ignatius "Frank" Frank gaze over their newly selected homestead on the Shoshone Project, with Heart Mountain in the background. "We came out here on the 14th of February [to pick a unit] and we knew we were coming to the end of the world. We packed. We brought sheepskin coats and overshoes and blankets and everything. When we got here, it was beautiful. In fact, I wore a suit all the while I was here. I didn't have a winter [coat] on. It was beautiful. . . . We didn't realize what it would entail at first," remembered Lola. (Photograph by C. L. Conway, 14 February 1947, Reclamation Photographs, NARA, Rocky Mountain Region)

first, before I did anyway, 'cause you'd get stuck down at the beet dump. But I loved it, I wouldn't miss it. I am still driving a beet truck. I'm sixty-seven years old. I hope they let me drive until I am seventy," boasted Edna McClaflin.[48]

Most who remained on or near their homesteads, rearing their families there and working to make the farm succeed, claim today that with the benefit of hindsight they would still do it all over again. Lola Frank was typical of many, admitting that her life was difficult but fulfilling rather than tragic: "I believe I would do it again. There were hardships, but in every walk of life you have certain hardships. . . . And it was a rewarding experience. Homesteading has been good for us really."[49] These women claim that homesteading possessed compensatory benefits that outweighed the hard work and privation.

Some viewed work on the farm as fulfilling in and of itself. When Phyllis Gies's husband, Ted, was about to retire he announced, "I'm done farming," but Phyllis retorted, "I'm not. You've got to buy me a big enough place I could continue to farm." Women were particularly proud of the vegetables and fruit that they grew and preserved. Through ingenuity, hard work, and judicious watering Violet Hurlburt managed to grow beautiful fruit and vegetables in the Tule Lake Basin, where it can freeze every month of the summer. Modestly, she deemed her successful gardening and her consequent ability to share fruit and vegetables with her neighbors to be "about all I ever did good."[50]

Some women credited a healthy self-image and mental outlook to their farmwork. Jo Miller, who had grown up in a family of five girls in Iowa and had regularly helped her father in the fields, "loved" fieldwork. When her only child turned one, she hired a woman to care for her daughter and to do the housework because "I really do enjoy working outside. . . . it was better than housework." Bob and Deloris Fram were dairy farmers when Bob was gored by a bull. Up until that time, Deloris, who had grown up on a dairy farm, had refused to do the milking. "He came in, and I was down . . . scrubbing the floor on my hands and knees and he says, 'You better get ready to take me to the hospital.' We had a toddler and a baby. So I called and we dropped them off on the way in and took him to the hospital." While her husband was away, Deloris had to manage the farm, including milk deliveries to Tucson. "So I'm sort of overseeing the dairy and the sheep and I had my kids home. . . . But anyway, my husband finally says, 'You're better off working.' And I am, I really am better off. So I started into something that summer and have been since."[51]

Although Deloris Fram felt better about herself when she assumed additional responsibilities, others like Lois Spiering were pleased that they had not regularly worked in the field. Spiering and her husband arrived at an "agreement" in which he would "do the farming" and she would "take care of the house."[52]

While women on homesteads viewed farmwork differently in retrospect, almost unanimously women who remained on the farm identified the homestead as an advantageous environment for mothers to rear children, one of their most significant responsibilities in their estimation. Virginia Reynolds maintained that the farm fostered "a closeness in family relationships" because "we had to work with our kids and teach them." The intertwining of the productive and the private sides of life on the farm assured children of frequent contact with their parents: "We were with our kids, and we were the ones that were teaching them their standards for life." Farm women did not have to choose between productive labor and motherhood; they could combine both and transcend what they saw as a false dichotomy between nurturing children and contributing economically to the family. The ability to harmonize productive and reproductive roles rather than having to choose one or the other was one of the greatest advantages of homesteading in the minds of many women.[53]

In addition to being able to work with and teach their children, women identified other advantages of farm life for their children, including the strong work ethic that they felt it fostered, although they recognized that farm labor limited some of their children's involvement in extracurricular activities. Verna Poore maintained that homesteading taught her children that "it's work that gets you somewhere in this life." Eleanor Bolesta claimed that her children acquired "so much knowledge and so many values . . . by working" on the farm. One of those values, according to Evaleen George, was a sense of responsibility. She described how her youngest son "was feeding our cows and putting them in the loader" by the time he was thirteen. Ruth Otto's daughter "was only ten years old and she could cook because I was out in the field and she had to help do laundry and help do the cooking." In giving them opportunities to make a difference through their labor, Deloris Fram believed that farm life gave children "a solid foundation," helping them to be "tied to more reality" and "really have their feet on the ground."[54]

Frances Johnson believed that farm life also taught children to be resourceful and creative. "Our children never really had to have a lot of things to play with. They had kids to play with." Likewise, Ruth Otto said that farm life taught the children to "make their own fun. They'd go down to the clubhouse and play baseball and just have fun together." Rather than engaging in organized sports, Lois Spiering's boys learned to "roam the hills," hunting, fishing, and target shooting.[55]

In their role as wives as well as in their maternal role, some women believed homesteading had been an asset because it had enabled them to share in and contribute to their husbands' welfare and contentment. Although she was temperamentally unsuited for farming, Pearl Mayfield sensed her husband's farming ambitions so keenly that his contentment and success pleased her deeply. In retrospect she reasoned, "He was a very, very good farmer; he did very, very well. It was what he loved and what he wanted and I'd be glad to do it over. I don't regret one day." Others, including Josephine Miller, felt closer to their husbands as a result of the sense of teamwork.

> A wife is damned important on a farm. . . . It is a job that you get so involved in together that I can't even consider that he could do it without me. . . . You know so much more about his job than you would if you worked away from each other. . . . On a farm, it is just like you are one thing, one unit, that is working to get this thing going.

Similarly, Edna McClaflin reflected, "You just learned to work together." Such statements corroborate Sarah Elbert's conclusion that modern farm women "have not been self-sacrificing so much as they have been self-actualizing through the sense of 'us' and 'ours' that characterizes family farms."[56]

The farm's success itself and the financial security it afforded instilled a sense of pride and accomplishment in some women. "It seems like your whole being goes into the land," explained Hannah Bodle. "I remember us wanting so desperately to get the land to grow, and when you see it grow, you were happy." Lois Spiering was proud that she and her husband had succeeded in "building a future, a home, a business for ourselves from scratch." Reflecting upon what homesteading had meant economically Anna Nelson was "sure we never would have had the assets or the net worth that we have now" if she and her husband had not homesteaded."[57]

Women also prized the opportunity that homesteading offered them to furnish their children with a productive inheritance. Edna McClaflin expressed her goal as "keep[ing] the farm for my kids." This aspiration was common among farm women of McClaflin's generation. In a study of farm women in the 1960s and 1970s Sarah Elbert found that "women share with men the goal of effecting an intergenerational transfer of a going farm enterprise."[58]

Journalists visiting homesteaders in the postwar era commented frequently on the seeming incongruity of middle-class feminine ideals purveyed by prescriptive literature and the realities of homestead life for women. A writer for the *Saturday Evening Post* visiting with Betty Brug on the Shoshone Project described her as "small, quick, blond and attractive." Although she sawed lumber, irrigated, and drove a tractor, the journalist reported that "she doesn't look as if she belongs on a farm."[59] Historically, nothing could have been more natural than a woman productively laboring on a farm; yet Americans in the face of industrialization, urbanization, and rising prosperity over the course of the previous century had recast the dominant definition of womanhood, making the union of economic productivity with motherhood and the home appear unnatural. In the modern West, economically productive labor was linked to wages, and it was something women engaged in outside the home and off the farm. In the home, by contrast, women engaged in reproductive labor, a socially valuable but economically marginal activity.[60] Such views may have been historically aberrant, but many women on postwar homesteads shared them and idealized them in their dreams. Their experiences with privation and rudimentary housing; the necessity of performing housework without running water or electricity; scant protection from extreme temperatures; the omnipresence of dirt and dust; pests such as snakes and insects; hazardous conditions; isolation from medical care; and loneliness only reinforced the appeal of ideals that insulated women and children in suburban communities with modern homes, new appliances, and sparkling floors. Most couples who homesteaded in the postwar era retreated from their farms within a few years, and the poor fit between the demands of homesteading and these women's expectations and dreams apparently impelled many of the departures. These women actively shaped their destinies.

While nearly everyone chafed under the rigors of homesteading, most women who remained on the land found that it had compensatory rewards and fulfilled many of their aspirations and dreams. They had built homes, cleared and fenced land, driven tractors, tended crops, driven farm trucks, grown and preserved fruit and vegetables, raised chickens, and run errands, and they took pride in having built a future for themselves and their families through their work. Their husbands had relied upon them, and in working with their spouses the women had come to know some of the most important dimensions of their partners' lives. This understanding and contribution translated into power in the household, pride, and self-respect. Farm life had also enabled these women to reject the artificial division of home and family from economic productivity. They felt that working productively with their husbands and children on the farm made them better in their roles as mothers, allowing them to supervise and teach their children the value of work and a sense of responsibility. On the farm, productivity and motherhood could be mutually reinforcing. As Edna McClaflin reflected,

> I just can't seem to thank God enough for giving us the land. Don't know what else to say, I just feel so good about it. I feel like if I take care of the land like my husband took care of it, that it will take care of me. Of course that is my goal now to keep it for my kids. . . . Mike and Patty are expecting to return here. One day they'll all be back. I hope I am around.[61]

6 "THE FIRM FOUNDATION OF OUR COMMUNITY" OPPORTUNITY AND ITS LIMITS ON THE BUREAU OF RECLAMATION'S RIVERTON PROJECT

We have seen that while homesteading fulfilled some men's and women's dreams, it dashed those of others. From a historical perspective, this was to be expected: homesteading had always been a gamble. In 1963 Commissioner of Reclamation Floyd Dominy recalled the conventional wisdom of seasoned westerners that "it took three generations of farmers to make an irrigation farm. The first one came in and subjugated the land and usually wore out and went broke. Another man would buy it. By the time he got it pretty well along he was also gone. It took the third investment before a fully successful family farm, economically sufficient, was available." Those who homesteaded in the postwar era knew that this had been the case but they had also been told that scientific surveys, modern machinery, loans to farmers, and technical advice and assistance had greatly increased their chances of success. In 1949 Reclamation Commissioner Michael W. Straus contrasted the early days of reclamation when under one-fifth of the homesteaders managed to retain their claims with the modern era when "almost 100 percent of the new settlers make good."[1]

In some places the rates of failure were greater than Straus cared to admit. Technology and science had not conquered every problem, and some of the most persistent and vexing challenges resulted ironically from an abundance of water, the Bureau's chief asset. In poorly drained areas underlain with tight subsoils, the soil worsened with each irrigation. As irrigation water evaporated, capillary action in the soil bore alkaline deposits to the surface, leaving a fine white crust behind and choking plant life. In their fifth year of farming, seventeen unlucky homesteaders in one heavily alkaline district of the Tule Lake Basin harvested only five sacks of grain per acre and a few potatoes from their stunted and discolored stands. On Asil Dobson's farm in the Wellton Mohawk Valley "the ground quit growing" after runoff from surrounding farms raised the water table to within 10 inches of the surface. Dobson recalled, "You could go out on any given day and take the shovel and dig down shovel depth in the dirt and hit water." As a result of deteriorating farm quality owing partly to seepage and alkaline soil, the Bureau estimated in 1953 that 430 landowners on reclamation projects (not all of them postwar homesteaders) could no longer grow enough to support themselves.[2]

Problems with drainage and alkali existed on every reclamation project, but they particularly plagued farmers on the Riverton Project. Similar problems had beset those who settled on the project's first two divisions earlier in the century, but the postwar homesteaders took up their lands in the wake of the New Deal, after the federal government had assumed vast new responsibilities for the welfare of citizens. The change was mirrored in the Bureau's approach and in the expectations of its clientele. As Commissioner Dominy observed in 1963, the postwar era was "a time when reclamation was going through something of a change in its entire philosophy encouraged by the Congress in which we were attempting to assume greater responsibility for the settlers' success." At Riverton, disgruntled settlers pushed the notion of governmental responsibility for the welfare of homesteaders so far that the element of risk for the settler all but disappeared. In the 1940s Congress had been unwilling to give homesteading veterans all the financial assistance that the Bureau requested. But in the context of the New Frontier and the Great Society, Congress responded to homesteaders' complaints by buying out the Riverton Project in the 1960s and writing off millions of dollars as a loss. By shifting the risks of homesteading almost exclusively to the government, the homesteaders at Riverton made the costs of future reclamation homesteading too great for the Bureau to bear.[3]

The Bureau of Reclamation awarded 159 homesteads on the Riverton Project between 1947 and 1950. Optimism and booster rhetoric suffused the speeches of dignitaries at each of the Riverton land drawings, just as it did elsewhere. For instance, at the 1947 drawing, state and local dignitaries praised the Bureau's "contribution to [the] welfare of veterans and community."[4] Notwithstanding such heady rhetoric, by 1951, only four years after the first postwar drawing for farms at Riverton, at least one-third of the settlers were complaining that the Bureau had grossly overestimated the productive capacity of their land. Seepage and alkaline soil, along with unstable subsoil that made traditional drains ineffective, were reducing harvests and turning the settlers' homesteading dreams into nightmares. Leonard and Eula Withington, who moved to the project from Kansas in 1948, were shocked to discover that "about half of our [land] was only six inches of [top]soil. The rest was hard[pan]." On Van and Isabell Sorensen's land, "all at once it started to get swampy." Van recalled, "You'd go out there at night and that alkali on everything, you'd swear it had snowed. Absolutely pure white. . . . There was not one living thing out there except for some cattails." A soil scientist who studied the problem informed the Sorensens that "underneath the surface was a layer of clay shale that was impermeable. . . . Some areas it might be within two feet of the surface and then you go for fifty yards and it would be down 100 feet." The water pooled atop the clay, forming "a reservoir full of water." The problems the Withingtons and Sorensens faced were common: after investigating conditions on the project in 1951, a board of review concluded, "It is extremely probable that within 10 years a majority of these farm units will lack sufficient irrigable land to support a family."[5]

Homesteaders at Riverton alleged that their complaints fell on deaf ears at the Bureau's local office, even though the Bureau had often made amends to farmers on its projects by scaling back indebtedness arising from engineering mistakes and cost overruns. Administrators strenuously denied that they were responsible for leading the settlers into unwinnable situations. One Bureau official replied to Van Sorensen's complaints by reminding him that homesteading had always entailed risk: "'Well that's the name of the game. That's the risk you take.'"[6]

Dissatisfied with administrators' seeming lack of interest in their plight, a few homesteaders shrewdly appealed to their senators, Joseph O'Mahoney and Lester Hunt, who arranged a meeting with representatives from the Bureau in Riverton. The meeting, which lasted until well after midnight, was "somewhat more pointed than many meetings of this character," noted a Bureau official, because of O'Mahoney's leverage as chair of the Senate Interior Committee. After gathering information in Wyoming, O'Mahoney and Hunt asked top officials in the Bureau to schedule a second conference with project, district, and regional personnel in Washington early in January

White alkaline deposits behind the automobile in this field on the Riverton Project were becoming a common sight when this photograph was taken in June 1951. (Photograph by H. Rinnan, Reclamation Photographs, NARA, Rocky Mountain Region)

1952. Charles Deckert, the former director of the irrigation district in Riverton, and Paul Petzold, an articulate homesteader who taught agricultural classes to the veterans, represented the settlers. At the conference, the duo averred that "farming was no longer profitable" in many fields due to alkali and seepage. They charged the Bureau with "moral responsibility" for the dilemma, because it had failed to detect these deficiencies prior to developing the project and had greatly misrepresented the land's productive capacity to the settlers when they first visited the project to investigate opportunities. The homesteaders wanted the government to reimburse them for their expenses in trying to reclaim marginal lands and requested cash assistance or emergency employment for all who were stranded on unproductive farms until the situation could be reversed. To correct the problems permanently, the homesteaders' representatives recommended that the Bureau permit some farmers to exchange their homesteads at Riverton for superior lands elsewhere, building upon a precedent Congress had established in 1924 when it had authorized homesteaders on unpatented lands to exchange their farms for raw lands on other irrigation projects. The productive portions of farms that were vacated could then be added to the holdings of remaining settlers so that each farmer would have close to 100 productive, irrigable acres. At O'Mahoney's suggestion, the Bureau's representatives pledged to incorporate the homesteaders' recommendations within a bill that he could submit to Congress.[7]

The following summer, the Bureau remapped the project's soils and studied drainage problems. The study upheld many of the settlers' complaints; a "relatively high salt and sodium content" plagued many farms. In some areas the soil would continue to deteriorate under irrigation because of subsurface shale. In the North Portal region, which had been farmed since 1950, nearly 38 percent of the farmland was deemed unirrigable. On farms that had been homesteaded in North Pavilion in 1949, the problem was even greater: nearly 48 percent of the land was unsuited for irrigation. In the Lost Wells area, where lands had been opened in 1947, "considerable acreages" were plagued with "shallow soils and slow permeable, high alkaline, moderate saline soils." More favorable soils predominated along the Pilot Extension, where about thirty veterans had settled. After reviewing the evidence, Assistant Commissioner H. F. McPhail concluded that the Bureau had made grave mistakes: "The facts clearly show that large amounts of money have been expended for construction of irrigation facilities on the newer portions of the project without reasonable certainty that the soils were irrigable." One settler recalled that at a meeting where the results of the study were shared with the homesteaders, they were told that "the original inspection of the soil was not done scientifically. The only method they used at the time they decided to test the soil was by feel and taste and sight."[8]

While McPhail as an administrator in the Bureau found the situation at Riverton "disconcerting," the debacle was heartbreaking and financially devastating for many of the homesteaders who had been misled by the Bureau's original classification of their land. Consider the case of Stanford Clark, a veteran who moved to Riverton from Salt Lake City after his name was drawn in the 1947 land lottery. When Clark visited Riverton to inspect the land and select a homestead, "a recent snow blanketed the ground and sage and it was 35 below zero." Unable to examine the soil because of the snow cover, Clark chose a farm on the basis of the Bureau's soil maps. The tract he selected had 115.6 acres of irrigable land, according to the map, including 38 acres of excellent, first-class land and 70 acres of decent, second-class land. Within a few weeks of selecting their homestead the Clarks moved there, intending to "make it a nice place for us to live for the rest of our lives." Although they worked long hours clearing, leveling, planting, and irrigating, investing their entire savings of $5,000 in improving the place, their first year's gross income barely topped $700. In subsequent years their disappointments continued. To make ends meet Clark's wife began teaching school, and he worked intermittently off the farm as his schedule permitted. By 1952 when the Bureau reclassified the soil on their farm, the land was "practically completely improved in all respects," but lakes and puddles had formed on 10 acres and the water was spreading. The Bureau's new investigations revealed that their farm actually contained no first-class land and only 49 acres of second-class land. Nearly 97 of their 160 acres were classified as 6 or 6W—marginal lands that should not be farmed. The couple estimated they had invested $12,690 of their own money in the place as well as $10,000 from the Farmers Home Administration. Yet in all their years on the project they had "never operated at a profit." Summing up his experiences, Clark wrote that he and his family had been "displaced for 7–8 years, live[d] on a lower standard of living than we were accustomed to, work[ed] harder than ever in our lives and face[d] more disappointment and hardships than a person should."[9]

Galvanized by the plight of scores of settlers with similar stories, Congress and officials in the Bureau worked to make amends. On 27 July 1953, Congress approved SB 887, permitting resettlement of some farmers and the redistribution of the remaining lands. On 13 August President Eisenhower signed the bill, which became Public Law 258. This statute committed the federal government to a far greater degree than ever before to ensuring that homesteaders on every reclamation project—not just Riverton—possessed "sufficient" farmland. As Commissioner of Reclamation Michael Straus observed when he announced that the Bureau intended to work with Congress to secure such a law, "the end purpose of the Bureau" had changed greatly. In light of congressional intent the agency's "basic philosophy" was now "to provide settlers with such irrigable properties as will permit them to make a living according to decent and acceptable standards."[10]

From the perspective of many old-timers in Riverton, who had experienced similar problems with seepage on their farms and had received little

Stanford Clark invested his entire savings and borrowed heavily from the Farmers Home Administration to construct this handsome farmstead on the Riverton Project, but his dream of a profitable farm collapsed as his lands became waterlogged. (Photograph by A. D. Perkins, 18 February 1953, Reclamation Photographs, NARA, Rocky Mountain Region)

relief from the government, the postwar homesteaders' willingness to trumpet their hardships and lobby for compensation seemed offensive, selfish, and potentially damaging to the market value of their own land. The homesteaders also managed to alienate many in Riverton's business community, who feared that negative publicity regarding the Riverton Project would jeopardize the project's future growth and ultimately diminish their profits in a place where irrigated agriculture provided "the firm foundation" for commercial growth.[11]

In the weeks surrounding the new law's enactment, boosters in Riverton endeavored to contradict or correct negative statements regarding the project. When Wyoming senator Lester C. Hunt stated that farm failures in Fremont County had risen over the past year, the *Riverton Ranger* disputed the statement. A few weeks later the newspaper assigned a reporter to visit the farms of homesteaders who had moved to the project after the war. "Project Crops Good," the headline for the resulting article proclaimed.[12]

Nothing demonstrated the negative implications of the homesteaders' complaints for the project's reputation or rallied the boosters to the defense of the project more than a week-long exposé of waste and mismanagement printed by the *Denver Rocky Mountain News* in early August. Written by reporter Morton Margolin after he received numerous documents from a disgruntled soil scientist who had once worked for the Bureau, the series charged that Reclamation had consistently developed irrigation canals and prepared land for settlement regardless of the land's agricultural potential. Margolin quoted the anonymous whistle-blower as saying, "Extension of the Riverton Project was one of the developments fostered by the urgent need for settlement opportunities for veterans returning from World War II. Congress and the Administration were alike in their desire to provide new farm lands as soon as possible. Political pressures dictated an expediting of construction, which prevented as thorough an investigation as the Bureau usually makes." Contradicting the Riverton newspaper's report of excellent crops and satisfied farmers, Margolin claimed that thirty-four of the thirty-six homesteaders in the Lost Wells region said they wanted to move because their prospects were "hopeless." One settler, thirty-three-year-old H. J. Merrigan, reportedly complained, "I've got 30 acres of seep and the shale is so shallow on the rest I can't plow it." His neighbor Herman Shott was quoted as saying, "This soil just doesn't produce and we're too far away from markets." Even the faint praise of one of the few optimists quoted in the series, Mrs. Delbert Edwards, was potentially damaging. She expressed faith that "we can make our home here" but acknowledged that they were not yet disappointed because their expectations were so low: "we didn't expect to make anything the first five years."[13]

The editor of Riverton's newspaper accused the Denver paper of "sensational" journalism and warmly defended the Bureau, the project, and self-reliant pioneering. Margolin's muckraking series forced the Wyoming editor to concede that some terrain on the project had been "opened for homesteading through a mistake," and that "some farmers [would] have to move off of [the] lands." The local editor maintained, though, that more than a few malcontents had failed because of "poor management and application" rather than through the shortcomings of their farms. "Many good" plots of land were scattered across the project. Quoting a Bureau spokesman, the

Riverton paper indicated that the average net worth of the postwar homesteaders was $13,859 and that the average settler had obtained a net gain of $5,281 on the project. "The modern homesteader has had many advantages over his forefathers," the editor pointed out, but the settlers should not expect the government to coddle them if the settlers themselves were negligent. In the American tradition of individual enterprise and self-reliance, "homesteading has always been a gamble. . . . The gamble still remains."[14]

Fearing farmers would leave the project en masse under the generous terms of Public Law 258, officials tried to persuade groups of farmers to remain. In one such attempt, they approached Van Sorensen, the leader of a small Mormon congregation on the project, asking him to encourage the Mormons to remain. Sorensen recalled the gist of the official's message: "We feel if we can get the Mormons to stay and stabilize this thing then the rest of them will kind of fall in line."[15]

On August 10, the homesteaders met to study their options under the new law, which created two categories of settlers: those who would remain in Riverton and those who would exchange theirs farms for a homestead elsewhere. Some husbands and wives disagreed with each other regarding whether or not they should move. Harold Holmes told a reporter in September that he wanted to relocate but his wife objected. "This has been a wonderful place to live, and I've enjoyed every minute of it," she said. By offering the settlers two options the law also created two competing interest groups, leading to what Van Sorensen called "a stressful time" between neighbors. Those who planned to leave wanted those who would take over their farms to compensate them fully for the improvements they had made. As Arnold Kuhlman pointed out, the person who stepped onto his farm if he relocated shouldn't automatically enjoy "full value" of the crops Kuhlman had planted. In terms of self-interest, though, it made sense for those who stayed to pay as little as possible for their neighbors' property. In light of the competing interests of the two groups and the costs of moving, Senator Lester Hunt warned that "administration of this act is going to be extremely difficult."[16]

Hunt's fears proved correct. Van Sorensen recalled, "To try to negotiate so everybody was happy was almost impossible." Different interests and opinions fueled "accusations" and "threats" and "finger pointing." Neighbors "start[ed] swearing at each other and threatening each other and blaming everyone else and calling each other liars."[17]

By late September, the plans for implementing PL 258 had been hammered out. Settlers who remained were entitled to at least 85 acres of first-class land or its equivalent. Anyone who possessed fewer than 160 irrigable acres could apply to relocate, though. A local committee of five homesteaders appointed by the secretary of the interior would gauge the relative severity of each homesteaders' plight so that those in greatest need would receive help first. Settlers who remained and acquired additional land would be required to compensate the former occupants for the buildings, crops, or other improvements on land. Those departing would be expected to deliver a clean title to the land, aside from any indebtedness to the Farmers' Home Administration; portions of those debts would be assumed by the new landowner; the balance would be written off by the government.[18]

By 1958, the exchange process was completed. Nearly half of the original postwar homesteaders at Riverton (49 percent) had exchanged their lands at Riverton for farms elsewhere. Most who remained behind had acquired portions of their departing neighbors' farms as amendments to their homesteads.[19]

The amendments increased the arable lands of those who remained in Riverton but did not resolve all of the remaining farmers' problems. The new lands some acquired were several miles distant from their original homesteads; workers and machinery had to be transported back and forth. Much of the newly acquired land, which had been abandoned by someone else, was marginal. Leonard and Eula Withington doubled the size of their homestead when they obtained a quarter section under the terms of PL 258. But portions of the land were so "seepy and wet," Leonard recalled, that even the "skeeters lying out there drowned out." Although he exaggerated, Dick Traweek voiced a common complaint: "Nobody gave us anything, except more of what we already had too much of."[20]

By 1957, just four years after PL 258 had been passed, some who remained in Riverton charged that even their newly amended farms were too small and unproductive to justify their prorated share of the project's construction charges, including ongoing drainage work. The issue was becoming pressing because the standard ten-year period in which settlers were exempt from construction payments would expire in 1960. With that date approaching, Bureau officials urged the farmers to form an irrigation district and negotiate a repayment contract. In 1958, after the Third Division Irrigation District had been formed, the homesteaders' representatives met with Bureau administrators to discuss the terms of repayment. The Bureau proposed a sliding repayment scale ranging from 40 cents to $2.40 per acre each year based upon the quality of the land, with the understanding that smaller annual payments would be permitted for the first 15 years. Over several generations, farmers on the project would be expected to repay $6,300,000 of the construction costs, or an average of $572 per acre. Individual settlers were free to propose revisions to the Bureau's classification of their lands, and many did so. Despite the leniency of the proposed contract, permitting repayment over multiple generations, the commissioners for the district spurned the Bureau, maintaining that the Third Division lands, with an average gross income of $30 per acre in 1960, were too unproductive to meet the repayment schedule. They pointed out that the repayment schedule would require centuries—438.8 years by one calculation—and that the charge of $572 per acre greatly exceeded the current worth of the land. "I came here so I could build up and leave a farm for my children—not a debt for generations to come," complained one homesteader. The commissioners audaciously proposed that "the entire construction obligation . . . be written off" as a loss and refused to submit the contract proposed by the Bureau to the farmers in the district for a vote.[21]

Attempting to prove that the construction charges were commensurate with the land's capacity to produce, the Bureau appointed three experts in irrigation and drainage—John A. Goe, J. R. Barkley, and James W. Legg—to survey the project thoroughly. In the summer of 1961 the trio concluded that the project's problems were not so severe or unusual as to prevent the farmers from repaying the proposed construction charges. They also recommended additional drainage work, which would increase the settlers' obligations to the government.[22]

Hoping to counter the experts' findings, some settlers persuaded Wyoming senator Joe Hickey to lead a congressional delegation to the project on 31 October 1961 to listen to their side of the story. Bureau officials suspected that the delegation's hearings on the project were rigged to discourage "favorable testimonials from either the settlers or other informed individuals." Most who spoke claimed that their incomes were so small that they could not meet the proposed construction charges. Whereas the Bureau had identified 11,831 acres as being irrigable on the project, Allen Talbott, secretary for the Third Division Irrigation District, claimed that a soil scientist formerly employed by the Bureau, Bill Peters, had predicted that within a few years, seepage and water logging would reduce the irrigable acreage to 5,000. Homesteader Delbert Edwards alleged that the Bureau's 1953 reclassification of lands on the project had "not [been] any more truthful than the original" and contended that many of the drains installed by the Bureau in the interim had not materially improved the situation. What reason was there to believe that more drains would protect the lands adequately? The idea of installing additional drains was like "spending $150 to doctor a $50 horse," scoffed one resident. Gene Tolman corroborated this argument, claiming that on his farm, "You can look out across it and see a big white seep crossed with three drains that are not serving their purpose."[23]

When one of the senators inquired about the possibility of writing off the construction charge and only assessing the settlers for the yearly expenses associated with operating and maintaining the irrigation system—the irrigation district commissioners' original proposal—Talbott shocked him by asserting that even such a radical concession would be insufficient. "There is nothing here to salvage," he averred. Instead, the government should buy out the remaining farmers, reimburse them for their improvements, and close the project. "You mean write off the whole $22,000,000 spent and forget about it?" queried an astonished Senator Quentin Burdick. "In my estimation, yes. That's the only thing to do," Talbott replied. "The position of the commissioners is that the Third Division will not carry its own weight."[24]

Only a few locals voiced any optimism at the hearing. A Riverton banker claimed that some farmers had increased their net worth and charged that many who had not done so had failed because of their own negligence. One project resident, Joe Chernick, corroborated the banker's claim, alleging that his net worth had risen by $26,000 over the previous decade.[25]

In light of the pessimistic tenor of the hearings, Senator Hickey asked the Bureau to appoint a second committee of outside experts to reexamine drainage problems on the project. This commission completed its investigation and review shortly before Christmas, reaffirming the previous committee's report regarding the general soundness of the project. Most of the drainage ditches—75 miles of them—were functioning properly, they found. By constructing 26 miles of additional drainage ditches and lining a 12-mile section of the main canal, most of the remaining drainage problems could be corrected. Talbott and others who endorsed a buyout of the farmers responded that the commission's findings were skewed by the fact that the investigators had examined the drainage system three months after the last irrigation occurred rather than when water was flowing in the canals.[26]

In March 1962, the Senate Interior Committee held hearings in Washington as a follow-up to their visit to the project the previous fall. Two of the farmers, Allen Talbott and Aubrey Traweek, who had dominated the hearings in Riverton late in 1961, traveled to Washington where they testified that 90 percent of farmers on the project believed it should be abandoned. Based upon a petition from seventeen farmers on the Third Division, Senator Hickey had introduced a bill to furnish irrigation water to the project for two more years, even though a repayment contract had not been signed. Talbot and Traweek claimed that most of the farmers were so convinced of the project's worthlessness that they did not want any irrigation water that year. Instead, they wanted "permanent legislation," according to a Riverton reporter who had spoken with Senator Hickey, that would entail a complete buyout and reimburse them for all the money they had invested. When Bureau employees contacted the farmers, they found that only one in five definitely did not want irrigation water and that over half were certain they wanted to farm and irrigate that season. An unsympathetic Bureau official complained after several meetings with Talbott and the other district commissioners that they sought "a payment from the government for [the sale of] their land holdings corresponding to the value of a fully improved farm in an area of the most productive farms in the United States."[27]

The commissioners' campaign for a buyout badly divided the homesteaders. Some, like Carroll Riggs, did not believe their lands were worthless but supported the proposed buyout because their amended homesteads consisted of widely separated fields. They hoped that a cash settlement would enable them to purchase a single, productive tract. Many, like Ethel Marlatt, believed the proposed buyout was a pipedream. "I just didn't think they could do it," she recalled. But they waited silently in the wings, preferring not to criticize a quixotic scheme that could enrich them if it somehow succeeded. A handful, including Stan and Eileen Huffman and Phyllis and Ted Gies, openly opposed a buyout, countering the dour appraisals of Talbott and others by sharing their success stories with a news reporter in September 1963. Huffman claimed he was "a contented and happy man" who had "a good ranch." "For ten years I have suffered the humiliation of seeing a small group of people tear down what I have been working hard to build up for 15 years. . . . I cannot remain silent any longer in the face of this terribly distorted picture," he said. Huffman averred that the much-maligned land "will produce with proper management" and claimed to be raising 3–4 tons of hay on land that former occupants had alleged was nearly worthless. By lining his ditches and carefully applying water he had stopped seepage. "You control seep by controlling your water," he maintained. Gies told a reporter, "We came here in 1950 to make our home, and we still believe we can do it. All it takes is some hard work."[28]

People who trumpeted their opinions were the subject of gossip and the butt of jokes. Ted and Phyllis Gies felt like "social outcasts" because they openly opposed the proposed buyout. Phyllis picked up their party-line telephone one day and heard a neighbor saying, "'That Ted Gies is so stupid he doesn't even know when people's trying to help him.'" Neighbors "would hardly speak to you on the street when they'd meet you," she recalled. "It was really tough." After a newspaper article was published indicating that the Gieses' recent purchase of a new car proved that money could be made on the Third Division, someone deflated the tires while the car was parked in town.[29]

Proponents of a government buyout cast enough doubt upon the Bureau's previous two studies that the House Interior and Insular Affairs Committee called for yet another investigation of the project's soils, drainage, and economic soundness in 1962. The Secretary of the Interior complied, appointing a five-man team in August. They finished their study early in 1963 and from the perspective of the Bureau of Reclamation "generally justified the activities of construction, drainage, and land classification" on the project. They estimated that the primary cause of the settlers' problems with drainage owed to seepage of as much as half of the water from the canal system into the surrounding soil. The investigators recommended the lining of additional canals and installation of new drains on the Third Division at the cost of $83 per acre. This additional expenditure was feasible, they believed. Summarizing the investigators' findings for a congressional committee, Assistant Secretary of the Interior Kenneth Holum stated, "Nowhere in the Western United States, the survey team concluded, can project-type irrigated land be developed as cheaply as the Riverton project land can be reclaimed and protected."[30]

Although the investigators' report showed that spending an added $83 per acre would be cheaper than developing a new project from scratch, the findings also supported the local commissioners' contention that the Bureau's investment in the Third Division, not including the additional drainage work that had been proposed, exceeded the value of the farms themselves. More than $21,000,000 had already been spent; that cost, divided by the 11,831 irrigable acres on those farms, amounted to roughly $1,775 per acre. The figure was inflated, for some of that cost entailed joint works shared with the Riverton Project's two older divisions. But one could safely assume that the Bureau had invested at least $1,200 per acre on the Third Division.[31]

While the Bureau contended that the value of crops produced over the long run along with the multiplier effect of federal dollars in the local economy justified such a heavy investment, many of the Third Division's residents argued that they and the nation's taxpayers would be further ahead financially if the government simply bought them out and wrote off the government's investment as a loss. In June Wyoming representative William Henry Harrison and Wyoming senator Milward Simpson introduced a bill to "pay off disgruntled settlers and junk the project's Third Division" by permitting the settlers to sue the Bureau in federal district court. The Third Division commissioners endorsed the bill as a mechanism for buying out the settlers at fair market value. That same year Joe Hickey, who had championed the discontented homesteaders' cause as a senator, retired from public office and resumed his law practice. Twenty-one of the Third Division's sixty-five landowners hired him as their attorney and filed suit in July, demanding payment of $2.4 million for their farms, or over $114,000 per farm.[32]

Shortly after the suit was filed, Wyoming senator Gale McGee introduced a bill drafted by the Bureau of Reclamation and based upon the recommendations of its most recent investigation of the project. The bill permitted the secretary of the interior to purchase at his discretion any land "which in his opinion has been rendered unsuitable for sustained irrigation production because of seepage from the project irrigation system and which it is not feasible to reclaim by draining or leaching or both." Moreover, the bill authorized the secretary to purchase additional lands "which the owners signify by written notice to the Secretary that they desire to convey to the United States." Rather than scrapping the Third Division, though, the bill permitted additional drainage work. In an attempt to make the financial obligations of Third Division farmers who chose to remain manageable, the bill applied funds from the sale of hydroelectric power to reduce construction charges. The Bureau estimated that under the bill $21,067,288 in power revenues would be applied to the construction charges, although at least half of that amount would be used to pay for drainage work on other divisions of the Riverton Project. Additionally, the Bureau proposed that $9,683,000 in construction charges for unproductive lands on the entire Riverton Project be written off, bringing the total charge for the Third Division farmer down to $473 an acre. Whether Congress bought out the farmers under the terms of the lawsuit or approved the bill proposed by the Bureau, it would still be heavily subsidizing the homesteaders.[33]

Those pressing for liquidation of the project objected to the Bureau's proposal, arguing that it unwisely allocated federal funds and granted "a complete subsidy" to farmers on a project where it was "practically impossible" to establish a viable farm. They objected, too, to the bill's reliance upon the Interior Department to determine which lands were unsuited for farming as well as the fair market value of other lands farmers desired to sell. "To permit the agency which is here in effect defending its mistakes [to arbitrate] would be to put the cat watching the mouse," Hickey contended.[34]

Features in the Harrison/Simpson and McGee bills were combined in compromise legislation, which the House Committee on Interior and Insular Affairs approved in November. A remarkably indulgent belief that "any settlers or landowners who want to leave the project should be able to do so" and should be treated "fairly and equitably" guided the committee in its deliberations. The compromise bill instructed the secretary of the interior to "negotiate" for the purchase of lands on the Third Division "at a price equal to the appraised value thereof and of the improvements thereon." The bill stipulated that lands that had been "represented as being suitable for sustained irrigation production" at the time they were homesteaded should be appraised "without reference to any deterioration in their irrigability." Thus lands that had been represented as prime irrigation land (Class 1) at the time they were homesteaded were to be bought at the current going rate for prime land—a handsome concession to the settlers who had already been given their former neighbors' land to compensate for the reduced value of their own farms. The bill permitted any landowner on the Third Division who preferred not to sell to continue to receive water for three years, during which time the Interior Department would determine whether those lands should be permanently classified as irrigable. The bill also authorized the government to resell irrigable lands it acquired through the buyout.[35]

The House and Senate approved the bill early in 1964 and President Lyndon Johnson signed it in March. So generous were the terms of the law that all but one of the sixty-five remaining landowners on the Riverton Project's Third Division decided to sell. When nearly everyone stepped forward to claim their share of the pie, those who had lobbied and fought for a buyout chided the others, accusing them of "freeload[ing]."[36]

Phyllis and Ted Gies, who had originally opposed the buyout, were among those who decided to sell. They did so, Phyllis recalled, "because we could see the writing on the wall." They feared that after three years with everyone else selling "we were going to have to sell." Moreover, the deal they were offered was sweet and without additional drains their seepage problem would worsen each year. "We could barely make a living on it at the last. So perhaps they [the proponents of the buyout] were right," Phyllis judged in retrospect.[37]

Eventually as part of the buyout the Bureau of Reclamation purchased 22,000 acres from settlers for $3.2 million, or over $145 per acre, ending the inglorious postwar homesteading saga on the project. Other farmers in the area leased the irrigable portions from the Bureau over the next six years. Early in 1971, the Bureau consolidated the land into forty-three farm units and auctioned them off for $1.4 million—a figure $245,750 higher than the minimum price affixed by appraisers prior to the sale but less than half the amount the government had paid the homesteaders for the property in the mid-1960s. New sprinkler technology, which made it possible to distribute water more efficiently and reduced drainage problems, increased the land's appeal for bidders. But by their enthusiastic bidding many local farmers showed they did not believe the veterans' assertions that the lands were worthless. Riverton's newspaper editor crowed, "Monday's bid was a vindication for those many people who worked for years to convince the Congress that Third Division has great value and a potential not unlike the potential of the rest of the Riverton irrigation project."[38]

The Bureau of Reclamation's quest to create homesteads for veterans veered out of control on the Riverton Project following World War II, becoming a public relations nightmare and a financial disaster. Riverton mayor W. B. Glass's assurances to the winning veterans at the first postwar land lottery on the project assume ironic undertones in light of the veterans' actual experiences. Glass had forecast, "We are sure you will find that the pioneering of this virgin soil will be your land of opportunity, and the extent of your success will depend entirely upon your own initiative."[39]

When Glass spoke of homesteaders succeeding on their own merits, he envisioned sturdy yeomen battling the elements and subduing the land through solitary enterprise and creativity. Instead, as their farms became water-logged, settlers creatively turned from farming the land to farming Congress—and succeeded in advancing their financial position as a result of their initiative.

In part the ill-fated outcome of postwar homesteading in Riverton occurred because of limitations, both in the area's natural resources and in the Bureau's scientific and technological data and expertise. Yet even in more favorable settings, large numbers of homesteaders had historically failed. As Bureau officials and old-timers reminded the veterans, homesteading had always been a gamble. What distinguished the postwar homesteaders from earlier generations of disappointed claimants and derailed the postwar homesteading program at Riverton was not so much the unproductive soil or the economic failure of the settlers. Instead, the mind-set of the settlers, including their sense of entitlement in their relationship to the federal government, their insistent perception of homesteading as a guaranteed investment, and their rejection of the notion that homesteading entailed real risk shackled the Bureau.

Earlier generations of homesteaders had complained loudly, too, and had wrested major concessions from Congress and the Bureau; debts had been written off and repayment periods had been lengthened. In this regard they were typical westerners, who have often sought "federal money as compensation for the West's failings." But the veterans at Riverton went further than earlier homesteaders on reclamation projects had done. In 1953–1954, they asked for more land or new homesteads and wound up persuading Congress to guarantee every postwar homesteader on federal reclamation projects whose lands were shown "to be insufficient to support a family" the chance to acquire additional lands or an entirely new farming opportunity. This was a substantial concession, but one that preserved the time-honored necessity of hard work on the settler's part. A decade later, a small cadre of settlers discredited repeated technical studies showing that their farms could be made sound. Having lived on their homesteads rent-free for as long as fifteen years, they convinced Congress that the government owed them more than the combined value of their land and improvements. Homesteading had become as soft as possible. The philosophy expressed in the nineteenth-century ballad, "How happy I am on my government claim, where I've nothing to lose and nothing to gain, Nothing to eat and nothing to wear, Nothing for nothing is honest and square," had been thoroughly repudiated. And with the passing of that philosophy, the financial risks for the federal government of homestead openings became excessive and unjustifiable. Meanwhile, on another front, homestead openings were becoming infeasible politically, too.[40]

A CONFLICT OF INTERESTS THE BATTLE OVER RECLAMATION HOMESTEADS

7

While settlers on the Riverton Project were eagerly liquidating their homesteads, thousands of other Americans remained interested in homesteading. Between 1956 and 1966, Americans claimed over 6,000 homesteads. Claims in Alaska predominated—only 416 of the entries involved reclamation homesteads—but many more Americans would have filed on reclamation projects if more farms had been offered. As an index of Americans' hunger for irrigated land, between 1946 and 1966 the Interior Department received over 150,000 applications for 3,041 farms. Moreover, as time passed interest in reclamation homesteading rose. When the government opened 20 homesteads on the Minidoka Project in 1961, nearly 4,000 citizens (almost 200 applicants for every farm available) applied; by contrast, the Bureau had received only 2,028 applications for the 86 farms it advertised in its first postwar land opening back in 1946. A study published by the Public Land Law Review Commission in 1969 noted that "a large number of citizens, and particularly . . . farmers" continued to clamor for public land openings.[1]

Nor was there any shortage of productive soil on the public domain; in 1969 the Bureau of Land Management reportedly administered 29,000,000 acres of public land suitable for farming, if irrigation water could be furnished. At a homestead drawing in Idaho in 1961, Commissioner of Reclamation Floyd Dominy averred, "All the way up the Snake River plain . . . there is land awaiting only water to add to your agricultural wealth." Secretary of the Interior Stewart Udall confirmed that plenty of water remained as well. "Land and water of superb quality and adequate amounts are still available for development," he observed in 1965. In 1969 the Bureau of Reclamation alone managed 800,000 acres of potentially irrigable public land including over 7,400 acres on the Minidoka Project and 50,000 acres on the Shoshone Project. The Bureau estimated that 230,000 additional farms could be created by 2000 if Congress would appropriate sufficient funds for reservoirs, canals, and high-lift pumping systems.[2]

Despite the availability of land and Americans' appetite for new homesteads, the Bureau's land development program inched forward at a snail's pace after 1957: in 1961 although other land openings were contemplated, the secretary of the interior announced what turned out to be the Bureau's final homestead drawing. The agency later sold some irrigable land, most notably in the Columbia Basin, but sales were infrequent: between 1962 and 1966, the Interior Department advertised only fifty-nine farms for sale in the Basin.[3]

The Bureau's homesteading program waned during the 1960s, partly because reclamation was so expensive. In 1960, the Bureau's estimates for developing new irrigated farmland ranged from $566 per acre in the Lower Arkansas River drainage to $2,780 per acre in southern California. The average cost stood at $920 an acre. By contrast, back in 1953 the Bureau had estimated the cost for developing irrigation facilities on the Columbia Basin Project to be $477 per acre. Despite rising costs, a lack of money was not the primary reason the Bureau, which continued to receive substantial appropriations, stopped developing new farmland. As Bureau officials pointed out, the increases in real dollars, adjusted for inflation, were more modest than the raw numbers suggested. Moreover, over half of the amount spent could be recovered relatively quickly from the sale of hydroelectric power generated by the Bureau's dams, and the multiplier effect of large tracts of new land being brought under construction was substantial for local economies, generating business, creating employment, and boosting tax revenues.[4]

A more significant factor involved changing national priorities and attitudes regarding western land and water. Some politicians opposed new irrigation projects feeling that water supplies should be developed instead for nonagricultural purposes. In his January 1965 budget message to Congress, President Lyndon Johnson noted that urban, industrial, and recreational requirements for water had "increased sharply in recent years" and that therefore "the relative priorities of many historic water uses including cropland" were diminishing. The Bureau of Reclamation's budget shifted to reflect competing demands for water. Whereas 86 percent of the agency's budget between 1921 and 1930 had been earmarked for irrigation development, that percentage dropped to 43 percent by 1961 and 25 percent in 1963. Hydroelectric power for cities and industry, water for municipalities, recreational development, and water for fish and wildlife conservation accounted for the majority of the budget. As Dominy told a congressional committee in 1965, reclamation had "evolved into a multipurpose undertaking to develop the limited and often grossly maldistributed Western water resources for all beneficial purposes." Advocates of reclamation insisted, though, that it was still important to develop new supplies of irrigation water. Assistant Secretary of the Interior Kenneth Holum told members of Congress that in some areas of the West "putting unused water on the land may well represent the best use of available water supply."[5]

A more potent criticism of reclamation projects revolved around the argument that the nation's remaining lands and rivers should remain undeveloped due to the intrinsic value of open space and free-flowing rivers. Regardless of whether they served urban or rural constituencies, environmental critics charged, reclamation projects violated Nature. In the relatively affluent postwar era, many Americans became less concerned about maximizing economic output and more concerned with the quality of experiences that the nation's land and water could provide. As Arizona Senator Paul Fannin observed in 1973, the nation's natural resources were being "revalued in a Nation where open space, clean air and room to stretch and roam are becoming priceless commodities." Increasingly Americans viewed the West, historian William Cronon notes, through the lens of "predominantly nonrural values" as a "nonworking" landscape or recreational space, as opposed to a productive, "working" space.[6]

Commissioner Dominy fretted that the Bureau of Reclamation's development of new irrigated land, which had been appreciated as progressive and patriotic in the 1940s, was now being portrayed by the agency's foes as archaic or even deleterious. Dominy bitterly derided reclamation's opponents, labeling the preservationist agenda "God-damned ridiculous." "Those who would have all forests and rivers remain pristine . . . ignore facts and play on emotions," he insisted. Having grown up on a dryland homestead in Nebraska and having worked with desperate ranchers on the bone-dry plains of Campbell County, Wyoming, during the Dust Bowl, Dominy regarded nature as "a pretty cruel animal" and saw reclamation as a means of improving upon nature by "putting water to work for man." "Let's *use* our environment. . . . The challenge to man is to do and save what is good but to permit man to progress in civilization," he reasoned.[7]

The Bureau was able to marshal statistics to counter arguments about agricultural surpluses and the nation's ability to consume farm products, and it adjusted its focus to accommodate urban water users. But under Dominy's leadership it failed in its attempts to use facts, figures, and bluster to persuasively counter arguments about wildlife, scenic waterways, and open space, arguments that resonated with the public's emotional and aesthetic sensibilities. Environmentalist organizations incessantly advanced such arguments. Reviewing the Bureau's recent history in 1973, former assistant commissioner of reclamation William E. Warne concluded that "attacks by environmentalists" had stymied the agency.[8]

A pivotal struggle pitting conservation and recreation interest groups against advocates of irrigated land development and homesteading occurred between 1951 and 1964 along the Oregon/California border. Local farmers and Bureau of Reclamation officials seeking to develop land for homesteading fought against a powerful alliance of metropolitan-based recreational and environmental interests, as well as farmers in the Central and Imperial Valleys and the U.S. Fish and Wildlife Service (FWS). This battle, which culminated in the passage by Congress of the Kuchel Act on Conservation of Wildlife Resources, demonstrated how popular attitudes toward western resource management had changed dramatically since the 1940s. The Kuchel Act banned additional homesteading only in northern California's Tule Lake Basin. But the values and perspectives undergirding the law had become so widespread by the time the act was passed that future homestead development by the Bureau of Reclamation anywhere in the West became politically untenable.[9]

Homesteads in the Tule Lake Basin were irrigated, but they were built upon rich sediment that had once been covered by marshes and shallow lakes. Between 1946 and 1949, the Bureau of Reclamation awarded 216 homesteads in the region, and it intended to award many more after constructing drainage works to prevent flooding during years of heavy runoff.[10]

The Bureau did not, however, unilaterally manage the public lands it intended to reclaim. The terrain was situated along the Pacific Migratory Bird Flyway and provided forage and shelter for hundreds of thousands of birds each year. In 1907 William Finley, western field representative of the National Association of Audubon Societies, had characterized the area as "perhaps the most extensive breeding ground in the West for all kinds of inland water birds." In a subsequent article he vividly described the profusion of wildlife and the sense of wonder it inspired.

> Avocets were swooping past with a loud "Whit-whit-ie!" Stilts were crying "Quit! Quit!" loud and fast. . . . Toward evening the ducks came in from the lake in bands and settled down for the night where the reedy bogs lay scattered about and the water was shallow. At dusk we lay in camp and listened to the rush of wings, as the night comers flocked in to their resting places. We could catch the faintest whir at first, which increased to a loud swish as the band passed. Out on the water came the light flappings, as flock after flock settled for the night.

Others shared Finley's sense of wonder and appreciation for wildlife. In 1916 negotiators from the United States and Great Britain/Canada agreed to protect birds migrating along the Pacific Flyway, a commitment that Congress ratified when it enacted the Migratory Bird Treaty Act in 1918 and the Migratory Bird Conservation Act in 1929. Additionally, in 1928, President Calvin Coolidge designated more than 10,000 acres of marshland at Tule Lake as the Tule Lake Bird Refuge, partly to offset reductions in the size of an older refuge two miles to the west. In 1936, Finley and other conservationists persuaded Franklin D. Roosevelt to triple the size of the Tule Lake refuge to encompass 37,300 acres. Thus, lands that had been withdrawn for homesteading came to be jointly managed by the Bureau of Reclamation and the FWS. The Executive Orders establishing and enlarging the refuge acknowledged that portions of the refuge might eventually be reclaimed and homesteaded. In anticipation of that time, the Bureau of Reclamation exercised its right to the land by leasing portions of the refuge to local grain farmers, with the stipulation that some of the grain they grew must be left as forage for migratory birds.[11]

In 1948 public support for the Bureau's homesteading program was strong. When the agency encroached upon the wildlife refuge to drain and open 2,300 acres for homesteading along its southern perimeter, the benefits for veterans were featured in an enthusiastic cover story for *Life Magazine* and were touted as well in newsreels. The *New York Times* celebrated the

Reclamation photographer Ben Glaha captured this image of Canada Honker Geese flying in formation over the Tule Lake Sump in September 1941. Note the reedy bog in the foreground. In the 1950s and 1960s, wildlife advocates and sportsmen successfully opposed plans to drain additional bogs in the sump area for homesteads. (Photograph by Ben D. Glaha, Reclamation Photographs, NARA, Rocky Mountain Region)

"miraculous transformation of the American wilderness" being wrought by the Bureau. In 1951, though, when the Bureau proposed opening thousands of additional acres to homesteading, the FWS tried to gain exclusive control of 15,232 acres on the refuge that had previously been jointly managed by the two agencies. After a committee of farmers and businessmen in the area protested vigorously by sending a brief to legislators and Interior Department officials, the FWS backed down but reiterated its opposition to reducing the size of the refuge. The Bureau, meanwhile, issued a conciliatory statement indicating that it had no current plans to drain "any additional areas now used for wildlife refuge purposes."[12]

Although the rivalry between the two agencies simmered for a time, it boiled over several months later when John Edmands, the editor of the *Tulelake Reporter*, printed a pro-development telegram from Undersecretary of the Interior Richard Searles to Bureau officials. Searles advised the Bureau to "energetically" pursue the agency's "established objective" of creating additional homesteads at Tule Lake. Searles urged that "the maximum acreage" that could be protected from seasonal flooding in the wildlife refuge should be homesteaded.[13]

After reading about Searles's telegram in the Tulelake paper, Seth Gordon, director of the California Division of Fish and Game, filed a protest with the Interior Department and mailed a copy to Jim Thomas, a reporter who wrote a regular "Outdoor Column" in the *San Francisco Chronicle*. Thomas represented Searles's statement to his readers as a "major threat to waterfowl conservation in the Pacific Flyway" and a menace to duck hunters everywhere. It would "wreck" the wildlife refuge system, "nullify" the government's multimillion dollar investment in the refuges, "eliminate" hunting in the Tule Lake refuge, and subject the grain fields of farmers in the Central Valley to "depradations" [*sic*] by migratory waterfowl. Thomas quoted an unnamed wildlife official who alleged that even though only one-third of the refuge would be homesteaded under Searles's proposal, "the value of Tule Lake" would be "shot to hell."[14]

Before long, others joined the fray. The *San Francisco Call-Bulletin* echoed the diatribe against Searles, the Bureau, and its supporters. Henry Clineschmidt, president of the Western States Federated Sportsmen, called upon sportsmen's groups throughout the West to oppose further homesteading and to urge the government to transfer all remaining public lands in the Tule Lake Basin to the FWS. The manager of the Tule Lake refuge, Tom Horn, also protested the proposed land openings. Estimating that at least 1,000 veterans hunted each year in the area, he asked, "Should we sacrifice hunting for 1,000 veterans each season in order to give 100 vets homesteads?"[15]

Having unwittingly unleashed a firestorm of opposition to homesteading, Edmands addressed an open letter to Thomas, pointing out that "our Tule Lake basin is more than a refuge for ducks and geese. It is also one of the most highly productive agricultural areas in the nation." Then he sketched out a broader regional and class-based critique, accusing urban Californians of failing to appreciate rural resources including the wildlife they supposedly loved. Edmands was willing to bet Thomas "a new typewriter that there are more real sportsmen among the 4,000 souls in this Tulelake area than you have in the entire city of San Francisco; and from what I have seen of hunting seasons past, I venture there are more real hunters in the local Business and Professional Women's Club than there are in the entire metropolis of Los Angeles." In another editorial, Edmands mocked San Francisco journalists as upper-class urban liberals "who chose to direct this basin from their vantage point atop the Mark Hopkins hotel."[16]

Thomas retorted that "millions of dollars of crop damage" would result if lands on the refuge were homesteaded. He did not doubt that the Tule Basin was highly productive agriculturally, nor did he disparage the work of farmers there. But he contended that removing lands from the refuge would "wreck the balance of the entire waterfowl refuge program in California and increase immeasurably the crop depradation [*sic*] problem in the Sacramento and San Joaquin valleys."[17]

This animated clash occasioned by Undersecretary Searles's telegram soon attracted attention in the nation's capital. In April 1952, Secretary of the Interior Oscar Chapman, a Colorado Democrat, ordered both the Bureau and the FWS to prepare recommendations regarding what should be done with the disputed land. Retreating from Searles's pro-development position, the Bureau's regional director, Richard Boke, met with nearly 100 farmers in the basin in August. Boke said he believed the Bureau could eventually develop a significant portion of the refuge. He asked the farmers to be patient and support his plan to defuse the issue by recommending no new homesteading in the basin for the time being. Instead, the Bureau would first survey reclamation prospects in the entire Klamath River drainage in south central Oregon and north central California.[18]

After Boke departed, pro-development sentiment regained the upper hand. The following month, about 300 residents met with Bureau officials, excluding Boke. After expressing frustration with "demands on their land by sportsmen and other government bureaus" they overwhelmingly endorsed a call for the Bureau to open new homesteads within the next year. Bureau officials in the meeting disagreed with each other regarding the advisability of the resolution, but it likely influenced Secretary Chapman's course of action.[19]

After collecting information and considering reports from the Bureau and from the FWS, Secretary Chapman signed a memorandum on 7 January 1953 as one of his last acts in office. Chapman's "lame-duck" directive promised something to both sides. It provided that 2,500 acres of land currently leased by the Bureau for farming on the Tule Lake refuge as well as several thousand acres in the Klamath Straits area in southern Oregon be opened to homesteading. The directive also stipulated, however, that all remaining public lands in the Tule Lake and Klamath Basins not needed to maintain the Bureau's activities be transferred to the FWS, thereby foreclosing any possibility of homesteading those lands in the future. Although the manager of the Tule Lake refuge was pleased with Chapman's decision, saying that it was based upon "the principle of the greatest good to the greatest number," most residents of the Basin condemned it. E. Layton Stephens, manager of the Bureau's Klamath project, expressed the prevailing sentiment of local residents. "Personally, I would not have favored releasing the lands in the Tulelake Basin for wildlife purposes; they are among the most valuable agricultural lands there are. I feel there is opportunity in the Basin to fulfill bird life requirements without their use."[20]

Not content with the Chapman compromise, local advocates of homesteading organized and pressed for more, anticipating that President Eisenhower's new interior secretary, the former Republican governor of Oregon, Douglas McKay, would favor their cause. Clyde Todd, commander of the American Legion post in Tulelake, traveled to Washington in February where he met with McKay as well as with the region's senators and representatives. The Tulelake Irrigation District leant its support by obtaining legal assistance from H. J. Horton, a southern California attorney specializing in water law.[21]

Meanwhile, hard-line opponents of all homesteading in the Associated Sportsmen of California, a powerful organization in the Golden State, also lobbied against Chapman's directive. The sportsmen asked Congress to permanently transfer the areas Chapman had slated for homesteading to the FWS. Representatives of the California Fish and Game Commission also persuaded the California Farm Bureau Federation and the State Chamber of Commerce to oppose Chapman's directive by arguing that rice and grain fields in central and southern California would be invaded by migratory birds before harvest time if the size of the Tule Lake refuge were reduced. The farm bureau and the state chamber selected Eugene Bennett, an attorney from San Francisco and leader in the California Duck Hunters Association, as their lobbyist.[22]

By the end of April, having heard complaints about Chapman's memorandum from both advocates and opponents of additional homesteading, McKay decided to ignore it. "At the present time we don't plan to do anything," a spokesman for the Department of the Interior announced. Everything was once again up for grabs.[23]

Trying to gain the upper hand, advocates of homesteading next turned their attention to persuading the California State Farm Bureau to reverse its stand against homesteading. At the farm bureau's convention in December, homesteader Stan Buckingham and American Legion commander Clyde Todd argued that there were more than enough marshlands in the area to sustain migratory birds even if the most fertile lands on the refuge were homesteaded. They persuaded the farm bureau to adopt a resolution calling for homesteading "no later than 1956" on two tracts that had been slated by Chapman for inclusion in the wildlife refuge.[24]

Next, supporters of homesteading tried to incorporate a guarantee that lands would be homesteaded within the Tulelake Irrigation District's repayment contract with the federal government. Several weeks after submitting their draft of the contract to the Interior Department in 1955, irrigation district directors Sam Anderson and Ivan Rose traveled to Washington to discuss the matter with Secretary McKay, only to be told that the secretary had been called out of town and still hadn't made up his mind regarding additional homesteads in the Basin. Anderson was "boiling" mad after having traveled across the country to meet with the secretary. He complained that McKay had known about the matter for over two years. Departmental undersecretary Fred Aandahl, a rock-ribbed North Dakotan experienced in power politics, was not about to be bullied, though. He icily warned Anderson and Rose that the Interior Department would not approve any contract that "lays down the conditions or creates pressure toward" opening lands for homesteading or leasing.[25]

The contract as finally approved and signed in the summer of 1956 offered no timetable or assurances regarding homesteading, but it did leave the door open by committing the United States to investigate the "feasibility of developing substitute wildlife habitat in other areas of the Klamath Basin." It also stated that "unentered public lands" lying within the district "should be open for homesteading as promptly as the United States may deem desirable consistent with other authorized uses." Representatives of the Tulelake Irrigation District delivered a carefully worded memorandum to governmental representatives at the signing ceremony. The irrigation district directors expressed their feeling "that your department has been lax in announcing its plans for the public lands in our district." They wanted the issue resolved promptly in order "to see the greatest amount of land in our district homesteaded and placed in private ownership." Speaking for the government, Clyde Spencer, regional director for the Bureau of Reclamation, stated in doublespeak, "We in Interior are . . . equally determined to protect and preserve our waterfowl as we are to see a maximum of farm families homesteading public lands."[26]

Nearly eight months after the repayment contract had been signed the government had still not opened any additional lands for settlement. Farmers in the Basin were "highly troubled" over the inability of the Bureau and the FWS to agree on "a program for the development of the water and land resources of our Basin." Following up on the government's contractual pledge to investigate the possibility of swapping lands within the Tule Lake Refuge for lands elsewhere in the region, a coalition of twenty water districts in the Klamath Basin proposed a plan to the secretary of the interior in May 1957. Under their plan, lands in the Tule Lake Basin would be opened immediately to homesteading and half a dozen tracts of public lands that were less suited to irrigation would be added to other wildlife refuges in the vicinity so that the total acreage of refuge land would not be diminished. They claimed that many groups of sportsmen would support the program.[27]

The new secretary of the interior, Fred Seaton, requested position papers from the Bureau of Reclamation and the FWS on the idea of a land swap. Unfortunately for proponents of homesteading, the director of the FWS, John L. Farley, was not known for compromising; Farley, who had blocked all recreational hunting in the Sacramento National Wildlife Refuge, opposed any reduction in the Tule Lake refuge even if substitute lands elsewhere were set aside for wildlife. He insisted that the Tule Lake refuge constituted "a key area" in the Pacific Flyway, and that therefore substitute acreage would be unacceptable. America's international honor was at stake; in a treaty with Canada and Mexico the United States had pledged to maintain "in perpetuity a chain of refuges and management areas throughout all flyways." Farley called for "adequate and firm water supplies" for the refuge, inclusion of additional land within the refuge, and placement of those lands under the permanent and exclusive jurisdiction of the FWS. By contrast, the Bureau of Reclamation recommended that 10,000 acres be homesteaded, claiming that substitute areas outside the refuge would afford ample food and shelter for wildlife.[28]

John Bennett, director of the Interior Department's Technical Review Staff, finished analyzing the two agencies' position papers by the end of January 1958. His report recommended against opening any refuge lands to homesteading for the time being. Some land on the wildlife refuges might be homesteaded eventually but only after substitute habitat had been fully developed. The Interior Department hailed Bennett's "impartial analysis." Privately the department's undersecretaries in charge of both irrigation and fish and wildlife believed its noncommital recommendations were "the best way to handle this difficult problem." But Sam Anderson, president of the Tulelake Irrigation District, was incensed: from the tenor of the report he would have guessed that Bennett "worked for the Fish and Wildlife Service," he fulminated, because it offered nothing concrete to proponents of reclamation.[29]

Acting upon the Bennett report Secretary Seaton decreed in April of 1958 that "controversial lands in the Lower Klamath–Tule Lake region must be used in a manner that will fully protect the valuable waterfowl resources of that area." Seaton's directive did not permanently quash the possibility of homesteading but indicated that the Bureau of Reclamation would have to "provide substitute wildfowl habitat in the area" as an "accomplished fact" and demonstrate the suitability of that substitute habitat before homesteading could be considered. George Difani, the secretary of the California Wildlife Federation, hailed the decision while the president of the Tulelake Irrigation District said he was "bitterly disappointed" and derided state and federal wildlife officials as "stupid."[30]

Seaton's decision once again preserved the status quo but held out the possibility—tantalizing for some and terrible for others—that lands on the refuge might eventually be homesteaded. In March 1960 the National Wildlife Federation lobbied Seaton to prepare a bill that would permanently ban homesteading on the refuge, and the Interior Advisory Committee of the Wildlife Management Institute subsequently helped to draft one and circulated it to members of Congress. In order to whip up support for it, C. R. "Pink" Gutermuth, the vice president of the Wildlife Management Institute, worked with reporters to "stir up some stories." A particularly influential one because of its national coverage appeared in *Audubon Magazine* under the title "Tule Lake Threat Must Be Removed." The editorial by Carl Bucheister, president of the Audubon Society, warned, "The remaining lands of Tule Lake are greatly coveted by private interests for speculative and homesteading purposes. . . . It is amazing that a few hundred individuals who stand to profit financially have been able to prevail against the interests of millions who use and enjoy the waterfowl." Bucheister characterized the advocates of homesteading as "raucous and constant" and depicted conservationists as "a big, silent majority . . . . [who] must speak up." Senator Thomas Kuchel of California supported the bill, but when the senior senator from the Golden State, Clair Engel, rebuffed Gutermuth and representatives from the Audubon Society, Kuchel became "skittish" about acting on his own.[31]

But the political winds in Washington changed with John F. Kennedy's inauguration in 1961. Kennedy's secretary of the interior, Stewart Udall, championed conservation and recreation much more vigorously than his recent predecessors. With an avid conservationist secretary, what had been a regional conflict over public lands management escalated into a cause celebre for conservation. In May 1961, Kuchel introduced the Wildlife Management Institute's bill, which would prevent further homesteading in the Tule Lake Basin by dedicating the lands that the Bureau had been managing there to waterfowl management. An Orange County attorney and Republican who had replaced Richard Nixon in the Senate, Kuchel insisted that he was not favoring "ducks" over "people." His support for the wildlife refuge resulted partly, he said, from his commitment to farmers in the Sacramento, San Joaquin, and Imperial Valleys. As was often the case in environmental victories in this era, sportsmen and conservationists, who were "evangelical" in support for Kuchel's bill and "unalterably opposed to any further reclamation of land in the Tule Lake area that would involve land presently in the duck preserve," found ways to ally with groups that had traditionally favored public lands development by appealing to their self-interest. Wildlife advocates had convinced Kuchel and at least some farmers in the Central Valley that migratory birds would arrive in their fields earlier in the season if portions of the Tule Lake refuge were homesteaded. As Kuchel told his colleagues in the Senate, "The capability of the Tule Lake–Klamath complex in holding the more than 7 million ducks and geese during their annual migration is vital to the successful harvesting of crops in the Sacramento, San Joaquin, and Imperial Valleys in California." Thus Kuchel was able to argue that his bill served the "interests of conservation, recreation, and agriculture."[32]

Sam Anderson, president of the Tulelake Irrigation District, criticized Kuchel's bill, and the "ever increasing emphasis" upon using land in the Basin for "fish and wildlife purposes to the detriment of the agricultural interests." Wildlife preservation, which had originally been "an incidental use of the land" under the executive order that established the wildlife refuge, was now being recast by Kuchel as "a primary use on a permanent basis." Anderson argued that Kuchel's bill violated the irrigation district's repayment contract, which stipulated that "unentered public lands" lying within the district should be open for homesteading. As Chet Langslet of the Klamath Basin Water Users Protective Association observed, the bill "abrogates the moral and contractual obligations of the government." Anderson pointed out that alternative tracts of wetland in the region were poorly suited to farming and recommended that those lands be substituted for valuable agricultural lands within the refuge. He insisted that opening additional lands to agriculture would not reduce forage for birds in the Tule Lake Basin. As Walt Radke, a reporter for the *San Francisco Chronicle*, observed, though, the farmers' opposition to creating a permanent "duck hotel" at Tule Lake was out of touch with the times: "Maybe the Tule Lake farmers do have present regulations on their side. But laws are revised to meet changing conditions. The Constitution is considered a legal masterpiece, but at last count it had been amended 23 times."[33]

Commissioner Dominy forthrightly opposed the bill, pointing out that it was "not consistent" with the Irrigation District's contract with the government. He also charged that the bill contradicted "the major policy decisions that have been announced publicly during the past ten years." Dominy preferred that the matter be handled administratively by interagency negotiations rather than legislatively. The headstrong commissioner was overruled, though, when the Department of the Interior officially endorsed the bill in November. In February 1962 Secretary Udall underscored the department's position with his own enthusiastic support of the bill. Udall told a Congressional subcommittee that preserving intact the boundaries of the Tule Lake refuge would be "one of the most important conservation decisions" Congress could make in that session. The bill was important to the entire nation because there was "probably no more important waterfowl area in the country" than the "refuges in the Upper Klamath Basin." Even the strong-willed, flamboyant commissioner was backed into the corner by Udall's decisive stand. Since the Bureau's "objections [had] been overruled," Dominy conceded, "we will go no further with our investigations of [opening] the Tule Lake sump area" to homesteading.[34]

In February 1962, the Senate Interior and Insular Affairs committee held hearings on the Kuchel bill. Five representatives from the Tulelake Irrigation District testified in opposition to the bill, as did a county supervisor and a representative of the Klamath Drainage district. Although there were thousands of individuals interested in obtaining homesteads, few even knew of the debate and they were not organized as a pressure group to promote their interests. Veterans' organizations, which had previously supported homesteading, now had no pressing reason to do so since the veterans preference legislation Congress had enacted in 1944 had expired in 1959. Veterans could still apply for homesteads, but only on the same footing as everyone else. Local agricultural and wildlife groups including the Klamath County Chamber of Commerce, the Tulelake Growers Association, the Siskiyou County Board of Supervisors, and the Oregon Wildlife Federation jointly proposed amendments to the bill that would augment the overall size of wildlife refuges within a 50-mile radius of Tule Lake while at the same time withdrawing 16,400 acres of the most valuable agricultural land on the Tule Lake refuge for homesteading. Arrayed against these primarily local groups were representatives of the Sport Fishing Institute, *National Wildland News*, the Wildlife Management Institute, the National Wildlife Federation, and the Izaak Walton League. Major California newspapers, California governor Edmund G. Brown, the Associated Sportsmen of California, the Citizens Committee of Natural Resources, the Southern Council of Conservation Clubs, and the International Association of Game, Fish and Conservation Commissioners also endorsed the bill. Kuchel had organized his supporters magnificently. They argued that Congress was faced with a choice between serving "the small interests of a very few" and meeting "the essential interests of future generations."[35]

Impressed by ringing endorsements of the bill from "every conservation organization in America," the committee on May 3 favorably reported the bill to the full Senate. The case for the Kuchel bill had been "presented mainly in fragments, and to uncritical metropolitan conservation audiences as a fight against government supported farmers who are already growing surplus crops," John Edmands of the *Tulelake Reporter* complained. Politicians like Kuchel and Brown were bowing to "multitudes of distant city hunters and conservation-minded voters" as well as "Sacramento Valley farmers, who outnumber us drastically at the ballot box." Locals complained that the Bureau of Reclamation, which had strongly campaigned for homestead openings, had imposed a gag order upon its employees after Secretary Udall endorsed the Kuchel bill.[36]

Venting local exasperation, Edmands printed an open letter to Kuchel in the Tulelake paper, criticizing him for discriminating against farmers in the Tule Lake Basin. The editor sarcastically proposed a wildlife refuge to be named in Kuchel's honor that would cover 9,000 square miles, extending 15 miles on either side of the entire length of the Sacramento River. "Your name will be on the lips of every farmer in those counties—not only as part of the title of the Sanctuary, but because you will have allowed them to share with us the Sacred Trust of protecting wildlife: a trust to which you have often referred in your news releases to Southern California sports columnists."[37]

On May 16, less than two weeks after the bill was reported to the Senate, it was approved by that body. Before endorsing the bill, the Senate amended it. The amendments clarified that the land would be "dedicated to wildlife conservation" and would "not be opened to homestead entry" but did authorize the Interior Department to lease lands within the refuge to farmers to the "optimum" amount that was "consistent" with wildlife needs. Oregon Senator Wayne Morse endorsed the amended bill, predicting that it would promote recreation, an enterprise he believed would soon "be the primary source of revenue" for his state.[38]

After it passed the Senate, the bill was referred in the House to its Subcommittee on Irrigation and Reclamation. Harold T. "Bizz" Johnson, who represented the Tule Lake Basin in Congress, served on the subcommittee. Directors of the Tulelake Irrigation District informed the subcommittee that they preferred to have the issues settled in local negotiations with the FWS where they believed they could exert greater influence than on Capitol Hill. Privately, they plotted strategy with Representative Johnson to amend the bill and if possible to prevent its passage in the current session. The strategy worked to "delay" the bill and thereby buy time for Johnson to engage the Department of the Interior in devising an alternative prior to the next session of Congress. The bill failed to reach the floor of the House before the legislative session ended.[39]

Knowing that Kuchel planned to reintroduce his bill, Johnson asked the Interior Department to draft an alternative that would safeguard agricultural interests more fully. Johnson was encountering pressure from conservationists in California and felt vulnerable politically. He persuaded a fellow Democrat, Senator Clair Engle, who had represented Johnson's district in the House for fourteen years before moving on to the Senate, to support the alternate bill in the Senate. But even this bill would "eliminate . . . the possibility of private ownership of any of the public lands" in the refuge. After Johnson and attorneys convinced representatives from the Tulelake Irrigation District that the opposition to homesteading was too numerous and influential to overcome, and that Johnson could not afford politically "to give an inch" on further homesteading, the irrigation district officers reluctantly agreed to "accept . . . the facts of political life" and abandon their campaign for additional homesteads. At least the Engle/Johnson bill would prioritize their claims upon water, ensuring that the wildlife refuge would not receive farmers' water during a drought. Convinced that the Engle bill was "as fair a compromise to the agriculture interest in the Tule Lake Basin as possible," the directors unanimously voted to support it.[40]

Reflecting on the turn of events, Lester Cushman, vice president of the Tulelake Irrigation District, remarked that he had "seen many changes take place" in the status of farmers over his twenty-seven-year career. Who could have predicted in the 1940s that homesteading would become such a dirty word? Who could have imagined just a few years earlier that the Tulelake Irrigation District would be supporting a bill that prohibited additional homesteading on land within the district?[41]

Unlike Cushman and his fellow commissioners, some local residents continued to campaign for additional homesteads. In June 1963 the Siskiyou County Republican Committee passed a resolution opposing the Johnson, Engle, and Kuchel bills and endorsing homesteading in order to increase the tax base. "There is no evidence," they claimed, "that the homesteading of

Homesteading was widely regarded nationwide as a noble enterprise when this photograph of Tulelake, California, was taken in March 1947. Land openings boosted the economy of small service centers nearby like Tulelake. As photographer J. E. Fluharty noted, "This town is quite new and is completely dependent on homesteaders for its existence. Naturally, it is quite happy over the prospect of getting new citizens to live within the trade area that it serves." (Reclamation Photographs, NARA, Rocky Mountain Region)

said lands would affect said bird refuge adversely." W. H. Weitkamp, who had homesteaded in the Basin, called the contention that homesteads would jeopardize harvests in the Central Valley "a lot of baloney." But this position had been relegated to the political fringe: Congress ignored the County Republican Committee's resolution.[42]

Gearing up for a battle over his bill, Kuchel solicited the support of wildlife interests ranging from environmentalists to duck hunters. Kuchel's friend J. P. Cuenin of the *San Francisco Examiner* pledged to "write articles which will induce many of Engle's constituents to ask if he is working for or against them." "Thank goodness for fine friends like you," Kuchel replied. Another of Kuchel's allies, Walt Radke, warned readers through his column in the *San Francisco Examiner* that the Engle bill would lift Basin farmers into "the driver's seat" and thereby perpetuate "the ancient conflict between waterfowl conservation and agriculture."[43]

The Senate Subcommittee on Irrigation and Reclamation held hearings on the Engle and Kuchel bills in April 1963. The main difference between the two bills involved the relative priorities they assigned to agriculture and wildlife in allocating water. In the event of a water shortage, should the interests of wildlife or irrigation prevail? Engle favored concessions to the farmers while Kuchel, who had already earned their enmity, was ready to repay it with interest. Engle said he had "hunted ducks on Tule Lake" and expressed "deep concern for the interests of ducks and geese, duck hunters, sportsmen, and wildlife conservationists." But he insisted that in order to win the support of farmers in the area and stave off a lawsuit, any bill providing for wildlife in the area should recognize the government's obligation under subsection 7 (b) of its contract with the Tulelake Irrigation District to provide water for farmers. Trying to undermine Engle's position, Kuchel asked him if he was saying that "you desire to have a compromise under which the conservation purposes of waterfowl management would be subordinate to the terms of the contract between the Tulelake Irrigation District and the Federal Government." Engle refused to be boxed into a corner: "What I am saying is that the Federal Government has to keep its contract, whatever the consequences of it." Frustrated with Kuchel's badgering, Engle pressed him to accept the wording in his bill and stop "nit-picking about . . . these arguments as to language." Kuchel retorted that it was Engle who was "nit-picking"; his reading of the irrigation contract was simply broader than Engle's.

> When you pick out the one section in that contract that says agricultural purposes shall be supreme, and you do not refer to the other section of the contract that says when there is a dispute the Secretary shall decide it, you give rise to a contention that the irrigation district would have the right to say the other provision of the contract does not apply to this piece of legislation.

Kuchel insisted that Congress must "recognize the need for optimal agricultural purposes" but "nevertheless subject those purposes to . . . the public interest in favor of conservation." At last the two Senators accepted compromise wording suggested by the Interior Department. It preserved Engle's stipulation that the Tule Lake sump "shall be operated and maintained in accordance with the provisions of section 7 (b) and (d) of the contract" but added the phrase "and at levels that are in the judgment of the Secretary adequate and practicable for waterfowl management purposes."[44]

When the Senate considered the compromise bill, both Engle and Kuchel endorsed it and downplayed their earlier disagreement. Engle said he preferred not to rehash the "unfortunate and unnecessary . . . controversy" and verbal sparring. Kuchel told his colleagues that under the bill in "all circumstances, the major purpose of conservation, sound waterfowl management, would remain supreme." Farmers in the Tule Lake Basin had contended that their interests would be harmed by legislation that gave preferential treatment to waterfowl over agriculture, but Kuchel averred that "with performance of the district's obligation to maintain the dikes and sumps, as provided in its contract, no conflict in the priorities ought to arise." With backing from Engle, Kuchel, and twelve other cosponsors the Senate approved the Kuchel bill on 15 July 1963. When the *San Francisco Examiner* praised Kuchel and Engle for having "worked tirelessly and effectively" to pass the bill, Kuchel's assistant, Warren B. Francis, griped to a coworker about the "free ride for Engle."[45]

Tulelake Irrigation District Manager Ed Lance felt that the compromise legislation was "not bad" but he hoped the House would restore Engle's original language. While the difference between the two versions was "not great" Engle's original bill offered more security to farmers in times of drought.[46]

In order to overcome opposition in the House to the Senate bill, California hunting, recreational, and environmental interests as well as farmers in the Central Valley mobilized. Bud Boyd, long an advocate of wildlife in his column "The Woodsman" in the *San Francisco Chronicle*, criticized Johnson in November 1963 for relegating Kuchel's bill "officially referred to as the most important conservation legislation of our time" to a "pigeon hole in Washington" where it stood "every chance of suffocation" unless Johnson's constituents who hunted ducks pulled their weight.[47]

When the House Committee on Interior and Insular Affairs met to review the Kuchel bill, they tried to soften its impact upon farmers. One amendment proposed by "Bizz" Johnson was intended, much like the original

Engle bill, as a concession to farmers in the Tule Lake area for whom the bill's prohibition of future homesteading in the Basin was "quite a blow." The amendment directed the secretary of the interior to regulate water levels for wildlife management in accordance with "the provisions of the contract between the United States and the Tule Lake Irrigation District." Kuchel's legislative assistant, Steve Horn, believed Johnson's amendment "would not harm the bill and would save face for [Johnson]," but Horn advised Kuchel and others to play hard ball and tell California sportsmen to oppose any amendments. House committee member John P. Saylor of Pennsylvania dissented from his colleagues on the committee, arguing Johnson's amendment "confuses rather than makes clear" the "priority in favor of waterfowl management" expressed in the Kuchel bill. Another amendment introduced by the chair of the committee, Walter Rogers, gave the state legislatures of either California or Oregon three years to force a reconsideration of the bill. Congress would then have to decide whether to sustain the state's objections or to reenact the statute. Saylor likewise opposed this amendment; "the bill really becomes no bill at all if this section is allowed to stand," he insisted. The committee reported the amended bill to the House on 19 December.[48]

The proposed amendments aroused particularly stiff opposition in the San Francisco Bay Area, where "a number of adverse editorials" appeared in newspapers. The latter amendment permitting state legislatures to reject the law attracted the most venom. Acting like a lightning rod, it deflected criticism that otherwise might have been focused on the amendment regarding the irrigation district's contract. By prior arrangement with Kuchel, Saylor worked behind the scenes to persuade the committee to delete that provision. He succeeded; on April 8, the House Committee on Interior and Insular Affairs removed the amendment regarding state legislatures from the bill. In return, Saylor endorsed the bill as a "constructive solution to an old, old problem." The House passed the Kuchel bill with Johnson's amendment on 20 April.[49]

Now Bizz Johnson tried to persuade Kuchel to support the bill as amended by the House. Claiming he had intended to discuss the Tule Lake situation with Kuchel for two years but had been unable to find time to do so because of "many, many things," Johnson wrote to the Senator explaining his position. The amendment was "very dear" to Johnson, he explained, because it offered the only ray of hope to the farmers. It "merely recognize[d]" the terms of the irrigation district's contract with the government. "Tom, you know when I took this job on, and made my stand in the Tulelake area and told the farmers that I would not go along with further homesteading, exchange or sale of public lands I really meant it," Johnson pleaded. He had "taken all the abuse that one could put up with" from people across the nation because of things that Kuchel or his allies had said. "I believe that certainly many facts have been misrepresented and misstated," he complained. He had been vilified as an enemy of wildlife when he was not. The least Kuchel could do was "accept the bill" as passed by the House. Kuchel tersely replied, "I frankly feel I cannot accept the amendment," although he invited Johnson to call him on the telephone.[50]

A conference committee representing the House and the Senate met over the following months to hammer out a compromise regarding the rights of the irrigation districts. Henry Jackson, Clinton Anderson, Frank Moss, Gordon Allott, and Kuchel represented the Senate while Joe Skubitz, Walter Rogers, Robert Duncan, Saylor, and Johnson represented the House. The committee received communications opposing the House version from the Pacific Flyway Council, the California Fish and Game Commission, the Nevada Fish and Game Commission, the National Rifle Association, the National Wildlife Federation, the Wildlife Management Institute, the Izaak Walton League, and the Rice Growers Association of California. Wildlife interests urged Kuchel to "hold fast for the Senate language and to permit the meeting to recess rather than to submit to any alternatives." But in the end Kuchel compromised with the House on this issue. The final version of the statute committed the secretary of the interior to "maintain" water levels in the wildlife refuge sump areas in conformance with the Tulelake Irrigation District's contract with the government. Unlike the Senate version, which had prioritized wildlife over farming, the final bill gently prioritized agriculture but added, "Such regulations shall accommodate to the maximum extent practicable waterfowl management needs." The House accepted the conference report on 18 August and the Senate did so the next day. President Johnson signed the bill on 2 September 1964.[51]

Wildlife interests were not entirely satisfied. Carl Wente of the Duck Hunters Association of California remarked that the bill "did not exactly give us what we wanted," and J. D. Flournoy, President of the California Wildlife Association, disliked the word "practicable" in the phrase "accommodate to the maximum extent practicable waterfowl management." Another prominent activist from the Duck Hunters Association, Gene Bennett, didn't "like it" either. But the *San Francisco Chronicle* praised the legislation as a "victory for common sense and the conservationists."[52]

After its quixotic, thirteen-year campaign to develop additional farms in the Tule Lake Basin, the Bureau was unable to open lands for homesteading anywhere in the nation. Plans to develop homesteads in the Basin aroused exceptionally vigorous opposition on a national level because they threatened a wildlife refuge. But even when the Bureau sought in the 1960s and 1970s to develop public lands for farming in districts outside national parks, monuments, and refuges, advocates of open space and wildlife staunchly opposed it. In 1965, for instance, the Bureau laid plans to develop and subdivide 7,400 acres into thirty homesteads on the Minidoka Project. The agency "immediately ran into a stalemate between pro-development and environmentalist groups." The Bureau argued that the land was inessential for pheasants and rabbits, but opponents countered that "any development" would jeopardize the animals. Although the Bureau tried to demonstrate in its proposal that it could mitigate the impact upon wildlife, the Interior Department vetoed the proposal because it was too controversial.[53]

The Bureau's inability to develop additional farms in places like the Tule Lake Basin and the Snake River Valley resulted largely from the ascendancy and popularity of preservationist sentiment in the relatively prosperous 1960s. The same forces stymied the Bureau in its larger campaign to build dams after 1960. Largely as a result of those forces, by the late 1960s, the Bureau gave up on developing additional homesteads anywhere in the West.[54]

REPEAL OF THE HOMESTEAD ACT

8

Although rising preservationist sentiment helped to prevent the Bureau of Reclamation from opening additional lands for homesteading after 1961, homesteading remained legally permissible under the Reclamation and Homestead Acts. In 1974, for instance, Kenneth Deardorff, a Vietnam veteran from California, claimed an 80-acre tract on Stony River, a remote tributary of the Kushkokwim River in southwestern Alaska. Deardorff arrived in the dead of winter and bivouacked in a nylon tent until he could construct a small cabin. A few months later his wife joined him, and together they built a larger log home from white spruce trees. The Deardorffs fulfilled the requirements of the Homestead Act, improving the land while they lived on it. They fished, hunted wild game, and traveled by dogsled over the deep snow. "It's been an exciting life," Deardorff recalled years later. "I always wanted to live where I could raise the window and shoot something. I certainly got that."[1]

The Homestead Act under which Deardorff claimed land was part of a complex web of federal land law that the government did not evaluate comprehensively until after the Public Land Law Review Commission was formed in 1964. Six years later, the Commission completed its report. In 1976, acting upon the commission's recommendation, Congress at last repealed the Homestead Act, ending the possibility of homesteading on the public domain.[2]

The process leading to the Homestead Act's repeal is poorly understood, an ironic gap in the history of public land law given the act's symbolic and practical eminence. Historians often conflate the passage of the Taylor Grazing Act in 1934 with the end of homesteading. Michael Malone and Richard Etulain, for instance, observe that the act "end[ed] the age-old policy of homesteading." The Taylor Act *was* monumental: in approving it, Congress embraced the view that most of the public domain was poorly suited for homesteading. But lawmakers fashioned loopholes in the Taylor Act that permitted homesteading to continue on a limited basis.[3]

After World War II, advocates of streamlined, efficient land sales raised the idea of rolling back the Homestead Act completely. In 1952 the House of Representatives appointed a special subcommittee of five chaired by Lloyd Bentsen Jr., a second-term congressman from Texas known for his pro-business outlook, to investigate ways of making the public land laws more efficient. The subcommittee held hearings in Alaska, Oregon, and California where prospective homesteaders along with representatives from business and labor organizations, government agencies, conservation groups, and extractive industries testified. In Alaska, would-be settlers wanted to retain the Homestead Act but repeal the statute that gave veterans preferential treatment in claiming land. Ben Culver, representing the All-Alaska Chamber of Commerce, urged the government to develop roads before opening land for homesteading. Ranchers in Oregon, eager to expand their holdings, said they preferred public land sales to homestead openings. Bentsen's committee reported its conclusions later that year. Stopping short of specifically recommending repeal of the Homestead Act, it instead advised that the tangle of laws regarding homesteads and desert land entries should be consolidated "into a coherent law which would permit title to be acquired to land suitable for agricultural purposes." They believed the federal government owned too much land and that "the main basis of our land policy" should be "transfer of Federal land in fee to non-Federal ownership." Congress generally failed to act upon the committee's recommendations until the 1960s.[4]

During the 87th Congress (1961–1962) Secretary of the Interior Stewart Udall renewed the call for streamlining land laws. Unlike Bentsen, Udall wanted to alter land laws in order to ensure "continued public ownership and management" in most cases. He urged Congress to repeal both the Homestead Act and the Desert Land Act, a statute that allowed individuals to buy up to 320 acres for a nominal price if they could successfully irrigate the land. Members of the House Committee on Interior and Insular Affairs agreed with Udall that land laws needed to be restructured, although not all of them shared Udall's preservationist sentiments. "It has been commonplace for many years to say that the 'good' agricultural lands have long since been settled; and that the 'easily' found minerals have been discovered and developed. The inference of these truisms is that the public land laws must be examined to ascertain whether they serve the changed conditions," the committee reported in 1963. They felt no need to substantiate these "truisms" because they were so widely shared in a largely metropolitan society. Regardless of the fact that lands suitable for irrigated agriculture remained in the public domain, most Americans believed otherwise.[5]

Congress responded to the committee's report by creating a bipartisan Public Land Law Review Commission in 1964. The nineteen-member committee consisted of six representatives, six senators, six citizens appointed by President Johnson, and a chair. The eighteen appointees elected Colorado Democrat Wayne Aspinall as their chair, a no-nonsense workaholic from the state's largely rural Western Slope who had dominated the House Interior and Insular Affairs Committee since 1959. A utilitarian conservationist, Aspinall was "the federal reclamation program's staunchest defender." Colleagues in the House accused him of dominating committees as if they were "his personal fiefdom" and of monitoring attendance like a "schoolteacher." While Udall sought to preserve the public domain, Aspinall often championed the pro-development views of the West's traditional extractive industries. As Sierra Club director David Brower quipped a few years later, environmentalists had seen "dream after dream dashed on the stony continents of Wayne Aspinall."[6]

Under Aspinall's chairmanship, the reviewers commissioned thirty-three studies on specialized topics related to land use. Several touched upon the history and status of reclamation homesteads, including a study of land laws related to agriculture conducted by a Sacramento legal firm. The authors of that study called the opening of irrigated lands under the Reclamation Act "one of the most important contributions to the agricultural development of the arid west." Times had changed, though, and "reclamation homesteads have been of diminishing significance in recent years," they correctly noted. The authors attributed the drop in homesteading, reclamation and otherwise, to the high cost of developing modern farms. Noting that "the very word [homesteads] conjures up a romantic picture of a pioneer family heading west in a covered wagon in search of new lands and opportunities," the authors claimed that the laws regarding homesteading, like the covered wagon, fit frontier conditions that had "long since passed from the scene." They concluded, "Not much of the remaining public domain is suitable for agriculture, and most of that is situated in arid or semi-arid regions where it is often expensive to put the land into cultivation." Treating the drop in homesteading as a historical inevitability dictated by environmental and economic forces, they neglected to discuss the role that changing public opinion and national priorities had played in the decline.[7]

Another study supervised by Max Myers, an economics professor at South Dakota State University who directed the university's Institute of Social Sciences on Rural Urban Research and Planning, concluded that the nation would be able to feed itself for the foreseeable future without developing additional irrigated farms. In previous decades, Reclamation Commissioner Floyd Dominy had repeatedly argued that the nation needed to develop its irrigable lands fully, citing the Agriculture Department's projection that the nation's farmland would decrease each year by about 1 million acres due to urbanization and increased recreational demands. Meanwhile, the nation's population would likely double by 2010. "Our presently diminishing agricultural lands will not be sufficient to feed the Nation," Dominy had warned.[8]

Myers and his colleagues questioned Dominy's claims. Population was projected to increase by 50–75 percent over the next four decades, but the nation's record of rising harvests due to advances in technology, plant genetics, and chemistry would likely continue and ensure sufficient food. If additional lands were needed, moreover, landowners who were being paid by the government to withhold 60 million acres on their farms from cultivation could be induced to plant that land. The authors cited a report by the National Advisory Commission on Food and Fiber, which predicted "no foreseeable shortage" in the nation's food supply.[9]

Even if the nation needed additional farmland, Myers and his colleagues maintained, it would be less expensive to clear and drain privately owned lands in the East than to develop public lands in the West for irrigation. In 1949, for instance, the Department of Agriculture estimated the costs of clearing, stumping, and draining lands in the Southeast to be between $60 and $75 per acre. In the intervening three decades, inflation had boosted costs but the authors averred that "millions of acres of uncleared and undrained lands [in the Southeast] could be brought under cultivation for well under $200 an acre," compared to the Bureau's estimated average cost of $921 for reclaiming an acre of western land. Although Bureau officials argued that the economic gains of reclamation totaled $1.60 for each dollar spent, Myers and his colleagues disputed the claim. They accused the Bureau of "double counting" the economic benefits of reclamation, citing University of Chicago economist Edward Renshaw's finding that the Bureau's methods of calculating the income benefits of reclamation were flawed. Having sifted the data, Myers and his associates concluded that irrigation development by the Bureau was "not economic."[10]

In support of their argument, Myers and his colleagues cited Illinois Senator Paul Douglas's blistering, witty, and memorable attack in 1955 upon the proposed Colorado River Storage Project that would benefit Wyoming, Utah, Colorado, and New Mexico.

> I have great affection not only for the Senators from the four States concerned, but also for the Senators from the great northern tier of States—Montana, North Dakota, Minnesota, Wisconsin, Michigan, and the upper New England area. They are all fine members, and their localities could also be benefited if Congress appropriated over $1.6 billion with which to erect hot-houses in which to grow bananas and luscious strawberries. Think of the employment which would be created in those regions if Congress decided, as a public project, to grow bananas in the wintertime, and thus alleviate the shortage of fruit. Prosperity would bloom throughout the northern area. But someone else would have to pay the bill.[11]

Turning from the cost of reclaiming lands to the question of whether the Bureau could reclaim enough western land to augment the nation's food supply significantly, Myers and his colleagues engaged in some statistical legerdemain of their own. The Bureau claimed 9.5 million acres in the West could be reclaimed economically by 2000 by impounding and pumping the waters of western rivers. But Myers erroneously assumed that the Bureau's only options for developing those lands involved diverting water from Northwestern rivers like the Yukon and Columbia and pumping it uphill thousands of miles. Accordingly, Myers and his colleagues pared down the number of acres in the public domain that the Bureau could reclaim to a mere 1.3 million acres—the acreage for which water was "presently physically and legally available" without any additional construction and storage. Those lands would support no more than 3,100 additional farms and would boost the nation's agricultural production by less than 1 percent.[12]

During the 1950s the Bureau had strenuously disputed criticisms of the costs and benefits of reclaiming western land for farming, but by the time the Myers report appeared in 1969, Reclamation and its allies in Congress had altered their strategy. Better to focus upon the ways that reclamation facilitated industrial and urban growth and recreation—causes that were easier to defend in an increasingly urban nation—than to promote agricultural expansion. Thus, when the House in 1968 debated HR 3300, a funding package for several water projects in the Southwest, supporters emphasized the urban, industrial, and recreational benefits. Representative Sherman Lloyd said he wanted to "emphasize the need for municipal and industrial use [of water] in Utah's urban areas," and Wayne Aspinall observed that "except for seaport cities, virtually every major population center west of the 98th meridian has had its origin at the site of a water project."[13]

The tone and conclusions of these Sacramento and South Dakota studies prefigured the Public Land Law Review Commission's recommendations in its final report, *One Third of the Nation's Land*, issued in 1970. Although the report generally favored planned development of natural resources over preservation, it recommended land sales in lieu of homesteading: the era of homesteading was essentially "over," the commissioners pointed out. Between 1950 and 1967 homesteaders had proved up on only 57,000 acres. Even in Alaska, where large tracts of public land were available, two-thirds of those who had attempted to homestead had never proved up. In the arid West where public land laws were more restrictive than in Alaska, 83 percent of the applications filed under the Desert Land Act during the 1950s had been denied by the Interior Department, generally because the department deemed the land better suited to uses other than farming. In view of these facts, the committee argued, "We can find no basic reason for maintaining the kind of agricultural settlement policies embodied in the homestead laws including provision for reclamation homesteads." The Bureau of Reclamation played vital roles in the West, such as the provision of "water power, recreation, flood control, and water for municipal and industrial purposes, as well as for irrigation," but the agency's original mission of developing the public lands for irrigation was "no longer necessary." That part of the Bureau's mission should be permanently abandoned. In lieu of homesteading, the committee recommended auctioning any remaining public lands suited to agriculture under competitive bidding. Even in Alaska future homesteading should be confined to state-owned lands. Whereas environmental concerns had galvanized opposition to homesteading in the Tule Lake Basin and on the Minidoka Project, a desire for efficiency and economy undergirded the commission's call for ending all homesteading.[14]

Environmental groups found no fault specifically with the commission's recommendation for repealing the Homestead Act, even though the commission's ultimate objective was not preservation. But they unanimously condemned other features of *One Third of the Nation's Land*, including its call for reexamining and possibly scaling back national forests, monuments, and reserves that had been established by presidential fiat. The Sierra Club asserted that these recommendations smacked of the "traditional view of the rural West" as a resource to be exploited. Stewart Udall charged that the report "worked against long-term environmental values" and was "oriented toward maximum immediate commercial exploitation."[15]

The commission's 289-page report and 137 recommendations provided considerable grist for the congressional mill; each year between 1971 and 1975 legislators considered bills based upon the report but could not agree on controversial provisions including public land sales and limiting the president's authority to withdraw land for national parks. Provisions regarding repeal of the Homestead Act excited less controversy. Most government employees charged with administering the public lands believed that repeal made sense. As Assistant Secretary of the Interior Harrison Loesch informed a Senate Committee in 1971, "Everyone in our department recognizes that the era of large-scale disposition of the public lands is long gone and it is probable that from now on . . . the land shall be retained for our descendants as a national trust, and that only in instances of either overriding public interest or for truly important management reasons, should public land be disposed of to individuals." Reflecting that view, the Interior Department issued Public Order 5418 in 1974 temporarily withdrawing the remaining 15 million acres of "unreserved public land" in Alaska from further homesteading until the land could be classified. The administrative action took most Alaskans by surprise. Curtis McVee, director of the Bureau of Land Management's Alaska office, said the withdrawal was intended to prevent potential claimants from sealing off "key access to adjacent public lands." Most of the land affected by the order was remote, often 100 or more miles from the nearest road.[16]

In congressional hearings only lawmakers from Idaho, where the Desert Land Act was still being used, and Alaska voiced reservations about the proposed repeal. In 1973 Idaho senator James McClure told his colleagues that "a great many" of his constituents were "still of the attitude that the public lands are there for acquisition by private interests." Influenced by that sentiment, the American Farm Bureau opposed repeal of the Desert Land Act in 1973 and Idaho senator Frank Church amended a public lands bill in 1974 that would have repealed the act.[17]

That same bill also "seriously worried" Alaska Senator Ted Stevens because it would eliminate homesteading and permit the government to transfer lands to private ownership only through competitive bidding, a process that favored the wealthy. The senator from the Last Frontier articulated the egalitarian sentiments that Americans had long associated with homesteading. "I cannot understand the direction we are taking which would shut off public lands to those people who are willing to put in what we call 'sweat equity' as they have in the past," he remarked. "I would hope there still would be a day when someone who had the sheer guts to go to our part of the country and make a home for himself and his family could do so without paying the Federal Government in cash for the Federal land." Stevens said he found the prospects of eliminating homesteading opportunities "abhorrent" when the federal government still controlled over 90 percent of Alaska. After Colorado senator Floyd Haskell questioned whether farming was even "a possibility in Alaska," demonstrating how abstract the issue of Alaskan homesteading was for many lawmakers, Stevens assured the Senate that his state contained "a vast amount of land that it is possible to develop for agricultural purposes." Stevens persuaded his colleagues to amend the bill to preserve the right to homestead in Alaska through June 1984. The amended bill passed 71 to 1, but the House failed to approve it before adjourning.[18]

When Congress reconvened advocates of land law reform in the Senate introduced a similar but more drastic bill. After Assistant Secretary of the Interior Jack Horton recommended that homesteading be eliminated in Alaska, too, because the homestead laws were "cumbersome," a Senate committee acquiesced.[19]

This time, Senator Stevens no longer insisted upon retaining the Homestead Act in Alaska. Instead, he proposed an amendment allowing individuals to settle and improve public land in Alaska under long-term leases. This would ensure that those with "guts, determination, and the will to settle a new land" would not lose out to "the highest bidder." The Senate approved the amendment.[20]

Meanwhile, a House committee was studying a "very similar" land reform bill, but one that permitted homesteading in Alaska to continue for another decade. On 22 July, the House approved the bill. In September a conference committee agreed to the House provision regarding homesteading in Alaska. The provision would have little practical application, though, because the Interior Department's temporary withdrawal of public lands from entry in Alaska dating from 1974 remained in force. The compromise bill, approved by the House and Senate, was signed by the president on 21 October, and the Federal Land Management Act of 1976 became law. Aside from a ten-year grace period for Alaska, Congress had finally repealed the Homestead Act, the most famous land law in American history and one of the foremost symbols of egalitarian economic opportunity and natural abundance.[21]

While the Federal Land Management Act permanently prevented further homesteading on reclamation projects, it did allow the federal government to sell lands that were well suited to agriculture. During the 1990s land-hungry individuals eyed close to 50,000 acres of irrigable land on the Wahluke Slope in the Columbia Basin that had constituted a buffer zone around the Department of Energy's Hanford Reservation during the Cold War. Canals built by the Bureau of Reclamation could furnish ready access to irrigation water. "There are a number of young families who are farming leased land. They would like to be able to own ground," explained Grant County Commissioner Helen Fancher. Over 300 people signed a petition requesting that the lands be opened to farming. Environmental and wildlife organizations including the Audubon Society countered with concerns about the implications for salmon, birds, mule deer, and other wildlife. In 1999 after Congress refused to preserve the land by designating the area as a Wild and Scenic River district, President Bill Clinton blocked land sales and agricultural development by adding 57,000 acres on the slope to the Saddle Mountain Wildlife Refuge.[22]

By the 1990s, the same metropolitan-based pressures and "nonrural values" that foreclosed development in the Tule Lake Basin in the 1960s and on the Wahluke Slope in the 1990s and brought an end to homesteading also affected those who farmed land that had been homesteaded after World War II. Secure in their land title, these homesteaders and their successors discovered that their entitlement to the water that made their lands productive was far from secure.[23]

9 "OUR DREAM WAS CHANGED INTO A NIGHTMARE" THE HOMESTEADERS AT THE DAWN OF THE TWENTY-FIRST CENTURY

In the arid West, bitter fights over water are legendary; in 1977 when President Jimmy Carter attempted to cancel funding for western water projects, Arizona Senator Barry Goldwater reportedly hectored the president, "There are three things we value in the West. We value women, we value gold, and we value water. And you can fool around with our women and with our gold. But damn you, Mr. President, don't touch our water!" Taken aback by the flinty resolve of Goldwater and his fellow westerners, Carter backed down. Even if he had held his ground, though, the postwar homesteaders and their successors on developed reclamation projects would have retained their water rights. Nevertheless, the skepticism regarding reclamation that undergirded Carter's threat boded ill for established western farmers including the homesteaders and their water rights.[1]

By replacing traditional water law with the doctrine of prior appropriation, nineteenth-century westerners tried to shield those who first diverted irrigation water from subsequent claimants. In apportioning water, though, frontier lawmakers overlooked or minimized Native American interests. In the Winters Case of 1908 attorneys for the Blackfeet successfully argued before the Supreme Court that their claims to water superseded all others. Winters established a legal precedent for other tribal claims against farmers and ranchers. It also portended an era when farmers' and ranchers' water rights would become increasingly unstable.[2]

Beginning in the 1970s explosive urban growth and suburban development in the West, along with passage of the Endangered Species Act in 1973, ushered in a new era of competition for farmers' water. Patricia Limerick's argument that "the clearest and most persistent case of continuity [in western history] involved disputes and conflicts over water" is true generally, but the relative power of western agriculture in those disputes changed radically after 1970. In the Colorado River drainage, Mexico's water demands also jeopardized farmers' activities. The homesteaders' patents vouchsafed them "the right to the use of water from the reclamation project in which the tract is situated, as an appurtenance to the irrigable lands" they possessed. Homesteaders interpreted this to mean that their water rights were inviolable, but shifting public priorities and competing demands for water suggested otherwise. As Secretary of the Interior Bruce Babbitt advised embattled growers in southern California in 1998, "What appears to be solid at one time may not be, particularly when public pressure mounts, particularly when there's a perception . . . of being unfair in the eyes of an audience of 40 million to 45 million [urban] people."[3]

Near the turn of the twentieth century, thousands of western farmers, like the Californians Babbitt addressed, were embroiled in acrimonious and expensive legal contests over water rights that had once seemed secure. Some of the most widely publicized disputes involved lands that the Bureau of Reclamation had developed for settlement and homesteading after World War II. Beginning in the 1970s, Mexican officials and farmers complained about salty runoff from irrigated land on the Bureau's Gila Project that had been settled after World War II. By the time the Colorado River reached Mexico it was too salty to use. One proposal for dealing with the problem involved eliminating irrigated farms in portions of the Wellton Mohawk Valley. In the Northwest, too, agriculture in the postwar homesteading districts came under fire. From the 1990s onward, homesteaders and their neighbors in the Columbia River Basin who had saved water by installing sprinklers battled environmentalists who argued that the surplus water should be returned to the river to safeguard salmon rather than be used for irrigating land above the ditch. Along the Snake River in 2004 owners of commercial fish hatcheries petitioned the government to shut down 1,300 irrigation wells serving postwar homesteaders and their neighbors in order to replenish the flow of groundwater into the river. The Bureau of Reclamation, which had exulted in 1951 that the aquifer was so vast that "no matter how long [their test] pumps operate there has been no appreciable drop in the water table" was forced to acknowledge that water levels were dropping rapidly. In 2003 the Secretary of the Interior and a federal court ruling forced farmers on homesteaded land in the Coachella Valley to reduce their use of irrigation water by one third in order to accommodate the needs of burgeoning California municipalities. Almost overnight, the price of irrigation water in the valley doubled. Water managers and farmers forecast "years of costly lawsuits."[4]

Although farmers battled to preserve their rights to water and land on many reclamation projects after 1970, the struggle was most acute in the Klamath Basin. In 2001, farmers there, including many postwar homesteaders and their descendants, fought tenaciously for water, appealing to Americans' sense of propriety and justice and arguing that the government had betrayed those who had homesteaded in good faith. For a few weeks, the farmers' protest attracted attention from national and even international media outlets, galvanized the White House to action, and created a groundswell of support for amending the Endangered Species Act. Although not all of the protesters were homesteaders, the protesters shrewdly highlighted those who had homesteaded, knowing that their story would resonate with the public's cherished beliefs and expectations regarding the American dream. Thus the Klamath Project homesteaders' experiences came to epitomize the challenges farmers faced in an urbanized West where many residents no longer viewed irrigated agriculture as the optimal use of land and water.[5]

At the center of the controversy were the Lost River sucker and shortnose sucker, two rare species valued by Indians in the Basin. According to tribal lore, the Indians' ancestors had narrowly averted starvation by eating the fish. By 1988, the two historically significant species seemed headed toward extinction; after biologists estimated that only a few thousand suckers remained the fish received federal protection under the Endangered Species Act of 1973 (ESA). Subsequent surveys showed that scientists had greatly underestimated the number of remaining fish: hundreds of thousands were still alive. Nevertheless, the fish retained their protective designation because biologists indicated that it was necessary to ward off extinction. In 1998, another species in the Klamath River drainage, the coho salmon, a commercially important fish, was designated as a threatened species—one step short of endangered status. The ESA prohibited any federal agency, including the Bureau of Reclamation, from undertaking activities that were "likely to jeopardize the continued existence of any endangered species or threatened species."[6]

In 2000, the Oregon Natural Resources Council, a privately funded grassroots environmental organization, sued the Bureau of Reclamation, contending that it had violated the ESA; the Bureau had withdrawn irrigation water from the Klamath River system in 2000 without first working with the National Marine Fisheries Service (NMFS) to ensure that the withdrawals would not harm salmon in the river. The Bureau symbolically protested the lawsuit by cutting off irrigation water to the Lower Klamath National Wildlife Refuge, ostensibly in order to maintain higher water levels for the salmon downstream. The agency resumed water deliveries within two weeks, having made its point: it lacked sufficient water, even in years with average precipitation, to satisfy all the demands for water imposed by Congress and the courts.[7]

Although the Bureau's protest in 2000 was strategic and symbolic, in 2001 the agency grappled with severe drought. The snowpack in mountains above the Klamath Basin was less than one third of normal, making 2001 the bleakest water year in a century. On January 22, the Bureau requested a biological opinion from the NMFS on the water needs of salmon that year. Three weeks later the Bureau requested a similar report from the Fish and Wildlife Service (FWS), the agency responsible for safeguarding the shortnose and Lost River suckers. In mid-March both agencies filed draft reports with the Bureau. The FWS recommended that the surface of Upper Klamath Lake be maintained at a level no lower than 4,140 feet above sea level to provide ample marshland habitat for maturing suckers, while the NMFS called for high stream flows in the Klamath River in order to safeguard salmon. When Bureau officials countered that the runoff would be insufficient to meet both agencies' recommendations, the FWS agreed to permit the release of an additional 75,000 acre feet of lake water in order to protect the salmon. This would lower the lake surface to 4,139 feet above sea level, or a water depth of about 4.8 feet. Nine years earlier during another drought, biologists at the FWS had permitted the lake level to drop to 4,137 feet above sea level but this time they insisted on a higher lake level. Spread out over the entire lake, the 2-foot difference added up to 150,000 acre feet—over 40 percent of the water farmers in the Basin would normally use for irrigation.[8]

Soon after the agencies released drafts of their biological opinions, U.S. District Judge Saundra Brown Armstrong resolved the previous year's lawsuit involving the Bureau and the Oregon Natural Resources Council. Brown ruled that the Bureau had violated the ESA in 2000, and she barred the agency from delivering water to farmers in 2001 without first ensuring the welfare of endangered species by consulting with federal agencies such as the NMFS.[9]

Doubly bound by Armstrong's recent decision and the ESA's safeguards for endangered and threatened species, the Bureau issued its 2001 Operations Plan on 6 April. The plan, devised without public input, surpassed farmers' worst fears. Many had expected their water allotments would be scaled back because of the drought, but they bristled at the Bureau's announcement that 90 percent of the farmers in the region, including all who cultivated lands homesteaded after World War II, would receive no irrigation water that season. According to Bureau representative Jeff McCracken the shutoff was "the biggest one we've ever seen in terms of the impact."[10]

Rather than attacking the ESA head-on, farmers' organizations accused the three government bureaus of applying the act in an "inflexible and narrow" fashion. The lake levels mandated by the FWS and NMFS were arbitrary and the benefits to fish were "illusory," charged Don Russell, president of the Klamath Water Users Association. Russell contended that the agencies' ruling was based on speculation rather than conclusive evidence. He indicated that algae, a key cause of sucker deaths in the past, bloomed more profusely in years of abundant water. Pointing out that without irrigation water, the Lower Klamath Wildlife Refuge, which received water from the irrigation canals, would also suffer, Tracy Liskey, a Basin farmer and officer in the Oregon Farm Bureau, likened the government's application of the ESA to a vise that was progressively "squeez[ing]" the Basin's lifeblood to the detriment of most humans and animals in the region.[11]

On April 9, farmers asked a U.S. district judge to force the government to furnish irrigation water until the lake reached the level to which it had fallen during the drought of 1992. Without any water, the grain they had planted the previous fall would die as would perennials like peppermint and horseradish. "Hundreds of farm and ranch families without income will not be able to support themselves. They will lack the ability to pay bills and service debt. Collateral will be forfeited. Bankruptcy will be common," they forecast. The suckers and salmon had endured the drought of 1992, they reasoned, so they should be able to "survive" at similar lake and river levels in 2001. Bob Gasser, the owner of a fertilizer store in the area, organized a rally attended by thousands including Oregon governor John Kitzhaber in support of the farmers' legal petition.[12]

Judge Ann Aiken sympathized with the plaintiffs but denied their request. There was "no question" farmers would "suffer severe economic hardship" without water. But Native Americans had equally compelling interests in safeguarding salmon and suckers. Members of the Klamath and Yurok tribes had been deprived of "food, income, employment opportunities, and sense of community" as the number of suckers and salmon had dropped. "Colliding communities and interests" prevented her from favoring one group of people over another. Moreover, despite the "harm" that might result to the farmers, the ESA "requires that endangered species be given the highest priority at all costs." In light of that fact, Aiken concluded, "I cannot find that the balance of hardship tips sharply in [the] plaintiffs' favor."[13]

Rebuffed by Aiken, water users vowed to continue fighting until Americans nationwide learned what was happening. Homesteader Paul Rogers believed that most Americans would agree that "any time a fish has precedence over a farmer, well, somebody has a screw loose." Don Russell vowed, "This is far too big to let it ride and let it go." The case was bound to generate sympathy for the farmers, he believed, especially when they learned that those who had been denied water included homesteaders and veterans who had been promised water by the government as a reward for their military service.[14]

One week after Aiken's ruling, the farmers made good on their pledge to continue fighting. A crowd of at least 13,000 converged on Klamath Falls while a Bucket Brigade passed fifty-one buckets of water—one for each state in the nation and the District of Columbia—from a city park on the shores of Lake Ewauna up Main Street and past the county courthouse to a bone-dry irrigation canal. Local businessmen Bob Gasser and Chris Moudry, who owned a fertilizer store, joined with farmers Nancy and Steve Kandra to spearhead the rally. They modeled the event loosely upon the Jarbidge Shovel Brigade, a well-known protest the previous year in which activists had opened a road in Nevada that federal authorities had blocked in order to protect an endangered fish. "We are hoping to speak to the nation through this rally," Gasser explained. In order to "get the message out to the mainstream media," the organizers hired a Sacramento public relations firm. Much to their delight, television crews from Portland, Los Angeles, CNN, and Fox News covered the event, as did reporters for the Associated Press, major west coast newspapers, and the *Christian Science Monitor*.[15]

Tule Lake Division homesteaders and their supporters at a rally protesting the shutoff of irrigation water, 2001. (Photograph courtesy of Anders Tomlinson)

Veterans who had homesteaded after World War II played pivotal, highly visible roles in the protest rally, pressing their entitlement as veterans and homesteaders to land and water. Jess Prosser, an eighty-five-year-old homesteader, kicked off the protest by wading into the lake to fill the first four-gallon bucket. He passed it to his fifty-year-old son, John, and grandchildren, Katie and James, signifying his family's deep roots on the land and the centrality of water to their family farm. The water closure had transformed the family's farming saga "from a dream to a nightmare," John said. "I couldn't believe they're giving suckers preference." Another veteran and homesteader, Marion Palmer, contrasted the image of the independent, sturdy yeoman farmer with welfare dependency. Addressing the crowd at the rally, he observed, "Fifty-nine years ago, we were welcomed home as heroes and asked to feed a hungry world. Today, we may be reduced to welfare recipients."[16]

Politicians and lobbyists voiced support for the farmers and basked in the free publicity. Oregon senator Gordon Smith told the crowd of protesters, "If the government chooses to save the sucker fish, it must not make suckers of Klamath County. We must never forget that it is not OK to say a sucker fish is of more value under the law than a family farm." When Lynn Cornell, representing the 246,000-member National Cattleman's Beef Association, addressed the crowd, she intensified the importance of the water shutoff for the nation, calling it "the first case where the Endangered Species Act has slammed head on into agriculture."[17]

Not all media coverage favored the farmers. An editorial in Portland's *Oregonian* maintained that the region's fundamental problem was insufficient water "even in years of average rainfall, to sustain all of the farms in the Klamath Basin." Countering the anthropocentric views of the protesters, the editor advocated a buyout of some farmers in order to free up more water for wildlife.[18]

While the Bucket Brigade rally publicized the farmers' plight, it did not restore their water. In a small gathering following the protest Senator Smith and Representative Greg Walden pledged to work on amending the ESA and said they would also pursue federal emergency relief funds for the farmers. In the meantime, some farmers substituted low-water crops like two-row barley for potatoes and onions, hoping the crops would survive with limited irrigation from wells. Others cut back on their acreage: the Prosser family normally planted 110 acres of potatoes, but in 2001 they only planted 18, figuring that they could improvise with pumps and irrigation pipelines to water that many acres from their well. Most farmers had to cut back even more: the owner of a packing shed in Tulelake signed contracts for only one tenth of the normal potato acreage.[19]

In mid-June Representative Walden brought six Republican members of the House Committee on Resources to the Klamath Basin for a hearing, hoping to gather data and build momentum for a campaign to amend the ESA. Ironic signs proclaiming "Welcome to the Klamath Project, largest water theft in history" and "Unemployed farmer will work 4 food" greeted the entourage. They passed a placard outside a local restaurant advertising a new addition to the menu: "Sucker Fish Sandwich" (really codfish). The restaurant owner pledged to donate part of the proceeds from each sandwich to the effort to repeal the ESA. A feisty, indignant mood suffused the Basin. Homesteader Paul Christy expressed that mood in an op-ed piece printed in the local newspaper shortly before the hearing convened; he charged that farmers in the region had become the "target of an agenda determined to return Tulelake to a primal marsh" despite "the fact that this would require the destruction of a very special civilization of very special people."[20]

The committee hearing at the county fairgrounds in Klamath Falls dragged on for six hours. One participant estimated that 6,000 attended although a news reporter believed the number was closer to 1,500. Representatives of the Yurok and Klamath Tribes, the Oregon Natural Resources Council, and the Pacific Coast Federation of Fishermen's Associations defended the cutoff and the ESA, but local elected officials, farmers and businessmen, and a representative from the California Waterfowl Association denounced the decision. David Vogel, a scientist from Natural Resource Scientists, Inc., a California-based environmental consulting firm, charged that the biological opinions that had precipitated the water cutoff had not been appropriately peer reviewed; instead they had been produced and reviewed in house by government employees who had "a vested interest" in the matter.[21]

Twenty-two veterans or spouses of veterans who had homesteaded following World War II filed complaints with the House committee. Many charged they had been betrayed by the government they had risked their lives to defend. Manuel Silva quoted from his patent to show that it vouchsafed "forever, land and water rights." Ruth Masterson recalled the "promise" of "never-failing water" she and her husband had verbally received when they homesteaded. Helen Newkirk alleged that a representative from the Bureau had described their water rights as "permanent" when she and her husband took up a homestead. Frances Johnson wrote, "We settled here in good faith, lived up to our commitments, and I believe that a promise by our government should be kept." Paul Christy's anger moved him to hyperbole: "what is happening is betrayal of our citizens of historic proportions equal to the Nazis and Communists." Similarly Kathleen Todd St. Peter compared the withholding of water from farmers in the Klamath Basin to Soviet Communism's expropriation of private property. Velma Robison remarked on the ironic twist that had transformed the Bureau of Reclamation from a "friend" to "our enem[y], taking from us what was awarded to us more than 50 years ago, and destroying the livelihoods of many." "Where is liberty and justice for all?" she queried. "We have been betrayed by our government." Adrian Witcraft, a Klamath tribal member, wondered why the homesteaders were shocked by the government's duplicity. "All I can say is, welcome to the party," he quipped.[22]

Whether the homesteaders personally farmed the land or had retired from farming and leased it to others, they emphasized that the water shutoff had crippled them economically at a vulnerable time in their lives when medical bills were soaring and their incomes were limited. "We're not talking about a group of people who can go out and do it all over again. Our honeymoon is over," Dorie Voorhees reminded the committee. For some, the loss amounted to more than the value of a single harvest: Helen Newkirk, who operated a horseradish farm on the family homestead with her daughter and son-in-law, feared that their horseradish, a perennial that "once planted is in for thirty years," would die and "we will lose everything." John Terry doubted his farm of fifty-one years would survive much longer: "our pasture is dying and cattle are starving." Joe and Mary Victorine relied upon monthly land payments from their son David, who was buying the homestead from them. Without irrigation water he could not continue making payments and the Victorines would fall behind in their bills. They had "farmed all our lives" and therefore received minimal Social Security benefits and no pensions. "Lights, power to pump water for the cows, heat and gas for the car more than take up our monthly [Social Security] check so we stretch it out by using from the land rent," they explained. The water shutoff had "hit us a terrible blow." They had "always figured we had the cows, for emergencies, and the value of the place either rented or sold," but now they were "having to sell the cows as the pasture is going without water, and the hay we had to carry over 'til they got out on the pasture is about gone."[23]

Most who addressed the committee wanted the ESA amended. They were incensed that the Bureau had made its decision to withhold water behind closed doors without consulting the "homesteaders and ranchers." Moreover, they charged that the Bureau had based its decision on speculative estimates rather than hard data regarding the water requirements of suckers and salmon. When a representative from the Oregon Natural Resources Council defended the ESA and proposed the government buy out the land and water rights of elderly couples like the Victorines for $4,000 an acre, Representative Walden sneered at the idea; it smacked of "someone offering to sell you air when their hands are around your neck, choking you to death." Walden's peer, Nevada congressman Jim Gibbons, opined, "It's time to amend the Endangered Species Act. We can't save every species, and maybe that's the way it should be."[24]

Hoping to communicate the personal impact of the water shutoff to a larger audience, reporter Jacqui Krizo, the daughter of homesteaders, posted the homesteaders' statements to the Committee on Resources on a

Protestors line Main Street in Klamath Falls, Oregon, passing buckets of water from Lake Ewauna to an irrigation canal as part of the Bucket Brigade, 7 May 2001. (Photograph courtesy of Anders Tomlinson)

Web site. She summarized the veterans' shock and sense of betrayal for readers:

> Our neighbors and parents were some of the lucky veterans whose deeds were signed by U.S. Presidents. They are in their 'golden years', and they cried and asked why? Why would their government take water off their land for the first time in all history? Why would their government break their promises? Why would their government say the fish are endangered when they will not tell us how many there are, how many there were, and how many they want? . . . Why would their government destroy the community that they spent their lives building from nothing?[25]

The Bucket Brigade, the hearing in Klamath Falls, and Krizo's Web site helped to publicize the farmers' plight, but some people felt they needed to act more aggressively to force the government's hand. As one woman observed, "Sympathy will not save this community." The possibility of more deliberate and dramatic protest simmered in the minds of malcontents for weeks. Shortly before Memorial Day a group of teenagers in Tulelake explored the idea in a skit at school. They role played a protestor defying the Bureau of Reclamation by opening the headgate of an irrigation canal so that farmers could water their fields. The skit concluded with the Supreme Court vindicating the protester.[26]

About a month later someone acted as the students had recommended in their skit. Between sunset on 29 June and dawn on the next day a person surmounted the chain link fence surrounding the Bureau's headgates in Klamath Falls, pried open a wooden headgate with a wrench, and released a stream of water into an irrigation canal at the rate of 80 cubic feet per second—about one tenth of the canal's capacity. It was a symbolic gesture of defiance, one that would not furnish enough water to salvage anyone's crops. Bob Gasser, one of the organizers of the Bucket Brigade, disclaimed responsibility for opening the gate. "We didn't want this to happen," he maintained. Activist Barron Knoll, who supported the headgate opening, later confirmed Gasser's innocence. Bureau employees soon closed the gate. The following Monday night, though, the gate was again opened. So on Tuesday Bureau employees again shut it, this time binding the control gears with tack welds.[27]

On Independence Day, a crowd of over 100 protesters converged on the bank of the canal near the headgate for a protest meeting. A mixture of sympathy for the homesteaders and other farmers and contempt for federal regulation of private property drove the protesters, who styled themselves as friends of the elderly veterans. The meeting had been called by Andrea Zingg, a thirty-year-old cosmetologist in Klamath Falls affiliated with the Klamath Freedom Cavalry, a group committed to defending private property rights against "excessive" environmental regulations. Zingg, who was so nervous about the public protest that she vomited four times on her way to the rally, depicted herself as a defender of the veterans who had homesteaded in the area. "People who fought and who would have died for this country were enticed to settle here and promised water, and are now being kicked in the pants. I just want to fix a wrong that has been perpetrated against these people," she stated. During the rally members of Zingg's Freedom Cavalry pulled up in a green pickup truck and stalked over to the headgate lugging a diamond-bladed chain saw and an acetylene cutting torch. While law enforcement officials and the press looked on, people in the crowd formed a human shield to protect Zingg's compatriots from being photographed, impeded, or arrested. The activists quickly severed the headgate's tack welds and cranked open the gate. The crowd cheered as water flowed into the canal. After it was over, Zingg claimed that "a lot more occurred than I thought would," but she said she was "glad the headgate was opened." One of the people who opened the headgate later spoke anonymously with a reporter. He justified his actions by asserting incorrectly that the "veterans built most of those canals by hand, and entrusted them to the government." Now the homesteaders and their neighbors were "afraid of losing everything, of losing their community." A woman who helped open the headgate identified herself as a rancher. She insisted she had always honored the law but said she had decided to disobey it at the headgate "for my daughter, for her future" on the ranch.[28]

After the Freedom Cavalry protest, 100 million gallons flowed into the canal before Bureau officials could seal the gate. Attempting to discourage further civil disobedience, the Bureau installed two sets of floodlights and announced that it would soon deploy surveillance cameras.[29]

The public reopening of the headgate once again focused media attention upon the plight of homesteaders in the Klamath Basin. Dozens of reporters from across the nation investigated the incident. Organizers of the Bucket Brigade disavowed any responsibility for the protest but Bob Gasser praised the protesters for bringing the media back to Klamath Falls. "I hate to say it, but breaking the law helped," he admitted. Ironically, "bad press is the only way you can get anyone to do anything," observed Susan Liskey, a farmer in the Basin. "They like blood and guts." The connections among veterans, homesteaders, and the water shutoff added to the salience of the story and countered images of the aggrieved farmers as slovenly rabble. A San Francisco reporter who traveled to Klamath Falls to cover the protest highlighted Eleanor Bolesta, a WAVE who had homesteaded near Tulelake. Bolesta had not helped to reopen the headgate but she told the reporter the government should have never placed the farmers in such a tight predicament. "It's really awful. It's just like we're in a bad dream and it's getting worse," she said.[30]

As unrest and talk of civil disobedience suffused the Klamath Basin, Oregon senator Gordon Smith proposed an amendment to the Interior Department Appropriation Bill on 12 July that would permit the Bureau of Reclamation to draw down the level of Upper Klamath Lake by 2 feet. The veterans were ideal poster children for Smith's cause. Displaying a 1947 issue of *Life* magazine celebrating the first postwar land opening for veterans in the

Basin, Smith reminded his colleagues of the spirit of the postwar era reflected in the magazine article; those who applied for farms following the war were "people who came home having saved liberty, having defended democracy," and Congress had rewarded them with land. "Look at the hopes and dreams in the faces of these people," Smith implored. "These were federal promises." He asked his colleagues to "remember the human faces in this picture, to remember the promises made, and to help me help these people," adding that the suckers "will survive, but my farmers will not, until we begin to reverse this." Smith's colleague California Senator Barbara Boxer, whose constituents included many of the veterans who had homesteaded in the lower Klamath Basin, called the situation "vexing" but countered Smith by staunchly defending the Endangered Species Act. Wildlife did not have a voice, Boxer said, so she and her colleagues had "to be their voice" and "protect God's creatures." Farmers would gain little from a release of irrigation water so late in the season, but fish would suffer, she predicted. Boxer moved to table Smith's amendment to the appropriation bill. By a narrow vote of 52–48 the Senate approved Boxer's motion. Support for Boxer's motion came primarily from the East and the Midwest, but ten senators from the eighteen westernmost states in the continental United States voted with Boxer, including both senators from Washington, California, and South Dakota. The next day, as expected, officials in the Interior Department refused to convene a seven-member committee dubbed the "God Squad" that might have temporarily set aside the ESA's strictures to release irrigation water.[31]

Although protesters, some reporters, and Senator Smith focused upon the plight of the homesteaders as "the human faces in this picture" the homesteaders were more circumspect than the protesters who claimed to represent them. The protest movement began to take on a life of its own as the businessmen, farmers, and homesteaders who had engineered and participated in the Bucket Brigade were supplanted by bolder activists, many of whom wanted to roll back government regulation on all fronts rather than merely amend the ESA or provide irrigation water for farmers. Back in May after the Bucket Brigade, the *Klamath Falls Herald and News* had boasted that civility had "reigned supreme" at the protest in contrast to more violent and acerbic activism elsewhere. Now, when a group who styled themselves the "Klamath Tea Party," led by Stan Thompson, a white-bearded, retired Union Pacific employee from Klamath Falls, called for yet another rally on 13 July in order to reopen the headgate, those who had organized the more restrained

Bucket Brigade scheduled a separate rally elsewhere for the same time. They feared that the rabble-rousing Thompson "might do more harm than good to the farmers' cause." The editor of the local paper likewise inveighed against Thompson, labeling him and his supporters "extremists" who were trying to "take over [the] farm protest." After Thompson refused to back down, a few farmers who called themselves Farmers Against Regulatory Madness (FARM) traveled to the headgate to protect the irrigation system from sabotage. One of them claimed, "That bald-headed Stan guy has nothing to do with us. We don't know who he is. The only thing that guy wants is his name in the paper and his picture on TV." As tension escalated, Thompson promised to cancel the rally and members of FARM departed.[32]

On Friday, 13 July, someone posted a sign near the headgates advising, "The only solution is to open the headgate today." That evening a crowd including television, radio, and newspaper reporters gathered, expecting something to occur. They were not disappointed. Shortly before 6:00 P.M., fifteen to twenty protesters including Thompson bowed in prayer near the headgates and then pried one open with a crowbar. Some in the motley group were farmers while others were townspeople like Thompson. None were homesteaders. One protester identified himself to a reporter as a "desperate farmer." Another, Walt Moden, a local part-time farmer and realtor, said, "We have to let the country know what's happening in this part of America. That's why we're here." Barron Knoll, a young farmer who had recently graduated from Oregon State University, claimed that even though he generally disliked radical antics, the federal government had forced his hand: "I wouldn't be down here doing what a lot of hippies do to get attention if I hadn't lost all hope," he told a reporter. When asked why he had come to the headgate after pledging to stay away, Thompson likened himself to a football quarterback. "When you get to the goal line and they hike the ball, do you tell everybody you're going to run around the end? We sure as hell don't." Joe Bair, a Klamath County native who held a master's degree in civil engineering from Portland State University and was convinced that God had brought him back to the Basin to fight for farmers' rights, chained himself to one of the headgates expecting to be arrested and "make the news."[33]

Instead, the sheriff arrested no one. Two hours after the headgate had been opened he ordered the protesters to leave the enclosure, sympathizing with their objectives but urging them to depart rather than face arrest. "I don't know if an arrest record is going to help your cause," he cautioned.

They complied although some remained in the general area. Later in the evening when two federal marshals arrived a small group blocked them from entering the enclosure. Projecting a flag-waving, god-fearing image, they broke out in patriotic songs and hymns. The protesters took courage when the marshals seemed "completely taken aback" by their singing and departed without arresting anyone.[34]

Perhaps the marshals were only outnumbered. They returned early the next morning with reinforcements: ten marshals and "twenty-five to thirty" local officers. One of the officers asked the protesters encamped at the headgate if anyone had the "key" they had used to open the gate. When they feigned ignorance, he asked if they had used a "wrench or pry bar." Someone jested that maybe it had fallen in the lake. Another jeered, "Don't steal our water." Others clasped hands and prayed. Faced with armed officers, the protesters parted to allow the marshals to escort a Bureau employee into the enclosure where he closed the gate. After it was shut, eight marshals remained on site to prevent anyone from opening it again.[35]

By afternoon a crowd of over 200, including many local farmers and sympathizers and some activists from outside the region, converged on the site for a prearranged protest. Organizers had erected a white canopy and arranged hay bales underneath it for seating. A banner flapped in the breeze emblazoned with a verse from the Old Testament: "If my people, which are called by my name, shall humble themselves, and pray, and seek my face, and turn from their wicked ways; then will I hear from heaven, and will forgive their sin, and will heal their land." At 2:30 P.M. the protest rally began. After a local gospel choir sang, the group recited the Pledge of Allegiance and sang the national anthem. Gavin Rajnus, a potato farmer in the Basin who had helped to organize the meeting and who would emerge as one of the major protest leaders, defended the activists' disobedience: "If we don't act on this and show a tremendous amount of backlash to what they've done to the economy and the ecology of this area, the country's never going to understand." Then Nevadan J. J. Johnson addressed the crowd, emphasizing Americans' constitutional rights and their duty to defend them. Johnson, an inveterate gadfly, edited *The Sierra Times*, an electronic publication dedicated to exposing governmental abuse of power, protecting agriculture and extractive industries, and persuading Americans that "those who privately own [natural] resources are in a position to manage them in the best interests of the environment as a whole."[36]

As evening approached, the crowd melted away. Fewer than three dozen protesters remained through the night. When the marshals guarding the enclosure turned spotlights on the protesters, several of them parked their trucks in a line and beamed their headlights back on the marshals.[37]

Discussing how to "re-acquire the initiative" and maintain media coverage now that the gates had again been closed, the small group remaining on site decided to circumvent the headgates entirely by siphoning lake water through a pipeline into the canal below the gate. "'That'll show 'em. Let 'em guard a gate we don't even use,'" protester Jeff Head remembered them saying. The group fanned out to spread news of their plan. Others hauled a pump and 700 feet of 8-inch pipe to the site. When two police officers tried to halt the two farmers who were installing the pump and pipe, several dozen people locked arms, forming a human shield around the men at work. One of the farmers involved in the effort, Doug Staff, told a reporter he was willing to be arrested if necessary. As the pumps started and water flowed through the pipe into the ditch at about 2:00 P.M. the crowd began to chant, "Let the water flow!" After about fifteen minutes, police asked the protesters to shut off the water in order to prevent the land surrounding the canal from eroding. In order for the symbolic protest to continue, park service police who had replaced federal marshals as guards permitted the protesters to extend the pipe through the headgate enclosure so that it would reach clear to the canal. Eager to fend off simplistic portrayals of the matter that could play into the hand of the protesters, FWS employee Patricia Foulk announced that since the lake level had not been drawn down sufficiently to violate the ESA, the agency did not plan to have the protesters arrested.[38]

The protest was made-to-order drama and spectacle for the nightly news nationwide—precisely what the activists wanted—and the more simplistic the portrayal of the issues, the better from their standpoint. When J. J. Johnson addressed a rally, television news crews filmed nearly 200 onlookers, the stars and stripes flying upside down in protest, and loudspeakers blaring the song "God Bless America"—a carnival atmosphere. The protesters issued daily news releases in an effort to maintain media interest. They even attracted a reporter from the London *Observer*, Lawrence Donegan, who dramatically dubbed the event the "'Battle of Klamath Falls.'" Donegan lavishly described the protest as "the last stand for something—if not for rural America, than for the most ecologically important tract of land west of the Mississippi, or for the already tattered reputation of George W. Bush's administration on environmental issues, or for the God-given right of Americans to live off the land regardless." Taking advantage of the fortuitous outpouring of publicity, Representative Greg Walden appealed for swift governmental action. "We have a Ruby Ridge in the making out there right now. This is not the time for bureaucratic foot-dragging," he warned. Under pressure from Oregon's and California's senators and representatives to do something, Congress appropriated $20 million in emergency aid for farmers, about a tenth of the farmers' anticipated losses for the year.[39]

The following Tuesday the activists unloaded a backhoe and announced they planned to install a 36-inch underground pipeline connecting the Link River to the canal. The water would be used to irrigate parched alfalfa and pasture, they said. The headgates themselves might be federal property, but protest organizer Barbara Martin, a real estate agent, claimed that county records showed an electric utility owned the land adjacent to the headgates. On Wednesday protesters started the engine on the backhoe, but when the federal guards grabbed some ominous-looking black bags, the protesters killed the engine.[40]

The protests, adverse publicity and pleas from law enforcement officials to defuse the tense situation goaded the Interior Department to act. For several days "very little work other than Klamath" was done by Secretary of the Interior Gayle Norton and the "upper levels of the Fish and Wildlife Service and the Bureau of Reclamation" as they looked for a way to release at least some irrigation water without violating the ESA. Jim Bryant, the Bureau's chief of water and lands in the Klamath Basin, devised a way. In the spring, Bryant and his colleagues had "wanted to be on the safe side" in complying with the ESA so they withheld all irrigation water. Now they revised their estimates downward and calculated that 75,000 acre feet of water—about a sixth of the water normally used by Basin farmers in a growing season—could be released without causing the lake to fall below the prescribed level. Biologists employed by the FWS had earlier recommended that any excess water in the lake be allocated for maintaining wetlands below the farmers' fields in the Lower Klamath National Wildlife Refuge. Although the scientists' recommendations were consistent with the ESA, Norton decided to release the water instead for mid- to late-summer irrigation. The late season water would revive pastures and might save perennials like mint and horseradish. Farmers who had been forced to rent expensive pasture elsewhere for their cattle would be able to bring their animals home sooner.[41]

On Tuesday, 24 July, Secretary Norton announced that the farmers would receive 70,000–75,000 acre feet of water in order to stave off a "confrontation that will lead to any more problems." In a conciliatory statement printed the following week, she expressed "hope that the water released will provide farmers with some relief" and expressed "disappoint[ment]" that no water was available for the wildlife refuges. As a further concession to the farmers, Norton's staff announced the following week that she would ask the National Academy of Sciences (NAS) to review the studies and calculations by the FWS that had led to the shutoff of irrigation water that year.[42]

Farmers including the homesteaders greeted Norton's announcements with guarded appreciation. Protest organizer Gavin Rajnus claimed that the water would "not benefit Klamath Basin farmers" economically, aside from recharging their domestic wells and reviving their pastures, but said that the government's decision was nevertheless a welcome "admission of error." Steve Kandra, chairman of the Klamath Irrigation District and one of the organizers of the Bucket Brigade, interpreted the opening of the gates as "a gesture to diffuse [*sic*] the situation" and cautioned that it would not "fix the problem." Still, as a county commissioner said, "If you're drowning and someone throws you a life preserver, you don't turn it down because you're waiting for a lifeboat."[43]

On Wednesday, 25 July, a crowd numbering close to 300 including thirteen television news crews gathered to watch as the headgates were raised to release water into the canal. The crowd cheered as the water flowed. A federal official unfurled an American flag and police permitted protesters to enter the headgate enclosure to "share in the victory."[44]

Despite some public complaints that the water release was skimpy and belated, farmers clearly believed it would help, and they swamped the irrigation district with water orders. Their eagerness was justified; economists later estimated that the water boosted crop production by $40 million.[45]

At the time Secretary Norton announced the water release, protesters Joe Bair and Bill Oetting were in Elko, Nevada, talking strategy with Grant Gerber, the man who had spearheaded the Jarbidge Shovel Brigade in 2000. Bair and Oetting hoped to raise money for farmers in the Basin. They also hoped to capitalize upon sympathy for the farmers in their drive to amend the ESA. They found an eager audience among Gerber's supporters, including people like Clarice Ryan, who hoped to expose the "problems" associated with government "control and regulation," which she felt "destroy the value of your property." Over the next two weeks Bair and Oetting worked with Gerber and others, planning what they hoped would be a media extravaganza. J. J. Johnson offered to drum up support using the *Sierra Times*. Relief convoys from Elko, Nevada; Kalispell, Montana; and Malibu, California, would transport donated money and goods to Klamath Falls for the drought-stricken farmers. The convoys would converge on Klamath Falls in August for a rally and protest parade. The event would resemble the Bucket Brigade in some respects and would memorialize that protest. A 10-foot-high bucket, crafted by a blacksmith in Elko, would be hauled through the town on a flatbed trailer and placed as a memorial on the county courthouse grounds. The event would bring together organizers of the Bucket Brigade and those like Bair who had broken the law in bolder protests at the headgates.[46]

On 31 July, organizers including Bair and Bill Ransom incorporated the Klamath Bucket Brigade to receive and disburse relief funds collected by the convoys. Three weeks later, on Freedom Day, 21 August, the convoys, consisting of a dozen semi trucks and trailers, fifty horses, and over fifty pickup trucks and passenger cars decorated with bunting and balloons, paraded through downtown Klamath Falls before a crowd of 4,000 spectators, many of whom chanted "Let the water flow!" John and Frank Prosser, sons of the World War II veteran homesteader who had been first in line in the original Bucket Brigade, sold 500 bottles of Sucker Beer to the crowd. The "beer bottles," which contained no water, barley, or alcohol, invited consumers to take a lighter view of the situation. Customers could purchase one bottle for $3, two for $5, or, if they were "suckers," three for $10. At the Klamath County Government Center the commemorative bucket was installed.[47]

Later in the day a fund-raising dinner and rally took place at the County Fairgrounds. Bob Gasser, who had organized the original Bucket Brigade, lauded participants in the protests, calling them "patriots who fought for justice, who took on the ESA and won." Former Idaho representative Helen Chenoweth Hage chastised the Interior Department for betraying the veterans who had homesteaded in the Basin but reserved her harshest criticism for "green bigots who call themselves environmentalists." "We're here, finally, to fight for each other. Let's keep up the fight. God bless you," she intoned.[48]

The convoys raised nearly $300,000 in goods and cash for the farmers but failed to persuade Congress to amend the ESA. Coincidentally, two days after the Freedom Day rally, federal officials closed the headgates as the lake approached the minimum water level agreed upon by the Bureau and scientists in the FWS the previous spring. The closure had been announced previously, and news crews were on hand to witness and record the event, but officials unobtrusively closed the gates in the predawn darkness leaving the media without any footage of the event. Several dozen protestors who had gathered hurled epithets at Bureau employees but otherwise remained peaceful. Stan Thompson, who had announced he intended to once again open the headgates at 10 A.M., arrived with a ladder and chains, intending to scale the fence and "take the head gates" by chaining himself to them. But Joe Bair and Bill Ransom persuaded him to wait at least "a couple of days," fearing that rash action might alienate the public. Instead of tampering with the headgates, the protesters reinstalled the 10-inch diversion pipe and began once again siphoning the water.[49]

One week after the gates had been closed, 500–700 people attended a mass meeting near the headgates. Real estate agent Barbara Martin presented her evidence that the land surrounding the headgate and enclosed by the Bureau's fence did not belong to the government. She urged the audience to scale the fence and seize the property. Robert Herd and Richard Mack, gun-rights advocates and defenders of local authority who had formerly served as sheriffs in California and Arizona, next spoke. Mack aroused the crowd, likening federal officials guarding the headgates to British redcoats who trampled on American colonists' rights. Farmers Rick Rodgers and Claude Hagerty counseled moderation and warned the group not to open the headgates, but they were shouted down. Then about 200 protesters beginning with Barron Knoll, one of the young farmers who had opened the headgate in July, breached the chain link fence to reclaim the land inside. Knoll presented a sheaf of documents to the Bureau rangers guarding the headgates, advising them that they were standing on private property. The guards then retreated to the catwalk spanning the irrigation canal. Some of the protesters removed the gate to the enclosure and passed tables, chairs, beans, and hotdogs into the area for a picnic. At dusk the crowd dispersed when large winged insects swarmed over the water under the spotlights that illuminated the enclosure. When one of the rangers tired of swatting insects and tried to extinguish the lights that were attracting them, a group of protesters blocked his path. He grabbed a shovel and smashed the light but tossed the shovel aside with no further violence.[50]

The protest simmered for the next few days. On 1 September, the pump being used to siphon water from the lake to the canal lost its prime. The next day the BLM rangers who had been guarding the headgates were replaced by FWS personnel from out of town. The agents fostered goodwill by helping the protesters to install a new mechanism for siphoning the water.[51]

Then the protest suddenly and unexpectedly ceased after the nation was attacked on 11 September. The day after the World Trade Center's twin towers collapsed in a terrorist attack, protest leaders Oetting, Bair, and Ransom met with government representatives and pledged to break camp and not tamper further with the headgates until after January 1, enabling the twenty officials who had been guarding the enclosure to perform more critical duties elsewhere. "We are patriotic Americans, and this national emergency takes precedence," Ransom declared. The county sheriff praised the protesters and their cause and vowed he would "not be put in a position next year of enforcing 'no water' to our people."[52]

Legislators representing the Basin who had been working to secure financial aid for the drought-strapped farmers adjusted their priorities, too. Representative Walden had drafted a bill granting $200 million in drought relief to the Klamath farmers and Senators Gordon Smith and Ron Wyden had been working to obtain $148 million, but approval seemed remote after 9/11. "Obviously we're faced with greater funding challenges today than we had two weeks ago," observed Josh Kardon, Wyden's chief of staff. Kardon gauged the mood in Congress correctly. When the House approved a $172 billion farm bill on October 5, it contained no aid for the Klamath Basin. The version of the farm bill passed by the Senate early in 2002 earmarked $175 million for the Basin, but a conference committee excised that provision before it became law.[53]

In the Tulelake Irrigation District, the value of crops produced in 2001 amounted to less than half of normal—a loss of $21.4 million. Extrapolating from that data, economist Susan Burke estimated that gross crop sales for the entire Klamath project probably were down by at least $59 million. Partially offsetting those losses were nearly $24 million in federal payments to farmers along with $3.6 million in direct payments by the state of California, although some of that money was earmarked for drilling wells. Individual farmers "went through hell," testified David Krizo, a farmer and homesteader's son, the following year. Krizo, who operated his father's homestead, had been forced to invest $80,000 in drilling a well and pumping water in order to keep his horseradish crop alive when the water was shut off. The water shutoff had forced at least five farmers—none of them homesteaders—into bankruptcy. Two farmers had committed suicide.[54]

Although the war on terrorism derailed the protest at the headgates and likely deprived the farmers of fuller compensation for their losses, it did not halt the NAS review of the federal agencies' biological opinions that had necessitated the water shutoff. The homesteaders and their peers who had lived for decades in the Basin's ecosystem had questioned the government's assertion that higher lake levels promoted the welfare of endangered suckers. The twelve scientists convened by the NAS to scrutinize the data were led by William Lewis Jr. of the University of Colorado at Boulder. In their interim report released in February 2002 the distinguished reviewers judged the alleged connection between healthy fish and higher lake levels to be speculative. The FWS biologists' contention that low water levels promoted growth of toxic algae in Upper Klamath Lake was unfounded. Algae had flourished and killed masses of fish even in high water years. Fish kills during the 1990s were "not associated with years of low water level," and there was "no clear evidence of a connection between the lake levels and the welfare of the two sucker species." A bigger concern, the scientists warned, was water quality. Moreover, there was insufficient evidence to support the contention that higher water levels in the Klamath River during the summer months benefited the coho salmon. In fact, the reverse might well be true; releasing warmer lake water into cold streams "might work to the disadvantage" of the salmon.[55]

While the report flayed some of the assumptions underlying the biological opinions from the FSW and NMFS, it did not entirely vindicate the farmers, either. The authors pointed out that in the absence of more data, it would have been unwise to permit the lake to fall to "mean minimum levels below the recent historical levels (1990–2000)," as the Bureau had originally proposed, because this might "pose unknown risks." During the 1992 drought, the lake had fallen to nearly the 4,137 foot level in September and October without imperiling fish. This was substantially below the minimum elevation of 4,139 feet that the FWS and NMFS had imposed, but it would have been imprudent to have drawn down the lake to that level earlier in the season or to have lowered it even more, as the Bureau had originally proposed. Without commenting specifically on the 2-foot margin of difference (4,139 feet vs. 4,137 feet) the panel found that at another lake in the Basin, a margin of 2 feet was "reasonable" in light of the possibilities for evaporation in drought conditions.[56]

Secretary Norton responded to the interim report by directing the FWS and the Bureau of Reclamation to review the report and respond to it within ten days. If 2002 had been as dry as the previous year, the report's impact might have been different. As it was, snow levels were above normal in the Klamath Drainage at the time the committee issued its report, though, so it seemed unlikely that the federal agencies would have to choose between fish and farmers that year. The report's criticism of some of the assumptions underlying the 2001 biological opinions, and the political pressure it generated, did speed approvals from the FWS and the NMFS for Reclamation's operations report for the Klamath Project that year, cutting down their review of the Bureau's proposal from "months" to "a few days," according to journalist Michael Milstein. On 29 March, Secretary Norton visited Klamath Falls and opened the irrigation season, releasing water into project canals as hundreds of cheering farmers looked on. Close to 100 Yurok Indians peacefully protested on the site. The tribe's executive director, Troy Fletcher, criticized Norton for "mak[ing] such a critical decision and fail[ing] to consult us and then hav[ing] a celebration for something that's devastating to our fish." But most of the 350 onlookers at the headgates enthusiastically chanted "Let the water flow!" as water raced into the canals. "A year ago I came here to tell you how sorry I was," said Senator Smith. "I'm delighted to be here today to tell you how delighted I am that we are righting that wrong."[57]

Water users in the Basin felt vindicated by the NAS's report, and some perceived the outcome as a "victory over extreme environmentalists and agenda-driven science in a difficult struggle for water." But they also recognized that the report itself was a hollow victory because it had not altered the provisions in the ESA that had precipitated the water shutoff; as long as those provisions remained on the books, the homesteaders and their neighbors would be vulnerable to future shutoffs and the market value of the farms they had developed would be diminished. Many landowners in the region felt they could no longer count on the government to treat them fairly. Nearly a year after the water shutoff had been announced homesteader Eleanor Bolesta told a reporter that she had become "very skeptical of the government." A similar sense of distrust politicized David and Jacqui Krizo, second-generation homesteaders. David had rarely read anything in the newspaper aside from comics and headlines prior to 2001 but after the government cut off their water, he and Jacqui organized a Web site to monitor political developments related to their water supply and the ESA.[58]

Three years after the water shutoff, members of the House Resources Subcommittee on Water and Power convened a field hearing in Klamath Falls on the water crisis and the ESA. One of the members of the committee, Greg Walden, who represented the Oregon portion of the Klamath Basin, had drafted a bill that would provide for independent peer review of government agencies' conclusions regarding the status and protection of wildlife. "There needs to be outside independent peer review of decisions to list or delist a species [as endangered or to] work on recovery programs," Walden maintained. By that point, the scientists empaneled by the NAS had released their final report, reiterating the conclusions of the interim document. Neither of those documents had called for independent peer review of federal agencies' decisions, but water users in the Basin were convinced that the reports produced by the blue ribbon committee demonstrated that peer review could provide an important corrective.[59]

One of the committee's objectives was to review the NAS report. "The field hearing is a great forum to focus the spotlight on preventing another injustice like the one that occurred in 2001 in the Klamath Basin. Constructive approaches can be taken to move in a new direction, and the road map that can take us there is the [NAS] report," said Dan Keppen, executive director of the Klamath Water Users Association. Among those who testified before the committee was David Carman, a homesteader who had participated in landings in the Aleutian Islands and at Kwajalein and Leyte during World War II. He traced the homesteaders' legendary saga, telling how he and his peers had "started a community" on "just bare ground" and had "united . . . to build schools, churches and a hospital." They had "liv[ed] the American dream" on the land in an era when few had that opportunity. A grateful nation had rewarded their military service with that precious opportunity. But, Carman testified, "In 2001 the Endangered Species Act came very close to destroying our dream. Our dream was changed into a nightmare." Calling the ESA "an Act that has become a tool to destroy rural America," Carman lobbied the Representatives to "never allow" them "to be betrayed" again. Deb Crisp of the Tulelake Growers Association, a nonprofit organization representing farmers in the region, informed the committee, "Words cannot begin to describe the hardships endured by our communities. Farm families have lost income. Long-term commodity supply contracts have been terminated. Debts will not be paid. Dreams are being shattered." The association alleged that not only the profitability of their farms but their identity as farmers and ranchers had been impaired because "there is no separation between our work and the rest of our lives."[60]

Four days after the hearing in Klamath Falls, the House Committee on Resources approved Walden's bill 26 to 15. When the full House failed to act on that bill before it adjourned at the end of the year, Walden joined with others on Capitol Hill including House Resources Committee Chairman Richard Pombo in drafting and sponsoring new reform legislation. On September 29, 2005, the House passed the Endangered Species Act Improvement Bill but it died in the Senate. Six years after the farmers called off their protest, the ESA had not yet been amended along the lines proposed by Walden and his colleagues.[61]

On a separate front, in 2005 federal judge Francis Allegra rejected a takings claim by thirteen landowners and fourteen water, irrigation, and drainage districts for $100 million as compensation for the government's shutoff of water. The farmers, including homesteader Fred Robison, had claimed in a lawsuit filed in October 2001 that their water rights amounted to property rights and that they were therefore entitled under the Fifth Amendment to compensation for seized property. Originally they had sought $1 billion but later amended their claim. The ruling deflated the homesteaders' assertion that their water rights were inviolable property rights. Allegra ruled that the patent deeds' conferral of "the right to the use of water from the Klamath Reclamation Project as an appurtenance to the irrigable lands" did not constitute a property right. Water right applications stipulated that in times of water shortage, allocations must be "equitable" but allowed the project manager to "take into consideration the character and necessities of the land" in allocating water. Moreover, in the event of shortages, the government would be immune from liability for "any damage direct or indirect arising therefrom." A contract entered into between the United States and homesteaders in the Tulelake Irrigation District in 1956 likewise provided that in the event of a drought, "in no event shall any liability accrue against the United States or any of its officers, agents, or employees for any damage, direct or indirect, arising therefrom." The plaintiffs' attorneys had argued that such provisions applied only to shortages brought about by "hydrologic causes" but Allegra disagreed: "the plain language of these provisions expressly absolves the United States from liability for all types of water shortages—not only the hydrologic causes." Further diminishing the farmers' water rights, the judge ruled that the farmers' water rights were "subservient to the prior interests not only of the United States" but also to those of Indian tribes in the Basin "whose interests carry a priority date of time immemorial."[62]

The outcomes of the agrarian protest in the Klamath Basin were thus mixed for the aging homesteaders, their descendants, successors, and neighbors. The water shutoff elicited sympathy for the farmers, especially because some of them possessed a distinctive relationship to the government as veterans and as homesteaders. The image of industrious yeomen whose hard work entitles them to competency and security continues to appeal to many Americans as a stock validation of the American Dream. Activists seized upon the homesteaders' plight as ammunition in their own larger quest to shore up private property rights. The combination of deeply revered myths and polarizing debate attracted national and even international media attention. Farmers and their allies in the Klamath Basin shrewdly capitalized upon media coverage to secure concessions including the late-season release of irrigation water—a limited abrogation of the ESA by the George W. Bush administration—and review of the FWS biological opinions by the NAS. Congress appropriated emergency relief funds for the farmers, and the House voted to amend the ESA. Reading the pulse of public opinion across the nation, though, the Senate chose not to tamper with the ESA. Meanwhile, the courts trimmed the scope of the homesteaders' water rights, making the resolution of future water disputes in the homesteaders' favor less likely. Times had changed and new political forces had gained ascendancy. To homesteaders of David Carman's generation the world had turned upside down. Their vision of themselves as agents of progress and virtue was no longer broadly shared. Feeling betrayed and angry, they complained that their agrarian dreams had metamorphosed into "a nightmare."

EPILOGUE

The repeal of the Homestead Act did not mark the end of "homesteading." Like other elements of the mythic West, homesteading retained its luster in Americans' collective memory and continued to inspire creative iterations as governments and individuals endeavored to perpetuate the perceived benefits of homesteading for new generations in a changing West.

In the 1970s, while opportunities to claim part of the public domain dwindled, Americans continued to "homestead" by migrating from urban areas to inexpensive farmland. As ethnographer Rebecca Gould has noted, participants in this migration generally opposed the ethos of Manifest Destiny and expansionism inherent in the Homestead Act but they nevertheless called themselves homesteaders and sought cheap land and "the same skills and fortitude as earlier pioneers." They employed the term *homesteading* much as Ralph Borsodi, the utopian experimenter and writer earlier in the century, had done. Borsodi described his family's "adventure in homesteading"—their attempts to be self-sufficient on a small farm—in his 1933 classic, *Flight from the City: An Experiment in Creative Living on the Land*. These self-styled homesteaders also drew inspiration from Wendell Berry's *The Long-Legged House* (1969), in which he invited readers to "reject the dependencies and artificial needs of urban life, and go into the countryside and make a home there in the fullest and most permanent sense: that is, live on and use and preserve and learn from and enrich and enjoy the land."[1]

Many of these self-described "homesteaders" who retreated into the countryside lacked a reformist social agenda, but others like Maynard and Sally Kaufman aggressively promulgated the homesteading movement. In 1973, the Kaufmans and their six children established a School of Homesteading on a 100-acre farm near Bangor, Michigan. There they taught idealistic students from Western Michigan University about "the full range of agricultural activities and whatever low-level technology and skills are appropriate to the means of the young subsistence homesteader."[2]

In the 1990s, another wave of homesteading ensued. Rebecca Gould characterized these 1990s homesteaders as sharing "a common commitment to on-the-ground environmental ethics, do-it-yourself pragmatics, and an improvisational, nature-based spiritual practice." They sought "to center [their] life around home, a home consciously built with attention to a particular place in the natural world." Thousands of Americans pursued this type of homesteading. In 1995 Jess Walter, a reporter for the Spokane *Spokesman-Review*, estimated that over 10,000 homesteading Americans had cut themselves off from the power grid in eastern Washington, Idaho's panhandle, and western Montana alone. Based upon their extensive network of homesteading contacts, Maynard Kaufman and Barbara Geisler divided end-of-the-century homesteaders into four categories: the most common were those who lived in ecologically sustainable, simple ways to conserve energy and preserve the environment. Others were vegetarians seeking a more organic and environmentally friendly lifestyle and a closer spiritual relationship with nature. A third group consisted of Christians trying to distance themselves from worldly ways by living close to nature, eating pure food, working toward self-sufficiency, and insulating the family through practices such as home schooling. Finally a fourth group was "politically motivated homesteaders" who retreated to the countryside in order to "get away from what they perceive to be the 'New World Order.'"[3]

Several magazines and advice manuals catered to participants in this turn-of-the-century homesteading movement. *Countryside & Small Stock Journal*, a publication billing itself as "the magazine of modern homesteading," equated homesteading with "seeking greater self-reliance." It printed articles on gardening, small-scale livestock raising, preserving food, frugality, and alterative energy sources. Another popular magazine, *Down to the Roots Organic Homesteading*, offered instruction in the art of "organic homesteading." Its editors defined homesteading as a "simple living philosophy" that might entail log cabin living and full-time organic farming or "just a few mere aspects" of the agrarian lifestyle practiced on a city lot or even an apartment balcony as people tried to be "eco-friendly, more self-reliant and grow many of [their] own foods."[4]

While some Americans late in the twentieth century aspired to the putative self-sufficiency and independence of homesteaders on the frontier by withdrawing from social, economic, and governmental institutions and conventions, governments experimented with "homesteading" programs, too, by offering land or other perquisites to those who were willing to move to sparsely populated locales. Many explicitly linked these programs to the Homestead Act because of its cachet. In 2002, North Dakota senator Byron Dorgan and Nebraska senator Chuck Hagel proposed a New Homestead Economic Opportunity Act to Congress. The senators hoped thereby to encourage Americans to relocate in rural areas. On the Great Plains, nearly 70 percent of rural counties had suffered a net loss of at least 30 percent of their population over the previous fifty years. Schools and churches were closing, rural businesses were losing money, and local tax bases were shrinking. As he introduced his bill, Dorgan reminded his colleagues of "the old Homestead Act" whereby Congress "decided to try to populate the middle of this country well over a century ago by offering land to people who would move to the center of the country and work to improve the land." He illustrated how the program had worked by recounting the heroism of his grandmother, a Norwegian widow who was drawn to South Dakota by the promise of free land. She and her six children bivouacked in a tent until they could build a house on their homestead. They were "strong people" who established themselves on the land and strengthened the community where they settled. Although Hagel and Dorgan's bill offered no land "because we don't have more land to give away," it did proffer economic incentives to individuals and businesses willing to relocate in rural regions. "People will go where there are opportunities. Jobs are part of that universe of opportunities," Hagel told his colleagues. The bill would waive up to $10,000 in student loan repayments for college graduates who were willing to move to any county where the population had fallen by at least 10 percent over the previous twenty years. It also offered tax credits of up to $45,000 for buyers of new homes and Individual Homestead Accounts—tax free savings accounts that could be used after five years of living in rural counties to pay medical bills or tuition, buy a home, or develop a small business. For businesses willing to relocate, Dorgan and Hagel proposed tax credits and a venture capital fund.[5]

Some senators questioned the lawmakers' "Norman Rockwell notion of small town" life, but the duo persisted. In 2003 they reintroduced their bill with backing from Senators Tim Johnson of South Dakota and Sam Brownback of Kansas. Johnson recalled for his colleagues how the Homestead Act had "made a commitment to populate rural America" by promising Americans like his great-grandfather who were "willing to travel to the midwest" that "if you stay and work the land for 5 years we will offer you a quarter section of land." Johnson wanted to use "this hugely popular and successful program" as a model for addressing rural depopulation. The Senate Finance Committee in 2004 incorporated portions of the New Homestead Act regarding financial incentives for business relocation within a corporate tax bill, but Congress later removed them. Undaunted, Dorgan, Hagel, and eight other senators reintroduced the New Homestead Act in 2005. In 2007 Dorgan and Hagel again introduced their bill, this time with the joint sponsorship of eleven colleagues. "There is good reason to think we will make significant progress on the New Homestead Act in the 110th Congress," Dorgan claimed. But Max Lu, a geographer at Kansas State University, was less sanguine. Noting that lawmakers from largely urban states had been uninterested in the bill since 2002, Lu opined in 2007, "The prospect of this bill passing into law in the foreseeable future is not very good."[6]

In 1977, Alaska developed a state-level version of the Homestead Act in which it offered a limited number of 5-acre "homesites" to state residents who would settle on the land, build a house, and remain there for at least thirty-five months. One couple who signed up for "free land," Ron and Denise Caldwell, wanted to escape "from the Anchorage rat race and see, for a change, some direct results of our labor." After two years of gathering the requisite supplies, they moved into a camper fitted for the bed of a pickup truck and a plywood annex and proceeded to clear the land and build a 20 x 24-foot home. Despite the large sums of money required and numerous unexpected setbacks, they achieved their objectives, and Denise felt it had been "more than worth the steep price we've paid."[7]

Beginning late in the twentieth century, municipalities also enacted "Mini-Homestead Acts," offering "free land" in an effort to revitalize their communities. In 1989, Koochiching County, a vast, sparsely populated region adjoining Minnesota's Canadian border, advertised 40-acre homesteads on land the county had repossessed. "Our real problem up here is that nobody's here anymore," said Lee Hervey, one of the architects of the homesteading program. Applicants were required to demonstrate the prospect of "sufficient" income in the county. Those who received land would have to build a house and live there for at least ten years. Some taxpayers worried that the free land program would attract riffraff. Because of their concerns, they persuaded the county to furlough its homestead program after only two homesteads had been awarded.[8]

Beginning in the 1990s other local governments in the rural West offered free town lots to prospective residents through their own "Mini-Homestead Acts." They looked to the original Homestead Act as a model. "We gave away the land to the first settlers, now we are giving it away again," observed Matt Wilson, a community leader in Eureka, Kansas.[9]

Hendrum, Minnesota, was one of the first towns to advertise free land. In 1994 town leaders began offering repossessed lots to people who would commit to move to the town and build there. By 2005, new homes stood on eighteen of the lots. In 1996 Lefors, Texas, held a lottery to give away fourteen repossessed lots. Nearly 600 people applied. “All that’s missing are the Conestoga wagons, bison herds and sod cabins of homesteading lore,” quipped reporter Verne Kopytoff. The town required winners to either move a house trailer to the lot or begin building a home within six months; after five years of residency, the occupants would receive title to the land.[10]

Hendrum’s and Lefor’s strategy for attracting new residents was adopted more widely in Kansas than in any other state. In 2007, geographer Max Lu identified twenty-one Kansas towns that were offering land to newcomers. Minneapolis, Kansas, advertised free lots beginning in 1999. Within eight years, twenty-eight lots had been taken. In Ellsworth County, community leaders in 2003 sweetened the offer by giving away not only land but building permits, free hookups to water and sewer lines, and passes to the municipal golf course and swimming pool. The towns also agreed to subsidize newcomers’ down payments with up to $3,000 if they enrolled children in local schools. Lenders also consented to reduce the required down payments on new homes by the value of the lots, an average of $8,000.[11]

Impressed by the success of Ellsworth County and Minneapolis, business leaders in Marquette, Kansas, bought 50 acres of vacant land on the west side of town for $100,000 in 2003. When the school board met to decide whether to cope with declining enrollment by closing the elementary school, Mayor Steve Piper unveiled Marquette’s plan to subdivide the land and give it away in order to attract young families. The board took the bait and agreed to keep the school open. In order to succeed, the plan needed publicity. An Associated Press reporter furnished that with an article that appeared nationwide in newspapers. Then on 22 May, CBS News highlighted Marquette’s land opening on its evening program. The next day, hundreds of phone calls swamped city employees. The fact that jobs were available in nearby Salina and Hutchinson made it feasible for people to move to Marquette. By 2005, eighty-two lots had been given away, twenty-three new homes were either finished or under way, and forty-five additional children had enrolled in school. Piper credited the giveaway with “sav[ing] our school and rekindl[ing] a lot of pride.”[12]

Mini-Homestead Acts in the Sunflower State received additional free advertising in February 2005 after Ellsworth's dynamic director of economic development, Anita Hoffhines, mailed press releases to media outlets. The press release caught the eye of a reporter for *USA Today*; his article quoted Hoffhines's promotional spiel. "If you want to be creative in Silicon Valley, the cost is very high. If you come to central Kansas, you can be very creative and have very low risk in comparison. And the quality of the people here is awesome." Within hours of the article's publication Hoffhines received close to 250 inquiries. A Telemundo news crew and reporters from the *New York Times*, *Time Magazine*, the *London Observer*, and the *Manchester Guardian* were soon in town. Eventually over thirty families from as far away as Nevada, Minnesota, Wyoming, and Oklahoma settled in Ellsworth. Although their interest had been piqued by the land offer, most decided it would be cheaper to buy houses already on the market than to build on a free lot. So few newcomers availed themselves of the free land that in August 2006, elected officials voted to deed a lot to a developer who was willing to build a spec home.[13]

Not all of the old-timers in Ellsworth were ecstatic about the land giveaway and the attention it brought to their community. After one news report highlighted the small-town, trusting atmosphere in Ellsworth and alleged that no one there needed to lock their homes or cars, longtime resident Peg Britton countered, "I lock my house and car and about everyone else I know does, particularly since it's been so well advertised world wide that it's so safe here we don't lock our houses or cars."[14]

Other towns continued to experiment with land giveaways although researchers Jon Bailey and Kim Preston at the Center for Rural Affairs warned in 2004 that Mini-Homestead Acts were not the elixir for all rural communities. Eureka, Kansas; Marne, Iowa; Lavilla, Texas; Chugwater, Wyoming; New Richland, Minnesota; and Kennesaw, Nebraska, were among the towns that advertised free land. In 2007, Anderson, Alaska, followed suit. High school students there persuaded the town council to offer twenty-six wooded lots of 1.3 acres each to the first twenty-six applicants who would commit to build either a summer home or a year-round residence. The offer spawned thousands of phone calls, some from as far away as Asia. On the day appointed for the land giveaway, forty-four people stood in line in Anderson to apply in person for the twenty-six lots; some had caught last-minute flights to Alaska, including one person from Florida.[15]

Applicants for free land shared many of the same aspirations as the postwar reclamation homesteaders. Some wanted a lifestyle that reminded them of their own past. Kimberly Bayless, who moved to Ellsworth, Kansas, from Las Vegas, said that the smell of "fresh-cut grass, the trees and the flowers" in Kansas made her feel "like I was home again." Maribel Juarez, a Salvadoran immigrant whose husband had been working as a hotel maintenance worker in the San Francisco Bay area before they moved to the Plains, liked the slow pace of life. "I found a place exactly like my hometown. . . . To us, this is our promised land," she said. Steven Thiessen, a fifty-eight-year-old retiree, wanted to travel back in time to a "cleaner" era. "We like the past. We basically are stuck about a half-century ago, and rural America really offers that to you," he told a reporter.[16]

The prospect of owning land and a home along with the attendant benefits of financial equity, stability, and independence attracted many. Sue and Paddy McCabe of Lancaster, Pennsylvania, applied for a lot in Marquette because they could see no prospect of ever buying a house in Pennsylvania on their income. "Where we were, it was very crowded and very expensive," Sue explained. Tom Kristensen, who retired at age fifty-three after suffering a stroke, learned he could build a house on free land in Hendrum for $70,000. The price seemed a pittance compared to metropolitan Dallas, where he had been living.[17]

Others sought a lifestyle that was tranquil and relatively free of crime. Angela and Roy Behanna had lived in a neighborhood in northern Virginia where shootings occurred and crime was rampant. They wanted a safer community. The Behannas recognized that problems existed everywhere but "compared to where we came from," Marquette was "very, very safe." Amy Eck liked the fact that her son would not "have to enter a metal detector" when he went to school because of the absence of gang violence.[18]

Many, like Patty and Peter Christidis, who moved to Kansas from Orange County, California, desired "something more family oriented"—an impulse that helped to bring many postwar homesteaders to the family farm. They wanted a place where children would be safe and sheltered and where neighbors would look out for one another. Jim Wymore of Chicago became interested in land in Marquette because his adolescent daughter was "getting a little too ghetto, a little too urban" and he wanted "someplace with family values." Kimberly Bayless wanted a home where her children could be safe playing outdoors and exploring. Ellsworth appealed to Billy Canaan of Baton Rouge because "you don't have to worry about your kids."[19]

At the dawn of the twenty-first century, then, free land and rural life continued to appeal to many Americans, much as they had to reclamation homesteaders earlier in the century. The Jeffersonian ideal with its equation of security and land ownership, along with conviction that hard work would yield economic independence, still burned brightly. Moreover, government leaders still found features of the Homestead Act relevant to modern problems.

Other continuities also linked the modern and historic Wests. As Patricia Limerick observed in 1987, westerners still competed, as they had for generations, "for the right to claim for oneself and for one's group the status of legitimate beneficiary of western resources." A prime example involved homesteaders' and other farmers' competition with urban, recreational, and wildlife interests for scarce water in places like the Klamath Basin and Coachella Valley. Confronted with limited water and other inadequacies, westerners also continued their old habit of agitating—often successfully—for federal programs to redress their grievances. The New Deal and the GI Bill nurtured the homesteaders' expectations and sense of entitlement. On reclamation projects, as Floyd Dominy observed, the government "assume[d] greater responsibility for the settlers' success" in the postwar era. The level of support climaxed in Congress's guarantee of a productive farm for all reclamation homesteaders in 1953 and its agreement to buy out the Riverton Project homesteaders in 1964.[20]

But there were significant differences as well between Turner's frontier of "free land," characterized by widespread agricultural settlement and homesteading, and the modern West, differences that were especially palpable in farm country. In making her case for "the unbroken past of the American West," Limerick acknowledged but downplayed these and other differences. She admitted that "a great deal had changed in the American West" by the 1980s; for instance, ranchers used pickup trucks [and] farmers used home computers." But she maintained that differences arising from new technology like the distinction between farming with "horse-drawn plows" and farming with "air-conditioned combines" explained "little about Western history" and certainly did not constitute a key disjuncture or temporal breaking point.[21]

In the rural West, the differences mattered more than Limerick suggested. Their impact was especially apparent in the lives of those who homesteaded after World War II because the contrasts between their lives and those of earlier homesteaders were so stark; they were participating in anachronistic frontier processes like land settlement and farm making in an era of rapid metropolitan growth, rural depopulation, and modernization. Much like earlier waves of homesteaders, the veterans claimed "free" land as the beneficiaries of government policies that had removed former occupants. Like earlier homesteaders they had to clear and fence the land; plow, plant, and irrigate; and grapple with environmental challenges including soil deficiencies and insect pests. Along with their predecessors they negotiated high interest rates and low commodity prices and dreamed of substantial homes and barns. They shared with earlier generations the desire to make money and to provide a stable home, and some hoped to establish a farm that would pass on to their children. But they perceived greater differences than similarities between themselves and homesteaders in the "pioneer" era. As Lyle Esser stated, "We did not consider ourselves pioneers."[22]

Some of the temporal differences involved the homesteading process itself. With concessions including reduced residency requirements; low-interest, federally financed loans; guidance from government experts and a ten-year reprieve from payments for the cost of their irrigation systems, nearly all were able to prove up—unlike previous homesteaders. They also received generous financial assistance under the GI Bill. Some even managed to borrow enough money to pay others to clear and level their lands or build their homes. Universal success in proving up had long been the goal of the Bureau of Reclamation for its homesteading program; ironically the agency came close to achieving that goal in the same generation that reclamation homesteading ceased. While the homesteaders' initial sense of loneliness and privation was keen because their lifestyle contrasted so sharply with the norm in postwar, electrified America, within a handful of years all obtained electricity and telephone service, which lessened the strenuousness of housekeeping and the isolation of farm life.

Other factors that separated the homesteaders' experiences from those of earlier generations were felt more widely, affecting most contemporary western farmers. Chemical fertilizer, pesticides, and new technology ranging from wind machines to sprinklers increased their capacity to produce and reduced the price of farm products relative to other consumer goods. The homesteaders like most farmers adopted tractors, combines, power mowers, pick up balers, and other specialized machinery in place of smaller horse-drawn implements, boosting their efficiency but also exponentially

Over their farming careers, Yuma homesteaders Fagan Tillman, Bill Gunlock, Bob Fram, and Eliot Waits (left to right), photographed in October 1998, adapted to changes in the scale, technology, and economics of farming. (Photograph courtesy of Pam M. Smith, *Desert Farm & Ranch, The [Yuma] Sun*)

increasing their need for operating capital. The scale of farming increased as did the costs and requisite business acumen. As David Danbom has observed, "Farmers had to be more sophisticated, better educated, more technologically literate, more willing to use complex business strategies, and more highly capitalized." Aside from the produce grown in their vegetable gardens, nearly all of the products of their farms were destined for the market. Modern transportation and communications and participation in federal farm programs provided new avenues for social and economic integration. Developments such as these helped to reshape the countryside. They forced many farmers like homesteader David Hunt out of business, increased the size of remaining farms, altered the dynamics of farmwork, and affected farmers' relationship to the land.[23]

The postwar homesteaders also experienced climactic transitions in the history of American agriculture in terms of the farm family's relationship to the market. Some husbands coped with the cost-price squeeze by working full-time off the farm, fewer farm families grew and preserved food for their own tables, many farm women abandoned traditional subsistence activities and "helping" on the farm and sought work in town for wages, and hired workers supplanted family members as farm laborers. The transition was gradual, and for many women on homesteads their off-farm employment began as their children grew older, making it easier for them to be absent from the home and farm during the workday. Few mothers with small children on homesteads worked outside the home in the 1950s and many ignored the advice of economists and social scientists and continued to grow and preserve their own food. Change was contested, and it was driven by economic opportunities, stage in the life cycle, and personal preference as well as financial constraints. But its ultimate impact upon the lifestyles of farm families was profound. By 1988, close to 45 percent of farm women under age sixty-five held off-farm jobs.[24]

Another significant discontinuity between the era of abundant homesteading opportunities and the modern West involved the Bureau of Reclamation and its influence in the West. The Bureau's orientation and leverage declined significantly in the second half of the twentieth century. Perhaps the postwar era marked the apogee of the Bureau's imperial power, as Donald Worster has argued, but that power was more short lived than he indicated. By Worster's reckoning, the Bureau's clout in Congress did not recede until after 1972. In reality, the agency's power was contested even in its glory days and it receded rapidly from 1960 onward. Reclamation homesteading was a small-ticket item on the Bureau's agenda by the 1940s and 1950s when it focused more of its budget upon large, multiple-use projects. But it was also the item that best fulfilled the Bureau's original legislative mandate as set forth in the Newlands Act. The fact that the agency had to modify its focus in order to retain its legitimacy and funding reflected its vulnerability and dependency. The Bureau's ability to secure congressional approval for its homesteading programs was haphazard even in the 1940s: Congress rejected veterans preference bills backed by the Bureau and its friends in 1944 and 1945. In the 1960s the agency wielded even less influence: Congress repeatedly discounted and overrode the Bureau's objections, legislating a buyout of homesteaders at Riverton and privileging the Fish and Wildlife Service over the Bureau in the Klamath Basin.[25]

Not only the experiences of the homesteaders and the legitimacy of the Bureau of Reclamation but societal values changed significantly in the years after World War II. The history of modern homesteading mirrors these fundamental and consequential changes that altered the entire West with its large amount of public land. Limerick characterized one manifestation of this change, Oregon's experiments with environmentally friendly policies in the 1960s and 1970s, as "one of the most significant events in western American history, an apparent reversal of the ruling trend toward ardent growth." But the events in Oregon were symptomatic of much broader, nationwide shifts in opinion. As fewer Americans relied upon extractive industries for their livelihood, citizens increasingly viewed rural landscapes through lenses that privileged aesthetics, recreation, and environmental protection over extraction of resources and maximum economic growth. In congressional hearings regarding postwar homesteading in the mid-1940s, opponents raised several objections to reclamation, but none of them concerned environmental degradation or threats to wildlife. Conversely, in governmental circles environmental concerns became paramount in debates over reclamation in the 1960s. The new values were reflected in the Bureau's cancellation of its plans for new reclamation homesteads, in the repeal of the Homestead Act, and in the priority accorded to wildlife over farmers' water rights. The change was profound. As Tule Lake homesteader Marion Palmer observed in 2001, "fifty-nine years ago, we were welcomed home as heroes and asked to feed a hungry world." But by the twenty-first century their water counted for more than what they could grow on their land.[26]

In 1953, Idaho Lieutenant Governor Edson Deal interpreted the fact that homesteaders were claiming land in the Snake River Valley as evidence that "new horizons have not vanished." In the twenty-first century farmers on irrigated lands in the West would still face new horizons, but bleaker ones. Whether the homesteaders' and their succeeding generation's thirst for irrigation water can be sustained over another century is uncertain in light of climatic shifts, metropolitan growth, and a keener sense of environmental consciousness. It will be a matter of more than passing academic interest to the region's residents.[27]

NOTES

INTRODUCTION

1. Frederick Jackson Turner, "The Significance of the Frontier in American History," in *Frontier and Section: Selected Essays of Frederick Jackson Turner*, ed. Ray Allen Billington (Englewood Cliffs, NJ: Prentice-Hall, 1961), 37, 62; David M. Wrobel, *The End of American Exceptionalism: Frontier Anxiety from the Old West to the New Deal* (Lawrence: University Press of Kansas, 1993).

2. E. Louise Peffer, *The Closing of the Public Domain: Disposal and Reservation Policies, 1900–1950* (New York: Arno Press, 1972), 3–4, 8, 134–137.

3. Walter Nugent, *Into the West: The Story of Its People* (New York: Vintage Books, 1999), 194; Geoff Cunfer, "Manure Matters on the Great Plains Frontier," *Journal of Interdisciplinary History* 34 (Spring 2004): 561–563; David B. Danbom, *Born in the Country: A History of Rural America* (Baltimore: Johns Hopkins University Press, 1995), 233–248.

4. Wrobel, *End of American Exceptionalism*, vii, 143; Henry Nash Smith, *Virgin Land: The American West as Symbol and Myth* (Cambridge, MA: Harvard University Press, 1950), 251.

5. Gerald D. Nash, *Creating the West: Historical Interpretations, 1890–1990* (Albuquerque: University of New Mexico Press, 1991), 49–158.

6. Patricia Nelson Limerick, *The Legacy of Conquest: The Unbroken Past of the American West* (New York: W. W. Norton, 1987), 25; Patricia Nelson Limerick, "Turnerians All: The Dream of a Helpful History in an Intelligible World," *American Historical Review* 100 (June 1995): 698; Richard White, *"It's Your Misfortune and None of My Own": A New History of the American West* (Norman: University of Oklahoma Press, 1991); Kerwin Lee Klein, "Reclaiming the 'F' Word, or Being and Becoming Postmodern," *Pacific Historical Review* 65 (May 1996): 179–215.

7. Limerick, "Turnerians All," 698; Wrobel, *End of American Exceptionalism*, vii, 146; James F. Brooks, *Captives and Cousins: Slavery, Kinship, and Community in the Southwest Borderlands* (Chapel Hill: University of North Carolina Press, 2002); Elliott West, *The Contested Plains: Indians, Goldseekers, and the Rush to Colorado* (Lawrence: University Press of Kansas, 1998); John Mack Faragher, ed., *Rereading Frederick Jackson Turner: "The Significance of the Frontier in American History" and Other Essays* (New Haven, CT: Yale University Press, 1999); Nugent, *Into the West*, 194.

8. Nugent, *Into the West*, 182, 279.

9. The fullest discussions of the Bureau's entire postwar homesteading program

are found in Paul W. Gates, *History of Public Land Law Development* (Washington, DC: GPO, 1968), 692–694; and William E. Warne, *The Bureau of Reclamation* (New York: Praeger, 1973).

10. Limerick, *Legacy of Conquest*, 130–131; Catherine McNicol Stock and Robert D. Johnston, eds., *The Countryside in the Age of the Modern State: Political Histories of Rural America* (Ithaca, NY: Cornell University Press, 2001), 4; Nugent, *Into the West*, 4, 131–132; Lisa McGirr, *Suburban Warriors: The Origins of the New American Right* (Princeton, NJ: Princeton University Press, 2001); James Noble Gregory, *American Exodus: The Dust Bowl Migration and Okie Culture in California* (New York: Oxford University Press, 1989), 243–244; R. Douglas Hurt, "Agricultural Politics in the Twentieth-Century American West," in *The Political Culture of the New West*, ed. Jeff Roche (Lawrence: University Press of Kansas), 2008, 71.

11. William Cronon, "Landscapes of Abundance and Scarcity," in *The Oxford History of the American West*, ed. Clyde A. Milner II, Carol A. O'Connor, and Martha A. Sandweiss (New York: Oxford University Press, 1994), 628.

12. William G. Robbins, *Landscapes of Conflict: The Oregon Story, 1940–2000* (Seattle: University of Washington Press, 2004); William G. Robbins, *Hard Times in Paradise: Coos Bay, Oregon, 1850–1986* (Seattle: University of Washington Press, 1988); William G. Robbins, *Colony and Empire: The Capitalist Transformation of the American West* (Lawrence: University Press of Kansas, 1994); William E. Riebsame et al., eds., *Atlas of the New West: Portrait of a Changing Region* (New York: W. W. Norton, 1997); David R. Wilson, "You Grow Where You're Planted: Community Building in Colstrip, Montana" (Ph.D. diss., Brigham Young University, 2000); Hal K. Rothman, *Devil's Bargains: Tourism in the Twentieth-Century American West* (Lawrence: University Press of Kansas, 1998); Carlos A. Schwantes, "Wage Earners and Wealth Makers," in Milner, O'Connor, and Sandweiss, *Oxford History of the American West*, 431–467; R. Douglas Hurt, ed., *The Rural West since World War II* (Lawrence: University Press of Kansas, 1998), 4, 5; James E. Sherow, "Environmentalism and Agriculture in the American West," in Hurt, *Rural West*, 58–75; Donald J. Pisani, "Federal Water Policy and the Rural West," in Hurt, *Rural West*, 119–146; Mark Friedberger, "Cattle Raising and Dairying in the Western States," in Hurt, *Rural West*, 190–212. See also Mark Friedberger, *Farm Families and Change in Twentieth-Century America* (Louisville: University Press of Kentucky, 1988), 241–243.

13. Stock and Johnston, *Countryside in the Age of the Modern State*, 6–7; Danbom, *Born in the Country*, 190–191; R. Douglas Hurt, *American Agriculture: A Brief History*, rev. ed. (West Lafayette, IN: Purdue University Press, 2002), 267–268; Brian Q. Cannon, "'We Are Now Entering a New Era': Federal Reclamation and the Fact Finding Commission of 1923–1924," *Pacific Historical Review* 66 (May 1997): 207–208.

14. U.S. Congress, Senate, Subcommittee on Irrigation and Reclamation, Committee on Interior and Insular Affairs, *Riverton Reclamation Project: Hearings before the Subcommittee on Irrigation and Reclamation . . . on S. 2035*, 88th Cong., 1st sess., 29–30 October 1963, 60; Stock and Johnson, *Countryside in the Age of the Modern State*, 6.

15. Donald Worster, *Rivers of Empire: Water, Aridity, and the Growth of the American West* (New York: Pantheon Books, 1985), 7, 239, 277, 310–326; Robert Dahl, *Who Governs? Democracy and Power in an American City* (New Haven, CT: Yale University Press, 1961); Nelson Polsby, *Community Power and Political Theory: A Further Look at Problems of Evidence and Inference* (New Haven, CT: Yale University Press, 1980); Raymond E. Wolfinger, *The Politics of Progress* (Englewood Cliffs, NJ: Prentice-Hall, 1974).

16. Allan Kulikoff, "Households and Markets: Toward a New Synthesis of American Agrarian History," *William and Mary Quarterly*, 3d series, 50 (April 1993): 343, 347, 348, 353.

CHAPTER 1. CREATING A "NEW FRONTIER OF OPPORTUNITY": WORLD WAR II VETERANS AND THE CAMPAIGN FOR WESTERN HOMESTEADS

1. Paul W. Gates, *History of Public Land Law Development* (Washington, DC: GPO, 1968), 249–284, 610–615; Richard K. Pelz, ed., *Federal Reclamation Laws and Related Laws Annotated*, 4 vols. (Washington, DC: GPO, 1972), 1: 515–516. In rare cases it was also still possible to purchase arid and semiarid land under the Desert Land Act if the purchaser could present feasible plans for irrigating the land. See ibid., 638–643, and "Can I Get Free Land from the Government?" *Changing Times, The Kiplinger Magazine*, March 1954, 44–45.

2. Geoff Cunfer, "Manure Matters on the Great Plains Frontier," *Journal of Interdisciplinary History* 34 (Spring 2004): 561–563; David B. Danbom, *Born in the Country: A History of Rural America* (Baltimore: Johns Hopkins University Press, 1995), 234–244; R. Douglas Hurt, *American Agriculture: A Brief History*, rev. ed. (West Lafayette, IN: Purdue University Press, 2002), 321.

3. U.S. Congress, House, Committee on Irrigation and Reclamation, *Settlement of Returning Veterans on Farms in Reclamation Projects*, 79th Cong., 1st sess., 12 April 1945, 90–92, 97; U.S. Congress, Senate, *Federal Reclamation by Irrigation*, 68th Cong., 1st sess., S. Doc. 92 (1924), 97. For information on abortive proposals to resettle veterans on farms following World War I, see Bill G. Reid, "Franklin K. Lane's Idea for Veterans' Colonization, 1918–1921," *Pacific Historical Review* 33 (November 1964): 447–461; and Bill G. Reid, "Agrarian Opposition to Franklin K. Lane's Proposal for Soldier Settlement, 1918–1921," *Agricultural History* 41 (Spring 1967): 167–179.

4. Andrew Weiss, "Special Report on 80 Soldier Entries of March 5, 1920, Fort

Laramie Division, North Platte Project," unpublished typescript, 1924, 151–152, Box 846, General Administrative and Project Records, 1919–1945, Record Group [RG] 115, Records of the Bureau of Reclamation, National Archives—Rocky Mountain Region, [NA], Denver.

5. U.S. Congress, House, Committee on Irrigation and Reclamation, *Settlement of Returning Veterans*, 92. Persistence rates on reclamation homesteads were comparable to the rates that Richard Bremer found in Nebraska from 1935 to 1945. Only 54 percent of the Nebraska farmers in Bremer's sample for 1935 remained on the same farms five years later, and by 1945 the figure had dropped to 35.9 percent. See Richard G. Bremer, *Agricultural Change in an Urban Age: The Loup Country of Nebraska, 1910–1970*, University of Nebraska Studies New Series no. 51 (Lincoln: University of Nebraska, 1976), 129.

6. Weiss, "Special Report," 3, 34, 68–89.

7. Andrew Weiss to Elwood Mead, 28 July 1924, Folder: "500 North Platte Colonization and Settlement—General, thru 1929," Box 846, RG 115, NA.

8. U.S. Congress, House, Committee on Irrigation and Reclamation, *Settlement of Returning Veterans*, 93; U.S. Congress, Senate, *Federal Reclamation by Irrigation*, 98, 202; Robert White, *Frannie-Deaver Proposition: A Chronicle of Optimism—and Alkali* (Cheyenne, WY: Frontier Printing, 1990), 159, 184–185.

9. Weiss, "Special Report," 33–34, 126–127; Vaughn Mechau, "Veteran, Wyoming," *Reclamation Era* 33, May 1947, 119.

10. Weiss, "Special Report," 62–63, 70–73, 126–127.

11. Ibid., 99–100, 161–162.

12. U.S. Congress, House, Committee on Irrigation and Reclamation, *Settlement of Returning Veterans*, 93.

13. U.S. Congress, Senate, *Federal Reclamation by Irrigation*, 47, 97–102, 123.

14. Pelz, *Federal Reclamation Laws*, 1: 316–327. For more information on the Fact Finders, see Brian Q. Cannon, "'We Are Now Entering a New Era': Federal Reclamation and the Fact Finding Commission of 1923–1924," *Pacific Historical Review* 66 (May 1997): 185–211.

15. John B. Holt, *An Analysis of Methods and Criteria Used in Selecting Families for Colonization Projects*, Social Science Research report no. 1 (Washington, DC: Farm Security Administration and Bureau of Agricultural Economics, 1937), 24, 33–36; John C. Page to Carl Hayden, 23 December 1937, Folder: "503 General Correspondence re: Selection of Settlers," 1936–1937, Box 835, General Correspondence File, 1930–45, RG 115, NA; Department of the Interior, "Information for Homeseekers," handbill dated 30 June 1927, Folder: "510.2 North Platte Publicity Methods thru 1929," Box 847, General Administrative and Project Records, 1919–1945, RG 115, NA.

16. U.S. Congress, House, Committee on Irrigation and Reclamation, Committee on Interior and Insular Affairs, *Preference to Ex-Servicemen for Entry to Public Lands on Reclamation Projects*, 78th Cong., 2d sess., 25 May 1944, 5.

17. John R. Murdock, "Veterans—Here's Your Farm," *Reclamation Era* 32, May 1946, 95–96; U.S. Congress, *Settlement of Returning Veterans*, 4.

18. U.S. Congress, House, 78th Cong., 2d sess., *CR* 90, pt. 4 (15 May 1944): 4509; U.S. Congress, *Preference to Ex-Servicemen*, 3.

19. U.S. Congress, *Preference to Ex-Servicemen*, 3.

20. Ibid., 21; U.S. Congress, House, 78th Cong., 2d sess. *CR* 90, pt. 4 (18 May 1944): 4667.

21. U.S. Congress, *Preference to Ex-Servicemen*, 1.

22. John M. Blum, *V Was for Victory: Politics and American Culture during World War II* (New York: Harcourt Brace Jovanovich, 1976), 59–60; Mark R. Grandstaff, "Visions of New Men and Prescriptions for Modern Life: American Society Addresses the World War II Veteran's Problem," paper presented at the meetings of the American Historical Association, Pacific Coast Branch, 6 August 2000, 4; U.S. Congress, *Preference to Ex-Servicemen*, 1, 2, 10–12, 14, 20–21. Until late in 1944, Congress's projections of the number of veterans who desired to farm following the war were based almost entirely upon estimates of the number of farm boys in the service. In 1944, however, the army's Information and Education Division attempted to determine the number of soldiers who planned on farming after the war. A cross-section of white enlisted men in the United States and smaller samples of black enlisted men, white officers, and troops in two overseas theaters were questioned regarding their postwar plans. On the basis of this survey, the Army estimated in a report printed in December of 1944 that 9–13 percent of white enlistees, 8–9 percent of African American soldiers, and 2 percent of army officers expected to farm following the war. All told, this meant that close to 800,000 officers and enlisted men in the army planned to farm. Of that group, 125,000 did not have a particular farm in mind and another 150,000 had a farm that they expected to buy or rent, but no assurance that the farm would actually be available to them. In light of the consolidation and mechanization of farms taking place, the planners estimated that many of these men would face "much stiffer" competition in finding a good farm than would have been the case prior to the war. Information and Education Division, *Soldiers' Plans for Farming after They Leave the Army*, Report B–131, 20 December 1944, Box 993, Entry 93, RG 330, Records of the Office of the Secretary of Defense, National Archives, College Park, MD. The study corroborated more conservative assertions that hundreds of thousands of veterans hoped to farm but because it focused only on the army it also provided some support for more extravagant estimates that as many as 1,000,000 soldiers hoped to

become established on a farm. The survey's findings, which the *Washington Post* reported in the spring of 1945, were alluded to briefly in congressional hearings that spring as proof that a substantial demand for farms existed. See U.S. Congress, *Settlement of Returning Veterans*, 337.

23. U.S. Congress, House, Special Committee on Post-war Economic Policy and Planning, *Post-War Agricultural Policy*, vol. 5 of *Post-War Economic Policy and Planning*, 79th Cong., 1st sess., 1301–1303.

24. U.S. Congress, *Settlement of Returning Veterans*, 3, 21, 22, 25–26.

25. *An Act to Allow Credit in Connection with Certain Homestead Entries for Military or Naval Service Rendered during World War II*, *United States Statutes at Large* 58, 747 (1944); U.S. Congress, House, Committee on Public Lands, *Allowing Credit in Connection with Certain Homestead Entries for Military or Naval Service Rendered during World War II*, 78th Cong., 2d sess., 1944, House Report 1646; U.S. Congress, Senate, Senate Committee on Public Lands and Surveys, *Allowing Credit in Connection with Certain Homestead Entries for Military or Naval Service Rendered during World War II*, 78th Cong., 2d sess., 1944, Senate Report 1084; Congress, House, 78th Cong., 2d sess., *CR* 90, pt. 5 (15 June and 19 June 1944), 6011, 6200; Congress, Senate, 78th Cong., 2d sess., *CR* 90, pt. 5 (14 June and 20 June 1944), 5933, 6247; Congress, Senate, 78th Cong., 2d sess., *CR* 90, pt. 6 (8 September, 13 September, 19 September 1944), 7608, 7721, 7907; Congress, House, 78th Cong., 2d sess., *CR* 90, pt. 6 (14 November 1944), 8162.

26. U.S. Congress, *Post-War Agricultural Policy*, 1233, 1249, 1302, 1413. The American capacity to consume could not keep pace with the growth of agricultural surpluses during the 1950s. Thus in 1954 Congress passed the Agricultural Trade Development and Assistance Act, which permitted the federal government to purchase surpluses and use them for foreign aid. Hurt, 323–324.

27. U.S. Congress, *Preference to Ex-Servicemen*, 12; U.S. Congress, Senate, Subcommittee on Irrigation and Reclamation, Committee on Interior and Insular Affairs, *Riverton Reclamation Project*, 88th Cong., 1st sess., 29–30 October 1963, 60.

28. U.S. Congress, *Preference to Ex-Servicemen*, 21; U.S. Congress, *Settlement of Returning Veterans*, 1–4, 336.

29. U.S. Congress, *Settlement of Returning Veterans*, 5, 9, 91, 209.

30. Ibid., 94, 98, 99, 100, 105, 118.

31. Ibid., 200, 203, 336.

32. Ibid., 237, 244.

33. Ibid., 24, 197.

34. Ibid., 207, 209.

35. Ibid., 213, 225.

36. Ibid., 232, 320.

37. U.S. Congress, House, *Facilitating Settlement of Returning Veterans on Farms in Projects Constructed, Operated, and Maintained by the Bureau of Reclamation*, 79th Cong., 1st sess., 1945, House Report 688, Serial 10933: 1–6.

38. Ibid., 4, 6; U.S. Congress, House, 79th Cong., 1st sess., *CR* 91, pt. 7 (19 September 1945): 8775, 8778–8779.

39. Congress, House, 79th Cong., 1st sess., *CR* 91, pt. 7 (19 September 1945): 8771, 8772, 8774.

40. Ibid., 8774–8775, 8779–8780, 8788.

41. Ibid., 8778, 8785.

42. Ibid., 8776, 8780, 8783.

43. Ibid., 8789, 8802.

CHAPTER 2. "AH, FOR THE LIFE OF A FARMER": THE CHIMERA OF FREE LAND

1. U.S. Congress, House, Committee on Irrigation and Reclamation, *Settlement of Returning Veterans on Farms in Reclamation Projects*, 79th Cong., 1st sess., 12 April 1945, 7–8, 22, 24, 118.

2. Bureau of Reclamation, *Summary Report of the Commissioner of the Bureau of Reclamation, 1966, and Statistical Appendix* (Washington, DC: Department of the Interior, 1966), 17.

3. Bureau of Reclamation, "Post-war Land Openings," mimeograph [1959], Historian's Office, Bureau of Reclamation, Denver; Public Notices 31–37 included in Annual Project Histories for Columbia Basin Project, 1960–1967, Boxes 81–82, Accession 8NN-115–88–053, Boxes 16, 31, Accession 8NN-115–92–130, RG 115, National Archives [NA], Lakewood, CO; Annual Project History, Columbia Basin Project, 1967, 35: 66, Box 224, Accession 8NN-115–92–130, RG 115, NA; Paul C. Pitzer, *Grand Coulee: Harnessing a Dream* (Pullman: Washington State University, 1994), 273, 280. Under the Water Conservation and Utilization Act of 1939, also known as the Wheeler-Case Act, Congress authorized the Bureau of Reclamation to develop small irrigation projects, known as Wheeler-Case projects, in areas that had formerly been dry-farmed, but responsibility for the development and settlement of farms on these projects was vested in the Farm Security Administration and the Soil Conservation Service. Individuals who had formerly owned or rented land on these projects received preferential treatment in applying to purchase these farms from the Soil Conservation Service. Any farms remaining were offered to veterans. The principal Wheeler-Case projects on which settlement occurred following the war were Buffalo Rapids in Montana, Buford Trenton in North Dakota, Mirage Flats in Nebraska, Angostura in South Dakota, and

Eden Valley in Wyoming. See John T. Phelan and Donald L. Basinger, *Engineering in the Soil Conservation Service* (Washington, DC: Soil Conservation Service, 1993), 15–16; "Modern Pioneers," *Reclamation Era* 40, November 1954, 83–84.

4. Interview with John Hansen, 30 June 1998, Caldwell, ID.

5. Bureau of Reclamation, "Narrative Report: Yuma Project Land Opening under Public Notice No. 59" (Boulder City, NV: Bureau of Reclamation, 1950), 2–3, copy in Regional Office Library, Bureau of Reclamation, Boulder City, NV; Robert L. Bee, "Quechan," in *Handbook of North American Indians*, ed. William C. Sturtevant, vol. 10, *Southwest*, ed. Alfonso Ortiz (Washington, DC: Smithsonian Institution, 1983), 94–95; Jay J. Wagoner, *Early Arizona: Prehistory to Civil War* (Tucson: University of Arizona Press, 1975), 232–235; Eric A. Stene, *Yuma Project and Yuma Auxiliary Project*, 3rd draft (Denver: Bureau of Reclamation History Program, 1996), http://www.usbr.gov/dataweb/html/yuma1.html, accessed 29 September 2003.

6. William J. Williams, "Homesteading Time in Yuma," *Reclamation Era* 34, May 1948, 89; Bureau of Reclamation, Land Use and Settlement Division of Operation and Maintenance, "Homesteading on Yuma Mesa—1949" (Yuma, AZ: Bureau of Reclamation, 1950), 1–2, copy in Regional Office Library, Bureau of Reclamation, Boulder City, NV; Bureau of Reclamation, Division of Operation and Maintenance, "Public Land Development and Settlement, Yuma Mesa Division, Gila Project" (Yuma, AZ: Bureau of Reclamation, 1949), 3–8, copy in Regional Office Library, Bureau of Reclamation, Boulder City, NV. Debra Trigg Conrad, *Yuma Mesa Homesteaders, 1948 and 1952: "It's There, All You Have to Do Is Irrigate"* (Yuma, AZ: Chameleon Computer Services, 2006), 51–58, reproduces the report entitled "Homesteading on Yuma Mesa, 1949."

7. Henry O. Harwell and Marsha C. S. Kelly, "Maricopa," in *Handbook of North American Indians*, ed. Sturtevant, vol. 10, *Southwest*, 71–75; "General Description and Plan, Gila Project, Arizona," http://www.usbr.gov/dataweb/html/gila.html, accessed 6 May 2003; "Sixteen Farm Units on Wellton-Mohawk Division, Gila Project, to be Sold by Reclamation," *Reclamation Era* 43, November 1957, 107.

8. Lowell John Bean, "Cahuilla," in *Handbook of North American Indians*, ed. Sturtevant, vol. 8, *California*, ed. Robert F. Heizer (Washington, DC: Smithsonian Institution, 1978), 583–586; "Coachella's Underground Lifeline," *Reclamation Era* 35, August 1949, 183–184; Annual Project History: All-American Canal—Coachella Division, vol. 9 (1954), 14–16, copy in Regional Office Library, Bureau of Reclamation, Boulder City, NV. The Coachella Valley's warm winter climate enabled farmers to grow lucrative crops including grapes, oranges, and lemons in seasons when most of the nation's farms were unproductive.

9. Theodore Stern, "Klamath and Modoc," in *Handbook of North American Indians*,

ed. Sturtevant, vol. 12, *Plateau*, ed. Deward E. Walker Jr. (Washington, DC: Smithsonian Institution, 1998), 447–460; Betty Lou Byrne-Shirley, "The Tule Lake–Lower Klamath Region: A Historical Overview," *Journal of the Modoc County Historical Society* 18 (1996): 6–11; Betty Lou Byrne-Shirley, "The Reclamation of Tule Lake," ibid., 49–61.

10. Helen H. Schuster, "Yakima and Neighboring Groups," in *Handbook of North American Indians*, ed. Sturtevant, vol. 12, *Plateau*, 327–346; *Yakima Project History*, 3rd draft (Denver: Bureau of Reclamation History Program, 1993), http://www.usbr.gov/dataweb/projects/washington/yakima/history.html, accessed 30 September 2003.

11. Jay Miller, "Middle Columbia River Salishans," in Sturtevant, ed., *Handbook of North American Indians*, vol. 12, *Plateau*, 253–254, 266–267; Columbia Basin Project Development, electronic document, http://www.usbr.gov/dataweb/html.columbia.html, accessed 30 September 2003, Pitzer, *Grand Coulee*, 21–80, 267–289; Annual Project History, Columbia Basin Project, 1967, 35:66, Box 224, Accession 8NN-115–92–130, RG 115, NA.

12. Robert F. Murphy and Yolanda Murphy, "Northern Shoshone and Bannock," in *Handbook of North American Indians*, ed. Sturtevant, vol. 11, *Great Basin*, ed. Warren L. D'Azevedo (Washington, DC: Smithsonian Institution, 1986), 286–287, 302–303; "Dream of Half Century Fullfilled [*sic*] in Black Canyon," *Caldwell News-Tribune*, 23 March 1950, 9; Annual Project History: Boise Project, 1946, 89, copy in historical files, Snake River Area Office—West, Bureau of Reclamation, Boise; *Boise Project History, 1920–1945*, Idaho State Historical Society Reference Series, no. 193, 1–5, http://www.idahohistory.net/Reference%20Series/0193.pdf, accessed 30 September 2003.

13. "Minidoka Project North Side Pumping Division Definite Plan Report," typescript (Boise, 1955), 8–11, copy in historical files, Bureau of Reclamation, Burley, ID [BOR-Burley]; Annual Project History: Minidoka Project, 1948, 45, Box 87, Accession 8NN-115–90–011, RG 115, NA; Annual Project History: Minidoka Project, 1949, 31, ibid.; Eric A. Stene, *The Minidoka Project*, 5th draft (Denver: Bureau of Reclamation History Program, 1997), http://www.usbr.gov/dataweb/projects/idaho/minidoka/history.html, accessed 30 September 2003.

14. Stene, *Minidoka Project*; "Opening New Frontiers," *Reclamation Era* 39, October 1953, 154–156; "North Side Pumping Division, Minidoka Project, Idaho, Report on Payment Capacity," typescript (1960), 2–8, copy in historical files, BOR-Burley; Acreage Summary: North Side Pumping Division Minidoka Project, [1959?], in Folder: "Minidoka North Side Pumping Division (Supp. Cert.) 53–59," BOR-Burley.

15. Fred W. Voget, "Crow," in *Handbook of North American Indians*, ed. Sturtevant, vol. 13, *Plains*, ed. Raymond J. DeMallie (Washington, DC: Smithsonian Institution, 2001), 695–698; Demitri B. Shimkin, "Eastern Shoshone," in *Handbook of North Amer-*

ican Indians, ed. Sturtevant, vol. 11, *Great Basin*, 308–309; Henry E. Stamm IV, *People of the Wind River: The Eastern Shoshones, 1825–1900* (Norman: University of Oklahoma Press, 1999), 34, 50, 53, 242–243; Robert Autobee, *Pick-Sloan Missouri River Basin Program: The Riverton Unit*, 3rd draft (1996), http://www.usbr.gov/dataweb/html/rvrton2.html, accessed 30 April 2003; U.S. Congress, House, Committee on Interior and Insular Affairs, *Authorizing the Secretary of the Interior to Acquire Lands . . . in the Third Division*, 88th Cong., 1st sess., 1963, House Report 1010, 3, 7.

16. Voget, "Crow," in *Handbook of North American Indians*, ed. Sturtevant, vol. 13, *Plains*, 695–698; H. H. Johnson, "Forty-Three Years on the Shoshone Project," *Reclamation Era* 33, June 1947, 124–127; Annual Project History: Shoshone Project, 1949, 66–67, historical files, Shoshone Irrigation District Office, Powell, WY.

17. U.S. War Department, *Final Report, Japanese Evacuation from the West Coast, 1942* (Washington, DC: GPO, 1943), 248–249; Audrie Girdner and Anne Loftis, *The Great Betrayal: The Evacuation of the Japanese-Americans during World War II* (London: MacMillan, 1969), 216; Roger Daniels, *Concentration Camps, North America: Japanese in the United States and Canada during World War II* (Malabar, FL: Robert E. Krieger, 1981), 93, 96. Agreements for improving Reclamation properties were part of the land transfers between the Bureau of Reclamation and the War Relocation Authority. For instance, in their initial memorandum of understanding regarding land transfers on the Shoshone Project, the WRA agreed to undertake canal repair work using the labor of internment camp residents. Douglas M. Tedd, "Cover Report, Engineering Section, Operations Division, Heart Mountain Relocation Center," typescript [1945], 4, Reel 63, Records of the War Relocation Authority [WRA], microfilm copy in Harold B. Lee Library, Brigham Young University, Provo, UT.

18. Tedd, "Cover Report," 4–5; Glen T. Hartman, "Final Report, Operations Division, Agricultural Section [1945]," 3–6, Reel 63, WRA; "A Trickle, Then a Stream—Water Courses through Canal," *Heart Mountain Sentinel*, 29 May 1943, 1.

19. Hartman, "Final Report"; Heart Mountain Weekly Report, 1–8 April 1943, Reel 62, WRA; "Water Reaches Fields, Outlook Good Despite Disruption by Storm," *Heart Mountain Sentinel*, 5 June 1943, 1; "Farm Activities Transform Barren Land," *Heart Mountain Sentinel*, 12 August 1944, 13–14. Initially administrators had envisioned preparing 6,000 to 8,000 acres at Heart Mountain for intensive cultivation, with the objective of marketing agricultural surpluses or earmarking them for lend-lease. But the population of camps began to fall in 1943 as some internees departed for jobs in the American interior. By the end of 1944, only 1,663 acres had been farmed. "Farm Program," Heart Mountain Glimpses, 25 February 1943, Miscellaneous Reports, Reel 57, WRA; Hartman, "Final Report," 3, 14.

20. Louis E. Rice and Rhuel D. Beebout, "Final Agricultural Section Report," typescript (1946), 6–13, 14–17, 33, Reel 89, WRA; "Final Engineering Report," typescript (1946), 33–34, Reel 89, WRA.

21. "Yearly Summary Report—Agriculture, 1943," 1, Operations Division: Agriculture, Reel 87, WRA; Minidoka Progress Report no. 11, 1942, Reel 88, WRA; Rice and Beebout, "Final Agricultural Section Report," 29–30; "Project Agriculture Department Proves Desert Sageland Can Be Made Productive," *Minidoka Irrigator*, 18 December 1943, 1.

22. "Raise 2000 Acres of Vegetables Here," *Tulean Dispatch*, 24 June 1942, 4; William T. Jarrett, "General Outline and History of the Agricultural Program at Tule Lake Center," n.d. ca. 1946, typescript, 2–4, Operations Division, Agriculture, Reel 114, WRA; "2500 Acres of Vegetables Planted," *Tulean Dispatch*, 17 August 1942, 2; "Farm Ditch Digging Project Is Launched," *Tulean Dispatch*, 30 March 1943, 1.

23. "Farmer's Life," *Tulean Dispatch*, 28 July 1942, 2; Memorandum no. 25 addressed to Edwin Bates, 26 August 1942, Project Reports, 1942, Reel 105, WRA; Girdner and Loftis, *Great Betrayal*, 231.

24. William T. Jarrett, "Personal Narrative," typescript (February 1946), Operations Division: Agriculture, Reel 114, WRA; Hartman, "Final Report," 3, 15; Heart Mountain Agriculture Quarterly Report, February 1943, 61, Reel 58, WRA; Jarrett, "General Outline and History," 5.

25. "Twenty-nine Farm Workers Injured in Second Accident, Five Are Critical," *Tulean Dispatch*, 16 October 1943, 1; Dorothy Swaine Thomas and Richard S. Nishimoto, *The Spoilage: Japanese American Evacuation and Resettlement* (Berkeley and Los Angeles: University of California Press, 1946), 113–124.

26. Thomas and Nishimoto, *Spoilage*, 125–130, 185; Allan Markley, "Development of the Farm Program," Special Report no. 13, Tule Lake Center, 15 March 1944, 1.

27. Thomas and Nishimoto, *Spoilage*, 142–147, 177, 178; Jarrett, "General Outline and History," 5.

28. "Veterans: Tule Lakers Now," *Newsweek* 28, 30 December 1946, 20; Girdner and Loftis, 224.

29. "Farm Land Returned to Bureau," *Minidoka Irrigator*, 3 February 1945, 1. For a representative public notice see, Bureau of Reclamation, "Report to the Commissioner on Land Opening of Part I, Heart Mountain Division, Shoshone Project," typescript (27 October 1947), Exhibits IV-1 and IV-2, historical files, Shoshone Irrigation District, Powell, WY.

30. Richard K. Pelz, ed., *Federal Reclamation Laws and Related Laws Annotated*, 4 vols. (Washington, DC: GPO, 1972), 1: 317; Minutes of public meeting held 30 March

1948, at Klamath Falls, 2, Folder 730, historical files, Office of the Bureau of Reclamation, Klamath Falls, OR; Bureau of Reclamation, "Report to the Commissioner on Land Opening of Part I, Heart Mountain Division," 7.

31. Robert V. Hine, *The American West: An Interpretive History* (Boston: Little, Brown and Company, 1973), 160; Stan Turner, *The Years of Harvest: A History of the Tule Lake Basin* (Eugene, OR: 49th Avenue Press, 1987), 300–301; Ten Broeck Williamson, "History of the 1946 Land Opening on the Tule Lake Division of the Klamath Project," typescript (August 1947), 9, Folder 732; F. D. Rockbice to Harold L. Ickes, 15 January 1946, Folder 730, historical files, Bureau of Reclamation, Klamath Falls, OR.

32. Williamson, "History of the 1946 Land Opening," vi–vii; Bureau of Reclamation, "Report to the Commissioner on Land Opening of Part I, Heart Mountain Division," 9.

33. Minutes of public meeting held 30 March 1948, at Klamath Falls, OR, 6, 10.

34. Bureau of Reclamation, "Narrative Report: Yuma Project Land Opening under Public Notice No. 59," 6; Williamson, "History of the 1946 Land Opening," 35–36.

35. Interview with Ruby Van Zant, 2 July 1998, Caldwell, ID; interview with Carlos "Jake" Colvin, 24 May 1997, Bard, CA; interview with Virginia Noel Reynolds by Amy Reynolds Billings, 31 July 1998, Cody, WY; interview with Violet Hurlburt, 12 August 1997, Tulelake, CA.

36. Interview with Phyllis Gies, 24 July 1998, Riverton, WY; Winifred Sawaya Wasden, ed., *Modern Pioneers* (Powell, WY: Northwest College Production Printing, 1998), 42; interview with Verna Poore, 30 October 1997, Indio, CA.

37. Wasden, *Modern Pioneers*, 24, 48.

38. Bureau of Reclamation, "Post-war Land Openings"; Public Notices 31–37 included in Annual Project Histories for Columbia Basin Project, 1960–1967, Boxes 81–82, Accession 8NN-115–88–053, Boxes 16, 31, Accession 8NN-115–92–130, RG 115, NA; Annual Project History, Columbia Basin Project, 1967, 35:66, Box 224, Accession 8NN-115–92–130, RG 115, NA.

39. Bureau of Reclamation, "Report to the Commissioner on Land Opening of Part I, Heart Mountain Division," 15; Williamson, "History of the 1946 Land Opening," 106; Bureau of Reclamation, "Narrative Report: Yuma Project Land Opening," 28.

40. Williamson, "History of the 1946 Land Opening," 62.

41. Interview with John K. ("Jack") Black, 20 July 1998, Lovell, WY.

42. Williamson, "History of the 1946 Land Opening," 66, 73.

43. Ibid., 103–105; Max Stern to Ray R. Best, 26 August 1946, Folder 730, historical files, Bureau of Reclamation, Klamath Falls, OR; "Farm Lottery," *Life* 22, 20 January 1947, 73–74.

44. Williamson, "History of the 1946 Land Opening," 115–116; Turner, *Years of Harvest*, 306.

45. Bureau of Reclamation, "Narrative Report: Yuma Project Land Opening," 42; "Land Opening," *Riverton Review*, 6 October 1949; "Land Opening Today Is Beginning of Vast Development Program," *Riverton Review*, 4 December 1947; Turner, *Years of Harvest*, 303; "Homesteads Awarded to Lucky Veterans," *Caldwell News-Tribune*, 25 March 1950.

46. *Twin Falls Times-News*, 5 August 1953; *Minidoka County News*, 6 August 1953.

47. Williams, "Homesteading Time in Yuma," 89; "Mecca Man Wins 1st Choice of Valley Homestead Lands," *Indio News*, 28 September 1954; Williamson, "History of the 1946 Land Opening," 303; "Homesteaders of '54," *Time Magazine* 64, 19 July 1954, 19; interview with Velma and Fred Robison, 12 August 1997, Tulelake, CA; "Veterans: Tule Lakers Now," 20; Norman Lobsenz and Amelia Lobsenz, "California Pioneers Model 1949," *Coronet* 25, April 1949, 79, 81; Bureau of Reclamation, "Narrative Report: Yuma Project Land Opening," 43.

48. Pitzer, *Grand Coulee*, 283–285.

49. Turner, *Years of Harvest*, 305–306; Annual Project History: Boise Project, 1949, typescript, 108, copy in historical files, Snake River Area Office—West, Bureau of Reclamation, Boise; interview with Eleanor Jane Bolesta, 11 August 1997, Tulelake, CA; Bureau of Reclamation to Lucy Evers, 4 April 1950, Folder 732, historical files, Snake River Area Office—West, Bureau of Reclamation, Boise. HR 5118, introduced abortively in the 79th Congress, would have eliminated the requirement that a person needed to be the head of a household in order to homestead. See Michael W. Strauss to George P. Miller, 27 March 1947, Folder 730: "Klamath Economic Reports—Applicants for Homestead Drawing 3/15/48 and 2/23/49," historical files, Bureau of Reclamation, Klamath Falls, OR.

50. Black interview.

51. Interview with Bill and Myrtle Gunlock, 22 May 1997, Yuma, AZ; Robison interview; interview with Eliot Waits, 23 May 1997, Yuma, AZ; interview with Wilbur Andrew, 1 July 1998, Caldwell, ID.

52. Turner, *Years of Harvest*, 307.

CHAPTER 3. PROVING UP AND PROVING THEMSELVES

1. Theodore Earl Aston, *Our Beautiful People* (Peachtree City, GA: Gibby Publishing, 1992), 130, 133; Matthew Basso, Laura McCall, and Dee Garceau, eds., *Across the Great Divide: Cultures of Manhood in the American West* (New York: Routledge, 2001), 5; C' de-Vere Fairchild, "I Finally Struck It Rich," *Reclamation Era* 33, January 1947, 3.

2. "Homesteaders of '54," *Time Magazine* 64, 19 July 1954, 19; interview with Van and Isabell "Bell" Sorensen, 14 September 2001, Mapleton, UT; interview with Bill Nolan, 17 August 1996, Quincy, WA.

3. *Riverton Review*, 12 February 1948.

4. Karl Jacoby, "We Are All New Western Historians Now," *Reviews in American History* 29, 4 (2004): 619; Basso, McCall, and Garceau, *Across the Great Divide*, 5; *Grand Coulee Dam: The Eighth Wonder of the World* (Coulee Dam, WA: Souvenirs, 1946), [27].

5. Mary Neth, *Preserving the Family Farm: Women, Community and the Foundations of Agribusiness, 1900–1940* (Baltimore: Johns Hopkins University Press, 1995), 217–218; Gail Bederman, *Manliness and Civilization: A Cultural History of Gender and Race in the United States, 1880–1917* (Chicago: University of Chicago Press, 1995), 19; Richard White, *The Organic Machine* (New York: Hill and Wang, 1995), 61; *Denver Post*, 30 November 1947.

6. White, *Organic Machine*, 61; Annette Kolodny, *The Lay of the Land: Metaphor as Experience and History in American Life and Letters* (Chapel Hill: University of North Carolina Press, 1975), 26–70, 136–137, 146–150, 153–154; Mark Fiege, *Irrigated Eden: The Making of an Agricultural Landscape in the American West* (Seattle: University of Washington Press, 1999), 19, 208. As Laura McCall has written, "The West's monumental scale and rugged beauty obscure the delicate ecosystems that characterize much of the region. Eco-feminists and environmental historians have suggested that the male desire to conquer and destroy has resulted in phenomenal environmental catastrophes." Basso, McCall, and Garceau, *Across the Great Divide*, 19.

7. Eleanor Bolesta, "A Woman Wins," *Journal of the Modoc County Historical Society* 18 (1996): 89–90.

8. Bureau of Reclamation, "Gila Project Annual Project History 1955," typescript, 179–185, Bureau of Reclamation, Yuma, AZ [BOR-Yuma]; Regional Director to Commissioner, 7 December 1955, Folder 730.01: "Land and Water Rights," Bureau of Reclamation, Klamath Falls, OR [BOR-Klamath]; Robert De Roos, "Sodbusting Pays Off," *Colliers* 133, 22 January 1954, 98; "Three June Deadlines for Reclamation Farm Applications," *Reclamation Era* 36, June 1950, 122; M. L. Tillery to Richard H. Seeley, 23 April 1959, Folder 231.5: "Finance—Project Cost Repayment North Side Pumping Division Settlers," historical files, Bureau of Reclamation, Burley, ID; interview with Bill and Joan Casper, 24 August 1996, Mesa, WA; Sorensen interview. Farmers could also meet the government's cultivation requirements for their homestead by growing for two years "a substantial stand of alfalfa, clover or other perennial grass" or by having fruit trees or vines on the land "of which 75 percent shall be in a thrifty condition." Phil Dickinson to Commissioner, 18 April 1947, Folder 30: "Klamath Econom-

ics Reports: Applicants for Homestead Drawing, 3/15/48 and 2/23/49," BOR-Klamath.

9. Richard L. Boke to R. W. Hollenberg, 8 April 1949; Project Manager to Regional Director, 13 November 1952, Folder 730: "Lands Settlement and Land Entries, 8/27/48–02/9/58," BOR-Klamath.

10. Interview with Asil and Windy Dobson, 17 June 1998, Tacna, AZ; Sorensen interview; interview with Glen C. Olsen, 3 July 1998, Caldwell, ID; interview with Claude Briddle, 24 July 1998, Riverton, WY; Phil Bare, "Homestead Commentary on the Northside Project of Rupert from 1955 to 1992" (tape recording), DeMary Memorial Library, Rupert, ID; Richard Lauterbach, "Homesteaders 1950," *Ladies' Home Journal* 67, October 1950, 219; *Powell Tribune*, 29 May 1947, 10 July 1947; Winifred Sawaya Wasden, ed., *Modern Pioneers* (Powell, WY: Northwest College Production Printing, 1998), 66–67.

11. Interview with Evaleen George, 18 July 1998, Cody, WY; *Powell Tribune* 31 July 1947; Wasden, ed., *Modern Pioneers*, 33, 60, 77; interview with Phyllis Gies, 24 July 1998, Riverton, WY; interview with Virginia Noel Reynolds by Amy Reynolds Billings, 31 July 1998, Cody, WY.

12. Gies interview; Sorensen interview.

13. Interview with Leon and Ruth Machen, 1 July 1998, Caldwell, ID; interview with Ed Hoff, 2 July 1998, Caldwell, ID; Olsen interview; interview with Carlos "Jake" Colvin, 24 May 1997, Bard, CA; Briddle interview; interview with Jack Grout, 17 June 1998, Wellton, AZ.

14. Typed draft of "Farming Guide" prepared by the Idaho Agricultural Extension Service for North Side Pumping Division of Minidoka Project (1953), 6–12, Folder: "Minidoka NS Pumping Division (Supp. Cert.) 53–59," historical files, Bureau of Reclamation, Burley, ID; "Coachella's Underground Lifeline," *Reclamation Era* 35, August 1949, 183–184; Reynolds interview; interview with Bill and Joan Ross, 18 July 1998, Cody, WY; interview with John Hansen, 30 June 1998, Caldwell, ID; Olsen interview; Bare, "Homestead Commentary."

15. *Powell Tribune*, 30 October 1947.

16. In addition to lands that had been developed and farmed by Japanese American internees at the Tule Lake, Heart Mountain, and Minidoka relocation centers, alfalfa had been planted by the Bureau of Reclamation during World War II on 5,000 acres near a military base on Yuma Mesa in order to minimize blowing sand and dust storms that might interfere with base operations. Homesteaders on these "predeveloped" lands on Yuma Mesa were billed for the Bureau's developmental work, an obligation that approximated $150 per acre.

17. Ian A. Briggs, "Gila Homesteaders Take Over," *Reclamation Era* 34, September 1948, 173–174; Acting Regional Director to Director, Branch of Operation and Maintenance, 4 November 1947, Folder 730: "Klamath Economic Reports—Applicants for Homestead Drawing 3/15/48 and 2/23/49," BOR-Klamath.

18. Interview with Ruth Otto, 18 July 1998, Powell, WY; Hoff interview; *Powell Tribune*, 17 April 1947, 7 August 1947; Sorensen interview; Orson W. Israelson, *Irrigation Principles and Practices*, 2d ed. (New York: John Wiley & Sons, 1950), 151–157, 317–333. Technically, small, relatively shallow furrows were called corrugations or rills. They were used in irrigating grain and alfalfa, where the plants grew close together. For row crops, the furrow method was used. Furrows were placed between crop rows or between every two rows and were much deeper than corrugations. "Farming Guide" for North Side Division, 8–9. Some farmers excavated field ditches to carry the water from the main supply ditch to the fields after the crops had been planted. "Riverton Project Annual Project History, 1950," typescript, 102.

19. Casper interview.

20. Ibid; interview with Jerry and Frances Johnson, 13 August 1997, Tulelake, CA.

21. Interview with Carroll Riggs, 29 September 2001, Riverton, WY; Tape recording of homesteading experiences related by Vernon and Mildred Egbert, 23 August 1991, DeMary Memorial Library, Rupert, ID; Olsen interview. In 1952 the costs for installing an irrigation system ranged from $70 to $120 per acre. "Farming Guide" for North Side Division, 7–8.

22. Egbert experiences; interview with Eldon Paulsen, 22 May 1997, Yuma, AZ; Bureau of Reclamation, "Homesteading on Yuma Mesa—1949," mimeograph, 1950, 4, Bureau of Reclamation, Boulder City, NV; Tape recording of homesteading experiences related by George Falkner, n.d., DeMary Memorial Library, Rupert, ID.

23. Wasden, ed., *Modern Pioneers*, 14; Paulsen interview; Bare, "Homestead Commentary."

24. "Farming Guide" for North Side Division, 11; Lauterbach, "Homesteaders 1950," 219; Esser interview; Egbert experiences, Olsen interview.

25. Esser interview; interview with Dale Lorensen, 2 July 1998, Caldwell, ID; interview with Mark D. Sweet, 1 July 1998, Nampa, ID; Egbert experiences; interview with Leonard and Eula Withington, 24 July 1998, Riverton, WY.

26. C. Marty Miller, "It's There: All You Have to Do Is Irrigate," in *Yuma Mesa Homesteaders, 1948–1952: "It's There, All You Have to Do Is Irrigate*, Debra Trigg Conrad (Yuma, AZ: Chameleon Computer Services, 2006), 161; Bureau of Reclamation, "Homesteading on Yuma Mesa—1949," 11; Dwight K. Parks, "Farm Family on Family Farm," *Reclamation Era* 42, August 1956, 58; Bureau of Reclamation, "North Side

Pumping Division Appendix to Report on Payment Capacity," typescript 1961, 40–45, historical files, Bureau of Reclamation, Burley, ID; Arthur Shultis et al., "Planning Your Farm in the Tule Lake Area," mimeograph, 1946, 2, File 732, BOR-Klamath.

27. Interview with Eleanor Jane Bolesta, 11 August 1997, Tulelake, CA; interview with Forrest Allen, 20 July 1998, Cody, WY; R. G. Howard to Regional Supervisor of Operation and Maintenance, 13 March 1950, Folder 730, "Lands Settlement and Land Entries, 8/27/48–2/7/58," BOR-Klamath; Otto interview; *Powell Tribune*, 25 September 1947, 6 November 1947; Briddle interview; Sweet interview.

28. North Side Pumping Division Irrigation Block 5, "Report of Field Check of Farm Units," Folder "Minidoka North Side Pumping Division (Supp. Cert.)" 53–59; Bureau of Reclamation, "Report on Payment Capacity: North Side Pumping Division," typescript, 1960, 11, Folder: "Minidoka North Side Pump (Post Cert.) 1959," historical files, Bureau of Reclamation, Burley; *Minidoka County News*, 16 September 1954; Briggs, "Gila Homesteaders Take Over," 173; Olsen interview; Ray C. King, "A Veteran's View," *Reclamation Era* 34 (July 1948):137; Bureau of Reclamation, "Public Land Development and Settlement: Yuma Mesa Division," mimeograph, 1949, 18, Bureau of Reclamation, Boulder City, NV.

29. Machen interview; interview with Pearl Mayfield, 20 May 1997, Indio, CA; Riggs interview; Ross interview; Nolan interview; *Powell Tribune*, 30 October 1947; *Riverton Ranger*, 8 September 1953; Gies interview; interview with Anthon and Norma Eppich Price, 24 August 1996, Mesa, WA. On the Yuma Mesa Project in 1949 farmers who applied 200 pounds of treble-superphosphate spent an average of $8.00 per acre. An extension agent on the Minidoka Project recommended an application of $12 worth of nitrogen per acre. Fertilizer amounts varied depending upon the crops grown. On the Minidoka project, fertilizing costs for sugar beets were seven times as high as the costs for alfalfa. Bureau of Reclamation, "Homesteading on Yuma Mesa—1949," 14; *Minidoka County News*, 16 September 1954; Bureau of Reclamation, "Report on Payment Capacity: North Side Pumping Division," 34.

30. Lorensen interview; Machen interview.

31. *Indio News*, 25 January 1955.

32. King, "A Veteran's View," 137; George interview; Olsen interview.

33. *Riverton Ranger*, 1 September 1953; Lauterbach, "Homesteaders 1950," 219; Marshall Bowen, *Utah People in the Nevada Desert: Homestead and Community on a Twentieth-Century Farmers' Frontier* (Logan: Utah State University Press, 1994), 75.

34. Paulsen interview; interview with Elliott Waits, 23 May 1997, Yuma, AZ.

35. Dobson interview.

36. Bureau of Reclamation, "Homesteading on Yuma Mesa—1949," 4; interview

with Lowell Kenyon, 13 August 1997, Tulelake, CA; Reynolds interview; *Minidoka County News*, 10 November 1955; *Seattle Times*, 30 March 1949; interview with Clarence B. Spencer, 27 July 1996, Yuma, AZ; Waits interview.

37. Sorensen interview; Bureau of Reclamation, "Riverton Project Annual History 1950," typescript, 1950, 84; Bureau of Reclamation, "Riverton Project Annual History 1951," typescript, 1951, 138.

38. Interview with Varian and Margaret Wells, 17 August 1996, Quincy, WA; interview with Bill and Myrtle Gunlock, 22 May 1997, Yuma, AZ.

39. *Indio News*, 26 April 1955; Egbert experiences; Paulsen interview; Esser interview.

40. Olsen interview; M. L. Tillery to Young Tractor Company, 4 March 1958, Folder 231.5, Finance, historical files, Bureau of Reclamation, Burley, ID.

41. Carlyle Butler, "Problems of a Present Day Homesteader," *Reclamation Era* 36, February 1950, 39; *Minidoka County News*, 26 May 1955; Kenyon interview; "Questionnaire for Area A Homesteaders Requesting Action under Public Law 258," 22 August 1954, Folder 730, "Lands Settlement and Land Entries Area A," BOR-Klamath; Bill Hosokawa, "Homesteaders, 1954," *Saturday Evening Post* 226, 2 January 1954, 36.

42. Bureau of Reclamation, "Yuma Mesa Homesteading—1949," 5; *Riverton Ranger*, 10 September 1953; Park County USDA Council, "An Introduction to Your Heart Mountain Homestead," mimeograph, [1947], 3, Exhibit IX in Bureau of Reclamation, "Report to the Commissioner on Land Opening of Part I, Heart Mountain Division, Shoshone Project," typescript, 1947, Shoshone Irrigation District, Powell, WY; Wayne L. Smith, "School Was Never Like This!" *Reclamation Era* 34, May 1948, 92–93.

43. Gunlock interview; R. G. Howard to Regional Supervisor of Operation and Maintenance, 13 March 1950; interview with David Hunt, 24 August 1996, Moses Lake, WA; Falkner interview; Spencer interview. In southern Idaho, the First Security Bank of Idaho did loan up to $4,000 to many GI's on the Hunt division of the Minidoka Project for equipment. The loans were repayable over three years at 4 percent interest. Butler, "Problems of a Present Day Homesteader," 39.

44. Olsen interview; *Minidoka County News*, 26 May 1956, 7 May 1957, 5 January 1959; Park County USDA Council, "Introduction to Your Heart Mountain Homestead," 6; Machen interview.

45. Bare experiences; Gies interview.

46. Riggs interview; *Minidoka County News*, 5 January 1959.

47. Falkner experiences; George interview; interview with Bob and Deloris Fram, 24 May 1997, Yuma, AZ.

48. Esser interview; Price interview; Hosokawa, "Homesteaders 1954," 26, 36.

49. *Riverton Ranger*, 1 September 1953, 15 September 1953; Alan R. Beals and Thomas McCorkle, *Lost Lake*, Kroeber Anthropological Society Papers no. 3 (Berkeley: University of California Department of Anthropology, 1950), 57, BOR-Klamath.

50. Nolan interview; interview with Art Over, 29 September 2001, Midvale, WY; George interview.

51. Gies interview; Beals and McCorkle, *Lost Lake*, 52; *Powell Tribune*, 31 July 1979; *Minidoka County News*, 12 February 1957.

52. Lauterbach, "Homesteaders 1950," 219; Stanford E. Clark to Joseph C. O'Mahoney, 21 January 1955, Homestead Entry Files, Fremont County Museum, Riverton; Olsen interview; Price interview.

53. Grout interview; Thomas L. Pierce to W. T. Nelson, 27 July 1957, Folder 231.5, Finance, historical files, Bureau of Reclamation, Burley, ID; Price interview; Dobson interview.

54. Beals and McCorkle, *Lost Lake*, 66.

55. Homesteader Files, Historical Section, Snake River Area Office, Bureau of Reclamation, Boise; Bureau of Reclamation, "Gila Project Annual Project History 1956," typescript, 18; *Minidoka County News*, 11 February 1954; Walter Nugent, *Into the West: The Story of Its People* (New York: Vintage Books, 1999), 71.

56. Price interview; Esser interview.

57. Sorensen interview; Bolesta interview; Briggs, "Gila Homesteaders Take Over," 174; Hosokawa, "Homesteaders 1954," 36.

CHAPTER 4. "GOLD MINE IN THE SKY": THE FARMERS' DREAMS FOR THEMSELVES AND THEIR LAND

1. U.S. Congress, Senate, Committee on Public Lands, *Exemption of Certain Projects from Land-Limitation Provisions of Federal Reclamation Laws*, 80th Cong., 1st sess., 5 May 1947, 216; Annette Kolodny, *The Lay of the Land: Metaphor as Experience and History in American Life and Letters* (Chapel Hill: University of North Carolina Press, 1975), 7.

2. Interview with Leon and Ruth M. Machen, 1 July 1998, Caldwell, ID; interview with Van and Isabell Sorensen, 14 September 2001, Mapleton, UT; interview with Robert "Butch" Woodman," 22 May 1997, Yuma, AZ.

3. Bill Hosokawa, "Homesteaders, 1954," *Saturday Evening Post* 226, 2 January 1954, 37; Bureau of Reclamation, "North Side Pumping Division Report on Payment Capacity," typescript (1960), 8, Folder: "Minidoka North Side Pumping (Post Cert.) 1959," Bureau of Reclamation, Burley, ID; Robert De Roos, "Sodbusting Pays Off," *Colliers* 133, 22 January 1954, 99; Bureau of Reclamation, "Homesteading on Yuma

Mesa, 1951," mimeograph (1952), historical files, Bureau of Reclamation, Boulder City, NV; U.S. Congress, Senate, Committee on Public Lands, *Exemption of Certain Projects*, 216.

4. Project Manager to Regional Director, 13 November 1952, Folder 730: "Lands Settlement and Land Entries 8/27/48–2/9/58," historical files, Bureau of Reclamation, Klamath Falls [BOR-Klamath]; Bureau of Reclamation, "Riverton Project Annual Project History, 1952," typescript, 87, Midvale Irrigation District Offices, Pavillion, WY.

5. Bureau of Reclamation, "Homesteading on Yuma Mesa, 1951," 3; interview with Mark D. Sweet, 1 July 1998, Caldwell, ID.

6. Interview with Roy L. and Mary Rucker, 29 October 1997, Payson, UT.

7. Richard White, *The Organic Machine: The Remaking of the Columbia River* (New York: Hill and Wang, 1995), 70; U.S. Congress, Senate, Committee on Public Lands, *Exemption of Certain Projects*, 101; "Report of Department of the Interior Hearing on the Land Limitation Provision of the Columbia Basin Project Act, 3 January 1957," Mesa, WA, typescript, 3, Box 1, Columbia Basin Commission Reports, State of Washington Archives, Olympia.

8. C' deVere Fairchild, "I Finally Struck It Rich," *Reclamation Era* 33, January 1947, 3–7; Orin Cassmore, "Gold Mine in the Sky," *Reclamation Era* 33, February 1947, 25.

9. Interview with Jerry H. Lindsey, 18 June 1998, Yuma, AZ.

10. Susan Sessions Rugh, "Pastoralism and the Rural Ideal," in *Encyclopedia of American Cultural and Intellectual History*, 3 vols., ed. Mary Kupiec Cayton and Peter W. Williams (New York: Charles Scribner's Sons, 2001), 2: 453; interview with Lyle Esser, 24 August 1996, Mesa, WA; interview with Eliot Waits, 23 May 1997, Yuma, AZ; interview with Bill Nolan, 17 August 1996, Quincy, WA.

11. Cassmore, "Gold Mine in the Sky," 28; interview with Carlos "Jake" Colvin, 24 May 1997, Bard, CA; interview with Ralph Issler, 17 June 1998, Yuma, AZ; interview with Glen C. Olsen, 3 July 1998, Caldwell, ID; interview with Dale Lorensen, 2 July 1998, Caldwell, ID.

12. Elliott West, *Growing Up with the Country: Childhood on the Far-Western Frontier* (Albuquerque: University of New Mexico Press, 1989), 247; Allan Kulikoff, "Households and Markets: Toward a New Synthesis of American Agrarian History," *William and Mary Quarterly*, 3d series, 50 (April 1993): 343–344; Catherine McNicol Stock and Robert D. Johnston, eds., *The Countryside in the Age of the Modern State: Political Histories of Rural America* (Ithaca, NY: Cornell University Press, 2001), 12. See also Allan Kulikoff, *The Agrarian Origins of American Capitalism* (Charlottesville: University of Virginia Press, 1992), especially 13–33.

13. James A. Henretta, "Families and Farms: *Mentalite* in Pre-Industrial America," *William and Mary Quarterly* 35 (January 1978): 19; West, *Growing Up with the Country*, 247; Kulikoff, "Households and Markets," 343–344. Some key works in the debate regarding the economic, familial, and communal values of farmers include Winifred Rothenberg, "The Market and Massachusetts Farmers, 1750–1855," *Journal of Economic History* 41 (1981): 283–314; Steven Hahn and Jonathan Prude, eds., *The Countryside in the Age of Capitalist Transformation: Essays in the Social History of Rural America* (Chapel Hill: University of North Carolina Press, 1985); Darrett B. Rutman, "Assessing the Little Communities of Early America," *William and Mary Quarterly*, 3d series, 43 (April 1986): 163–178; John Mack Faragher, *Sugar Creek: Life on the Illinois Prairie* (New Haven, CT: Yale University Press, 1986); Christopher Clark, *The Roots of Rural Capitalism: Western Massachusetts, 1780–1860* (Ithaca, NY: Cornell University Press, 1990); Hal S. Barron, *Mixed Harvest: The Second Great Transformation of the Rural North, 1870–1930* (Chapel Hill: University of North Carolina Press, 1997).

14. Kulikoff, "Households and Markets," 343, 347, 348, 353.

15. "Report of Department of the Interior Hearing," 3, 16.

16. Ibid., 2; U.S. Congress, Senate, Committee on Public Lands, *Exemption of Certain Projects*, 101; Paul W. Gates, *History of Public Land Law Development* (Washington, DC: GPO, 1968), 387–529; Donald J. Pisani, *Water and American Government: The Reclamation Bureau, National Water Policy, and the West, 1902–1935* (Berkeley: University of California Press, 2002), xv–xvi, 1–4, 273–277; Donald Worster, *Rivers of Empire: Water, Aridity, and the Growth of the American West* (New York: Pantheon, 1985), 167–169; Doris Ostrander Dawdy, *Congress in Its Wisdom: The Bureau of Reclamation and the Public Interest* (Boulder, CO: Westview Press, 1989), 207. The spouse of a reclamation homesteader could *purchase* and irrigate an additional 160 acres, but homesteaders generally lacked the cash to avail themselves of this option during the early years of farming.

17. U.S. Congress, Senate, Committee on Public Lands, *Exemption of Certain Projects*, 104, 126; "Report of Department of the Interior Hearing," 2; Paul C. Pitzer, *Grand Coulee: Harnessing a Dream* (Pullman: Washington State University Press, 1994), 269, 273.

18. Interview with Eleanor Jane Bolesta, 11 August 1997, Tulelake, CA; "Report of Department of the Interior Hearing," 10, 16.

19. Assistant Regional Solicitor to Klamath Project Manager, 18 December 1978, Folder 730: "Lands," historical files, BOR-Klamath; "Report of Department of the Interior Hearing," 14; Pitzer, *Grand Coulee*, 296–297; interview with Forrest Allen, 20 July 1998, Cody, WY; Bureau of Reclamation, Gila Project Annual Project History, 1951, 7, copy in Bureau of Reclamation, Boulder City, NV.

20. Dawdy, *Congress in Its Wisdom*, 177–178; interview with Wilbur Andrew, 1 July 1998, Caldwell, ID; interview with Claude B. Briddle, 24 July 1998, Riverton, WY.

21. Dawdy, *Congress in Its Wisdom*, 177–178; interview with Bill and Joan Casper, 24 August 1996, Mesa, WA.

22. *Minidoka County News*, 7 May 1957; Bureau of Reclamation, "North Side Pumping Division Report on Payment Capacity," 7; Allen interview; interview with Asil and Windy Dobson, Tacna, AZ, 17 June 1998; Theodore Earl Aston, *Our Beautiful People* (Peachtree, GA: Gibby Publishing, 1992), 151.

23. Hosokawa, "Homesteaders, 1954," 37. Payments for irrigation and drainage systems were scheduled to begin after ten years of farming, and they were repayable over periods as great as fifty years, with estimated charges varying from $75 to $88 per acre on the Yuma and Klamath Projects to $115 on the Minidoka Project and $200 on the Shoshone and Gila Projects. Bureau of Reclamation, "Farming Guide," typescript (1953), 17; Folder: "Min NS Pumping Div (Supp Cert) 53–59," historical files, Bureau of Reclamation, Burley, ID; Carlyle Butler, "Problems of a Present Day Homesteader," *Reclamation Era* 36, February 1950, 40; interview with Vernon E. McVey by John A. Leveritt, transcript in Folder 730: "Lands Settlement and Land Entries 3/5/47 thru 6/18/48," historical files, BOR-Klamath; *Yuma Daily Sun*, 19 May 1948; "Next Month More G.I. Homesteaders Will Join Heart Mountain's Pioneers," *Rocky Mountain Empire Magazine* (Sunday Supplement to *Denver Post*), 30 November 1947.

24. Interview with Ralph Wright, 1 July 1998, Caldwell, ID; Waits interview; Casper interview; interview with Carroll Riggs, 29 September 2001, Riverton, WY.

25. Interview with Eldon Paulsen, 22 May 1997, Yuma, AZ; Casper interview. On the other hand, "up times" helped to offset economic downturns. Prices could rise as rapidly as they could fall; Van Sorensen liked to remember the year when the price of barley doubled practically overnight or the season when the price of sugar beets soared so high that "the income tax got serious." Roy Rucker's neighbor in the Coachella Valley "made over a million bucks" on forty acres of bell peppers. Sorensen interview; Rucker interview.

26. *Columbia Basin Herald*, 15 March 1951; *Seattle Post Intelligencer*, 29 April 1952, 1; telephone interview with Saron K. Minden, 23 August 1996, Tacoma, WA, notes in author's possession.

27. Persistence rates on the Northside Pumping Division of the Minidoka Project were calculated using county real estate records for a cluster sample. This cluster sample includes all settlers whose patents were dated 1956 or 1957 and officially recorded in the Minidoka County Recorder's Office by 15 July 1959. Additionally, it includes patents dated 1958 for settlers with surnames beginning with the letters A–L

that were recorded through page 71 of Minidoka County Patent Book 6. Persistence rates for the Yuma project were calculated using Yuma city and county directories located in the Yuma Public Library. Persistence rates at Tule Lake through 1952 are based upon a survey conducted by the Bureau of Reclamation in 1952 and reported in "Report on Progress of Settlers on Farm Units in Reclamation Projects Opened to Settlement, 1945–1952," Folder 730: "Lands Settlement and Land Entries, 8/27/48–2/9/58," Historical Records, BOR-Klamath. Information regarding settler persistence through 1968 was calculated from a list of the settlers attached to Reunion Committee to Mr. Lawrence, 11 July 1968, Folder 730: "Klamath Settlement (Homestead Reunion)," BOR-Klamath. Persistence rates were not unusually low; they were generally somewhat better than persistence rates that Richard Bremer found in Nebraska from 1935 to 1945. Only 54 percent of the Nebraska farmers in Bremer's sample for 1935 remained on the same farms five years later, and by 1945 the figure had dropped to 35.9 percent. See Richard G. Bremer, *Agricultural Change in an Urban Age: The Loup Country of Nebraska*, 1910–1970, University of Nebraska Studies New Series no. 51 (Lincoln: University of Nebraska, 1976), 129.

28. Waits interview.

29. Interview with David Hunt, 18 August 1996, Moses Lake, WA.

30. Interview with Lowell Kenyon, 13 August 1997, Tulelake, CA; *Klamath Falls Herald and News*, 12 August 1997, 13–14.

31. Interview with Jack Grout, 17 June 1998, Wellton, AZ; Lindsey interview; interview with Clarence B. Spencer, 27 July 1996, Yuma, AZ.

32. Lorensen interview.

33. Esser interview; Wright interview.

34. Interview with Ed Hoff, 2 July 1998, Caldwell, ID; Ed Hoff, Personal History, typescript, copy in author's possession.

35. Machen interview.

36. Olsen interview.

CHAPTER 5. THE BEST YEARS OF THEIR LIVES? WOMEN ON WESTERN HOMESTEADS

1. Interview with Evaleen George, 18 July 1998, Cody, WY.

2. Sandra Schackel, "Ranch and Farm Women in the Contemporary American West," in *The Rural West since World War II*, ed. R. Douglas Hurt (Lawrence: University Press of Kansas, 1998), 99; Katherine Jellison, *Entitled to Power: Farm Women and Technology, 1913–1963* (Chapel Hill: University of North Carolina Press, 1993), 178; Murray A. Straus, "The Role of the Wife in the Settlement of the Columbia Basin Project,"

Marriage and Family Living 20 (February 1958): 59–64; Susan Armitage, "Through Women's Eyes: A New View of the West," in *The Women's West*, ed. Susan Armitage and Elizabeth Jameson (Norman: University of Oklahoma Press, 1987), 9–17.

3. Richard L. Neuberger, "The GI's Look Westward," *Foreign Service* 33 (January 1946): 22; interview with Phyllis Gies, 24 July 1998, Riverton, WY; Straus, "Role of the Wife," 62–64.

4. Joan Jensen, *With These Hands: Women Working on the Land* (Old Westbury, NY: Feminist Press, 1981), xxiii; Schackel, "Ranch and Farm Women," 104; Jellison, *Entitled to Power*, 178–179, 212; interview with Anton and Norma Eppich Price, 24 August 1996, Basin City, WA. Historians have noted a disjuncture between the fact that women's work on the farm and outside the family increased in the 1950s, on the one hand, and "the celebration of domesticity by public figures and popular culture" and the tendency of farm families "to view women's primary role as that of homemaker," on the other hand. Interpreting that disjuncture is more difficult. Some women likely embraced fieldwork or farmwork as preferable alternatives to domestic roles; others likely did so as extensions of their roles as wife and mother and believed their activities on the farm and in the home to be complementary. One survey of Iowa farm women found that just under half of farm women worked at least occasionally in the fields and that of that group, 46 percent preferred fieldwork to housework. Thus, women were fairly evenly divided in their experience with fieldwork and in their assessment of it. Katherine Jellison contends that those who worked on the farm "might sometimes publicly downplay their role as farm producers in order to conform outwardly to the era's domestic ideology" in order to "deflect criticism." But they could have also tried to harmonize their activities with socially prescribed roles because they viewed facets of the domestic ideal such as motherhood as significant and desirable roles. Susan M. Hartmann, "Women's Employment and the Domestic Ideal in the Early Cold War Years," in *Not June Cleaver: Women and Gender in Postwar America, 1945–1960*, ed. Joanne Meyerowitz (Philadelphia: Temple University Press, 1994), 84, 86, 97; Jellison, *Entitled to Power*, 167, 168, 179, 180.

5. Deborah Fink, *Agrarian Women: Wives and Mothers in Rural Nebraska, 1880–1940* (Chapel Hill: University of North Carolina Press, 1992), 186, 196; Barbara Handy-Marchello, *Women of the Northern Plains: Gender and Settlement on the Homestead Frontier, 1870–1930* (St. Paul: Minnesota Historical Society Press, 2005), 78, 166.

6. Winifred Sawaya Wasden, ed., *Modern Pioneers* (Powell, WY: Northwest College Production Printing, 1998), 188, 233–234.

7. Seena B. Kohl, "Image and Behavior: Women's Participation in North Ameri-

can Family Agricultural Enterprises," in *Women and Farming: Changing Roles, Changing Structures*, ed. Wava G. Haney and Jane B. Knowles (Boulder, CO: Westview Press, 1988), 99; George interview; interview with Roy L. and Mary Rucker, 29 October 1997, Payson, UT; "Homesteads Awarded to Lucky War Veterans," *Caldwell News-Tribune*, 25 March 1950, 1; Applicant files, Folder 732: Historical Records, Snake River Area Office—West, Bureau of Reclamation, Boise, ID; "The Klamath Basin Drought New 'Dust Bowl' Saddening," *Portland Oregonian* 14 July 2001, D07.

8. Wasden, *Modern Pioneers*, 27, 152, 230; Gies interview; Bill Hosokawa, "Homesteaders, 1954," *Saturday Evening Post* 226, 2 January 1954, 26.

9. Wasden, *Modern Pioneers*, 61, 170; interview with Pearl Mayfield, 20 May 1997, Indio, CA.

10. Rucker interview; interview with Virginia Noel Reynolds by Amy Reynolds Billings, 31 July 1998, Cody, WY; Mildred Egbert interview, 23 August 1991, tape recording, DeMary Library, Rupert, ID; Wasden, *Modern Pioneers*, 130.

11. Interview with Windy and Asil Dobson, 17 June 1998, Tacna, AZ; interview with Nelda Haney by Clinton Christensen, 13 March 1997, Nephi, UT.

12. *Minidoka County News*, 30 August 1956; *Time Magazine*, July 19, 1954; undated newspaper clipping entitled "Ex-Captain, Ex-Crewman to be Neighbors on North Side; Both from Corn State," appearing in Minidoka County Newsclipping Scrapbook for 1954, 137, DeMary Library, Rupert, Idaho.

13. Wasden, *Modern Pioneers*, 24, 48, 60, 61, 74; interview with Verna Poore, 30 October 1997, Provo, UT; Rucker interview.

14. Mayfield interview; interview with Fran Didier, Myrtle Paulsen, and Joanne Livingston, 21 May 1997, Yuma, AZ; interview with Jerry and Frances Johnson, 13 August 1997, Tulelake, CA; Poore interview; Rucker interview; Gies interview.

15. Price interview.

16. Wasden, *Modern Pioneers*, 38, 157; interview with Ruth Otto, 18 July 1998, Powell, WY. Jellison, *Entitled to Power*, 163, notes the primacy of the homemaking role for farm women generally in the 1950s.

17. Gies interview; *Salt Lake Tribune*, 11 May 1959; Wasden, *Modern Pioneers*, 29.

18. Poore interview; Wasden, *Modern Pioneers*, 38, 44, 67, 114; Didier, Paulsen, and Livingston interview; *Powell Tribune*, 28 August 1947.

19. Wasden, *Modern Pioneers*, 15, 18, 27, 33, 34, 71, 80, 114.

20. Ibid., 63; Otto interview; Mayfield interview.

21. Otto interview; Price interview; Didier, Paulsen, and Livingston interview; Hosokawa, "Homesteaders, 1954," 36; Wasden, *Modern Pioneers*, 78.

22. Wasden, *Modern Pioneers*, 129, 216.

23. Ibid., 51, 64; interview with Bill and Joan Casper, 24 August 1996, Basin City, WA; Otto interview.

24. Mayfield interview; Didier, Paulsen, and Livingston interview; Wasden, *Modern Pioneers*, 197.

25. Barbara Krizo, "The Krizos: 1946 Homesteaders," *Journal of the Modoc County Historical Society* 18 (1996): 125; Price interview; Didier, Paulsen, and Livingston interview; Poore interview.

26. Robert De Roos, "Sodbusting Pays Off," *Colliers* 133, 22 January 1954, 98; Johnson interview.

27. Didier, Paulsen, and Livingston interview; Price interview.

28. Richard Lauterbach, "Homesteaders 1950," *Ladies' Home Journal* 67, October 1950, 217–219; Wasden, *Modern Pioneers*, 198; Johnson interview; Didier, Paulsen, and Livingston interview; interview with Bill Nolan, 17 August 1996, Quincy, WA.

29. Wasden, *Modern Pioneers*, 43; Otto interview.

30. Rucker interview; Reynolds interview.

31. Fink, *Agrarian Women*, 54–55.

32. Didier, Paulsen, and Livingston interview; Wasden, *Modern Pioneers*, 45; Mayfield interview; Egbert interview; George Falkner interview, 1990, DeMary Library, Rupert, ID; Lauterbach, "Homesteaders 1950," 209, 216.

33. *Twin Falls Times-News*, 7 September 1962; Didier, Paulsen, and Livingston interview; Wasden, *Modern Pioneers*, 56; interview with Ruth Machen, 1 July 1998, Caldwell, ID.

34. Casper interview; Wasden, *Modern Pioneers*, 71.

35. Machen interview.

36. Hosokawa, "Homesteaders, 1954," 36.

37. Lauterbach, "Homesteaders 1950," 219; Otto interview; Wasden, *Modern Pioneers*, 219.

38. Wasden, *Modern Pioneers*, 77, 79; Otto interview; Casper interview; Price interview; George interview; *Twin Falls Times-News*, 7 September 1992; Straus, "Role of the Wife," 61; "Does Your Wife/Husband Help?" *Wallace's Farmer*, 20 September 1958, 60.

39. Wasden, *Modern Pioneers*, 79; Price interview; George interview; interview with Eliot Waits, 23 May 1997, Yuma, AZ; Mary Victorine, "The Victorines, 1949 Homesteaders," *Journal of the Modoc County Historical Society* 18 (1996): 135–138; Otto interview.

40. Jellison, *Entitled to Power*, 165; Wasden, *Modern Pioneers*, 61, 77; Mayfield interview; Straus, "Role of the Wife," 61.

41. Reynolds interview; Mayfield interview; Wasden, *Modern Pioneers*, 193; Straus, "Role of the Wife," 61.

42. Wasden, *Modern Pioneers*, 70; Jellison, *Entitled to Power*, 156–160.

43. Straus, "Role of the Wife"; Jellison, *Entitled to Power*, 155, 156; Fink, *Agrarian Women*, 27. For an excellent discussion of efforts by professionals to segregate women's fieldwork from women's work in the home and some farm women's insistence that the two were inseparable prior to World War II, see Mary Neth, *Preserving the Family Farm: Women, Community and the Foundations of Agribusiness, 1900–1940* (Baltimore: Johns Hopkins University Press, 1995), 214–243.

44. Wasden, *Modern Pioneers*, 17; Otto interview; *Salt Lake Tribune*, 11 May 1959.

45. Reynolds interview.

46. John Mack Faragher, "History from the Inside-Out: Writing the History of Women in Rural America," *American Quarterly* 33 (1981): 550; Wasden, *Modern Pioneers*, 45, 62, 78; interview with Ruby Van Zant, 2 July 1998, Caldwell, ID.

47. Interview with Wilbur Andrew, 1 July 1998, Caldwell, ID.

48. Fink, *Agrarian Women*, 62; Wasden, *Modern Pioneers*, 17, 199.

49. Wasden, *Modern Pioneers*, 46.

50. Gies interview; interview with Violet Hurlburt, 12 August 1997, Tulelake, CA.

51. Wasden, *Modern Pioneers*, 205; interview with Bob and Deloris Fram, 24 May 1997, Yuma, AZ.

52. Wasden, *Modern Pioneers*, 240.

53. Reynolds interview. Similarly, Barbara Handy-Marchello has found, "family concerns still motivate many women to remain on the farm and work long hours. They prefer to be home when their children are, and they believe the farm is the best place to raise a family." Thereby they "integrate" household (reproductive) labor and farm (productive) labor. Handy-Marchello, *Women of the Northern Plains*, 149, 164.

54. Wasden, *Modern Pioneers*, 243; Poore interview; Bolesta interview; George interview; Otto interview; Fram interview.

55. Johnson interview; Otto interview; Wasden, *Modern Pioneers*, 243.

56. Mayfield interview; Wasden, *Modern Pioneers*, 199, 206–207; Sarah Elbert, "Women and Farming: Changing Structures, Changing Roles," in *Women and Farming*, ed. Haney and Knowles, 262.

57. Wasden, *Modern Pioneers*, 150, 219, 244–245.

58. Ibid., 200; Elbert, "Women and Farming," 262.

59. Norman Lobsenz and Amelia Lobsenz, "California Pioneers Model 1949," *Coronet* 25, April 1949, 81; Hosokawa, "Homesteaders, 1954," 26.

60. On the distinction between productive and reproductive labor, see Joan Kelly,

"The Doubled Vision of Feminist Theory: A Postscript to the 'Women and Power' Conference," *Feminist Studies* 5 (Spring 1979): 216–227.

61. Wasden, *Modern Pioneers*, 200.

CHAPTER 6. "THE FIRM FOUNDATION OF OUR COMMUNITY": OPPORTUNITY AND ITS LIMITS ON THE BUREAU OF RECLAMATION'S RIVERTON PROJECT

1. U.S. Congress, Senate, Subcommittee on Irrigation and Reclamation, Committee on Interior and Insular Affairs, *Riverton Reclamation Project*, 88th Cong., 1st sess., 29–30 October 1963, 60; *Riverton Review*, 29 September 1949.

2. U.S. Congress, Senate, Subcommittee on Irrigation and Reclamation, Committee on Interior and Insular Affairs, *Riverton Reclamation Project*, 65–66; "Tabulation of Crop Survey of Area A Homesteaders Declared Eligible for Amended or Lieu Units," typescript, 1954, Folder 730: "Lands Settlement and Land Exchanges (Area A)," historical files, Bureau of Reclamation, Klamath Falls, OR; interview with Asil and Windy Dobson, 17 June 1998, Tacna, AZ; *Riverton Ranger*, 11 August 1953. Over a two-year period (1961–1962) the number of acres under cultivation in the Wellton Mohawk Valley fell by over 4 percent because of drainage problems. "Annual Project History: Gila Project, 1961," typescript, 14; "Annual Project History: Gila Project, 1962," typescript, 14, copies in Bureau of Reclamation, Yuma, AZ.

3. U.S. Congress, Senate, Subcommittee on Irrigation and Reclamation, Committee on Interior and Insular Affairs, *Riverton Reclamation Project*, 60.

4. *Riverton Review*, 9 October 1947; 4 December 1947; 29 September 1949; 6 October 1949; 31 August 1950; "Riverton Farm Drawing," *Reclamation Era*, October 1950, 188–189.

5. Interview with Leonard and Eula Withington, 24 July 1998, Riverton, WY; interview with Van and Isabell "Bell" Sorensen, 14 September 2001, Mapleton, UT; *Denver Rocky Mountain News*, 7 August 1953.

6. Sorensen interview.

7. *Riverton Review*, 10 January 1952, 24 July 1952; I. B. Hosig and C. R. Maierhafer, 6 February 1952, Folder "Riverton 844," Box 402, Accession 115–66-AU–447, Federal Records Center [FRC], Denver; U.S. Congress, Senate, *Permitting the Exchange and Amendment of Farm Units on Federal Irrigation Projects*, 83rd Cong., 1st sess., Senate Report no. 531, 3.

8. Bureau of Reclamation, "Annual Project History: Riverton Project, 1952," vol. 35, mimeograph, 87; Bureau of Reclamation, "Annual Project History: Riverton Project, 1953," vol. 36, mimeograph, 19–22; H. F. McPhail to Regional Director, 17 December 1953, Folder "Riverton 740," Box 402, Accession 115–66-AU–447, FRC;

Theodore Earl Aston, *Our Beautiful People* (Peachtree City, GA: Gibby Publishing, 1992), 141. Copies of Annual Project Histories for Riverton are in the headquarters of the Midvale Irrigation District, Pavillion, WY.

9. H. F. McPhail to Regional Director, 17 December 1953, Folder "Riverton 740," Box 402, Accession 115–66-AU–447, FRC; Stanford E. Clark to Bureau of Reclamation, 18 December 1947, Homestead Entry Files, Fremont County Museum, Riverton; Stanford E. Clark to Joseph C. O'Mahoney, 27 January 1955, Homestead Entry Files, Fremont County Museum, Riverton.

10. *Riverton Review*, 24 July 1952; Bureau of Reclamation, "Annual Project History: Riverton Project, 1953," vol. 36, mimeograph, 10, 75–77; Richard K. Pelz, ed., *Federal Reclamation Laws and Related Laws Annotated*, 4 vols. (Washington, DC: GPO, 1972), 2: 1118–1122.

11. Interview with Phyllis Gies, 24 July 1998, Riverton, WY; *Riverton Ranger*, 6 August 1953.

12. *Riverton Ranger*, 11 June 1953, 28 July 1953.

13. *Denver Rocky Mountain News*, 2–9 August 1953. See also U.S. Congress, Senate, Subcommittee on Irrigation and Reclamation, Committee on Interior and Insular Affairs, *Third Division Irrigation District of the Riverton Project*, 87th Cong., 1st sess., 31 October 1961, 69.

14. *Riverton Ranger*, 6 August 1953.

15. Sorensen interview.

16. Ibid.; *Riverton Ranger*, 20 August 1953, 25 August 1953, 8 September 1953.

17. Sorensen interview.

18. *Riverton Ranger*, 18 August 1953, 17 September 1953, 29 September 1953, 13 October 1953; U.S. Congress, Senate, Subcommittee on Irrigation and Reclamation, Committee on Interior and Insular Affairs, *Third Division Irrigation District*, 27–28; interview with Ethel Marlatt, 24 July 1998, Riverton, WY.

19. U.S. Congress, Senate, Subcommittee on Irrigation and Reclamation, Committee on Interior and Insular Affairs, *Riverton Reclamation Project*, 30, 74; Bureau of Reclamation, "Annual Project History: Riverton Project, 1954," vol. 37, mimeograph, 15; Bureau of Reclamation, "Annual Project History: Riverton Project, 1958," vol. 41, mimeograph, 16. The financial gains and hazards of relocating are demonstrated in the experiences of Ted Aston, who relinquished his homestead at Riverton and sold his improvements on the farm for $6,000. The Bureau of Reclamation canceled Aston's debt of $831 for land development. But he was required to repay his obligations to other creditors. After selling his livestock, machinery, and some furniture and repaying his debts, he had $3,200 with which to start anew at farming in Idaho. By con-

trast, Aston claimed, he had arrived in Riverton with farm machinery and $9,000. Theodore Aston to George V. Hansen, [June 1953], Homestead Entry Files, Fremont County Museum, Riverton; Floyd Dominy to George V. Hansen, 16 November 1965, Homestead Entry Files, Fremont County Museum, Riverton. Another couple who chose to relocate, Walter and Dorothy White, moved to a homestead in southern Arizona. In addition to the disappointments associated with farming shallow soils at Riverton, Walter had lost part of his right arm there in a combine accident. The couple traveled to Roll, Arizona, with their six children in their farm truck, pulling a house trailer. They camped out in their trailer for several months until they completed a modest two-bedroom home, and they spent three months clearing their new land. Water for their home was drawn from a nearby canal. They also struggled to learn new irrigation methods used in the Southwest. After having been away from Wyoming for over a year, Walter told a reporter he still missed Wyoming's climate and the home they had left behind there, but he expressed the conviction that he ultimately would fare better in Arizona than in Wyoming. "Farm Family on Family Farm," *Reclamation Era* 42, August 1956: 57–58, 76. The Whites remained on their homestead in Roll for only five more years. See Yuma City Directories for 1961 and 1962 in Yuma Public Library. Russ Mohlman was eager to leave Riverton but suspicious of whether or not he could profitably farm his new homestead on the Minidoka Project in Idaho. Until he knew that he could make a living on the new homestead, he housed his family in a garage on his new land rather than investing in a house. Some who took lieu units on other projects eventually departed, but Mohlman fared well on the Minidoka Project, gradually acquired additional lands, and eventually left a ranch large enough to support three of his sons and their families. *Twin Falls Times-News*, 7 September 1992.

20. Gies interview; Withington interview; U.S. Congress, Senate, Subcommittee on Irrigation and Reclamation, Committee on Interior and Insular Affairs, *Third Division Irrigation District*, 74.

21. U.S. Congress, Senate, Subcommittee on Irrigation and Reclamation, Committee on Interior and Insular Affairs, *Third Division Irrigation* District, 2, 11, 74, 78–79; Bureau of Reclamation, "Annual Project History: Riverton Project, 1958," vol. 41, mimeograph, 8; Bureau of Reclamation, "Annual Project History: Riverton Project, 1959," vol. 42, mimeograph, 6–7; Bureau of Reclamation, "Annual Project History: Riverton Project, 1960," vol. 43, mimeograph, 6–7; Bureau of Reclamation, "Annual Project History, Riverton Project, 1961," vol. 44, mimeograph, 12–13; Bureau of Reclamation, "Annual Project History, Riverton Project, 1962," vol. 45, mimeograph, 7–9.

22. Bureau of Reclamation, "Annual Project History: Riverton Project, 1961," vol. 44, mimeograph, 12; *Riverton Ranger*, 31 October 1961.

23. *Riverton Ranger*, 31 October 1961; 1 November 1961; *Denver Rocky Mountain News*, 1 November 1961; Bureau of Reclamation, "Annual Project History: Riverton Project, 1961," vol. 44, mimeograph, 12–13; U.S. Congress, Senate, Subcommittee on Irrigation and Reclamation, Committee on Interior and Insular Affairs, *Third Division Irrigation District*, 14, 54–55, 79.

24. U.S. Congress, Senate, Subcommittee on Irrigation and Reclamation, *Third Division Irrigation District*, 14, 54–55, 79.

25. *Riverton Ranger*, 31 October 1961; *Denver Rocky Mountain News*, 1 November 1961; U.S. Congress, Senate, Subcommittee on Irrigation and Reclamation, Committee on Interior and Insular Affairs, *Third Division Irrigation District*, 56–67.

26. Bureau of Reclamation, "Annual Project History: Riverton Project, 1962," vol. 45, mimeograph, 8–9; *Denver Rocky Mountain News*, 4 February 1962.

27. *Riverton Ranger*, 16 March 1962, 19 March 1962; Bureau of Reclamation, "Annual Project History: Riverton Project, 1962," vol. 45, mimeograph, 7–9.

28. Bureau of Reclamation, "Annual Project History: Riverton Project, 1962," vol. 45, mimeograph, 8; interview with Carroll Riggs, 29 September 2001; Marlatt interview; Gies interview; *Riverton Ranger*, 19 September 1963, 20 September 1963; U.S. Congress, Senate, Subcommittee on Irrigation and Reclamation, Committee on Interior and Insular Affairs, *Third Division Irrigation District*, 23.

29. Gies interview; U.S. Congress, Senate, Subcommittee on Irrigation and Reclamation, Committee on Interior and Insular Affairs, *Riverton Reclamation Project*, 18.

30. Bureau of Reclamation, "Annual Project History: Riverton Project, 1963," vol. 45, mimeograph, 8–9; Bureau of Reclamation, "Annual Project History: Riverton Project, 1963," vol. 46, mimeograph, 10; U.S. Congress, Senate, Subcommittee on Irrigation and Reclamation, Committee on Interior and Insular Affairs, *Riverton Reclamation Project*, 6, 66, 78.

31. *Riverton Ranger*, 31 October 1961; U.S. Congress, Senate, Subcommittee on Irrigation and Reclamation, Committee on Interior and Insular Affairs, *Third Division Irrigation District*, 2, 13. Commissioner Floyd Dominy informed a Senate committee that the cost per acre on the Third Division amounted to $642, but that excluded over half of the cost of the entire Riverton project that the Bureau proposed should be repaid from hydro power revenue. In the Missouri River Basin, Dominy reported, the Bureau typically invested $800–$900 per acre in constructing an irrigation system. U.S. Congress, Senate, Subcommittee on Irrigation and Reclamation, Committee on Interior and Insular Affairs, *Riverton Reclamation Project*, 70.

32. U.S. Congress, Senate, Subcommittee on Irrigation and Reclamation, Committee on Interior and Insular Affairs, *Riverton Reclamation Project*, 4, 29; *Riverton Ranger*, 22 June 1963, 30 October 1963. The suit was dismissed in October "on the contention that the motion was not specific and the court does not have jurisdiction, and the case involves a type of tort action from which the Government is exempt." Bureau of Reclamation, "Annual Project History: Riverton Project, 1963," vol. 46, mimeograph, 10.

33. U.S. Congress, Senate, Subcommittee on Irrigation and Reclamation, Committee on Interior and Insular Affairs, *Riverton Reclamation Project*, 3, 5–6, 69–70.

34. Ibid., 36–37, 42, 44.

35. U.S. Congress, House, Committee on Interior and Insular Affairs, *Authorizing the Secretary of the Interior to Acquire Lands . . . in the Third Division*, 88th Cong., 1st sess., 1963, House Report 1010, 1–2, 5; *Riverton Ranger*, 28 October 1963, 30 October 1963, 13 November 1963, 27 November 1963.

36. Bureau of Reclamation, "Annual Project History: Riverton Project, 1963," vol. 46, mimeograph, 10; Bureau of Reclamation, "Annual Project History: Riverton Project, 1964," vol. 47, mimeograph, 10; Pelz, *Federal Reclamation Laws*, 3: 1740–1742; *Riverton Ranger*, 25 March 1964; Marlatt interview. The only landowner on the Third Division who did not sell was Keith Blankenship.

37. Gies interview.

38. Bureau of Reclamation, "Annual Project History: Riverton Project, 1971," vol. 54, mimeograph, 14–15; Bureau of Reclamation, "Annual Project History: Pick Sloan Missouri Basin Program, Riverton Unit, 1985," vol. 68, typescript; *Riverton Ranger*, 4 February 1971; 9 February 1971; 10 February 1971.

39. *Riverton Review*, 4 December 1947.

40. Patricia Nelson Limerick, *The Legacy of Conquest: The Unbroken Past of the American West* (New York: Norton, 1987), 138; Michael P. Malone, "Beyond the Last Frontier: Toward a New Approach to Western American History," *Western Historical Quarterly* 20 (November 1989): 418; Lane County Bachelor, "Starving to Death on a Government Claim," http://lonehand.com/cowboy_songs_iii.htm#S, accessed 6 May 2005.

CHAPTER 7. A CONFLICT OF INTERESTS: THE BATTLE OVER RECLAMATION HOMESTEADS

1. Paul W. Gates, *History of Public Land Law Development* (Washington, DC: GPO, 1968), 613; Ten Broeck Williamson, "History of the 1946 Land Opening on the Tule Lake Division of the Klamath Project," mimeograph, 1947, v, Folder 732, historical files, Bureau of Reclamation, Klamath Falls, OR [BOR-Klamath]; "1961 Annual His-

tory of the Minidoka Project," typescript, 1961, 502, Box 107, Accession 8NN 115–90–011, RG 115, National Archives, Lakewood, CO; Stanley W. Kronick et al., *Legal Study of Federal Public Land Laws and Policies Relating to Intensive Agriculture* (Springfield, VA: National Technical Information Service, 1969), 2: S9.

2. Kronick, *Legal Study*, 174; *Minidoka County News*, 21 August 1961; U.S. Congress, House, Committee on Interior and Insular Affairs, *Policies, Programs, and Activities of the Department of the Interior*, 89th Cong., 1st sess., 26 January 1965, 1: 11; H. H. Johnson, "Forty-Three Years on the Shoshone Project," *Reclamation Era* 33, June 1947, 124; Project Superintendent to Regional Director, 16 March 1965, historical files, Bureau of Reclamation, Burley, ID; U.S. Congress, Senate, Select Committee on National Water Resources, *Water Resources Activities in the United States: Future Needs for Reclamation in the Western States*, 86th Cong., 2d sess., 1960, Committee Print 32, 18, 21, 26.

3. U.S. Congress, House, *Establishing Public Land Policy; Establishing Guidelines for Its Administration; Providing for the Management, Protection, Development, and Enhancement of the Public Lands; and for Other Purposes*, 94th Cong., 2d sess., 1976, HR 1163, Serial 13134–7, 120–123; *Minidoka County News*, 11 May 1961; Annual Project History for Calendar Year 1962, Columbia Basin Project, mimeograph, 1962, 66; Annual Project History for Calendar Year 1963, Columbia Basin Project, mimeograph, 1963, 57; Annual Project History for Calendar Year 1965, Columbia Basin Project, mimeograph, 1965, 61; Annual Project History for Calendar Year 1966, Columbia Basin Project, mimeograph, 1966, 55, copies in RG 115, National Archives, Rocky Mountain Region, Lakewood, CO.

4. U.S. Congress, Senate, Select Committee on National Water Resources, *Water Resources Activities*, 18–19, 26; Rudolph Ulrich, "Relative Costs and Benefits of Land Reclamation in the Humid Southeast and the Semiarid West," *Journal of Farm Economics* 35 (February 1953): 67; Stephen C. Sturgeon, *The Politics of Western Water: The Congressional Career of Wayne Aspinall* (Tucson: University of Arizona Press, 2002), 69–122; Steven C. Schulte, *Wayne Aspinall and the Shaping of the American West* (Boulder: University Press of Colorado, 2002), 177–218; Donald Worster, *Rivers of Empire: Water, Aridity, and the Growth of the American West* (New York: Pantheon, 1985), 275.

5. U.S. Congress, House, Committee on Interior and Insular Affairs, *Policies, Programs, and Activities*, 1: 11, 121, 127, 142.

6. U.S. Congress, Senate, Committee on Interior and Insular Affairs, *Management of National Resource Lands*, 94th Cong., 1st sess., 7 March 1975, 2; William Cronon, "Landscapes of Abundance and Scarcity," in *The Oxford History of the American West*, ed. Clyde A Milner II, Carol A. O'Connor, and Martha A. Sandweiss (New York: Oxford University Press, 1994), 628; Samuel P. Hays, *Beauty, Health and Permanence: Environ-*

mental Politics in the United States, 1955–1985 (New York: Cambridge University Press, 1987).

7. U.S. Congress, House, Committee on Interior and Insular Affairs, *Policies, Programs, and Activities of the Department of the Interior*, 91st Cong., 1st sess., 18 February 1969, 5: 90–91; *Minidoka County News*, 21 August 1961; John McPhee, *Encounters with the Archdruid* (New York: Farrar, Straus and Giroux, 1971), 154–157, 172–173.

8. William E. Warne, *The Bureau of Reclamation* (New York: Praeger, 1973), 16.

9. This episode is briefly explored in Doug Foster, "Refuges and Reclamation: Conflicts in the Klamath Basin, 1904–1964," *Oregon Historical Quarterly* 103 (Summer 2002): 178–180.

10. Stan Turner, *The Years of Harvest: A History of the Tule Lake Basin* (Eugene, OR: 49th Avenue Press, 1987); Betty Lou Byrne-Shirley, "The Refuges," *Journal of the Modoc County Historical Society* 18 (1996): 32–36.

11. Byrne-Shirley, "Refuges," 31–34; Foster, "Refuges and Reclamation," 173. Copies of the executive orders establishing wildlife refuges in the area are found in U.S. Congress, Senate, Subcommittee on Irrigation and Reclamation, Committee on Interior and Insular Affairs, *Tule Lake, Lower Klamath, and Upper Klamath National Wildlife Refuges*, 87th Cong., 2d sess., 23 February 1962, 11–18.

12. *Tulelake Reporter* [TR], 22 March 1951; 19 April 1951; 26 April 1951; 24 May 1951; 28 June 1951; *New York Times*, 5 October 1947, SM30; Ten Broeck Williamson, "History of the 1946 Land Opening on the Tule Lake Division of the Klamath Project," typescript (1947), 104, Folder 732, historical files, BOR-Klamath.

13. TR, 13 December 1951.

14. *San Francisco Chronicle*, 30 December 1951.

15. TR, 3 January 1952; 17 January 1952; 6 March 1952.

16. TR, 10 January 1952; 31 January 1952.

17. *San Francisco Chronicle*, 13 January 1952.

18. TR, 14 August 1952.

19. TR, 25 September 1952.

20. TR, 15 January 1953; 30 April 1953.

21. TR, 12 February 1953; 5 March 1953; 19 March 1953; 9 April 1953.

22. TR, 22 January 1953; 2 April 1953; 9 April 1953.

23. TR, 30 April 1953.

24. TR, 10 December 1953.

25. TR, 19 May 1955; 26 May 1955.

26. TR, 30 August 1956; 13 September 1953; B. J. Weddell, K. L. Gray, and J. D. Foster, "Summary of Historical Documents Relating to the Klamath Basin National

Wildlife Refuges," (1994), 44, copy in Tule Lake National Wildlife Refuge Headquarters, Tulelake, CA.

27. TR, 2 May 1957; 9 May 1957; Klamath Basin Water Users Protective Association to Fred A. Seaton, 22 April 1957, Folder 730: "Lands Settlement," historical files, BOR-Klamath.

28. Weddell, Gray, and Foster, "Summary of Historical Documents," 45; Harold Mayfield, "The Seventy-Second Stated Meeting of the American Ornithologists' Union," *Auk* 72 (January 1957): 75.

29. Klamath Basin Water Users Protective Association, 7 February 1962, Folder 751: "Klamath Land and Water Rights," historical files, BOR-Klamath; Fred G. Aandahl and Ross Leffler to Secretary of the Interior, 31 January 1958, Folder 730: "Lands," historical files, BOR-Klamath; TR, 3 April 1958.

30. TR, 3 April 1958; Department of the Interior, press release, 1 April 1958, Folder "730 Lands," historical files, BOR-Klamath.

31. C. R. Gutermuth to State Directors of the Wildlife Management Institute, 6 June 1960; Gutermuth to Robert A. Wenke, 15 August 1960; Merrell F. Small to WBF, n.d. [August 1961]; Charles H. Callison to Small, 29 June 1960, all in Folder "Tule Lake 63–64", Box 458, Thomas Kuchel Papers, Bancroft Library, University of California, Berkeley; Carl W. Buchheister, "Tule Lake Threat Must Be Removed," *Audubon Magazine* (July-August 1960): 153–155.

32. Klamath Basin Water Users Protective Association to Clinton P. Anderson, 7 February 1962, Folder 751: "Klamath Land and Water Rights," historical files, BOR-Klamath; TR, 20 April 1961 and 14 December 1961; "Thomas Henry Kuchel, (1910–1994)," http://bioguide.congress.gov/scripts/biodisplay.pl?index=K000335, accessed 6 March 2007; U.S. Congress, Senate, Subcommittee on Irrigation and Reclamation, Committee on Interior and Insular Affairs, *Tule Lake, Lower Klamath*, 18, 19, 24, 27–28, 29.

33. Sam Anderson to Stewart L. Udall, 15 August 1961, Folder 730: "Lands Settlement," historical files, BOR-Klamath; C. L. Langslet to Thomas L. Kimball, 7 September 1961, Folder 751: "Exchange of Lands," BOR-Klamath; TR, 28 December 1961; U.S. Congress, Senate, Subcommittee on Irrigation and Reclamation, Committee on Interior and Insular Affairs, *Tule Lake, Lower Klamath*, 28–29.

34. U.S. Congress, Senate, Subcommittee on Irrigation and Reclamation, Committee on Interior and Insular Affairs, *Tule Lake, Lower Klamath*, 4–8, 18–25; Floyd E. Dominy to Kenneth Holum, 7 August 1961, Folder 730: "Lands Settlement," historical files, BOR-Klamath; Floyd E. Dominy to Assistant Secretary Holum, 17 January 1962, Folder 751: "Klamath Land and Water Rights," historical files, BOR-Klamath.

35. U.S. Congress, Senate, Subcommittee on Irrigation and Reclamation, Committee on Interior and Insular Affairs, *Tule Lake, Lower Klamath*, 18–45, 137–153; TR, 1 March 1962; John A. Marshall and C. L. Langslet to Clinton P. Anderson, 7 February 1962, Folder 751: "Klamath Land and Water Rights," historical files, BOR-Klamath; Edwin V. Lance to H. P. Dugan, 8 February 1962, historical files, BOR-Klamath; Thomas Kuchel to Sports Editors, 9 February 1962, Folder "Tule Lake 63–64," Box 458, Kuchel Papers. In 1954 Congress broadened preferential rights for veterans in applying for homesteads to include veterans of the Korean War and it extended those rights through 1959. *An Act to allow credit in connection with certain homestead entries for military or naval service rendered during the Korean conflict and for other purposes, Statutes at Large* 68, 253–254 (1955); Congress, Senate, 83rd Cong., 2d sess., *Congressional Record* [*CR*] 100, pt. 5 (4 May 1954): 5930.

36. U.S. Congress, Senate, Subcommittee on Irrigation and Reclamation, Committee on Interior and Insular Affairs, *Tule Lake, Lower Klamath*, 18; TR, 3 May 1962, 10 May 1962; U.S. Congress, Senate, 87th Cong., 2d sess., *CR*, 108, pt. 6 (16 May 1962): 8545; Floyd E. Dominy to Assistant Secretary Holum, 17 January 1962, Folder 751: "Klamath Land and Water Rights," historical files, BOR-Klamath.

37. TR, 10 May 1962.

38. U.S. Congress, Senate, 87th Cong., 2d sess., *CR*, 108, pt. 6 (16 May 1962): 8544–8551.

39. U.S. Congress, Senate, 88th Cong., 1st sess., *CR*, 109, pt. 9 (15 July 1963): 12551; Tulelake Irrigation District, Minutes of Board of Directors, 16 August 1962, Folder "832—TID Meetings," historical files, BOR-Klamath.

40. U.S. Congress, Senate, 88th Cong., 1st sess., *CR*, 109, pt. 9 (15 July 1963):12553; Tulelake Irrigation District, Minutes of Board of Directors, 10 April 1963, Folder 832: "TID Meetings," historical files, BOR-Klamath; TR, 2 May 1963; Warren B. Francis to Thomas Kuchel, 26 November 1962, Folder "Tule Lake 63–64"; Pop to EH, 3 December 1962, Folder "Tule Lake 63–64," Box 458, Kuchel Papers.

41. TR, 20 June 1963.

42. Ibid.; W. H. Weitkamp to Thomas Kuchel, 27 February 1963, Folder "Tule Lake 63–64," Box 458, Kuchel Papers.

43. Thomas Kuchel to Carl F. Wente, 8 March 1963; J. P. Cuenin to Kuchel, [March 1963]; Kuchel to Cuenin, 30 April 1963, Folder "Tule Lake 63–64," Box 458, Kuchel Papers; *San Francisco Examiner*, 13 March 1963.

44. U.S. Congress, Senate, Subcommittee on Irrigation and Reclamation, Committee on Interior and Insular Affairs, *Tule Lake–Klamath Wildlife Refuge*, 88th Cong., 1st. sess., 24 April 1963, 8, 13, 17, 23, 27.

45. Congress, Senate, 88th Cong., 1st sess., *CR*, 109, pt. 9 (15 July 1963): 12550–12559; *San Francisco Examiner*, 23 July 1963, with attached undated memo from Warren B. Francis to Steve Horn, Folder "Tule Lake '63," Box 461, Kuchel Papers.

46. *TR*, 18 July 1963.

47. *San Francisco Chronicle*, 7 November 1963; Wallace R. Lynn to Thomas Kuchel, 14 March 1963; Lynn to Paul Fay, 13 November 1963, Folder "Tule Lake 63–64," Box 458, Kuchel Papers.

48. U.S. Congress, House, *CR*, 110, pt. 6 (20 April 1964): 8382–8385; U.S. Congress, House, Committee on Interior and Insular Affairs, 88th Cong., 1st sess., *Promoting the Conservation of the Nation's Wildlife Resources on the Pacific Flyway*, House Report 1072 (1963), 16–17; Harold T. "Bizz" Johnson to Wallace R. Lynn, 13 March 1964, Folder "Tule Lake 64," Box 485, Kuchel Papers.

49. U.S. Congress, House, 88th Cong., 2d sess., *CR*, 110, pt. 6 (20 April 1964): 8381–8385; Dick Andrews to Thomas Kuchel, 21 February 1964, Folder "Tule Lake 63–64," Box 458, Kuchel Papers.

50. Harold T. "Bizz" Johnson to Thomas Kuchel, 17 April 1964; Kuchel to Johnson, 27 April 1964, Folder "Tule Lake 63–64," Box 458, Kuchel Papers.

51. U.S. Congress, House, 88th Cong., 2d sess., *CR*, 110, pt. 6 (20 April 1964): 110: 20154–20155, 20457–20459; U.S. Congress, House, Committee on Interior and Insular Affairs, *Promoting the Conservation*; Richard D. Andrews to Senate Conferees, 22 July 1964, Folder "Tule Lake 63–64"; Thomas Kuchel to Martin Winton, 13 May 1964, Folder "Tule Lake 64"; C. R. Gutermuth to Walter P. Shannon, 12 May 1964, Folder "Tule Lake 64," Box 458, Kuchel Papers.

52. Carl F. Wente to Thomas Kuchel, 5 October 1964; J. D. Flournoy to Kuchel, 18 August 1964, Folder "Tule Lake 64," Box 458, Kuchel Papers; *San Francisco Chronicle*, 28 August 1964.

53. Walter H. Muller to Reclamation Bureau, 27 January 1964, Folder 730: "Lands Settlement," historical files, BOR-Klamath; Project Superintendent to Regional Director, 16 March 1965; Chief of Planning Field Branch to Regional Planning Officer, 21 March 1975; E.M. to G. Osborne, "Northside Extension," 29 October 1987; "North Side Pumping Division Drainwater Management Study, Minidoka Project, Idaho," 1990, all in folder labeled "Wildlife MNSPD Extension," Bureau of Reclamation, Burley, ID.

54. Richard W. Etulain, *Beyond the Missouri: The Story of the American West* (Albuquerque: University of New Mexico Press, 2006), 383.

CHAPTER 8. REPEAL OF THE HOMESTEAD ACT

1. National Park Service, "Found! America's Last Homesteader," http://www.nps.gov/home/historyculture/lasthomesteader.htm?eid=122894&root_aId=135.; Alaska Trappers Association, "Oral History Interviews: Ken Deardorff," n.d., http://www.alaskatrappers.org/bio_sketch_ken_deardorff.html, accessed 26 April 2007.

2. When Congress repealed the Homestead Act, those who were in the process of proving up on their claims were permitted to continue with the process.

3. Michael P. Malone and Richard W. Etulain, *The American West: A Twentieth-Century History* (Lincoln: University of Nebraska Press, 1989), 96. See also Walter Nugent, *Into the West: The Story of Its People* (New York: Vintage Books, 1999), 251.

4. *Anchorage Alaska Daily News*, 26 September 1952, 27 September 1952; U.S. Congress, House, *Revision of the Public Land Laws*, 82nd Cong., 2d sess., 1952, HR 2511, Serial 11578, 1–9.

5. U.S. Congress, House, *Establishment of Public Land Law Review Commission*, 88th Cong., 1st sess., 1963, House Report 1008, Serial 12545, 5–6; David M. Wrobel, *The End of American Exceptionalism: Frontier Anxiety from the Old West to the New Deal* (Lawrence: University Press of Kansas, 1993), viii. As William Cronon has observed, "In the nineteenth century, the frontier had stood in the minds of many Americans for the unworked abundance of a savage or prehuman landscape awaiting the touch of human hands to become the site of prosperous farms. . . . The reclamation dream had extended this vision of frontier plenty even into the drylands of the arid West. . . . [But] perceived abundance gradually gave way to perceived scarcity. . . . By the late twentieth century, the wilderness, which had once stood as America's most potent icon of limitless abundance, seemed, in the eyes of many, to be its scarcest resource." William Cronon, "Landscapes of Abundance and Scarcity," in *The Oxford History of the American West*, ed. Clyde A. Milner II, Carol A. O'Connor, and Martha A. Sandweiss (New York: Oxford University Press, 1994), 633.

6. Public Land Law Review Commission, *One Third of the Nation's Land: A Report to the President and to the Congress by the Public Land Law Review Commission* (Washington, DC: GPO, 1970), ix; Steven C. Schulte, *Wayne Aspinall and the Shaping of the American West* (Boulder: University Press of Colorado, 2002), 2, 72, 227, 234–244.

7. Stanley W. Kronick et al., *Legal Study of Federal Public Land Laws and Policies Relating to Intensive Agriculture* (Springfield, VA: National Technical Information Service, 1969), S1–2, 91, 328–329.

8. Ibid., 149; U.S. Congress, Senate, Senate Select Committee on National Water Resources, *Water Resources Activities in the United States: Future Needs for Reclamation in the Western States*, 86th Cong., 2d sess., 1960, Committee Print 32, 9; *Minidoka County News*, 21 August 1961.

9. Max Myers et al., *Federal Public Land Laws and Policies Relating to Intensive Agriculture* (Brookings, SD: South Dakota State University Economics Department, 1969), 2: 224, 235–236.

10. Ibid., 238, 240; Edward F. Renshaw, "Appraisal of Federal Investment in Water Resources," in University of Illinois Land Economics Institute, *Modern Land Policy: Papers of the Land Economics Institute* (Urbana: University of Illinois Press, 1960), 235, 244–247. See also Edward F. Renshaw, *Toward Responsible Government* (Chicago: Idyia Press, 1957).

11. Myers et al., *Federal Public Land Laws*, 238; U.S. Congress, Senate, 84th Cong., 1st sess., *Congressional Record* [CR] 101, pt. 4 (18 April 1955): 4575.

12. Myers et al., *Federal Public Land Laws*, 226, 254–256.

13. U.S. Congress, House, 90th Cong., 2d sess., *CR* 114, pt. 10 (15 May 1968): 13404, 13447.

14. Public Land Law Review Commission, *One Third of the Nation's Land*, 1, 178, 179.

15. Schulte, *Wayne Aspinall*, 242.

16. U.S. Congress, Senate, *National Resource Lands Management Act*, 94th Cong., 1st sess., 1975, SR 583, Serial 13096, 36–37; U.S. Congress, Senate, Committee on Interior and Insular Affairs, *Legislation to Revise the Public Land Laws*, 92d Cong., 1st sess. (21 September 1971): 74; "Homesteading in Alaska a Thing of the Past," *Mother Earth News* 31 (January/February 1975), http://www.motherearthnews.com/Modern-Homesteading/1975-01-01/Land-Closed-To-Homesteading.aspx, accessed 9 February 2007; *New York Times*, 20 May 1974, 24; *Anchorage Daily News*, 29 March 1974.

17. U.S. Congress, Senate, Committee on Interior and Insular Affairs, *Management of National Resources Land*, 93rd Cong., 1st sess. (1 March 1973): 29, 186; U.S. Congress, Senate, 93rd Cong., 2d sess., *CR* 120, pt. 17 (8 July 1974): 22269–22277, 22280.

18. U.S. Congress, Senate, 93rd Cong., 2d sess., *CR* 120, pt. 17 (2 July 1975): 22280–22285. Only Jesse Helms of South Carolina voted against the bill, believing that it gave too much discretionary authority to the secretary of the interior.

19. U.S. Congress, Senate, Committee on Interior and Insular Affairs, *Management of National Resource Lands*, 94th Cong., 1st sess. (7 March 1975): 65.

20. U.S. Congress, House, *Establishing Public Land Policy; Establishing Guidelines for Its Administration; Providing for the Management, Protection, Development, and Enhancement of the Public Lands; and for Other Purposes*, 94th Cong., 2d sess., 1976, House Report 1163, Serial 13134-7, 33; U.S. Congress, Senate, Committee on Interior and Insular Affairs, *Management of National Resource Lands*, 61, 65, 155; U.S. Congress, Senate, 94th Cong., 2d sess., *CR* 122, pt. 4 (23 February 1976): 4055.

21. U.S. Congress, House, Subcommittee on Public Lands, Committee on Interior

and Insular Affairs, *Public Land Policy and Management Act of 1975*, 94th Cong., 1st sess., 21 March 1975, 1, 225; U.S. Congress, House, *Providing for the Management, Protection, and Development of National Resource Lands, and Other Purposes*, 94th Cong., 2d sess., 1976, House Report 1724, Serial 13134–13, 49, 66; U.S. Congress, House, 94th Cong., 2d sess., *CR* 122, pt. 19 (22 July 1976): 23483–23484; U.S. Congress, House, 94th Cong., 2d sess., *CR* 122, pt. 26 (29 September 1976): 33500–33503; 34512, 35087.

22. *Tri-City Herald*, 19 June 1997; *Seattle Post-Intelligencer*, 6 November 1999.

23. Cronon, "Landscapes of Abundance and Scarcity," 628.

CHAPTER 9. "OUR DREAM WAS CHANGED INTO A NIGHTMARE": THE HOMESTEADERS AT THE DAWN OF THE TWENTY-FIRST CENTURY

1. Senator Jake Garn's report of Goldwater's comments quoted in Adam R. Eastman, "From Cadillac to Chevy: Environmental Concern, Compromise, and the Central Utah Project Completion Act" (M.A. thesis, Brigham Young University, 2006), 1.

2. On the Winters case and its legacy, see Norris Hundley Jr., "The Dark and Bloody Ground of Indian Water Rights: Confusion Elevated to Principle," *Western Historical Quarterly* 9 (October 1978): 454–482; John Shurts, *Indian Reserved Water Rights: The Winters Doctrine in Its Social and Legal Context, 1880s–1930s* (Norman: University of Oklahoma Press, 2000).

3. Patricia Nelson Limerick, *The Legacy of Conquest: The Unbroken Past of the American West* (New York: W. W. Norton, 1987), 135; copy of patent deed recorded in Deeds Vol. 179, 92, Modoc County Recorder's Office, electronic copy available at http://www.klamathbasincrisis.org/Homesteaders/original_deed.htm, accessed 26 September 2006; *Riverside Press-Enterprise*, 20 October 1998, A04.

4. Evan R. Ward, *Border Oasis: Water and the Political Ecology of the Colorado River Delta, 1940–1975* (Tucson: University of Arizona Press, 2003), 120–121, 128–129; interview with Lyle Esser, 18 August 1996, Mesa, WA; Save Our Wild Salmon Coalition, "Illegal Irrigation Hurting Salmon," press release, 19 May 2000, http://www.wildsalmon.org/pressroom/press-detail.cfm?docID=85, accessed 31 January 2008; "Multimillion-dollar Idaho Water Rights Deal Approved," *U.S. Water News Online* (April 2004), http://www.uswaternews.com/archives/arcconserv/4multdoll4.html, accessed 19 October 2006; Hu Blonk, "Tapping Lost River," *Reclamation Era* 37, April 1951, 67; *San Diego Union-Tribune*, 10 May 2003, A-3; *Los Angeles Times*, 23 June 2003, B-1; *Riverside Press-Enterprise*, 4 July 2003, A-1.

5. *San Francisco Chronicle*, 14 August 2001. Documentary filmmaker and playwright Stephen Most briefly narrates portions of the farmers' protest in his engaging popu-

lar history of the Klamath Basin, *River of Renewal: Myth and History in the Klamath Basin* (Portland: Oregon Historical Society Press, and Seattle: University of Washington Press, 2006), xxx–xxxiv, 230–243. Historian William G. Robbins briefly relates the story in *Landscapes of Conflict: The Oregon Story, 1940–2000* (Seattle: University of Washington Press, 2004), 110–112.

6. *Portland Oregonian*, 6 May 2001, A-1; 8 May 2001, A-1; 21 March 2001, D-4; Endangered Species Act of 1973, http://www.fws.gov/laws/digest/ESACT.html, accessed 19 October 2006.

7. *Oregonian*, 5 April 2001, B-2; 21 September 2000, E-1.

8. *Oregonian*, 16 June 2001, D-8; 15 March 2001, B-7; 21 March 2001, D-4; 20 July 2001, A-1; *Klamath Falls Herald and News*, 9 April 2001; *Steven Lewis Kandra et al. v. United States, Klamath Tribes and Wilderness Society*, Opinion and Order, 30 April 2001, http://www.klamathbasincrisis.org/articles/Archives/archive1/injunctiondenied.htm, accessed 24 January 2006; William S. Braunworth et al., *Water Allocation in the Klamath Reclamation Project, 2001: An Assessment of Natural Resource, Economic, Social, and Institutional Issues with a Focus on the Upper Klamath Basin* (Eugene: Oregon State University Extension Service, 2002), 13.

9. *Oregonian*, 5 April 2001, B-2.

10. *Klamath Falls Herald and News*, 9 April 2001.

11. *Oregonian*, 15 March 2001, B-7; 10 April 2001, B-9; 7 April 2001, A-1; 8 May 2001, A-1.

12. *Klamath Falls Herald and News*, 9 April 2001; 11 June 2001; *San Francisco Chronicle*, 16 July 2001; *Oregonian*, 12 April 2001, C-1; 15 April 2001, C-4; 7 July 2001, D-1.

13. *Kandra v. United States*.

14. Jeff Barnard, "Judge Denies Klamath Farmers' Desperate Plea for Water," Associated Press Release, 1 May 2001, http://www.klamathbasincrisis.org/articles/Archives/archive1/Judge-AP5-1-01.htm, accessed 24 January 2006; *Medford Mail Tribune*, 22 May 2001.

15. *Klamath Falls Herald and News*, 25 April 2001; 8 May 2001; *Oregonian*, 7 July 2001, D–1; Chris Moudry, "Klamath Basin Crisis—Endangered Species Act Gone," n.d., http://www.klamathbasincrisis.org/articles/Archives/archive1/basinfertilizer.htm, accessed 24 January 2001.

16. *Klamath Falls Herald and News*, 7 May 2001; *Oregonian*, 8 May 2001, A-9.

17. *Oregonian*, 8 May 2001, D-7; *Klamath Falls Herald and News*, 8 May 2001.

18. *Oregonian*, 13 May 2001, D-4.

19. *Klamath Falls Herald and News*, 30 April 2001; 8 May 2001; 18 September 2001; *San Francisco Chronicle*, 16 July 2001.

20. *Oregonian*, 8 May 2001, A-1; *Klamath Falls Herald and News*, 11 June 2001.

21. *San Francisco Chronicle*, 7 July 2001; *Oregonian*, 17 June 2001, A-17; *Klamath Falls Herald and News*, 22 June 2001; Braunworth et al., *Water Allocation in the Klamath Reclamation Project*, 191.

22. Testimonials of Manuel Silva, Ruth Masterson, Helen Newkirk, Frances Johnson, Paul Christy, Kathleen Todd St. Peter, and Velma Robison, http://www.klamathbasincrisis.org/Homesteaders/homesteaders.htm, accessed 17 January 2006; *Oregonian*, 8 May 2001, A-1.

23. Testimonials of Dorie Voorhees, Helen Newkirk, John Terry, and Joe and Mary Victorine, http://www.klamathbasincrisis.org/Homesteaders/homesteaders.htm, accessed 17 January 2006.

24. Testimonial of Paul Christy, ibid.; *Oregonian*, 17 June 2001; 2 August 2001.

25. Jacqui Krizo, "Where Is the Klamath Basin, Who Is Our Community, Who Is KBC, and Who Are the Caretakers?" http://www.klamathbasincrisis.org/aboutus/about%20us.htm, accessed 13 November 2006.

26. *Klamath Falls Herald and News*, 23 May 2001; 8 July 2001.

27. Ibid., 2 July 2001; 3 July 2001; 5 July 2001; 30 August 2001.

28. J. J. Johnson, "Klamath Falls: Where Civil Rights Meets Water Rights," *Sierra Times*, 7 July 2001, http://www.sierratimes.com/archive/files/jul/07/arjj070701.htm, accessed 13 November 2006; Signature and affiliation of Andrea Zingg, Petition of Environmental Conservation Organization, http://www.freedom.org/WTC/response/who/signed-A.shtml, accessed 22 August 2006; *Herald and News*, 5 July 2001; 8 July 2001.

29. *Klamath Falls Herald and News*, 11 July 2001.

30. Ibid., 8 July 2001; *San Francisco Chronicle*, 7 July 2001.

31. *Oregonian*, 13 July 2001, A-1; U.S. Congress, Senate, 107th Cong., 1st sess., *Congressional Record* 147, pt. 97 (12 July 2001): 7554.

32. *Klamath Falls Herald and News*, 9 May 2001; 10 July 2001; 12 July 2001.

33. Ibid., 15 July 2001; 30 August 2001; *Oregonian*, 14 July 2001, A-1; 15 July 2001, A-1.

34. *Klamath Falls Herald and News*, 15 July 2001; *Oregonian*, 14 July 2001, A-1; Jeff Head, "The Stand at Klamath Falls," 17 July 2001, http://www.jeffhead.com/klamath/account1.htm, accessed 14 November 2006.

35. Head, "Stand at Klamath Falls"; *Oregonian*, 15 July 2001, A-1; *Klamath Falls Herald and News*, 15 July 2001.

36. *Klamath Falls Herald and News*, 15 July 2001; 18 July 2001; 20 March 2006; *Montana Human Rights Network News*, September 2001, http://www.mhrn.org/news

archive/0901Klamath.html, accessed 16 August 2006; "About the Sierra Times," http://www.sierratimes.com/mission/htm, accessed 16 August 2006.

37. *Oregonian*, 16 July 2001, A-1.

38. Head, "Stand at Klamath Falls"; *Oregonian*, 16 July 2001; *Klamath Falls Herald and News*, 16 July 2001.

39. *Oregonian*, 16 July 2001, A-1; 22 July 2001, A-1; *London Observer*, 29 July 2001; *Klamath Falls Herald and News*, 19 July 2001.

40. *Oregonian*, 19 July 2001, A-1; *Klamath Falls Herald and News*, 19 July 2001.

41. *Oregonian*, 20 July 2001, A-1; 25 July 2001, A-1; 26 July 2001; 2 August 2001, A-1; 3 August 2001, D-12; 8 August 2001, A-1.

42. *Oregonian*, 25 July 2001, A-1; 29 July 2001, A-17; 2 August 2001, A-1; 7 August 2001, A-1.

43. *Klamath Falls Herald and News*, 25 July 2001; 28 July 2001; *Oregonian*, 26 July 2001.

44. *Klamath Falls Herald and News*, 25 July 2001.

45. Ibid.; Braunworth et al., *Water Allocation in the Klamath Reclamation Project*, 257.

46. *Klamath Falls Herald and News*, 2 August 2001; 5 August 2001; 12 August 2001; 20 August 2001; *Pasco Washington Tri-City Herald*, 15 August 2001.

47. *Klamath Falls Herald and News*, 18 September 2001; 12 March 2006; "A History of the Klamath Bucket Brigade," n.d., http://www.klamathbucketbrigade.org/a_history_of_KBB.htm, accessed 14 November 2006.

48. *Oregonian*, 19 August 2001, A-1; 22 August 2001, A-1; *Montana Human Rights Network News*, September 2001, http://www.mhrn.org/newsarchive/0901Klamath.html, accessed 16 August 2006; *Klamath Falls Herald and News*, 21 August 2001; 24 August 2001.

49. Braunworth et al., *Water Allocation in the Klamath Reclamation Project*, 189; *Oregonian*, 24 August 2001, C-6; *Klamath Falls Herald and News*, 23 August 2001.

50. *Klamath Falls Herald and News*, 30 August 2001; Sean Finnegan, "Klamath: Pitchforks Not Required," *Sierra Times* (30 August 2001), http://www.sierratimes.com/mission/htm, accessed 22 August 2006.

51. *Klamath Falls Herald and News*, 2 September 2001; 3 September 2001.

52. *Oregonian*, 13 September 2001, B-15; *Klamath Falls Herald and News*, 12 September 2001; 13 September 2001.

53. *Oregonian*, 18 September 2001, C-5; 27 September 2001, B-7; 5 October 2001, C-8; 12 October 2001, C-8; 26 April 2002, A-1; 27 April 2002, B-1.

54. Braunworth et al., *Water Allocation in the Klamath Reclamation Project*, 12, 22, 258; *Klamath Falls Herald and News*, 4 February 2002; 29 March 2002.

55. Committee on Endangered and Threatened Fishes in the Klamath River Basin,

Scientific Evaluation of Biological Opinions on Endangered and Threatened Fishes in the Klamath River Basin: Interim Report (Washington, D.C.: National Academy Press, 2002), 4, 17, 19, 24, http://www.nap.edu/openbook/0309083249/html/26.html, accessed 14 November 2006.

56. Ibid., 14, 16, 20, 26. Some politicians and administrators greeted the report as definitive evidence, but dissenting scientists including fisheries professor Douglas Markle and graduate student Michael Cooperman charged that the document contained "multiple errors that detract from its scientific usefulness." *Oregonian*, 14 November 2002, B-9. One week after the scholars appointed by the National Academy of Sciences released their final report in October 2003, a separate panel of scientists from Oregon State University and the University of Idaho upheld the strategy of withholding water in Upper Klamath Lake as a reasonable and appropriate one. *Oregonian*, 22 October 2003, A-1; 29 October 2003, C-10.

57. *Oregonian*, 5 February 2002, A-1; 28 February 2002, E-4; 30 March 2002, A-1; *Klamath Falls Herald and News*, 29 March 2002.

58. *Klamath Falls Herald and News*, 31 March 2002; 14 May 2002.

59. Christine Souza, "Klamath ESA Congressional Hearing," California Farm Bureau Ag Alert, 21 July 2004, http://www.klamathbasincrisis.org/esa/esahearing0704/esaagalerthearing072104.htm, accessed 12 September 2006; Testimony of Tulelake Growers Association to the Committee on Natural Resources, 17 July 2006, http://www.klamathbasincrisis.org/esa/esahearing0704/testimonytga071704.htm, accessed 12 September 2006.

60. Souza, "Klamath ESA Congressional Hearing"; Testimony of Tulelake Growers Association; David Carman, testimony before Committee on Natural Resources, 17 July 2006, http://www.klamathbasincrisis.org/esa/esahearing0704/testimonydcarman071704.htm, accessed 21 November 2006.

61. "Walden Bipartisan ESA Modernization Bill Approved by House Resources Committee," press release by Greg Walden, 21 July 2004, http://www.klamathbasincrisis.org/esa/esa%20lawsuits/waldenesabillapproved072104.htm, accessed 12 September 2006; "Walden Cosponsors Bipartisan Critical Habitat Legislation to Update ESA," press release, 15 March 2005, http://www.klamathbasincrisis.org/esa/waldensponsors031705.htm; *Klamath Falls Herald and News*, 11 October 2005; 4 July 2006; Richard W. Pombo, "Environment vs. Property Rights: Endangered Species Act Reform Needed?" *San Francisco Chronicle*, 5 July 2006.

62. Francis M. Allegra, Opinion, *Klamath Irrigation District et al., v. US*, US Federal Claims Court, 31 August 2005, http://www.klamathbucketbrigade.org/Allegra_DecisioninFederalCourtofClaims090205.htm, accessed 31 January 2008.

EPILOGUE

1. Rebecca Kneale Gould, *At Home in Nature: Modern Homesteading and Spiritual Practice in America* (Berkeley: University of California Press, 2005), 2; Ralph Borsodi, *Flight from the City: The Story of a New Way to Family Security* (New York: Harper and Bros., 1933), 7, 89; Wendell Berry, *The Long-Legged House* (New York: Harcourt, Brace and World, 1969), 89; Maynard Kaufman and Sally Kaufman, "Information about the School of Homesteading" (1973), http://www.michiganlandtrust.org/compilation/info1973.html, accessed 17 January 2008. For additional information on back-to-the-land impulses including the idea of subsistence homesteads, see Paul K. Conkin, *Tomorrow a New World: The New Deal Community Program* (Ithaca, NY: Cornell University Press, 1959), 11–36.

2. Kaufman and Kaufman, "Information about the School of Homesteading."

3. Gould, *At Home in Nature*, 2; Philip Weiss, "Off the Grid," *New York Times Magazine*, 8 January 1995, http://query.nytimes.com/gst/fullpage.html?res=990CE3DA1F3AF93AA15752C0A963958260, accessed 27 September 2007; Barbara Geisler and Maynard Kaufman, "Homesteading in the 1990s" http://www.michiganlandtrust.org/compilation/Barmay.htm, accessed 3 January 2008. Jack Dody, the webmaster for a site dedicated to "Christian Homesteading," defined homesteading for a new age in 2003. He indicated that homesteaders "share some of the following characteristics: They usually live in the country, although there are urban homesteaders. They grow some of their own food. They are financially responsible, choosing to work their way out of debt. They homeschool their children. They embrace new alternative energy technologies like solar and wind power. They depend less upon government and more upon themselves." http://www.christianhomesteaders.org/, accessed 27 September 2007.

4. *Countryside & Small Stock Journal* homepage, http://www.countrysidemag.com/, accessed 3 January 2008; *Down to the Roots Organic Homesteading Magazine* homepage, http://www.downtotherootsmagazine.com, accessed 3 January 2008.

5. U.S. Congress, Senate, 107th Cong., 2d sess., *Congressional Record* [CR], 148, pt. 14 (14 February 2002): S793.

6. Ibid.; U.S. Congress, Senate, 108th Cong., 1st sess., *CR*, 149, pt. 41 (13 March 2003): S3664; U.S. Congress, Senate, 109th Cong., 1st sess., *CR*, 151, pt. 33 (17 March 2005): S675; U.S. Congress, Senate, 110th Cong., 1st sess., *CR*, 153, pt. 59 (12 April 2007): S4437; Max Lu, "Homesteading Redux: New Community Initiatives to Reverse Rural Depopulation in the Great Plains," *Journal of the West* 46 (Winter 2007): 76.

7. Teresa Hull and Linda Leask, "Dividing Alaska, 1867–2000: Changing Land Ownership and Management," *Alaska Review of Social and Economic Conditions* 32 (No-

vember 2000): 6; Denise Caldwell, "Author Decides to Homestead in Alaska and Shares Her Experiences," http://freeamericandream.blogspot.com/, accessed 3 January 2008. A Hawaii statute permitted native Hawaiians to lease "homesteads"—either agricultural or residential tracts—from the state. Department of Hawaiian Homelands, *Applying for Hawaiian Homelands* (Honolulu: State of Hawaii, n.d.), http://hawaii.gov/dhhl/applicants, accessed 9 January 2007.

8. "Rural County Offers Land to Get People," *New York Times*, 15 January 1988, http://www.nytimes.com/gst/fullpage.html?res=940DE0DA1731F936A25751C1A96E948260&sec=&spon=&pagewanted=1, accessed 4 January 2008; *Anchorage Daily News*, 17 March 2007.

9. In 2004, Jon M. Bailey and Kim Preston, researchers at the Center for Rural Affairs in Lyons, Nebraska, applied the term "Mini-Homestead Acts" to these free land programs. Jon M. Bailey and Kim Preston, *Fresh Promises: Highlighting Promising Strategies of the Rural Great Plains and Beyond* (Lyons, NE: Center for Rural Affairs, 2004), 25–26. Many others also likened the free land programs to the vaunted 1862 act. See Marti Attoun, "Where the Land Is Free," *American Profile* (30 April 2006), http://www.americanprofile.com/article/5285.html, accessed 4 January 2008; Paul Harris, "Meet America's New Pioneer Breed," *Observer Magazine, Manchester Guardian*, 29 May 2005, http://www.guardian.co.uk/world/2005/may/29/usa.paulharris, accessed 3 January 2008; and Jeffrey Spivak, "Kansas Says: Take This Land . . . Please!" *Planning* (November 2007), http://www.entrepreneur.com/tradejournals/article/print/172168549.html , accessed 3 January 2008.

10. Verne G. Kopytoff, "Free-Land Lottery Withers on a Prairie in Texas," *New York Times*, 4 May 1997, http://www.nytimes.com/gst/fullpage.html?res=9F02E3D61031F937A35756C0A961958260, accessed 27 September 2007; Attoun, "Where the Land Is Free."

11. Lu, "Homesteading Redux," 76; Spivak, "Kansas Says: Take This Land"; John Ritter, "Towns Offer Free Land to Newcomers," *USA Today*, 8 February 2005, http://usatoday.com/news/nation/2005-02-08-land-cover_x.htm, accessed 27 September 2007; Tom Leonard, "Free Land for Families Tempts New Pioneers to the Prairies," *London Daily Telegraph*, 26 July 2005, http://www.telegraph.co.uk/news/worldnews/northamerica/usa/1494860/Free-land-for-families-tempts-new-pioneers-to-the-prairies.html, accessed 27 July 2008; Mark Kudlowitz and Lance George, *Turning Challenges into Opportunities: Housing and Community Development Strategies in Rural Population Loss Counties* (Washington, DC: Housing Assistance Council, 2007), 37–40.

12. Ritter, "Towns Offer Free Land"; "Marquette, Kansas/Free Land," Fox Evening

News Television Broadcast, 22 May 2004, http://openweb.tvnews.vanderbilt.edu/; accessed 17 January 2008; Spivak, "Kansas Says: Take This Land"; Daniel Kadlec, "Double Take," *Time Magazine*, 5 July 2005, http://www.time.com/time/magazine/article/0,9171,1079474,00.html, accessed 21 February 2008; Susan Lahey, "There's Still Free Land out West," *Grit*, January/February 2007, http://www.grit.com/article/2007/01/Land-Out-West.html, accessed 4 January 2008.

13. *Newton Kansan*, 27 April 2006; Ellsworth City Council, Minutes, 28 August 2006, http://blog.ellsworthks.net/minutes/2007/03/august–2006.html, accessed 3 January 2008; Kudlowitz and George, *Turning Challenges into Opportunities*, 41.

14. Peg Britton, blog response to Paul Harris, 29 May 2005, http://www.kansasprairie.net/kansasprairieblog/?m=200505, accessed 8 January 2008.

15. Ric Hanson, "Marne Gets Some Takers on Free Land," KJAN radio broadcast, 26 April 2006, http://www.radioiowa.com/gestalt/go.cfm?objectid=0546CE56-A6E8-48C5-ABAE98E5A37DC200, accessed 27 September 2007; Bailey and Preston, *Fresh Promises*, 25, 26; Kudlowitz and George, *Turning Challenges into Opportunities*, 23; "Alaska Town Giving Away Free Land," 16 March 2007, http://www.foxnews.com/story/0,2933,259264,00.html, accessed 18 February 2008; "Alaska: Free Land Is Snapped Up in Hours," *New York Times*, 20 March 2007, www.newyorktimes.com/2007/03/20/us/20brfs-land.html, accessed 18 February 2008.

16. *Salina [KS] Journal*, 6 May 2004; Darrin Stineman, "New Homesteaders," *Salina Journal*, 12 February 2005, A01; *Topeka Capital-Journal*, 29 August 2005.

17. Attoun, "Where the Land Is Free."

18. John Gordon, "Kansas Church Welcomes Families Drawn by Promise of Free Land," 19 April 2005, United Methodist News Service, http://archives.umc.org/interior.asp?ptid=2&mid=7250, accessed 4 January 2008; *Topeka Capital-Journal*, 29 August 2005.

19. *Salina Journal*, 6 May 2004; Ritter, "Towns Offer Free Land"; Spivak, "Kansas Says: Take This Land"; Kadlec, "Double Take."

20. Patricia Nelson Limerick, *The Legacy of Conquest: The Unbroken Past of the American West* (New York: W. W. Norton, 1987), 138; U.S. Congress, Senate, Subcommittee on Irrigation and Reclamation, Committee on Interior and Insular Affairs, *Riverton Reclamation Project*, 88th Cong., 1st sess., 29–30 October 1963, 60.

21. Limerick, *Legacy of Conquest*, 24, 134.

22. Interview with Lyle Esser, 24 August 1996, Mesa, WA.

23. David B. Danbom, *Born in the Country: A History of Rural America* (Baltimore: Johns Hopkins University Press, 1995), 234.

24. Ibid., 251.

25. Donald Worster, *Rivers of Empire: Water, Aridity, and the Growth of the American West* (New York: Pantheon, 1985).

26. Limerick, *Legacy of Conquest*, 148; Eric Bailey, "Parched Farmers Pour Out Frustrations over Water Policy," *Los Angeles Times*, 8 May 2001, http://articles.latimes.com/2001/may/08/local/me-60844, accessed 25 July 2008.

27. *Minidoka County News*, 6 August 1953.

BIBLIOGRAPHY

MANUSCRIPT COLLECTIONS AND ARCHIVES

Bureau of Reclamation, Klamath Basin Area Office, Klamath Falls, OR

Bureau of Reclamation, Library, Denver Office, Lakewood, CO

Bureau of Reclamation, Lower Colorado Regional Office, Boulder City, NV

Bureau of Reclamation, Snake River Area Office—East, Burley, ID

Bureau of Reclamation, Snake River Area Office—West, Boise, ID

Bureau of Reclamation, Yuma Area Office, Yuma, AZ

Columbia Basin Commission Papers, State of Washington Archives, Olympia

DeMary Memorial Library, Rupert, ID

Fremont County Museum, Riverton, WY

Thomas Kuchel Papers, Bancroft Library, University of California, Berkeley

Midvale Irrigation District, Pavillion, WY

Minidoka County Recorder's Office, Rupert, ID

Modoc County Recorder's Office, Alturas, CA

Records of the Bureau of Reclamation, Federal Records Center [FRC], Lakewood, CO

Records of the Bureau of Reclamation, Record Group [RG] 115, National Archives, Rocky Mountain Region, Lakewood, CO

Records of the Office of the Secretary of Defense, RG 330, National Archives, College Park, MD

Records of the War Relocation Authority, RG 210, microfilm copy, Harold B. Lee Library, Brigham Young University, Provo, UT

Shoshone Irrigation District, Powell, WY

Tule Lake National Wildlife Refuge Headquarters, Tulelake, CA

Yuma Public Library, Yuma, AZ

INTERVIEWS (TRANSCRIPTS IN AUTHOR'S POSSESSION)

Allen, Forrest. Interview by author, 20 July 1998, Cody, WY.

Andrew, Wilbur. Interview by author, 1 July 1998, Caldwell, ID.

Black, John K. "Jack." Interview by author, 20 July 1998, Lovell, WY.

Bolesta, Eleanor Jane. Interview by author, 11 August 1997, Tulelake, CA.

Briddle, Claude. Interview by author, 24 July 1998, Riverton, WY.

Casper, Bill and Joan. Interview by author, 24 August 1996, Mesa, WA.

Colvin, Carlos "Jake." Interview by author, 24 May 1997, Bard, CA.

Didier, Fran, Myrtle Paulsen, and Joanne Livingston. Interview by author, 21 May 1997, Yuma, AZ.

Dobson, Asil and Windy. Interview by author, 17 June 1998, Tacna, AZ.

Esser, Lyle. Interview by author, 24 August 1996, Mesa, WA.

Fram, Bob and Deloris. Interview by author, 24 May 1997, Yuma, AZ.

George, Evaleen. Interview by author, 8 July 1998, Cody, WY.

Gies, Phyllis. Interview by author, 24 July 1998, Riverton, WY.

Grout, Jack. Interview by author, 17 June 1998, Wellton, AZ.

Gunlock, Bill and Myrtle. Interview by author, 22 May 1997, Yuma, AZ.

Haney, Nelda. Interview by Clinton Christensen, 13 March 1997, Nephi, UT.

Hansen, John. Interview by author, 30 June 1998, Caldwell, ID.

Hoff, Ed. Interview by author, 2 July 1998, Caldwell, ID.

Hunt, David. Interview by author, 24 August 1996, Moses Lake, WA.

Hurlburt, Violet. Interview by author, 12 August 1997, Tulelake, CA.

Issler, Ralph. Interview by author, 17 June 1998, Yuma, AZ.

Johnson, Jerry and Frances. Interview by author, 13 August 1997, Tulelake, CA.

Kenyon, Lowell. Interview by author, 13 August 1997, Tulelake, CA.

Lindsey, Jerry H. Interview by author, 18 June 1998, Yuma, AZ.

Lorensen, Dale. Interview by author, 2 July 1998, Caldwell, ID.

Machen, Leon and Ruth. Interview by author, 1 July 1998, Caldwell, ID.

Marlatt, Ethel. Interview by author, 24 July 1998, Riverton, WY.

Mayfield, Pearl. Interview by author, 20 May 1997, Indio, CA.

Minden, Saron K. Interview by author, 23 August 1996, Tacoma, WA. (Notes only in author's possession.)

Nolan, Bill. Interview by author, 17 August 1996, Quincy, WA.

Olsen, Glen C. Interview by author, 3 July 1998, Caldwell, ID.

Otto, Ruth. Interview by author, 18 July 1998, Powell, WY.

Over, Art. Interview by author, 29 September 2001, Midvale, WY.

Paulsen, Eldon. Interview by author, 22 May 1997, Yuma, AZ.

Poore, Verna. Interview by author, 30 October 1997, Provo, UT.

Price, Anthon and Norma Eppich. Interview by author, 24 August 1996, Mesa, WA.

Reynolds, Virginia Noel. Interview by Amy Reynolds Billings, 31 July 1998, Cody, WY.

Riggs, Carroll. Interview by author, 29 September 2001, Riverton, WY.

Robison, Velma and Fred. Interview by author, 12 August 1997, Tulelake, CA.

Ross, Bill and Joan. Interview by author, 18 July 1998, Cody, WY.

Rucker, Roy L. and Mary. Interview by author, 29 October 1997, Payson, UT.

Sorensen, Van and Isabell "Bell." Interview by author, 14 September 2001, Mapleton, UT.

Spencer, Clarence B. Interview by author, 27 July 1996, Yuma, AZ.

Sweet, Mark. Interview by author, 1 July 1998, Nampa, ID.

Van Zant, Ruby. Interview by author, 2 July 1998, Caldwell, ID.

Waits, Eliot. Interview by author, 23 May 1997, Yuma, AZ.

Wells, Varian and Margaret. Interview by author, 17 August 1996, Quincy, WA.

Withington, Leonard and Eula. Interview by author, 24 July 1998, Riverton, WY.

Woodman, Robert "Butch." Interview by author, 22 May 1997, Yuma, AZ.

Wright, Ralph. Interview by author, 1 July 1998, Caldwell, ID.

NEWSPAPERS

Anchorage Daily News, 1952, 1974, 2007

Caldwell [ID] News-Tribune, 1950

Columbia Basin [Moses Lake, WA] Herald, 1951

Denver Post, 1947

Denver Rocky Mountain News, 1953, 1961, 1962

Heart Mountain [WY] Sentinel, 1943–1944

Indio [CA] News, 1954–1955

Klamath Falls [OR] Herald and News, 1997, 2001–2002, 2006

London Daily Telegraph, 2005

London Observer, 2001, 2005

Los Angeles Times, 2001, 2003

Manchester Guardian, 2005

Medford [OR] Mail Tribune, 2001

Minidoka County [ID] News, 1953–1957, 1959, 1961

Minidoka [ID] Irrigator, 1943, 1945

Newton Kansan, 2006

New York Times, 1947, 1988, 1995, 1997, 2007

Portland Oregonian, 2001

Powell [WY] Tribune, 1947, 1949

Riverside [CA] Press-Enterprise, 1998, 2003

Riverton [WY] Ranger, 1953, 1961–1964, 1971

Riverton [WY] Review, 1947–1949, 1952

Salina [KS] Journal, 2005

Salt Lake Tribune, 1959

San Diego Union-Tribune, 2003

San Francisco Chronicle, 1951–1952, 1963–1964, 2001, 2006

San Francisco Examiner, 1963

Seattle Post Intelligencer, 1952, 1999

Seattle Times, 1949

Sierra Times, 2001

Topeka Capital-Journal, 2005

Tri-City [WA] Herald, 1997, 2001

Twin Falls [ID] Times-News, 1953, 1962, 1992

Tulean [CA] Dispatch, 1942–1943

Tulelake [CA] Reporter, 1951–1953, 1955–1958, 1961–1963

USA Today, 2005

Yuma Daily Sun, 1948

CONGRESSIONAL HEARINGS

U. S. Congress. House. Committee on Interior and Insular Affairs. *Policies, Programs, and Activities of the Department of the Interior.* 89th Cong., 1st sess., pt. 1, 26 January 1965.

———. *Policies, Programs, and Activities of the Department of the Interior.* 91st Cong., 1st sess., pt. 5, 18 February 1969.

U.S. Congress. House. Committee on Irrigation and Reclamation. *Settlement of Returning Veterans on Farms in Reclamation Projects.* 79th Cong., 1st sess., 12 April 1945.

U.S. Congress. House. Special Committee on Post-War Economic Policy and Planning. *Post-War Economic Policy and Planning.* 79th Cong., 1st sess., 23 August 1944.

U.S. Congress. House. Subcommittee on Irrigation and Reclamation. Committee on Interior and Insular Affairs. *Preference to Ex-Servicemen for Entry to Public Lands on Reclamation Projects.* 78th Cong., 2d sess., 25 May 1944.

U.S. Congress. House. Subcommittee on Public Lands. Committee on Interior and Insular Affairs. *Public Land Policy and Management Act of 1975.* 94th Cong., 1st sess., 21 March 1975.

U.S. Congress. Senate. Committee on Interior and Insular Affairs. *Legislation to Revise the Public Land Laws.* 92d Cong., 1st sess., 21 September 1971.

———. *Management of National Resource Lands.* 94th Cong., 1st sess., 7 March 1975.

U.S. Congress. Senate. Committee on Public Lands. *Exemption of Certain Projects from Land-Limitation Provisions of Federal Reclamation Laws.* 80th Cong., 1st sess., 5 May 1947.

U.S. Congress. Senate. Select Committee on National Water Resources. *Water Re-*

sources Activities in the United States: Future Needs for Reclamation in the Western States. 86th Cong., 2d sess., 1960, Committee Print 32.

U.S. Congress. Senate. Subcommittee on Irrigation and Reclamation. Committee on Interior and Insular Affairs. *Riverton Reclamation Project: Hearings before the Subcommittee on Irrigation and Reclamation . . . on S. 2035.* 88th Cong., 1st sess., 29–30 October 1963.

———. *Third Division Irrigation District of the Riverton Project.* 87th Cong., 1st sess., 31 October 1961.

———. *Tule Lake–Klamath Wildlife Refuge.* 88th Cong., 1st. sess., 24 April 1963.

———. *Tule Lake, Lower Klamath, and Upper Klamath National Wildlife Refuges.* 87th Cong., 2d sess., 23 February 1962.

———. *Management of National Resource Lands.* 93rd Cong., 1st sess., 1 March 1973.

CONGRESSIONAL REPORTS

U.S. Congress. House. *Establishing Public Land Policy; Establishing Guidelines for Its Administration; Providing for the Management, Protection, Development, and Enhancement of the Public Lands; and for Other Purposes.* 94th Cong., 2d sess., 1976. House Report 1163. Serial 13134-7.

———. *Establishment of Public Land Law Review Commission.* 88th Cong., 1st sess., 1963. House Report 1008. Serial 12545.

———. *Facilitating Settlement of Returning Veterans on Farms in Projects Constructed, Operated, and Maintained by the Bureau of Reclamation.* 79th Cong., 1st sess., 1945. House Report 688, Serial 10933.

———. *Providing for the Management, Protection, and Development of National Resource Lands, and Other Purposes.* 94th Cong., 2d sess., 1976. House Report 1724. Serial 13134–13.

———. *Revision of the Public Land Laws.* 82d Cong., 2d sess., 1952. House Report 2511. Serial 11578.

U.S. Congress. House. Committee on Interior and Insular Affairs. *Promoting the Conservation of the Nation's Wildlife Resources on the Pacific Flyway.* 88th Cong., 1st sess., 1963. House Report 1072.

———. *Authorizing the Secretary of the Interior to Acquire Lands . . . in the Third Division.* 88th Cong., 1st sess., 1963. House Report 1010.

U.S. Congress. House. Committee on the Public Lands. *Allowing Credit in Connection with Certain Homestead Entries for Military or Naval Service Rendered during World War II.* 78th Cong., 2d sess., 1944. House Report 1646.

U.S. Congress. Senate. *Federal Reclamation by Irrigation.* Report prepared by Elwood Mead et al. 68th Cong., 1st sess., 1924. S. Doc. 92.

———. *National Resource Lands Management Act.* 94th Cong., 1st sess., 1975. Senate Report 583. Serial 13096.

———. *Permitting the Exchange and Amendment of Farm Units on Federal Irrigation Projects.* 83rd Cong., 1st sess., 1953. Senate Report 531.

U.S. Congress. Senate. Committee on Public Lands and Surveys. *Allowing Credit in Connection with Certain Homestead Entries for Military or Naval Service Rendered during World War II.* 78th Cong., 2d sess., 1944. Senate Report 1084.

CONGRESSIONAL DEBATES AND PROCEEDINGS

U.S. Congress. House. 78th Cong., 2d sess., *Congressional Record* 90, pt. 4 (15 May 1944); pt. 5 (15–19 June 1944); pt. 6 (14 November 1944).

———. 79th Cong., 1st sess., *Congressional Record* 91, pt. 7 (19 September 1945).

———. 88th Cong., 2d sess., *Congressional Record* 110, pt. 6 (20 April 1964).

———. 90th Cong., 2d sess., *Congressional Record* 114, pt. 10 (15 May 1968).

U.S. Congress. Senate. 78th Cong., 2d sess., *Congressional Record* 90, pt. 5 (14–20 June 1944); pt. 6 (8–19 September 1944).

———. 83rd Cong., 2d sess., *Congressional Record* 100, pt. 5 (4 May 1954).

———. 84th Cong., 1st sess., *Congressional Record* 101, pt. 4 (18 April 1955).

———. 87th Cong., 2d sess., *Congressional Record* 108, pt. 6 (16 May 1962).

———. 88th Cong., 1st sess., *Congressional Record* 109, pt. 9 (15 July 1963).

———. 93rd Cong., 2d sess., *Congressional Record*, 120, pt. 17 (8 July 1974).

———. 94th Cong., 2d sess., *Congressional Record* 122, pt. 4 (23 February 1976); pt. 19 (22 July 1976); pt. 26 (29 September 1976).

———. 107th Cong., 1st sess., *Congressional Record* 147, pt. 97 (12 July 2001).

———. 107th Cong., 2d sess., *Congressional Record* 148, pt. 14 (14 February 2002).

———. 108th Cong., 1st sess., *Congressional Record* 149, pt. 41 (13 March 2003).

———. 109th Cong., 1st sess., *Congressional Record* 151, pt. 33 (17 March 2005).

———. 110th Cong., 1st sess., *Congressional Record* 153, pt. 59 (12 April 2007).

LEGISLATION

An Act to Allow Credit in Connection with Certain Homestead Entries for Military or Naval Service Rendered during the Korean Conflict and for Other Purposes. United States Statutes at Large 68 (1955).

An Act to Allow Credit in Connection with Certain Homestead Entries for Military or Naval Service Rendered during World War II. United States Statutes at Large 58 (1944).

GENERAL PUBLISHED WORKS

"Alaska Town Giving away Free Land." 16 March 2007. http://www.foxnews.com.

Alaska Trappers Association. "Oral History Interviews: Ken Deardorff." n.d. http://www.alaskatrappers.org/bio_sketch_ken_deardorff.html, accessed 26 April 2007.

Allegra, Francis M. Opinion in *Klamath Irrigation District et al., v. US*. *US Federal Claims Court*, 31 August 2005. http://www.uscfc.uscourts.gov/Opinions/Allegra/07/ALLEGRA.Klamathsovopd.pdf

Armitage, Susan. "Through Women's Eyes: A New View of the West." In *The Women's West*, ed. Susan Armitage and Elizabeth Jameson, 9–18. Norman: University of Oklahoma Press, 1987.

Aston, Theodore Earl. *Our Beautiful People*. Peachtree City, GA: Gibby Publishing, 1992.

Attoun, Marti. "Where the Land Is Free." *American Profile*, 30 April 2006. http://www.americanprofile.com/article/5285.html.

Autobee, Robert. *Pick-Sloan Missouri River Basin Program: The Riverton Unit*, 3rd draft. 1996 http://www.usbr.gov/dataweb/html/rvrton2.html.

Bailey, Jon M., and Kim Preston. *Fresh Promises: Highlighting Promising Strategies of the Rural Great Plains and Beyond*. Lyons, NE: Center for Rural Affairs, 2004.

Barnard, Jeff. "Judge Denies Klamath Farmers' Desperate Plea for Water." Associated Press Release. 1 May 2001. http://www.klamathbasincrisis.org/articles/Archives/archive1/Judge-AP5-1-01.htm.

Barron, Hal S. *Mixed Harvest: The Second Great Transformation of the Rural North, 1870–1930*. Chapel Hill: University of North Carolina Press, 1997.

Basso, Matthew, Laura McCall, and Dee Garceau, eds., *Across the Great Divide: Cultures of Manhood in the American West*. New York: Routledge, 2001.

Beals, Alan R., and Thomas McCorkle. *Lost Lake*. Kroeber Anthropological Society Papers no. 3. Berkeley: University of California Department of Anthropology, 1950.

Bean, Lowell John. "Cahuilla." In *Handbook of North American Indians*, ed. William C. Sturtevant, vol. 8, *California*, ed. Robert F. Heizer, 575–587. Washington, DC: Smithsonian Institution, 1978.

Bederman, Gail. *Manliness and Civilization: A Cultural History of Gender and Race in the United States, 1880–1917*. Chicago: University of Chicago Press, 1995.

Bee, Robert L. "Quechan." In *Handbook of North American Indians*, ed. William C. Sturtevant, vol. 10, *Southwest*, ed. Alfonso Ortiz, 86–98. Washington, DC: Smithsonian Institution, 1983.

Berry, Wendell. *The Long-Legged House*. New York: Harcourt, Brace and World, 1969.

Blonk, Hu. "Tapping Lost River." *Reclamation Era* 37, April 1951, 67.

Blum, John M. *V Was for Victory: Politics and American Culture during World War II*. New York: Harcourt Brace Jovanovich, 1976.

Bolesta, Eleanor. "A Woman Wins." *Journal of the Modoc County Historical Society* 18 (1996): 89–90.

Borsodi, Ralph. *Flight from the City: The Story of a New Way to Family Security*. New York: Harper and Bros., 1933.

Bowen, Marshall. *Utah People in the Nevada Desert: Homestead and Community on a Twentieth-Century Farmers' Frontier*. Logan: Utah State University Press, 1994.

Braunworth, William S., et al. *Water Allocation in the Klamath Reclamation Project, 2001: An Assessment of Natural Resource, Economic, Social, and Institutional Issues with a Focus on the Upper Klamath Basin*. Corvallis: Oregon State University Extension Service, 2002.

Bremer, Richard G. *Agricultural Change in an Urban Age: The Loup Country of Nebraska, 1910–1970*. University of Nebraska Studies New Series no. 51. Lincoln: University of Nebraska, 1976.

Briggs, Ian A. "Gila Homesteaders Take Over." *Reclamation Era* 34, September 1948, 173–174.

Britton, Peg. Blog response to Paul Harris, 29 May 2005. http://www.kansasprairie.net/kansasprairieblog/?m=200505.

Brooks, James F. *Captives and Cousins: Slavery, Kinship, and Community in the Southwest Borderlands*. Chapel Hill: University of North Carolina Press, 2002.

Buchheister, Carl W. "Tule Lake Threat Must Be Removed." *Audubon Magazine*, July-August 1960, 153–155.

Bureau of Reclamation. "Columbia Basin Project Development." n.d. http://www.usbr.gov/dataweb/html/columbia.html.

Bureau of Reclamation. *Summary Report of the Commissioner of the Bureau of Reclamation, 1966, and Statistical Appendix*. Washington, DC: Department of the Interior, 1966.

Butler, Carlyle. "Problems of a Present Day Homesteader." *Reclamation Era* 36, February 1950, 39.

Byrne-Shirley, Betty Lou. "The Reclamation of Tule Lake." *Journal of the Modoc County Historical Society* 18 (1996): 49–61.

———. "The Refuges." *Journal of the Modoc County Historical Society* 18 (1996): 31–48.

———. "The Tule Lake–Lower Klamath Region: A Historical Overview." *Journal of the Modoc County Historical Society* 18 (1996): 6–11.

Caldwell, Denise. "Author Decides to Homestead in Alaska and Shares Her Experiences." n.d. http://freeamericandream.blogspot.com/.

"Can I Get Free Land from the Government?" *Changing Times, The Kiplinger Magazine*, March 1954, 44–45.

Cannon, Brian Q. "'We Are Now Entering a New Era': Federal Reclamation and the Fact Finding Commission of 1923–1924."*Pacific Historical Review* 66 (May 1997): 185–211.

Carman, David. Testimony before House Committee on Natural Resources. 17 July 2006. http://www.klamathbasincrisis.org/esa/esahearing0704/testimonydcarman071704.htm.

Cassmore, Orin. "Gold Mine in the Sky." *Reclamation Era* 33, February 1947, 25–29.

Clark, Christopher. *The Roots of Rural Capitalism: Western Massachusetts, 1780–1860*. Ithaca, NY: Cornell University Press, 1990.

"Coachella's Underground Lifeline." *Reclamation Era* 35, August 1949, 183–184.

Committee on Endangered and Threatened Fishes in the Klamath River Basin. *Scientific Evaluation of Biological Opinions on Endangered and Threatened Fishes in the Klamath River Basin: Interim Report*. Washington, D.C.: National Academy Press, 2002. http://www.nap.edu/openbook/0309083249/html/26.html.

Conkin, Paul K. *Tomorrow a New World: The New Deal Community Program*. Ithaca, NY: Cornell University Press, 1959.

Conrad, Debra Trigg. *Yuma Mesa Homesteaders, 1948 and 1952: "It's There, All You Have to Do Is Irrigate."* Yuma, AZ: Chameleon Computer Services, 2006.

Countryside & Small Stock Journal homepage. http://www.countrysidemag.com/.

Cronon, William. "Landscapes of Abundance and Scarcity." In *The Oxford History of the American West*, ed. Clyde A. Milner II, Carol A. O'Connor, and Martha A. Sandweiss, 603–638. New York: Oxford University Press, 1994.

Cunfer, Geoff. "Manure Matters on the Great Plains Frontier." *Journal of Interdisciplinary History* 34 (Spring 2004): 539–567.

Dahl, Robert. *Who Governs? Democracy and Power in an American City*. New Haven, CT: Yale University Press, 1961.

Danbom, David B. *Born in the Country: A History of Rural America*. Baltimore: Johns Hopkins University Press, 1995.

Daniels, Roger. *Concentration Camps, North America: Japanese in the United States and Canada during World War II*. Malabar, FL: Robert E. Krieger, 1981.

Dawdy, Doris Ostrander. *Congress in Its Wisdom: The Bureau of Reclamation and the Public Interest*. Boulder, CO: Westview Press, 1989.

Department of Hawaiian Homelands. *Applying for Hawaiian Homelands*. Honolulu: State of Hawaii, n.d. http://hawaii.gov/dhhl/applicants.

De Roos, Robert. "Sodbusting Pays Off." *Colliers* 133, 22 January 1954, 96–99.

"Does Your Wife/Husband Help?" *Wallace's Farmer*, 20 September 1958, 60.

Doty, Jack. "Christian Homesteading." http://www.christianhomesteaders.org/.

Down to the Roots Organic Homesteading Magazine homepage. http://www.downtotherootsmagazine.com.

Eastman, Adam R. "From Cadillac to Chevy: Environmental Concern, Compromise, and the Central Utah Project Completion Act." M.A. thesis, Brigham Young University, 2006.

Elbert, Sarah. "Women and Farming: Changing Structures, Changing Roles." In *Women and Farming: Changing Roles, Changing Structures*, ed. Wava G. Haney and Jane B. Knowles, 245–264. Boulder, CO: Westview Press, 1988.

Ellsworth KS City Council. Minutes. 28 August 2006. http://blog.ellsworthks.net/minutes/2007/03/august-2006.html.

Endangered Species Act of 1973. http://www.fws.gov/laws/digest/ESACT.html.

Environmental Conservation Organization. Petition. n.d. http://www.freedom.org/WTC/response/who/signed-A.shtml222.

Etulain, Richard W. *Beyond the Missouri: The Story of the American West*. Albuquerque: University of New Mexico Press, 2006.

Fairchild, C' deVere. "I Finally Struck It Rich." *Reclamation Era* 33, January 1947, 3.

Faragher, John Mack. "History from the Inside-Out: Writing the History of Women in Rural America." *American Quarterly* 33 (1981): 537–557.

———. *Sugar Creek: Life on the Illinois Prairie*. New Haven, CT: Yale University Press, 1986.

———, ed. *Rereading Frederick Jackson Turner: "The Significance of the Frontier in American History" and Other Essays*. New Haven, CT: Yale University Press, 1999.

"Farm Family on Family Farm." *Reclamation Era* 42, August 1956, 57–58, 76.

"Farm Lottery." *Life* 22, 20 January 1947, 73–74.

Fiege, Mark. *Irrigated Eden: The Making of an Agricultural Landscape in the American West*. Seattle: University of Washington Press, 1999.

Fink, Deborah. *Agrarian Women: Wives and Mothers in Rural Nebraska, 1880–1940*. Chapel Hill: University of North Carolina Press, 1992.

Foster, Doug. "Refuges and Reclamation: Conflicts in the Klamath Basin, 1904–1964." *Oregon Historical Quarterly* 103 (Summer 2002): 150–187.

Friedberger, Mark. "Cattle Raising and Dairying in the Western States." In *The Rural West since World War II*, ed. R. Douglas Hurt, 190–212. Lawrence: University Press of Kansas, 1998.

———. *Farm Families and Change in Twentieth-Century America.* Louisville: University Press of Kentucky, 1988.

Gates, Paul W. *History of Public Land Law Development.* Washington, DC: GPO, 1968.

Geisler, Barbara, and Maynard Kaufman. "Homesteading in the 1990s." n.d. http://www.michiganlandtrust.org.

"General Description and Plan, Gila Project, Arizona." http://www.usbr.gov/dataweb/html/gila.html.

Girdner, Audrie, and Anne Loftis. *The Great Betrayal: The Evacuation of the Japanese-Americans during World War II.* London: MacMillan, 1969.

Gordon, John. "Kansas Church Welcomes Families Drawn by Promise of Free Land." United Methodist News Service, 19 April 2005. http://archives.umc.org/interior.asp?ptid=2&mid=7250.

Gould, Rebecca Kneale. *At Home in Nature: Modern Homesteading and Spiritual Practice in America.* Berkeley: University of California Press, 2005.

Grand Coulee Dam: The Eighth Wonder of the World. Coulee Dam, WA: Souvenirs, 1946.

Grandstaff, Mark R. "Visions of New Men and Prescriptions for Modern Life: American Society Addresses the World War II Veteran's Problem," 2000. Paper presented at the meetings of the American Historical Association, Pacific Coast Branch, 6 August 2000. Typescript Ms. Copy in author's possession.

Gregory, James Noble. *American Exodus: The Dust Bowl Migration and Okie Culture in California.* New York: Oxford University Press, 1989.

Hahn, Steven, and Jonathan Prude, eds. *The Countryside in the Age of Capitalist Transformation: Essays in the Social History of Rural America.* Chapel Hill: University of North Carolina Press, 1985.

Handy-Marchello, Barbara. *Women of the Northern Plains: Gender and Settlement on the Homestead Frontier, 1870–1930.* St. Paul: Minnesota Historical Society Press, 2005.

Hanson, Ric. "Marne gets some takers on free land." KJAN radio broadcast, 26 April 2006. http://www.radioiowa.com/gestalt/go.cfm?objectid=0546CE56-A6E8-48C5-ABAE98E5A37DC200.

Harris, Paul. "Meet America's New Pioneer Breed." *Observer Magazine, Manchester Guardian,* 29 May 2005. http://www.guardian.co.uk/world/2005/may/29/usa.paulharris.

Hartmann, Susan M. "Women's Employment and the Domestic Ideal in the Early Cold War Years." In *Not June Cleaver: Women and Gender in Postwar America, 1945–1960,* ed. Joanne Meyerowitz. Philadelphia: Temple University Press, 1994.

Harwell, Henry O., and Marsha C. S. Kelly. "Maricopa." In *Handbook of North American*

Indians, ed. William C. Sturtevant, vol. 10, *Southwest*, ed. Alfonso Ortiz, 71–85. Washington, DC: Smithsonian Institution, 1983.

Hays, Samuel P. *Beauty, Health and Permanence: Environmental Politics in the United States, 1955–1985*. New York: Cambridge University Press, 1987.

Head, Jeff. "The Stand at Klamath Falls." 17 July 2001. http://www.jeffhead.com/klamath/account1.htm.

Henretta, James A. "Families and Farms: *Mentalite* in Pre-Industrial America." *William and Mary Quarterly* 35 (January 1978): 3–32.

Hine, Robert V. *The American West: An Interpretive History*. Boston: Little, Brown and Company, 1973.

"A History of the Klamath Bucket Brigade," n.d., http://www.klamathbucketbrigade.org/a_history_of_KBB.htm.

Hoff, Ed. Personal History, n.d. Typescript Ms. Copy in author's possession.

Holt, John B. *An Analysis of Methods and Criteria Used in Selecting Families for Colonization Projects*. Social Science Research report no. 1. Washington, DC: Farm Security Administration and Bureau of Agricultural Economics, 1937.

"Homesteaders of '54." *Time* 64, 19 July 1954, 19.

"Homesteading in Alaska a Thing of the Past." *Mother Earth News* 31, January/February 1975. http://www.motherearthnews.com/Modern-Homesteading/1975-01-01/Land-Closed-To-Homesteading.aspx.

Hosokawa, Bill. "Homesteaders, 1954." *Saturday Evening Post* 226, 2 January 1954, 26–37.

Hull, Teresa, and Linda Leask. "Dividing Alaska, 1867–2000: Changing Land Ownership and Management." *Alaska Review of Social and Economic Conditions* 32 (November 2000): 6.

Hundley, Norris, Jr. "The Dark and Bloody Ground of Indian Water Rights: Confusion Elevated to Principle." *Western Historical Quarterly* 9 (October 1978): 454–482.

Hurt, R. Douglas. "Agricultural Politics in the Twentieth-Century American West." In *The Political Culture of the New West*, ed. Jeff Roche. Lawrence: University Press of Kansas, 2008.

———. *American Agriculture: A Brief History*. Rev. ed. West Lafayette, IN: Purdue University Press, 2002.

———, ed. *The Rural West since World War II*. Lawrence: University Press of Kansas, 1998.

Idaho State Historical Society. *Boise Project History, 1920–1945*. Reference Series no. 193. n.d. http://www.idahohistory.net.

Israelson, Orson W. *Irrigation Principles and Practices.* 2d ed. New York: John Wiley & Sons, 1950.

Jacoby, Karl. "We Are All New Western Historians Now." *Reviews in American History* 29, 4 (2004): 614–620.

Jellison, Katherine. *Entitled to Power: Farm Women and Technology, 1913–1963.* Chapel Hill: University of North Carolina Press, 1993.

Jensen, Joan. *With These Hands: Women Working on the Land.* Old Westbury, NY: Feminist Press, 1981.

Johnson, H. H. "Forty-Three Years on the Shoshone Project." *Reclamation Era* 33, June 1947, 124–127.

Kadlec, Daniel. "Double Take." *Time Magazine,* 5 July 2005. http://www.time.com/time/magazine/magazine/article/0,9171,1079474,00.html.

Kaufman, Maynard, and Sally Kaufman. "Information about the School of Homesteading."1973. http://www.michiganlandtrust.org/compilation/info1973.html.

Kelly, Joan. "The Doubled Vision of Feminist Theory: A Postscript to the 'Women and Power' Conference." *Feminist Studies* 5 (Spring 1979): 216–227.

King, Ray C. "A Veteran's View." *Reclamation Era,* July 1948, 137.

Klein, Kerwin Lee. "Reclaiming the 'F' word, or Being and Becoming Postmodern." *Pacific Historical Review* 65 (May 1996):179–215.

Kohl, Seena B. "Image and Behavior: Women's Participation in North American Family Agricultural Enterprises." In *Women and Farming: Changing Roles, Changing Structures.* ed. Wava G. Haney and Jane B. Knowles, 89–108. Boulder, CO: Westview Press, 1988.

Kolodny, Annette. *The Lay of the Land: Metaphor as Experience and History in American Life and Letters.* Chapel Hill: University of North Carolina Press, 1975.

Krizo, Barbara. "The Krizos: 1946 Homesteaders." *Journal of the Modoc County Historical Society* 18 (1996): 125–127.

Krizo, Jacqui. "Where Is the Klamath Basin, Who Is Our Community, Who Is KBC, and Who Are the Caretakers?" http://www.klamathbasincrisis.org/aboutus/about%20us.htm.

Kronick, Stanley W., et al. *Legal Study of Federal Public Land Laws and Policies Relating to Intensive Agriculture.* Springfield, VA: National Technical Information Service, 1969.

Kudlowitz, Mark, and Lance George. *Turning Challenges into Opportunities: Housing and Community Development Strategies in Rural Population Loss Counties.* Washington, DC: Housing Assistance Council, 2007.

Kulikoff, Allan. *The Agrarian Origins of American Capitalism.* Charlottesville: University of Virginia Press, 1992.

———. "Households and Markets: Toward a New Synthesis of American Agrarian History." *William and Mary Quarterly*, 3d series, 50 (April 1993): 342–355.

Lahey, Susan. "There's Still Free Land out West." *Grit*, January/February 2007. http://www.grit.com/article/2007/01/Land-Out-West.html.

Lane County Bachelor. "Starving to Death on a Government Claim." http://lonehand.com/cowboy_songs_iii.htm#S.

Lauterbach, Richard. "Homesteaders 1950." *Ladies' Home Journal* 67, October 1950, 207–219.

Limerick, Patricia Nelson. *The Legacy of Conquest: The Unbroken Past of the American West.* New York: W. W. Norton, 1987.

———. "Turnerians All: The Dream of a Helpful History in an Intelligible World." *American Historical Review* 100 (June 1995): 697–716.

Lobsenz, Norman, and Amelia Lobsenz. "California Pioneers Model 1949." *Coronet* 25, April 1949, 78–82.

Lu, Max. "Homesteading Redux: New Community Initiatives to Reverse Rural Depopulation in the Great Plains." *Journal of the West* 46 (Winter 2007): 74–80.

Malone, Michael P. "Beyond the Last Frontier: Toward a New Approach to Western American History." *Western Historical Quarterly* 20 (November 1989): 409–427.

Malone, Michael P., and Richard W. Etulain. *The American West: A Twentieth-Century History.* Lincoln: University of Nebraska Press, 1989.

"Marquette, Kansas/Free Land." Fox Evening News Television Broadcast, 22 May 2004. http://openweb.tvnews.vanderbilt.edu/.

Mayfield, Harold. "The Seventy-Second Stated Meeting of the American Ornithologists' Union." *Auk* 72 (January 1957): 75.

McGirr, Lisa. *Suburban Warriors: The Origins of the New American Right.* Princeton, NJ: Princeton University Press, 2001.

McPhee, John. *Encounters with the Archdruid.* New York: Farrar, Straus and Giroux, 1971.

Mechau, Vaughn. "Veteran, Wyoming." *Reclamation Era* 33, May 1947, 119.

Miller, C. Marty. "It's There: All You Have to Do Is Irrigate." In Debra Trigg Conrad, *Yuma Mesa Homesteaders, 1948 and 1952: "It's There, All You Have to Do Is Irrigate."* Yuma, AZ: Chameleon Computer Services, 2006.

Miller, Jay. "Middle Columbia River Salishans." In *Handbook of North American Indians*, ed. William C. Sturtevant, vol. 12, *Plateau*, ed. Deward E. Walker Jr., 253–270. Washington, DC: Smithsonian Institution, 1998.

"Modern Pioneers." *Reclamation Era* 40, November 1954, 83–84.

Montana Human Rights Network News, September 2001. http:// www.mhrn.org/newsarchive/0901Klamath.html.

Most, Stephen. *River of Renewal: Myth and History in the Klamath Basin.* Portland: Oregon Historical Society Press, and Seattle: University of Washington Press, 2006.

Moudry, Chris. "Klamath Basin Crisis—Endangered Species Act Gone." n.d. http://www.klamathbasincrisis.org/articles/Archives/archive1/basinfertilizer.htm.

"Multimillion-dollar Idaho Water Rights Deal Approved." *U.S. Water News Online* (April 2004). http://www.uswaternews.com/archives/arcconserv/4multdoll4.html.

Murdock, John R. "Veterans—Here's Your Farm." *Reclamation Era* 32, May 1946, 95–96.

Murphy, Robert F., and Yolanda Murphy. "Northern Shoshone and Bannock." In *Handbook of North American Indians*, ed. William C. Sturtevant, vol. 11, *Great Basin*, ed. Warren L. D'Azevedo, 284–307. Washington, DC: Smithsonian Institution, 1986.

Myers, Max, et al. *Federal Public Land Laws and Policies Relating to Intensive Agriculture.* Brookings, SD: South Dakota State University Economics Department, 1969.

Nash, Gerald D. *Creating the West: Historical Interpretations, 1890–1990.* Albuquerque: University of New Mexico Press, 1991.

National Park Service. "Found! America's Last Homesteader." http://www.nps.gov/home/historyculture/lasthomesteader.htm?eid=122894&root_aId=135.

Neth, Mary. *Preserving the Family Farm: Women, Community and the Foundations of Agribusiness, 1900–1940.* Baltimore: Johns Hopkins University Press, 1995.

Neuberger, Richard L. "The GI's Look Westward." *Foreign Service* 33 (January 1946): 22.

Nugent, Walter. *Into the West: The Story of Its People.* New York: Vintage Books, 1999.

"Opening New Frontiers." *Reclamation Era* 39, October 1953, 154–156.

Parks, Dwight K. "Farm Family on Family Farm." *Reclamation Era* 42, August 1956, 58.

Peffer, E. Louise. *The Closing of the Public Domain: Disposal and Reservation Policies, 1900–1950.* New York: Arno Press, 1972.

Pelz, Richard K. ed. *Federal Reclamation Laws and Related Laws Annotated*, 4 vols. Washington, DC: GPO, 1972.

Phelan, John T., and Donald L. Basinger. *Engineering in the Soil Conservation Service.* Washington, DC: Soil Conservation Service, 1993.

Pisani, Donald J. "Federal Water Policy and the Rural West." In *The Rural West since World War II*, ed. R. Douglas Hurt, 119–146. Lawrence: University Press of Kansas, 1998.

———. *Water and American Government: The Reclamation Bureau, National Water Policy, and the West, 1902–1935.* Berkeley: University of California Press, 2002.

Pitzer, Paul C. *Grand Coulee: Harnessing a Dream.* Pullman: Washington State University, 1994.

Polsby, Nelson. *Community Power and Political Theory: A Further Look at Problems of Evidence and Inference.* New Haven, CT: Yale University Press, 1980.

Public Land Law Review Commission. *One Third of the Nation's Land: A Report to the President and to the Congress by the Public Land Law Review Commission.* Washington, DC: GPO, 1970.

Reid, Bill G. "Agrarian Opposition to Franklin K. Lane's Proposal for Soldier Settlement, 1918–1921." *Agricultural History* 41 (Spring 1967):167–179.

———. "Franklin K. Lane's Idea for Veterans' Colonization, 1918–1921." *Pacific Historical Review* 33 (November 1964): 447–461.

Renshaw, Edward F. "Appraisal of Federal Investment in Water Resources." In *Modern Land Policy: Papers of the Land Economics Institute,* University of Illinois Land Economics Institute, 235–247. Urbana: University of Illinois Press, 1960.

———. *Toward Responsible Government.* Chicago: Idyia Press, 1957.

Riebsame, William E., et al., eds. *Atlas of the New West: Portrait of a Changing Region.* New York: W. W. Norton, 1997.

"Riverton Farm Drawing." *Reclamation Era,* October 1950, 188–189.

Robbins, William G. *Colony and Empire: The Capitalist Transformation of the American West.* Lawrence: University Press of Kansas, 1994.

———. *Hard Times in Paradise: Coos Bay, Oregon, 1850–1986.* Seattle: University of Washington Press, 1988.

———. *Landscapes of Conflict: The Oregon Story, 1940–2000.* Seattle: University of Washington Press, 2004.

Rothenberg, Winnifred. "The Market and Massachusetts Farmers, 1750–1855." *Journal of Economic History* 41 (1981): 283–314.

Rothman, Hal K. *Devil's Bargains: Tourism in the Twentieth-Century American West.* Lawrence: University Press of Kansas, 1998.

Rugh, Susan Sessions. "Pastoralism and the Rural Ideal." In *Encyclopedia of American Cultural and Intellectual History,* 3 vols., ed. Mary Kupiec Cayton and Peter W. Williams, 2: 453–461. New York: Charles Scribner's Sons, 2001.

Rutman, Darrett B. "Assessing the Little Communities of Early America." *William and Mary Quarterly,* 3d series, 43 (April 1986): 163–178.

Save Our Wild Salmon Coalition. "Illegal Irrigation Hurting Salmon." 19 May 2000. http://www.wildsalmon.org/pressroom/press-detail.cfm?docID=85.

Schackel, Sandra. "Ranch and Farm Women in the Contemporary American West." In *The Rural West since World War II,* ed. R. Douglas Hurt, 99–118. Lawrence: University Press of Kansas, 1998.

Schulte, Steven C. *Wayne Aspinall and the Shaping of the American West.* Boulder: University Press of Colorado, 2002.

Schuster, Helen H. "Yakima and Neighboring Groups." In *Handbook of North American Indians*, ed. William C. Sturtevant, vol. 12, *Plateau*, ed. Deward E. Walker Jr., 327–346. Washington, DC: Smithsonian Institution, 1998.

Schwantes, Carlos A. "Wage Earners and Wealth Makers." In *The Oxford History of the American West*, ed. Clyde A. Milner II, Carol A. O'Connor, and Martha A. Sandweiss, 431–467. New York: Oxford University Press, 1994.

Sherow, James E. "Environmentalism and Agriculture in the American West." In *The Rural West since World War II*, ed. R. Douglas Hurt, 58–75. Lawrence: University Press of Kansas, 1998.

Shimkin, Demitri B. "Eastern Shoshone." In *Handbook of North American Indians*, ed. William C. Sturtevant, vol. 11, *Great Basin*, ed. Warren L. D'Azevedo, 308–335. Washington, DC: Smithsonian Institution, 1986.

Shurts, John. *Indian Reserved Water Rights: The Winters Doctrine in Its Social and Legal Context, 1880s–1930s.* Norman: University of Oklahoma Press, 2000.

"Sixteen Farm Units on Wellton-Mohawk Division, Gila Project, to be Sold by Reclamation." *Reclamation Era* 43, November 1957, 107.

Smith, Henry Nash. *Virgin Land: The American West as Symbol and Myth.* Cambridge, MA: Harvard University Press, 1950.

Smith, Wayne L. "School Was Never Like This!" *Reclamation Era* 34, May 1948, 92–93.

Souza, Christine. "Klamath ESA Congressional Hearing." California Farm Bureau Ag Alert, 21 July 2004. http://www.klamathbasincrisis.org/esa/esahearing0704/esa agalerthearing072104.htm.

Spivak, Jeffrey. "Kansas Says: Take This Land . . . Please!" *Planning* (November 2007). http://www.entrepreneur.com/tradejournals/article/print/172168549.html.

Stamm, Henry E., IV. *People of the Wind River: The Eastern Shoshones, 1825–1900.* Norman: University of Oklahoma Press, 1999.

Stene, Eric A. *The Minidoka Project*, 5th draft. Denver: Bureau of Reclamation History Program, 1997. http://www.usbr.gov/dataweb/html.yuma1.html.

———. *Yuma Project and Yuma Auxiliary Project*, 3rd draft. Denver: Bureau of Reclamation History Program, 1996. http://www.usbr.gov/dataweb/html.yuma1.html.

Stern, Theodore. "Klamath and Modoc." In *Handbook of North American Indians*, ed. William C. Sturtevant, vol. 12, *Plateau*, ed. Deward E. Walker Jr., 446–466. Washington, DC: Smithsonian Institution, 1998.

Steven Lewis Kandra et al. v. United States, Klamath Tribes and Wilderness Society. Opinion and Order, 30 April 2001. http://www.klamathbasincrisis.org/articles/Archives/archive1/injunctiondenied.htm.

Stock, Catherine McNicol, and Robert D. Johnston, eds. *The Countryside in the Age of the Modern State: Political Histories of Rural America*. Ithaca, NY: Cornell University Press, 2001.

Straus, Murray A. "The Role of the Wife in the Settlement of the Columbia Basin Project." *Marriage and Family Living* 20 (February 1958): 59–64.

Sturgeon, Stephen C. *The Politics of Western Water: The Congressional Career of Wayne Aspinall*. Tucson: University of Arizona Press, 2002.

Testimonials. http://www.klamathbasincrisis.org/Homesteaders/.

Thomas, Dorothy Swaine, and Richard S. Nishimoto. *The Spoilage: Japanese American Evacuation and Resettlement*. Berkeley and Los Angeles: University of California Press, 1946.

"Thomas Henry Kuchel, (1910–1994)." http://bioguide.congress.gov/scripts/biodisplay.pl?index=K000335.

"Three June Deadlines for Reclamation Farm Applications." *Reclamation Era* 36, June 1950, 122.

Tulelake Growers Association to the Committee on Natural Resources. Testimony. 17 July 2006. http://www.klamathbasincrisis.org/esa/esahearing0704/testimonytga071704.htm.

Turner, Frederick Jackson. "The Significance of the Frontier in American History." In *Frontier and Section: Selected Essays of Frederick Jackson Turner*, ed. Ray Allen Billington, 37–62. Englewood Cliffs, NJ: Prentice-Hall, 1961.

Turner, Stan. *The Years of Harvest: A History of the Tule Lake Basin*. Eugene, OR: 49th Avenue Press, 1987.

Ulrich, Rudolph. "Relative Costs and Benefits of Land Reclamation in the Humid Southeast and the Semiarid West." *Journal of Farm Economics* 35 (February 1953): 62–73.

U.S. War Department. *Final Report, Japanese Evacuation from the West Coast, 1942*. Washington, DC: GPO, 1943.

"Veterans: Tule Lakers Now." *Newsweek* 28, 30 December 1946, 20.

Victorine, Mary. "The Victorines, 1949 Homesteaders." *Journal of the Modoc County Historical Society* 18 (1996): 135–138.

Voget, Fred W. "Crow." In *Handbook of North American Indians*, ed. William C. Sturtevant, vol. 13, *Plains*, ed. Raymond J. DeMallie, 695–717. Washington, DC: Smithsonian Institution, 2001.

Wagoner, Jay J. *Early Arizona: Prehistory to Civil War*. Tucson: University of Arizona Press, 1975.

"Walden Bipartisan ESA Modernization Bill Approved by House Resources Committee." 21 July 2004. http://www.klamathbasincrisis.org/esa/esa%20lawsuits/waldenesabillapproved072104.htm.

"Walden Cosponsors Bipartisan Critical Habitat Legislation to Update ESA." 15 March 2005. http://www.klamathbasincrisis.org/esa/waldensponsors031705.htm.

Ward, Evan R. *Border Oasis: Water and the Political Ecology of the Colorado River Delta, 1940–1975*. Tucson: University of Arizona Press, 2003.

Warne, William E. *The Bureau of Reclamation*. New York: Praeger, 1973.

Wasden, Winifred Sawaya, ed. *Modern Pioneers*. Powell, WY: Northwest College Production Printing, 1998.

Weiss, Philip. "Off the Grid." *New York Times Magazine*, 8 January 1995. http://query.nytimes.com/gst/fullpage.html?res=990CE3DA1F3AF93AA15752C0A963958260.

West, Elliott. *The Contested Plains: Indians, Goldseekers, and the Rush to Colorado*. Lawrence: University Press of Kansas, 1998.

———. *Growing Up with the Country: Childhood on the Far-Western Frontier*. Albuquerque: University of New Mexico Press, 1989.

White, Richard. *"It's Your Misfortune and None of My Own": A New History of the American West*. Norman: University of Oklahoma Press, 1991.

———. *The Organic Machine: The Remaking of the Columbia River*. New York: Hill and Wang, 1995.

White, Robert. *Frannie-Deaver Proposition: A Chronicle of Optimism—and Alkali*. Cheyenne, WY: Frontier Printing, 1990.

Williams, William J. "Homesteading Time in Yuma." *Reclamation Era* 34, May 1948, 89.

Wilson, David R. "You Grow Where You're Planted: Community Building in Colstrip, Montana." Ph.D. diss., Brigham Young University, 2000.

Wolfinger, Raymond E. *The Politics of Progress*. Englewood Cliffs, NJ: Prentice-Hall, 1974.

Worster, Donald. *Rivers of Empire: Water, Aridity, and the Growth of the American West*. New York: Pantheon, 1985.

Wrobel, David M. *The End of American Exceptionalism: Frontier Anxiety from the Old West to the New Deal*. Lawrence: University Press of Kansas, 1993.

Yakima Project History. 3rd draft. Denver: Bureau of Reclamation History Program, 1993. http://www.usbr.gov/dataweb/projects/washington/yakima/history.html.

INDEX